Equitable Damages

Hugh McCalmont Cairns, 1st Earl Cairns, 1819–85

Equitable Damages

Peter M McDermott

LLB (Hons) (Qld), LLM (Qld)
Senior Lecturer in Law, University of Queensland
Barrister of the Supreme Court of Queensland

with a foreword by

The Right Honourable Sir Robert Megarry

Formerly the Vice-Chancellor of the Supreme Court of England and Wales

Butterworths
Sydney Adelaide Brisbane Canberra Melbourne Perth
1994

AUSTRALIA   BUTTERWORTHS 271-273 Lane Cove Road, North Ryde 2113
111 Gawler Place, Adelaide 5000
King George Tower, 71 Adelaide Street, Brisbane 4000
53-55 Northbourne Avenue, Canberra 2601
160 William Street, Melbourne 3000
178 St Georges Terrace, Perth 6000

CANADA   BUTTERWORTHS CANADA LTD Toronto and Vancouver

IRELAND   BUTTERWORTH (IRELAND) LTD Dublin

MALAYSIA   MALAYAN LAW JOURNAL SDN BHD Kuala Lumpur

NEW ZEALAND   BUTTERWORTHS OF NEW ZEALAND LTD Wellington and Auckland

PUERTO RICO   BUTTERWORTH OF PUERTO RICO INC San Juan

SINGAPORE   BUTTERWORTHS ASIA Singapore

SOUTH AFRICA   BUTTERWORTH PUBLISHERS (PTY) LTD Durban

UNITED KINGDOM   BUTTERWORTH & CO (PUBLISHERS) LTD London and Edinburgh

USA   BUTTERWORTH LEGAL PUBLISHERS Carlsbad, California;
Salem, New Hampshire

National Library of Australia Cataloguing-in-Publication entry

McDermott, Peter M. (Peter Malcolm), 1953 – .
Equitable damages

Includes index.
ISBN 0 409 30973 7.

1. Damages — Australia. I. Title.

344.94077

Inquiries should be addressed to the publishers.

Typeset in Horley Old Style

Printed in Australia by Ligare Pty Ltd

to Fiona

Acknowledgments

The author and publishers gratefully acknowledge the following copyright owners who have given their permission for work to be reproduced in this book:

United Kingdom
Controller of Her Majesty's Stationary Office: Judicature (Northern Ireland) Act 1978; Supreme Court Act 1981; Reports of Patent Cases.
Incorporated Council of Law Reporting for England and Wales: Law Reports.
Modern Law Review Limited: Modern Law Review.
National Portrait Gallery: Photograph of Lord Cairns by Lock & Whitfield.

Australia
New South Wales Council of Law Reporting: New South Wales Law Reports.
Administrator (Crown Copyright and Intellectual Property): Queensland Law Reform Commission, Report on the Supreme Court Acts.
Incorporated Council of Law Reporting for the State of Queensland: Queensland Reports.
Victorian Council of Law Reporting: Victorian Reports.
Law Book Co: Commonwealth Law Reports, South Australian State Reports and texts.

Canada
Winnipeg Courts: Queen's Bench Act.
Ministry of the Attorney General, Ontario: Courts of Justice Act.
Deputy Minister of Justice and Deputy Attorney General, Saskatchewan: Queen's Bench Act.

United States
Mead Data Central, provider of LEXIS®/NEXIS®: Unreported judgment.

Hong Kong
By courtesy of the Hong Kong Government: Supreme Court Ordinance.

While every care has been taken to trace and acknowledge copyright of the extracts reproduced in this book, the author and publishers tender their apologies for any accidental infringement where copyright has proved untraceable.

Contents

Foreword

Section 2 of the Chancery Amendment Act 1858 has long been familiarly known as *Lord Cairns' Act, tout court*. Its purpose was to empower the courts of equity to award damages in claims for injunctions or specific performance. The Act authorised the award of damages 'either in addition to or in substitution for' such orders. This proved to be a beneficial enlargement of jurisdiction, and in time corresponding provisions were enacted in over twenty jurisdictions. Such damages came to be known as 'equitable damages', and they form the subject of this welcome book.

It had been thought that damages awarded 'in substitution for' specific performance were not limited to damages at common law but should be such damages as would provide a true substitute for the decree that was not being made. This would put the party concerned into the same position as if specific performance had been ordered, so far as money could do it. But in *Johnson v Agnew*[1] the House of Lords laid down that the measure of such damages 'is exactly what it would be at common law',[2] apparently whether or not it provides a true substitute for specific performance. The author observes that, strictly speaking, what was said on the point was obiter, and that in any case it had not been argued. It may also be observed that in rejecting the view based on substitution the statutory words 'in substitution for' were quoted as being 'in lieu of';[3] and not every thing that is given instead of another is a substitute for it. It will be interesting to see what view is taken in other jurisdictions of the basis for confining a statutory addition to equity's discretionary remedies within the uncertain straitjacket of damages at common law. Even on quantum, the distinction between equitable damages and common law damages cannot be said to have vanished, and in any case there is more to equitable damages than merely the measure of them. This the author conveniently summarises in his Introduction.

The author has ranged far and wide in his research for this book. It is remarkably comprehensive and thorough, both geographically and within the various jurisdictions. The Appendix sets out the terms of section 2, together with the corresponding statutory provisions in every other jurisdiction; and the text duly examines these in the light of a critical appraisal of all the authorities. Most of them, of course, are reported cases; but many are unreported. For these, Australia heads the list, though

---

1 [1980] AC 367.
2 *William Sendall Plc v Cambridgeshire County Council* [1994] 1 WLR 1016 at 1037 per Hoffmann LJ, obiter.
3 *Johnson v Agnew* [1980] AC 367 at 400.

there are numerous contributions from other jurisdictions. Such authorities pose problems, especially for practitioners. In England, unreported decisions of the Court of Appeal may be seen at the Royal Courts of Justice; but overseas decisions are another matter, as are unreported decisions at first instance. But even though the day is yet to come when there are convenient systems for retrieving such judgments throughout the common law world, it is at least helpful to have unreported decisions cited in their proper context. Pursuit, however burdensome, may then be made for any case reasonably suspected of filling some crucial void.[4]

This book provides a valuable conspectus of its subject, and an excellent tool for research, both professional and academic. It cannot, of course, yield a solution for every problem, but it does everything possible to provide the means for a solution. Apart from case law, there is a very full range of references to text books, articles and other material in many jurisdictions, including at least one reference to an unpublished thesis. Some of the references, indeed, are to books or articles that at first sight seem to have little prospect of providing anything useful either on equity or damages; but the nuggets are there. The reader is left with the comfortable feeling that all that is available in any country has been included, set out with lucidity, and that he (or she) can build on a firm foundation. Both the organisation of the text and its arrangement are well conceived and admirably executed. All in all, this book illuminates an important segment of equity that has too long lain in the shadows, and has not yet finished developing. *Floreat!*

Lincoln's Inn
Michaelmas Day, 1994

---

4 Pursuit of this kind soon convinced one judge of the unwisdom of having cited an unreported decision of his own in a book.

Preface

Much of the literature on equitable remedies is devoted to specific relief in the form of an injunction or specific performance, and has been the subject of learned treatises such as Spry's *Equitable Remedies* and Sharpe's *Injunctions and Specific Performance*. In comparison the literature on equitable monetary remedies appears to be not as extensive.

Useful material on equitable damages may be found in the leading equity texts such as Spry's *Equitable Remedies*; Pettit's *Equity and the Law of Trusts* and Meagher, Gummow and Lehane's *Equity — Doctrines and Remedies*. These texts stimulated my interest in equitable damages. However, for some time now I have thought that the subject of equitable damages warranted discrete treatment in a book where the leading authorities on *Lord Cairns' Act* are gathered for the convenience of practitioners.

I am honoured that the Rt Hon Sir Robert Megarry took the time to write the foreword to this book. Many consider Sir Robert to be one of the leading equity and property scholars in the common law world. The subject of *Lord Cairns' Act* assumed prominence after his Lordship delivered judgment in *Wroth v Tyler* [1974] Ch 30. At that time Professor Jolowicz remarked that his Lordship's judgment was an 'obviously correct award of damages in equity' (*Cambridge Law Journal*, 1975, pp 233–4). That view was later endorsed in Australia by Meagher, Gummow and Lehane in *Equity — Doctrines and Remedies* (2nd ed, Butterworths, 1984, p 614).

I wish to also mention the assistance which has been generously given to me by W A Lee Esq. Mr Lee encouraged me to undertake the task of writing this book.

Beechvale
Redland Bay
October 1994

Table of Cases

Table of Statutes

Australia

Zambia

Introduction

The term 'equitable damages' is used by the writer to refer to statutory equitable damages which are awarded under s 2 of the Chancery Amendment Act 1858 (*Lord Cairns' Act*),[1] or a successor provision such as s 50 of the Supreme Court Act 1981.[2] It is in this sense that the term is generally used in the leading equity texts[3] and by the courts.[4] The use of the term 'equitable damages' is appropriate to refer to the remedy of damages under *Lord Cairns' Act* which was awarded by the Court of Chancery prior to the introduction of the Judicature system. The term continued to be used after the introduction of the Judicature system. In *Barbagallo v J & F Catelan Pty Ltd*[5] McPherson J remarked: 'Even after the *Judicature Act* it is common to speak of the remedy as equitable, and of such damages as equitable damages'.[6] The jurisdiction to award equitable damages is quite distinct from the jurisdiction to grant equitable compensation.[7] The term 'equitable damages' is also sometimes used in the context of the compensatory jurisdiction of a court of equity to grant restitution, or relief in respect of a breach of a fiduciary duty.[8]

Lord Cairns' Act was passed to prevent a multiplicity of proceedings in courts of law and equity where a plaintiff sought the common law remedy of damages, and equitable relief in the form of a decree for an injunction or specific performance. A suitor who sought an injunction or specific performance, and also damages, was generally obliged to commence proceedings both at law and in equity. However it should be appreciated

---

1 21 & 22 Vict c 27. For the text of s 2 of the Chancery Amendment Act 1858 (*Lord Cairns' Act*): see Appendix at p 281.

2 1981 c 54. For the text of s 50 of the Supreme Court Act 1981: see Appendix at p 281.

3 I C F Spry, *Equitable Remedies*, 4th ed, Law Book Co, Sydney, 1990, p 615; R P Meagher, W M C Gummow and J R F Lehane, *Equity — Doctrines and Remedies*, 2nd ed, Butterworths, Sydney, 1984, p 615.

4 *Norton v Angus* (1926) 38 CLR 523 at 534; *Hooper v Rogers* [1975] Ch 43 at 47; *Newmont Pty Ltd v Laverton Nickel NL* [1981] 1 NSWLR 215 at 218; *Wentworth v Woollahra Municipal Council* (1982) 149 CLR 672 at 678–9; *Ansdell v Crowther* (1984) 55 BCLR 216 at 221; *Kelly v Desnoe* [1985] 2 Qd R 477 at 491; *McEwan v Dick* (1985) 9 ACLR 1011 at 1017; *Barbagallo v J & F Catelan Pty Ltd* [1986] 1 Qd R 245 at 252, 265.

5 [1986] 1 Qd R 245.

6 [1986] 1 Qd R 245 at 252.

7 *United States Surgical Corp v Hospital Products International Pty Ltd* [1982] 2 NSWLR 766 at 815.

8 *Prudential Assurance Co Ltd v Newman Industries Ltd* [1981] Ch 257 at 298; *Markwell Bros Pty Ltd v CPN Diesels (Qld) Pty Ltd* [1983] 2 Qd R 508 at 523; (1982) 7 ACLR 425 at 437; *Daly v Sydney Stock Exchange Ltd* [1982] 2 NSWLR 421 at 427; *Taylor v National Union of Mineworkers* [1985] IRLR 99 at 104; *Fraser Edmiston Pty Ltd v AGT (Qld) Pty Ltd* [1988] 2 Qd R 1 at 13; *Ryde Holdings Ltd v Sorenson* [1988] 2 NZLR 157 at 159.

that the Court of Chancery possessed jurisdiction to grant damages, particularly where that remedy was ancillary to a decree of specific performance or other relief.

There were also other procedural difficulties prior to the introduction of the Judicature system. Where a plaintiff sought an injunction to protect a legal right it was often necessary to initially establish the existence of that right by proceedings at law. Even after the enactment of *Lord Cairns' Act* the Court of Chancery was reluctant to exercise the jurisdiction which had been conferred by the Act, and also determine legal questions. That is why the Chancery Regulation Act 1862 (*Sir John Rolt's Act*)[9] was passed. *Sir John Rolt's Act*, with a number of reservations, required the Court of Chancery to determine every question of fact or law upon which a plaintiff's entitlement to equitable relief was dependent.

Upon the commencement of the *Judicature Acts*[10] the jurisdiction which was vested in the Court of Chancery under *Lord Cairns' Act* was transferred to the newly-created High Court of Justice. It should be appreciated that *Lord Cairns' Act* was not merely a procedural statute which enabled the Court of Chancery to award those damages which could be awarded by a common law court at Westminster. The statute also enabled damages to be awarded which were unavailable at law. The jurisdiction to award equitable damages survived the commencement of the *Judicature Acts*. That is why the jurisdiction which was conferred by *Lord Cairns' Act* still has relevance today.

Equitable damages may be awarded in England (and Wales), Northern Ireland, the Republic of Ireland, Australia, New Zealand, Canada and a number of Commonwealth countries. This is because legislation derived from *Lord Cairns' Act*, or a successor provision, has been passed in some countries, or the courts in those countries possess the same jurisdiction as the High Court. In *Commissioner of Highways v George Eblen Pty Ltd*[11] Wells J mentioned that *Lord Cairns' Act* 'has been reproduced in other jurisdictions whose legal traditions are those of England'.[12]

Under *Lord Cairns' Act* a court has a discretion to award equitable damages in addition to or in substitution for an injunction or specific performance. The jurisdiction under *Lord Cairns' Act* may be exercised where a plaintiff, at the time of commencement of proceedings or later, possesses an equity to an injunction or specific performance. Accordingly the jurisdiction has potential in a case in which such specific relief might be ordered. The cases where equitable damages may be awarded include cases of nuisance, obstruction of light, trespass, restrictive covenants, easements, *quia timet* relief, infringements of equitable interests, breach of confidence, vendor and purchaser, part performance and equitable estoppel. The jurisdiction also has potential where there is a breach of a statutory duty.

---

9   25 & 26 Vict c 42.
10 Supreme Court of Judicature Act 1873 (36 & 37 Vict c 66); Supreme Court of Judicature Act 1875 (38 & 39 Vict c 77).
11 (1975) 10 SASR 384.
12 (1975) 10 SASR 384 at 398.

There are certain procedural advantages in seeking an award of equitable damages. Proceedings for the specific performance of a contract, and equitable damages in addition to or in substitution for such relief, may be instituted before any breach of contract has taken place. There may be a deficiency of pleading in a case so that common law damages are unavailable, and consequently it may be necessary to consider whether equitable damages may be awarded.[13] Common law damages are also unavailable where there has been a failure to comply with a statute which requires a notice to be served before an action is commenced, although in such circumstances a court may grant equitable damages. Common law damages may not be awarded where a repudiation of a contract has not been accepted, nor where the plaintiff has put an end to the contract; but equitable damages may be awarded in such a case.

There are also differing rules for the assessment of equitable damages and these may advantage a plaintiff who seeks equitable damages instead of common law damages. Common law damages are generally awarded only in respect of damage sustained up to the date of the issue of a writ. A limited exception to this principle exists where rules of court permit an assessment of damages in respect of a continuing cause of action; in such a case damages may be assessed down to the date of assessment. Equitable damages may be awarded for loss sustained prior to the date of the trial, or for prospective loss.

In the context of a discussion of the jurisdiction to award equitable damages it has been found necessary to also mention some other monetary remedies which may be relevant in an equity suit.

---

13 I C F Spry, *Equitable Remedies*, 4th ed, Law Book Co, Sydney, 1990, p 607.

1

Jurisdiction of the Court of Chancery to Award Damages[*]

1.1 Medieval conception of damages

In modern times the remedy of damages is often regarded as a common law remedy and specific relief as the exclusive province of equity.[1] From an historical perspective it should be appreciated that from the earliest times the Royal Courts gave relief which was essentially of a proprietary nature, by which a suitor could recover some thing of which he had been deprived.[2] A suit would accordingly be instituted to recover a thing (whether land or a chattel), rather than damages. Prior to the time of Edward I the Royal Courts gave specific relief in a suit which was a real action, or was obviously connected with a real action.[3] It was only by a

---

[*] This chapter is a revised version of: P M McDermott, 'Jurisdiction of the Court of Chancery to Award Damages', *Law Quarterly Review*, vol 108, 1992, p 652.

1 Compare J Berryman, 'The Specific Performance Damages Continuum: An Historical Perspective', *Ottawa Law Review*, vol 17, 1985, 295 at p 296.

2 G T Washington, 'Damages in Contract at Common Law', *Law Quarterly Review*, vol 47, 1931, p 345.

3 W S Holdsworth, *History of English Law*, vol II, 4th ed, Methuen, London, 1936, p 247; A W B Simpson, *A History of the Common Law of Contract*, Oxford University Press, Oxford, 1975, p 14.

series of later developments that they awarded compensatory damages as ancillary relief to a claim for proprietary relief. This was one of the instances, by reason of statutory reform, in which damages could be awarded at law.

During the thirteenth century various statutes were passed which extended the circumstances in which land and damages (*dampna*) could be obtained in the one suit.[4] The Statute of Merton[5] enabled a widow 'deforced' of her dower to recover damages in a writ of dower.[6] The Statute of Marlborough provided for damages to be given to a feoffee,[7] against a lord, for distress sustained by a tenant in a suit[8] and in cases of waste.[9] The Statute of Gloucester[10] provided for damages to be given against the tenant in a writ of entry for disseisin and other writs. The assise of novel disseisin, from which the action of trespass originated, initially only gave recovery of land, and it was always uncertain whether chattels could be recovered. The Statute of Gloucester enabled the award of damages representing the value of those chattels removed in the course of the disseisin where restoration was impossible.[11] The Statute of Westminster II[12] provided for damages in *quare impedit*, and *darrain presentment* in the case of the usurpation of an advowson.

An award of damages was not restricted to compensatory damages. In some medieval cases an award of damages included the costs of a party. There are many instances where the award of damages by a medieval court included the costs of the clerks of the court which became known in the vernacular as 'damages cleer' (from *damna clericorum*).[13] One Year Book records the award of 'Damages: thirteen pounds, sixteen shillings, whereof forth shillings to the clerks' (*Dampna xiii libr' xvi s', unde clericis xl s–2*).[14] The medieval notion that costs are part of 'damages' has continued to prevail.[15]

The term 'damages' sometimes did not include the costs of a party. The

---

4   F Pollock and F W Maitland, *The History of English Law Before the Time of Edward I*, vol II, Cambridge University Press, Cambridge, 1985, pp 521–2. See also A W B Simpson, *A History of the Common Law of Contract*, Oxford University Press, Oxford, 1975, p 14.

5   20 Hen III c 1 (1235).

6   J Biancalana, 'The Writs of Dower and Chapter 49 of Westminster I', *Cambridge Law Journal*, vol 49, 1990, p 91.

7   52 Hen III c 6 (fraudulent feoffments) (1267). See also W S Holdsworth, *History of English Law*, vol IV, 3rd ed, Methuen, London, 1945, p 537.

8   52 Hen III c 9 (1267).

9   52 Hen III c 23 (1267).

10 6 Ed I c 1 (1278).

11 T F T Plucknett, *A Concise History of the Common Law*, 5th ed, Butterworths, London, 1956, p 369.

12 13 Ed I c 5 (1285).

13 W S Holdsworth, *History of English Law*, vol 1, 7th rev ed, Methuen, London, 1956, p 255; J J S Wharton, *Law Lexicon*, 14th ed, Stevens, London, 1938, p 296. See also B H Putnam, *Sir William Shareshull, Chief Justice of Common Pleas*, Cambridge University Press, Cambridge, 1950, p 89.

14 *Year Books of Edward II*, vol XXV, 12 Edw II, 1319, Selden Society, vol 81, 1964, p 126. See also *Select Cases of Trespass from the King's Courts 1307–1399*, vol 1, Selden Society, vol 100, 1984, p 6; *The Notebook of Sir John Port*, Selden Society, vol 102, 1986, pp 21, 161.

15 Co Litt 257a; *Phillips v Bacon* (1808) 9 East 298; 103 ER 587; *O'Loughlin v Fogarty* (1842) 5 Ir LR 54 at 63; *Andrews v Barnes* (1888) 39 Ch D 133 at 139.

Statute of Gloucester made a distinction between 'Damages' and 'Costs'. This statute is now regarded as the foundation for the law of costs, as the reference in the statute to 'Costs of his Writ purchased' has been liberally construed to include the legal costs of a suit.[16] The statute also provided that a plaintiff who recovered damages should also recover his costs.

The remedy of damages was not the exclusive province of the common law courts. Damages were awarded in both the Exchequer and Chancery. These were both offices of administration and were probably located in the same building.[17] By the late thirteenth century the Exchequer was holding the inquisition *ad quod damnum*: this procedure was particularly used with reference to mortmain.[18] From the fourteenth century the term 'damages' was used in cases in which the Chancellor exercised his jurisdiction to grant an account,[19] although now an account is regarded as an equitable claim for money had and received rather than damages.[20] In *Cardinal Beaufort's* case,[21] where a feoffee in trust wrongfully enfeoffed a third party, it is stated: 'I shall have a *subpoena* against my feoffee and recover damages for the value of the land'.[22] This case may have been an instance of indemnity or restitution.

In medieval times a suitor in Chancery was required by statute to find a sufficient surety. A fifteenth century statute provided that:

> ... no Writ of *Subpoena* be granted from henceforth until Surety be found to satisfy the Party so grieved and vexed for his Damages and Expenses, if so that the matter cannot be made good, which is contained in the Bill.[23]

The subpoena was the initial process of Chancery requiring under pain that the defendant appear.[24] Legislation requiring petitioners to find sureties that they would pay damages should their suit prove unfounded was generally not effective. In the fifteenth century, no sureties were accepted in the Court of Chancery unless they were of sufficient standing.[25] By the end of the sixteenth century, sureties were no longer required in Chancery. At that time West sought a revival of the practice. West, like Coke, recognised the practice of requiring sureties to be based upon statute.[26]

---

16 A Goodhart, 'Costs', *Yale Law Journal*, vol 38, 1929, 849 at p 852.
17 R P L Poole, *The Exchequer in the Twelfth Century*, Clarendon Press, Oxford, 1912, p 184.
18 S Raban, 'Mortmain in Medieval England', *Past and Present*, No 62, 1974, 3 at pp 18, 20.
19 W P Baildon (ed), *Select Cases in Chancery (AD 1364 to 1471)*, Selden Society, vol 10, 1896, pp 1, 107, 121.
20 *Watson v Holliday* (1882) 20 Ch D 780 at 784.
21 (1453) 31 Hen VI, Stratham Abr, Subpena, pl [1].
22 J H Baker and S F C Milsom, *Sources of English Legal History — Private Law to 1750*, Butterworths, London, 1986, p 95.
23 15 Hen VI c 4 (1436).
24 W J Jones, *The Elizabethan Court of Chancery*, Oxford University Press, Oxford, 1967, p 503.
25 M E Avery, 'An Evaluation of the Effectiveness of the Court of Chancery under the Lancastrian Kings', *Law Quarterly Review*, vol 86, 1970, 84 at p 96.
26 W J Jones, *The Elizabethan Court of Chancery*, Oxford University Press, Oxford, 1967, p 503. See also W West, *Second Part of Symboleography ('Of the Chancerie')*, C Yetsweirt (pub), London, 1594, p 39.

1.2 Ancient Chancery statutory jurisdiction

An ancient statute which was passed in the reign of Richard II enabled the Chancellor to award damages.[27] A leading American equity commentator said that this statute was a solemn recognition by parliament of the court as a distinct and permanent tribunal, having a separate jurisdiction and its own modes of procedure and of granting relief; and that the enactment was an important event in the legal history of the Court of Chancery.[28] The statute provided:

> For as much as People be compelled to come before the King's Council, or in the Chancery by Writs grounded upon untrue Suggestions; that the Chancellor for the Time being, presently after that such Suggestions be duly found and proved untrue, shall have Power to ordain and award Damages according to his Discretion, to him which is so troubled unduly, as afore is said.[29]

This jurisdiction was later required to be observed by a statute of Henry VI which empowered the Chancellor to take security for costs.[30] The term 'Damages' in the statute of Richard II is a reference to the costs that a defendant had sustained by reason of some false claim in Chancery. This was recognised by one legal historian, Burroughs, who said that this statute gave the Chancery 'Consistency, Discipline, and Order',[31] and that 'without a Power to give costs, it could scarce have any appearance, much less any Vigour of a Court of Equity'.[32]

The statute of Richard II did not extend to every Chancery suit where a petition was dismissed. The statute only conferred jurisdiction upon the Chancellor in a cause where a suggestion of a plaintiff was 'duly proved untrue'. Coke said that the statute 'extendeth not to a demurrer in law upon a bill, but upon hearing of the cause'.[33] As Bohun observed, the jurisdiction could only be exercised 'where the Truth of the Plaintiff's Suggestion is tried, & c which is not done upon a Demurrer where the Fact is confess'd',[34] although the actual practice in Chancery was contrary to the statute.[35] As the jurisdiction conferred by the statute could only be

---

27 17 Ric II c 6 (1393).

28 J N Pomeroy, *Pomeroy's Equity Jurisprudence*, vol 1, 3rd ed, Bancroft-Whitney, San Francisco, 1905, p 39, para 38.

29 O Ruffhead (ed), *Statutes at Large*, M Basket (pub), London, 1769, p 410. See also *Andrews v Barnes* (1888) 39 Ch D 133 at 139.

30 15 Hen VI c 4 (1436).

31 *History of the Chancery Relating to the Judicial Power of that Court and the Rights of the Masters*, J Wathoe (pub), London, 1726, p 50. (The authorship of this work is attributed to S Burroughs: see C E A Bedwell, *Middle Temple Catalogue*, vol 1, London, 1914, p 180.)

32 Burroughs, n 31 above, p 51.

33 E Coke, *Institutes of the Laws of England*, vol 4, W Clarke & Sons, London, 1817, cap 8, p 83. The common law jurisdiction of the Lord Chancellor included the grant of common law demurrers: see W J Jones, *The Elizabethan Court of Chancery*, Oxford University Press, Oxford, 1967, p 157.

34 W Bohun, *Course of Proceedings in the High Court of Chancery & c*, 2nd ed, J Wathoe, London, 1723, p 209.

35 D E C Yale (ed), *Lord Nottingham's 'Manual of Chancery Practice' and 'Prolegomena of*

exercised on or after the hearing of a cause, it could not be the foundation of the wide jurisdiction that the Chancellor possessed, from an early date, to award costs in all stages of a Chancery suit.[36]

Lord Hardwicke LC considered that the jurisdiction of the Court of Chancery to award costs was inherent, and was derived not 'from any authority, but from conscience'.[37] General Orders were periodically issued under which the Court of Chancery exercised a wide discretion as to costs. These General Orders did not have any statutory foundation, but were issued under the inherent authority of the Lord Chancellor.[38] The jurisdiction of the Chancellor in respect of costs was wide. The Court of Chancery not only possessed jurisdiction to allow for costs between party and party, but could also allow so much of the costs as between solicitor and client as was equitable.[39]

---◁◦▷---

1.3 Jurisdiction after the Middle Ages

It has already been mentioned that damages are traditionally regarded as a common law remedy. This appears from the following passage in Coke's *Institutes of the Laws of England*:

> 'Damages'. *Damna* in the common law hath a special signification for the recompence that is given by the jury to the plaintife or defendant,[40] for the wrong the defendant hath done onto him.[41]

Similarly, Blackstone in his *Commentaries* spoke of 'damages given to a man by a jury, as a compensation and satisfaction for some injury sustained'.[42]

The Court of Chancery generally regarded the remedy of damages as the province of the courts of common law.[43] However, the Court of Chancery could also award damages in an appropriate case. In the sixteenth and seventeenth centuries there were instances of the award of 'damages' by the Court of Chancery.[44] At this time, it would seem that the court would generally only intervene where no remedy at law was available. This was because there were instances where a defendant demurred to a bill upon

---

Chancery and Equity', Cambridge University Press, Cambridge, 1965, p 188, n 7.

36 *Andrews v Barnes* (1888) 39 Ch D 133 at 139; W S Holdsworth, *History of English Law*, vol IX, 3rd ed, Methuen, London, 1944, p 536; *Latoudis v Casey* (1990) 170 CLR 534 at 557 per Dawson J.

37 *Burford Corporation v Lenthall* (1743) 2 Atk 551 at 552; 26 ER 731 at 732.

38 *Andrews v Barnes* (1888) 39 Ch D 133 at 138.

39 *Sprague v Ticonic National Bank* (1939) 307 US 161 at 165 per Frankfurter J.

40 A note in the text states that the word 'defendant' seems to be printed in this place by mistake, instead of 'demandant'.

41 E Coke, *Institutes of the Laws of England*, vol II, 19th ed, London, 1832, 2572.

42 Blackstone, *Commentaries*, vol 2, 1766, p 438.

43 *Wiseman v Roper* (1645–1646) 1 Chan Rep 158 at 160; 21 ER 537; *Ranelaugh v Hayes* (1683) 1 Vern 189 at 190; 23 ER 405 at 406.

44 *Picketon v Littlecote* (1579–1580) Cary 93; 21 ER 49; *Johnson v Glemham* (1582–1583) Choyce Cas 169; 21 ER 98; 'Damages' (1588–1640) Tothill 51; 21 ER 121.

the ground that a plaintiff had a sufficient remedy at law.[45] Damages could be awarded as ancillary to an equitable remedy. One instance was where an injunction was granted to restrain waste. Damages were awarded in Chancery as compensation for waste committed upon woods.[46] Another example was the court's direction for the payment of debts beyond the Statute of Limitations where a will contained a direction for the payment of the debts.[47] The latter instance is clearly a case where equity fastened upon the conscience of a party, and provided a remedy where no remedy was available at law. There was one obvious limitation upon the jurisdiction: the court would not be concerned with trifles. The Court of Chancery would accordingly not entertain claims for small sums.[48]

It should be appreciated that at this time the term 'damages' had various meanings. In one Exchequer case the term 'damages' was used to refer to mesne profits.[49] Yale has pointed out that in early Chancery cases the term 'damages' had two primary senses: the term was used to refer to an indemnity[50] or to the payment of interest[51] and costs.[52] It may have been in the first sense that the term was used in *Cleaton v Gower*[53] where the plaintiff exhibited a bill for the execution of an agreement to work mines. The defendant submitted that as a tenant for life he was liable to account for waste, and therefore could not execute the agreement. The defendant had obviously contrived this reason to put in another tenant. The report of the case states that in addition to decreeing the execution of the 'Agreement *in Specie*, as far as he was capable of doing it', the defendant was required to 'satisfy the Plaintiff such Damages as he hath sustained in not enjoying the Premisses according to the Agreement'.[54] This decree may have been an order for indemnification for the expenditure for works as there was a complaint in the bill relating to the expenditure. It has been

45 *Wood v Tirrell* (1576–77) Cary 59; 21 ER 32.
46 *Browne v Dom' Bridges* (1588–89) Tothill 51–2; 21 ER 121. See also *Anonymous* Cary 2; 21 ER 1. The Chancery would forbid waste which was punishable at law in a case of 'wrong to the inhabitants, and hurt to the commonwealth', see *Anonymous* (1604) Cary 26; 21 ER 14. See also *Worsley v Stuart* (1711) 4 Brown 377; 2 ER 255. An injunction to stay waste could be granted where no remedy was available at law because ejectment proceedings could not be brought prior to the expiry of a notice to quit: see *Kane v Vanderburgh* (1814) 1 Johns Ch 11.
47 *Halsted v Little* (1632) Tothill 53; 21 ER 121.
48 *Knighton v Allen* (1579) Cary 80; 21 ER 43; *Marbar v Kempester* (1579) Cary 83; 21 ER 44.
49 *Dale v Sotherton* (Ex 1631) Hargr 30 f 277.
50 Compare *King v Atkins* (1332) 1 Sid 442; 82 ER 1206.
51 In some cases the term is clearly used to refer to 'interest' (see *Roo v Aspley* (1670) 1 Sid 442; 82 ER 1206 (*le Court taxer les damages (scil interest)*)), however, the term 'interest' (OF) was also then used to refer to compensation for injury, damages, or loss: see *Oxford English Dictionary*, 2nd ed, Oxford University Press, Oxford, p 1099; *Shorter Oxford English Dictionary*, vol 1, 3rd rev ed, Oxford University Press, Oxford, 1968, p 1027.
52 D E C Yale, *Lord Nottingham's Chancery Cases — Vol II*, Selden Society, vol 79, 1961, Introduction, p 15, n 3. See also *Robert Pilford's Case* (1613) 10 Co Rep 1156 at 1162; 77 ER 1102 at 1103. ('And that in all cases where a man should recover damages he should recover costs, which is meant of all cases where he should recover damages.')
53 (1674) Rep Temp Finch 164; 23 ER 90.
54 (1674) Rep Temp Finch 164; 23 ER 90.

suggested that this case is an example of an award of 'damages'.[55] It is however unlikely that the award was granted for compensatory damages, as the bill did not mention any such complaint. Sir Edward Fry in his classic work on specific performance regarded the decree as an early instance of an award of compensation.[56]

Quantum damnificatus

The Court of Chancery had an established jurisdiction to ascertain compensation or damages by either directing an issue, *quantum damnificatus*, to be tried at law by a jury, or by giving a reference to a master or a chief clerk.[57] It would appear that the usual course was to direct an issue to be tried before a jury, but in some cases a reference was given to the master to settle the amount of damages.[58] There are a number of cases which recognise the existence of this jurisdiction. In *Phillips v Thompson*,[59] a New York Chancery case, Chancellor Kent remarked:

> The cases are numerous in which the Court of Chancery has caused damages to be assessed, either by an issue or by a master, at its discretion. (2 Fonb 441; *Hedges v Everard;*[60] *Cudd v Rutter;*[61] *Errington v Aynesly*[62]). I believe that the more usual course, where the damages are not a matter of mere computation, is by awarding an issue.[63]

The jurisdiction to direct an issue was recognised as early as the seventeenth century. In *Ranelaugh v Hayes*[64] Lord Keeper North decreed performance in specie of an indemnity given by an assignee in respect of the assignment of several shares of the excise of Ireland, while observing that 'the court then might, if there should be occasion, direct a trial at law in a *quantum damnificatus*'.[65] The Lord Keeper gave as one reason for the decree:

> That the computation of damages in such a cause must depend upon examination of long and intricate accounts of the revenue of Ireland, which cannot be made upon a trial at law, and a jury cannot foretel what damages will after happen, but must give their verdict upon uncertainties, which will afterwards occasion suits in this court.[66]

---

55 R P Meagher, W M C Gummow and J R F Lehane, *Equity — Doctrines and Remedies*, 2nd ed, Butterworths, Sydney, 1984, p 517 [2304]; 3rd ed, Butterworths, Sydney, 1992, p 639 [2305].

56 E Fry, *Specific Performance of Contracts*, 6th ed, Stevens, London, 1921, p 583.

57 D E C Yale, *Lord Nottingham's Chancery Cases — Vol II*, Selden Society, vol 79, 1961, Introduction, p 15, n 3; R M Jackson, *The History of Quasi-Contract in English Law*, Cambridge University Press, Cambridge, 1936, p xiii. See also *Denton v Stewart* (1786) 17 Ves 280n; 34 ER 108; *Greenaway v Adams* (1806) 12 Ves 395; 33 ER 149.

58 *Wade v Paget* (1784) 1 Bro CC 363 at 368; 28 ER 1180 at 1182; *Greenaway v Adams* (1806) 12 Ves 395 at 402; 33 ER 149 at 152; *Sutton v Mashiter* (1829) 2 Sim 513 at 514; 57 ER 880. See also *McNulty v Hamill* (1815) Beat 544 at 549 (account).

59 (1814) 1 Johns Ch 130.

60 1 Eq Cas Abr 18, pl 7.

61 1 P Wms 570.

62 2 Bro 341.

63 (1814) 1 Johns Ch 130 at 151.

64 (1683) 1 Vern 189; 23 ER 405.

65 (1683) 1 Vern 189 at 190; 23 ER 405 at 406.

66 (1683) 1 Vern 189 at 190 n 3; 23 ER 405 at 406.

11

An issue, *quantum damnificatus*, was directed in *City of London v Nash*[67] where the municipality sought specific performance of a building lease. It was clear that specific relief was inappropriate as it would have resulted in the demolition of needed housing. The equity suit was really brought to recover damages. Lord Hardwicke LC remarked: 'It would be of no service to the city of London to make such a decree, for all they want is to be compensated in damages, and therefore the court ought not to make a decree for a specific performance'.[68] The Lord Chancellor added: 'The relief must be by way of inquiry of damages before a jury; and I am more inclined to this, than to decree a specific performance'.[69]

It would seem that the usual practice of the Court of Chancery in not directing an issue was not derived from any lack of jurisdiction of the Chancery to assess damages, but because the Chancery at this time lacked adequate judicial resources.[70] It was not until the nineteenth century that the number of judicial officers in the Chancery was significantly increased. In 1813 the arrears of Chancery business which accumulated under Lord Eldon's tenure of the woolsack resulted in the appointment of a Vice-Chancellor.[71] The procedural jurisdiction of the Master of the Rolls was extended in 1833.[72] In 1841 two more Vice-Chancellors were appointed after the equity jurisdiction of the Exchequer[73] was transferred to the Court of Chancery.[74] In 1851 two Lord Justices of Appeal were appointed.

The procedure of directing an issue was invoked where the Court of Chancery exercised jurisdiction to relieve against a penalty or forfeiture upon terms that the defaulting party paid damages.[75] This is reflected in the ancient maxim of equity that:

---

67 (1747) 3 Atk 512; 26 ER 1095. The existence of this authority disproves the assertion that the Chancery Amendment Act 1858 (*Lord Cairns' Act*) (21 & 22 Vict c 27) 'gave the Court [of Chancery] power to award damages in lieu of specific performance, a power, the existence of which despite *Denton v Stewart* (1786) 1 Cox Eq Cas 258; 29 ER 1156, one must doubt prior to 1858': R P Meagher, W M C Gummow and J R F Lehane, *Equity — Doctrines and Remedies*, 2nd ed, Butterworths, Sydney, 1984, p 519 [2306]; 3rd ed, Butterworths, Sydney, 1992, p 640 [2307].

68 (1747) 3 Atk 512 at 516; 26 ER 1095 at 1097.

69 (1747) 3 Atk 512 at 517; 26 ER 1095 at 1098.

70 Compare J H Langbein, 'Fact Finding in the English Court of Chancery: A Rebuttal', *Yale Law Journal*, vol 83, 1974, 1620 at pp 1629–30.

71 R E Megarry, 'The Vice-Chancellors', *Law Quarterly Review*, vol 98, 1982, 370 at p 371.

72 See Megarry, n 71 above, p 372, n 6.

73 As to the equity jurisdiction of the Exchequer: see W H Bryson, *The Equity Side of the Exchequer*, Cambridge University Press, Cambridge, 1975.

74 T F T Plucknett, *A Concise History of the Common Law*, 5th ed, Butterworths, London, 1956, pp 209–10; R E Megarry, 'The Vice-Chancellors', *Law Quarterly Review*, vol 98, 1982, 370 at p 377.

75 D E C Yale, *Lord Nottingham's Chancery Cases — Vol II*, Selden Society, vol 79, 1961, Introduction, p 15, n 3; A W B Simpson, *A History of the Common Law of Contract*, Oxford University Press, Oxford, 1975, p 120. See also J L Barton, 'Penalties and Damages', *Law Quarterly Review*, vol 92, 1976, p 20.

Equity suffers not Advantage to be taken of a Penalty or Forfeiture, where Compensation can be made.[76]

An example of the exercise of this jurisdiction is *Errington v Aynesly*[77] where the Court of Chancery directed an issue, *quantum damnificatus*, where a plaintiff was relieved from a penalty due under a bond. The plaintiff contracted to build a bridge over the river Tyne for £9,000, and entered into a sum, conditioned for the performance of the contract. He built the bridge, but it was destroyed by a flood and it was found that no bridge built on that site could stand. He filed a bill to be relieved against the bond by seeking an issue of *quantum damnificatus* upon his building a bridge where it could not properly be built. Upon submitting to an issue, he was relieved from the penalty.[78]

In the exercise of this jurisdiction an issue would not be directed where compensation was not thought possible or damages could not be assessed.[79]

---◄○►---

1.4 *Hooker v Arthur; Stafford v Mayor of London*

The decisions in *Hooker v Arthur*[80] and *Stafford v Mayor of London*[81] have caused some difficulties, and provoked much discussion. The decisions have been regarded by several commentators as authority for the proposition that the Court of Chancery would not exercise any jurisdiction to either award or assess damages. In one leading Australian equity text it is said that the decision in *Hooker v Arthur*[82] 'established that Chancery would not entertain an action for damages, in that case for breach of covenant in a lease, where this was the principal relief sought'.[83] Another commentator has remarked that both cases evidence 'a reluctance on the part of the Court of Chancery to assess damages'.[84] It is submitted that these views of the cases cannot be supported.

---

76 R Francis, *Maxims of Equity*, 2nd ed, London, 1739, p 44 (Maxim XII); D E C Yale, *Lord Nottingham's Chancery Cases — Vol II*, Selden Society, vol 79, 1961, Introduction, p 16; A W B Simpson, *A History of the Common Law of Contract*, Oxford University Press, Oxford, 1975, p 121.

77 (1788) 2 Bro CC 341; 29 ER 191.

78 See also *Davis v Hone* (1805) 2 Sch & Lef 341 at 351.

79 A W B Simpson, *A History of the Common Law of Contract*, Oxford University Press, Oxford, 1975, p 121.

80 (1671–1672) 2 Chan Rep 62; 21 ER 616.

81 (1719) 6 Vin Abr 472 pl 10.

82 (1671–1672) 2 Chan Rep 62; 21 ER 616.

83 R P Meagher, W M C Gummow and J R F Lehane, *Equity — Doctrines and Remedies*, 2nd ed, Butterworths, Sydney, 1984, p 517 [2304]; 3rd ed, Butterworths, Sydney, 1992, p 638–9 [2304].

84 C Harpum, 'Specific Performance with Compensation as a Purchaser's Remedy', *Cambridge Law Journal*, vol 40, 1981, 47 at p 70, n 37.

In *Hooker v Arthur*[85] the plaintiff had been the defendant to an action at law in which he alleged that damages were improperly claimed, and he unsuccessfully sought to invoke the jurisdiction of the Court of Chancery to review a judgment at law. It should be borne in mind that at this time there was a general principle that 'a Cause shall not be examined upon Equity in the Court of Requests, Chancery, or other Court of Equity, after Judgment at the Common Law'.[86] (There was an exception, which was not relevant in this case, where a common injunction could issue if a party had unconscionably obtained a judgment in a common law court.[87]) In these circumstances the court ordered the parties to proceed at law upon the covenant. The case was therefore not authority for the proposition that the Court of Chancery did not have any jurisdiction to award or assess damages, but rather that the Court of Chancery would not act as an appellate tribunal to review an action at law.

The report by Viner of *Stafford's* case is brief and merely states: 'Breach of Covenant is triable at law, for equity will not settle damages'.[88] Similarly, a note of the case in *A General Abridgment of Cases in Equity* states: 'Breach of Covenants triable at law; for Equity will not settle damages'.[89] *Stafford's* case, which was more extensively reported by Brown,[90] concerned proceedings in error upon a judgment at law that was taken on appeal to the House of Lords from the Court of Exchequer. In a second action the municipality obtained judgment by default for arrears of rent due upon a lease. In the first action the plaintiffs pleaded in abatement that one lessee who was reported dead was living: the plea of abatement was presumably made because of the non-joinder of a necessary party. The arguments of the parties before the House of Lords were primarily directed towards whether the City of London owned various properties which the municipality could properly demise, and towards the exceptions in the grant of lease. As a subsidiary argument the municipality submitted: 'That whether the respondents had broken any of their covenants or not was a matter properly triable at law; as the damages (supposing a breach) could not be settled without such trial'.[91] This argument appears extracted as a headnote in Brown's report although the report does not disclose that this subsidiary argument was central to the case. That the Court of Chancery at this time possessed jurisdiction to award damages may be seen from one case in which the principal relief sought was arrears of rental not recoverable at law, although there was no ground in equity to grant relief.[92]

———◦———

85 (1671–1672) 2 Chan Rep 62; 21 ER 616.
86 1 Eq Cas Abr 130; 21 ER 935.
87 *Earl of Oxford's Case* (1615) 1 Rep Ch 1.
88 (1719) 6 Vin Abr 472 pl 10.
89 (1719) 1 Eq Cas Abr 18; 21 ER 840.
90 (1719) 4 Brown 635; 2 ER 433 (HL).
91 (1719) 4 Brown 635 at 639; 2 ER 433 at 435.
92 *Episcopus Sarum v Nosworthy* (1671–1672) 2 Chan Rep 60; 21 ER 616.

1.5 Eighteenth century

By the eighteenth century it was clear that the Court of Chancery could award or assess damages in an appropriate case. In *Lannoy v Werry*[93] it was considered that the Court of Chancery could settle a difference in damages where there was sufficient evidence before the court. Lord Chancellor Harcourt remarked that the court could assess damages where it was 'unlikely, that any better evidence than was already before the Court could be had before a jury'.[94] A similar case is the Irish case of *Martyn v Blake*[95] where it was held that if a covenant sounding in damages is collateral to a matter in equity, a court of equity acquires jurisdiction to award damages in order to prevent a circuity of action. Sir Edward Sugden LC (of Ireland) observed:

> If I were to send this case to trial in a court of law, for damages, I know what the measure of damages would be, namely, the amount of the arrears of the annuity and interest on those arrears.[96]

At this time the Court of Chancery also assumed jurisdiction to award damages where specific performance for the sale of land was sought, but where it was impossible to decree specific relief because of misconduct by the vendor in selling the land to another party.[97] In *Denton v Stewart*[98] a bill contained a prayer for the specific performance of a partly executed parol agreement to assign a lease. The court could not decree specific performance as the lease had been assigned to another person for valuable consideration without notice of the agreement. The Statute of Frauds 1677[99] also precluded an action at law for damages.[100] Sir Lloyd Kenyon MR provided a remedy to the innocent plaintiff by directing a reference to the Master of the Rolls to inquire into what damages the plaintiff had sustained. However, the purpose of the decree was primarily intended to award the costs of the suit to the plaintiff. J Mansfield, for the defendant, unsuccessfully objected to the form of the decree as it was probable that the plaintiff had not sustained any damage. The Master of the Rolls said that even if the plaintiff was only entitled to nominal damages, the defendant had acted so dishonestly that he ought to pay the costs of the suit.[101] In these circumstances the case may be of limited value as a precedent, although at the time the decision was regarded as authority for the proposition that damages could be awarded in equity. Soon after in

---

93 (1717) 4 Brown 630; 2 ER 429.
94 (1717) 4 Brown 630 at 634; 2 ER 429 at 432.
95 (1842) 3 Dr & War 125; 61 RR 27.
96 (1842) 3 Dr & War 125 at 141; 61 RR 27 at 32.
97 *Denton v Stewart* (1786) 17 Ves 280n; 34 ER 108; *Greenaway v Adams* (1806) 12 Ves 395; 33 ER 149.
98 (1786) 17 Ves 280n; 34 ER 108.
99 29 Chas II c 3 s 4.
100 C Harpum, 'Specific Performance with Compensation as a Purchaser's Remedy', *Cambridge Law Journal*, vol 40, 1981, p 71, n 41. See also *Lavery v Pursell* (1888) 39 Ch D 508 at 518.
101 (1786) 17 Ves 280n; 34 ER 108.

Brodie v St Paul[102] J Scott (Solicitor-General, later Sir John Scott and subsequently Lord Eldon) remarked in argument that *Denton v Stewart*[103] was decided on the principle that: 'If a lease is not made to him, because Defendant covenanted to do, what he could not do, he ought to put Plaintiff in the same situation'.[104]

The decision in *Denton v Stewart*[105] was followed with some apparent reluctance in *Greenaway v Adams*.[106] In this case, specific performance of an agreement to assign a lease could not be decreed because there was a subsequent sale and assignment of that lease to a third party. Sir William Grant MR stated that a party injured by the non-performance of a contract could either resort to a court of law for damages or to a court of equity for a specific performance. Sir William Grant expressed the view that if a court of equity did 'not think fit to decree a specific performance, or finds, that the contract cannot be specifically performed, either way I should have thought there was equally an end of its jurisdiction'.[107] However, Sir William Grant recognised that:

> ... the case of *Denton v Stuart* is a decision in point against that proposition; and the species facti is precisely the same as in this case; for in that the inability of the party to perform the contract grew out of an act done by the party, after the contract had been entered into.[108]

Sir William Grant directed a reference to the Master, remarking: 'I shall yield my doubts to the authority of Lord Kenyon'.[109] Earlier in *Hall v Warren*[110] Sir William Grant had commented: 'it is as much of course in this Court to decree a specific performance, as it is to give damages at Law'.[111]

It may have been arguable that *Greenaway v Adams*[112] was distinguishable from *Denton v Stewart*[113] as in the latter case the court provided a remedy where no remedy at law was available. In *Greenaway v Adams*[114] it appears that there was no obstacle to the plaintiff commencing an action for damages. *Denton v Stewart*[115] was followed in the New York case of *Phillips v Thompson*[116] where an issue, *quantum damnificatus*, was directed even though the doctrine of part performance could not be applied to take a case out of the Statute of Frauds. Chancellor Kent remarked: 'Justice demands that the plaintiff should have relief, and I

---

102 (1791) 1 Ves 326; 30 ER 368.
103 (1786) 17 Ves 280n; 34 ER 108.
104 (1791) 1 Ves 326 at 329; 30 ER 368 at 370.
105 (1786) 17 Ves 280n; 34 ER 108.
106 (1806) 12 Ves 395; 33 ER 149.
107 (1806) 12 Ves 395 at 401; 33 ER 149 at 152.
108 (1806) 12 Ves 395 at 401–2; 33 ER 149 at 152.
109 (1806) 12 Ves 395 at 402; 33 ER 149 at 152. In discussing this passage Lord Brougham LC referred to Lord Roslyn instead of Lord Kenyon: see *Jenkins v Parkinson* (1833) 2 My & K 5 at 12; 39 ER 846 at 849.
110 (1804) 9 Ves 605; 32 ER 738.
111 (1804) 9 Ves 605 at 608; 32 ER 738 at 739.
112 (1806) 12 Ves 395; 33 ER 149.
113 (1786) 17 Ves 280n; 34 ER 108.
114 (1806) 12 Ves 395; 33 ER 149.
115 (1786) 17 Ves 280n; 34 ER 108.
116 (1814) 1 Johns Ch 130.

am apprehensive he would be remediless without the aid of this court'.[117] Later in *Hatch v Cobb*[118] Chancellor Kent explained that in *Phillips v Thompson*,[119] 'The bill was filed for discovery and for specific performance, and the plaintiff made out a case of very clear equity to relief, and the remedy was precarious at law'.[120] It might be mentioned that there are some obstacles to an award of damages in a case of part performance. Despite earlier suggestions that damages could be awarded at law where there was part performance,[121] it was decided by Sir Frederick Pollock LCB in *Massey v Johnson*[122] that there was 'no foundation for any such doctrine'.[123]

In *Gwillim v Stone*[124] Sir William Grant MR reiterated his doubts as to whether damages ought to be awarded in equity. In that case a bill prayed the delivery up of a contract on account of the defective title of the vendor, and sought compensation. A decree for the delivery up of the instrument was made without prejudice to an action. Sir William Grant was not disposed to direct an inquiry as the case was 'more proper for an action'.[125] The Master of the Rolls distinguished *Denton v Stewart*[126] and *Greenaway v Adams*[127] by stating: 'In those cases the object of the bill was a specific performance; and in the latter I had some doubt upon the principle'.[128]

----◄◦►----

1.6 Todd v Gee

A distinct change in the attitude of the Court of Chancery was evident after the decision in *Todd v Gee*,[129] where damages were sought in the alternative to specific performance of an agreement for the sale of an estate.

---

117 (1814) 1 Johns Ch 130 at 151.
118 (1820) 4 Johns Ch 559.
119 (1814) 1 Johns Ch 130.
120 (1820) 4 Johns Ch 559 at 561. See also *Wiswall v McGowan* (1839) 1 Hoff Ch 125.
121 *Whitbread v Brockhurst* (1784) 1 Bro CC 404 at 417; 28 ER 1205 at 1211 per Lord Thurlow LC. ('There certainly are cases which have considered an agreement which has been partly executed as never having been within the original view of the statute; and this has been a ground to induce the Court of King's Bench, as I am told, to determine this case to be entirely out of the statute'); *Brodie v St Paul* (1791) 1 Ves 326 at 333; 30 ER 368 at 372 per Buller J ('As to the part performance; Courts of law have lately adopted the same sort of reasoning, that prevails in this Court; that there can be but one true construction upon the Statute of Frauds. Whatever it is, it ought to hold equally both in Courts of Law and of Equity; and that, as it is settled in Equity, that a part-performance takes it out of the statute, the same rule shall hold at law').
122 (1847) 1 Ex 241; 154 ER 102.
123 (1847) 1 Ex 241 at 252; 154 ER 102 at 107. The Chancery Amendment Act 1858 (*Lord Cairns' Act*) (21 & 22 Vict c 27) enabled equitable damages to be awarded in a case of part performance: see P M McDermott, 'Equitable Damages in Nova Scotia', *Dalhousie Law Review*, vol 12, 1989, 131 at pp 140–2.
124 (1807) 14 Ves 128; 33 ER 469.
125 (1807) 14 Ves 128 at 129; 33 ER 469 at 470.
126 (1786) 17 Ves 280n; 34 ER 108.
127 (1806) 12 Ves 395; 33 ER 149.
128 (1807) 14 Ves 128 at 129; 33 ER 469 at 470.
129 (1810) 17 Ves 273; 34 ER 106.

The plaintiff charged that the defendants were unable to perform the agreement as the estate was devised in trust to pay debts and legacies. It was held that accounts could be taken to determine whether title could be made. However, Lord Eldon took exception to the claim for damages, and ruled:

> ... except in very special cases, it is not the course of proceeding in Equity to file a Bill for specific performance of an agreement; praying in the alternative, if it cannot be performed, an issue, or an inquiry before the Master, with a view to damages. The Plaintiff must take that remedy, if he chooses it, at Law.[130]

The Lord Chancellor also commented: 'In *Denton v Stewart* the Defendant had it in his power to perform the agreement; and put it out of his power pending the suit. The case, if it is not to be supported upon that distinction, is not according to the principles of the Court'.[131]

Todd v Gee[132] was followed in New York by Chancellor Kent who remarked in *Hatch v Cobb*[133] that 'though equity, in very special cases, may possibly sustain a bill for damages, on a breach of contract, it is clearly not the ordinary jurisdiction of the court'.[134] Later in *Kempshall v Stone*[135] Chancellor Kent observed: 'The more I have reflected on the subject, the more strongly do I adhere to that opinion'.[136] Chancellor Kent considered that a bill filed for the 'sole purpose of assessing damages for a breach of contract ... is a matter strictly of legal, and not of equitable jurisdiction'.[137] Chancellor Kent placed great reliance on English Chancery precedents.[138]

The decision of Lord Eldon detracted from any authority that was previously accorded to the decisions in *Denton v Stewart*[139] and *Greenaway v Adams*.[140] In *Williams v Higden*[141] Sir Lancelot Shadwell VC remarked that 'the authorities giving damages in this Court, by reason of a vendor's selling property that was not his own, have been reviewed of late years and overruled'.[142] In *Jenkins v Parkinson*[143] Lord Brougham LC observed that 'It may now be affirmed that those two cases are no longer law'.[144] In *Sainsbury v Jones*[145] Lord Cottenham LC commented:

---

130 (1810) 17 Ves 273 at 279; 34 ER 106 at 108.
131 (1810) 17 Ves 273 at 279; 34 ER 106 at 108.
132 (1810) 17 Ves 273; 34 ER 106.
133 (1820) 4 Johns Ch 559.
134 (1820) 4 Johns Ch 559 at 560.
135 (1821) 5 Johns Ch 193.
136 (1821) 5 Johns Ch 193 at 195.
137 (1821) 5 Johns Ch 193 at 195.
138 J T Horton, *James Kent: A Study in Conservatism, 1763–1847*, Appleton-Century Co, New York, 1939, p 207.
139 (1786) 17 Ves 280n; 34 ER 108.
140 (1806) 12 Ves 395; 33 ER 149.
141 (1828) CP Cooper 500; 47 ER 619.
142 (1828) CP Cooper 500 at 500–1; 47 ER 619.
143 (1833) 2 My & K 5; 39 ER 846.
144 (1833) 2 My & K 5 at 12; 39 ER 846 at 849.
145 (1839) 5 My & Cr 1; 41 ER 272.

... my having known the profession sufficiently long to recollect the time when the decision of Lord Kenyon in *Denton v Stewart* had not been formally overruled; but, at that time, very little weight was attached to it.[146]

The Lord Chancellor added: 'Lord Eldon, in 1810, in *Todd v Gee* expressly overruled *Denton v Stewart*'.[147] The decision in *Todd v Gee*[148] was followed by the Court of Chancery for more than forty years. After the decision the court disclaimed any jurisdiction to award damages where purchasers unsuccessfully sought specific performance of a contract for an estate.[149] Also the court would not entertain claims for damages whether in respect of a defect in a vendor's title[150] or for the misconduct of a solicitor.[151]

The Court of Chancery declined to grant a *ne exeat regno* (or *regnum*) for the amount obtained upon an action for the breach of a covenant in a lease.[152] The Court of Chancery possessed jurisdiction to issue a writ *ne exeat regno*[153] where there were circumstances present which would constitute an equity, such as fraud or the liability to account. The writ would issue on a money demand in the nature of an equitable demand or equitable debt,[154] but not on a legal demand for a sum for which the defendant would be held to bail.[155]

---

146 (1839) 5 My & Cr 1 at 3; 41 ER 272 at 273.

147 (1839) 5 My & Cr 1 at 3; 41 ER 272 at 273.

148 (1810) 17 Ves 273; 34 ER 106.

149 *Blore v Sutton* (1817) 3 Mer 237 at 248; 36 ER 91 at 95; *Sainsbury v Jones* (1839) 5 My & Cr 1 at 3–4; 41 ER 272 at 273. See also *Kempshall v Stone* (1821) 5 Johns Ch 193 at 195; *Aberaman Ironworks v Wickens* (1868) LR 5 Eq 485 at 515; *Pearl Life Assurance Company v Buttenshaw* [1893] WN 123.

150 *Williams v Higden* (1828) CP Cooper 500; 47 ER 619. See also *Kempshall v Stone* (1821) 5 Johns Ch 193 at 195; *Malden v Fyson* (1846) 9 Beav 347; 50 ER 377.

151 *Tylee v Webb* (1851) 14 Beav 14 at 16; 51 ER 192 at 193.

152 *Jenkins v Parkinson* (1833) 2 My & K 5 at 12; 39 ER 846 at 849. The plaintiff died before judgment was perfected, and his executors instituted proceedings in equity for a *ne exeat* to obtain the costs of the action which would be otherwise lost. Lord Brougham LC regarded the amount of the verdict to be 'damages', and considered that the executors were in no better position than if their bill had prayed compensation for the breach of the lease. The suit for a *ne exeat* was obviously filed in an attempt to obviate the general rule in equity that if costs are not taxed they die with the person: see *Kemp v Mackrell* (1744) 2 Ves 580; 28 ER 370. Although where a plaintiff died after a decree for costs and before taxation, the costs could be recovered by the personal representatives of that party by a bill of revivor: see *Morgan v Scudamore* (1796) 3 Ves 195; 30 ER 965; *Travis v Waters* (1814) 1 Johns Ch 85.

153 The history of the writ *ne exeat regno* was reviewed by Megarry J in *Felton v Callis* [1969] 1 QB 200. See also *Al Nahkel for Contracting and Trading Ltd v Lowe* [1986] QB 235; *Allied Arab Bank Ltd v Hajjar* [1988] QB 787.

154 *King v Smith* (1741) Dick 82; 21 ER 199; *Anonymous* (1741) 2 Atk 210; 26 ER 530; *Cock v Ravie* (1801) 6 Ves 283; 31 ER 1053; *Jones v Sampson* (1803) 8 Ves 593; 32 ER 485; *Jackson v Petrie* (1804) 10 Ves 164 at 165; 32 ER 807; *Genet v Tallmadge* (1814) 1 Johns Ch 1; *Genet v Tallmadge* (1814) 1 Johns Ch 1; *Glover v Walters* (1950) 80 CLR 172 (ne exeat colonia). See also *Ex parte Duncombe* (1774) Dick 503; 21 ER 365.

155 *Pearne v Lisle* (1749) Amb 75 at 76; 27 ER 47 at 48; *Crosley v Marriot* (1783) Dick 609; 21 ER 408.

The availability of the writ *ne exeat regno* has been discussed in a number of judgments. In *Genet v Tallmadge*[156] Chancellor Kent observed:

> The writ of *ne exeat* cannot be granted for a debt due and recoverable at law. As a general rule it is applicable only to equitable demands.[157]

Similarly in *Glover v Walters*[158] Sir Owen Dixon remarked:

> It is a prerogative writ used for the purpose of preventing a subject quitting the country without giving bail or security to answer a money claim of an equitable nature.[159]

The attitude of the Court of Chancery at that time was reflected in contemporary texts. Fonblanque wrote that 'the Chancery cannot assess damages'.[160] Hovenden remarked: 'If the performance of the contract be impossible, the vendee's remedy is, generally speaking, only to be had at law, by an action for damages, which cannot be given in Equity'.[161] In *Bacon's Abridgement* it is stated that 'whenever the matter of the bill is merely in damages, there the remedy is at law, because the damages cannot be ascertained by the conscience of the Chancellor, and therefore must be settled by a jury'.[162] Maddock, of Lincoln's Inn, commented that:

> ... it seems that compensation will not be granted for the loss sustained by the failure of the Contract, though the Bill pray, in the alternative, a specific performance, or an Issue, or an Inquiry before the Master with a view to damages, that being more properly the subject of an Action.[163]

From an historical perspective it should be appreciated that *Todd v Gee*[164] was decided at a time of decline of the Court of Chancery. The deterioration of Chancery procedure is a perennial theme of English legal history. The Court of Chancery was established in the fourteenth century because of its superior modes of procedure and proof; but by the nineteenth century the court was the setting for Charles Dicken's *Bleak*

---

156 (1814) 1 Johns Ch 1.
157 (1814) 1 Johns Ch 1 at 1–2.
158 (1950) 80 CLR 172.
159 (1950) 80 CLR 172.
160 J Fonblanque, *A Treatise of Equity*, vol 1, 5th ed, London, 1820, p 44.
161 J E Hovenden, *Jurisdiction of Courts of Equity in Matters of Fraud & c*, vol II, Sweet, England, 1825, p 38.
162 M Bacon, *New Abridgement of the Law*, vol I, 7th ed, A Strahan, London, 1832, p 134. This passage appears to be derived from the following sentence in Lord Chief Baron Gilbert's *The History and Practice of the High Court of Chancery (Forum Romanum)*, London, 1758, p 219: 'And it is a general rule, that wherever the matter of a Bill is merely in damages, there the remedy is at law, because the damages cannot be ascertained by the conscience of the chancellor, and therefore must be settled by a jury at law; and therefore the Chancery never tries the quantum of the damages in a quantum damnificatus, where you demur to the bill, unless there be matter of fraud mixed with damages'. Forum Romanum (sometimes cited as *Gil For Rom*) is not regarded as accurately depicting Chancery practice as established when the work was written: see W H Maxwell and L F Maxwell, *Legal Bibliography of the British Commonwealth*, vol I, 2nd ed, Sweet & Maxwell, London, 1955, p 338.
163 H Maddock, *A Treatise of the Principles and Practice of the High Court of Chancery*, vol I, 3rd ed, London, 1837, p 557.
164 (1810) 17 Ves 273; 34 ER 106.

House.[165] In the early nineteenth century the growth of formalism coincided with the decline of equity. Atiyah observed: 'The Court of Chancery itself went into a period of decline towards the beginning of this period from which it never wholly recovered. Partly, if not chiefly, this decline was due to the purely fortuitous nature of Lord Eldon's disposition'.[166] Formalism is another perennial theme in the history of the Court of Chancery: the growing formality of Chancery procedure was also evident in the Elizabethan period.[167]

------◄○►------

1.7 Mid-nineteenth century

An interesting development occurred prior to the enactment of the Chancery Amendment Act 1858 (*Lord Cairns' Act*, which vested the Court of Chancery with a statutory jurisdiction to award damages) by which the Court of Chancery reasserted a jurisdiction to award damages.[168] In *Phelps v Prothero*[169] the plaintiff brought an action at law, which was later compromised, for damages for breaches of covenants in a lease. The defendant had sought specific performance of the compromise, and later commenced an action at law for damages for breach of the compromise. It was inconsistent for a party to simultaneously seek both specific performance and damages at law in reference to the same subject-matter.[170] This was recognised by Turner LJ who remarked: 'The Defendant had originally the right to proceed, either at law, for breach of the agreement, or in this Court, for the specific performance of it'.[171] The Lords Justices of Appeal held that a party who commenced proceedings in equity was bound to submit a claim for damages to the judgment of the court of equity. Turner LJ remarked:

> ... a Plaintiff, who has legal rights, and comes to this Court for its aid, is bound to put his legal rights under the control of the Court, and that that principle reaches the present case. The Plaintiff, therefore, having sued in equity for specific performance, was bound, in my opinion, to submit his

---

165 J H Langbein, 'Fact Finding in the English Court of Chancery: A Rebuttal', *Yale Law Journal*, vol 83, 1974, 1620 at pp 1628–9.

166 P S Atiyah, *The Rise and Fall of Freedom of Contract*, Oxford University Press, Oxford, 1979, pp 392–3.

167 W J Jones, *The Elizabethan Court of Chancery*, Oxford University Press, Oxford, 1967, p 309.

168 *Phelps v Prothero* (1855) 7 De GM & G 722; 44 ER 280; *Gedye v Montrose, Duke of* (1858) 26 Beav 45; 53 ER 813.

169 (1855) 7 De GM & G 722; 44 ER 280.

170 *Fennings v Humphery* (1841) 4 Beav 1 at 6; 49 ER 237 at 239; *Beaufort v Glynn* (1856) 3 Sm & G 213 at 226; 65 ER 630 at 636; *Kell v Nokes* (1863) 32 LJ Ch 785; *Tredegar v Windus* (1875) LR 19 Eq 607 at 613–15. A plaintiff who recovered damages in respect of a contract could not then claim specific performance: see *Sainter v Ferguson* (1849) 1 Mac & G 286.

171 (1855) 7 De GM & G 722 at 733–4; 44 ER 280 at 285.

claim for damages to the judgment of this Court, and was not entitled to proceed at law otherwise than by leave of this Court.[172]

A similar development occurred in the United States of America where a plaintiff in an equity suit who made no demand for damages or failed to introduce proof as to damages was precluded from later maintaining an action at law to recover damages.[173] A court of equity could, in addition to giving equitable relief, award damages to finally determine a controversy over which it had jurisdiction.[174] In an equity suit damages could be awarded where specific performance was not an appropriate remedy, particularly where clauses were too indefinite to be the subject of an order.[175]

In *Raineri v Miles*[176] Lord Edmund-Davies expressed an opinion, in reliance on remarks of Turner LJ in *Phelps v Prothero*,[177] that upon a vendor's default a purchaser who proceeded in a court of equity 'could recover damages whether or not he had also sought specific performance'.[178] Although Turner LJ had only considered a case where a plaintiff had sought specific performance, there should be no reason, in principle, why the jurisdiction should not have been exercised where a suitor sought other equitable relief. On the other hand, it had been held that a purchaser who had sought the delivery up of a contract could not recover damages.[179] In the United States a plaintiff in an equity suit would be awarded damages in order to obtain complete relief where a remedy other than specific performance was sought.[180] So that in a late eighteenth century copyright suit in the equity side of a federal court in which it seems that the plaintiff sought an interlocutory injunction to restrain a breach of copyright, the plaintiff was awarded damages for lost profits.[181]

Even after the decision in *Todd v Gee*[182] the Court of Chancery would award damages in an appropriate case. It is submitted that, contrary to the views of some commentators,[183] the Court of Chancery could award damages for delay in completing a contract. An instance is *Gedye v Duke of*

---

172 (1855) 7 De GM & G 722 at 734; 44 ER 280 at 285.
173 *American Jurisprudence*, 2nd ed, Lawyers Co-operative, Rochester NY, 1966, §112.
174 *Wright v Scotton* (1923) 13 De Ch 402; *Steindler v Virginia Public Service Co* (1934) 175 SE 888; *Marwede v Commercial Hotel Inc* (1948) 273 App Div 984; 78 NYS 2d 438. See also *American Digest*, vol 44, West Publishing Co, New York, 1903, col 1866 et seq.
175 *Holden v Efficient Craftsman Corp* (1923) 138 NE 85 at 86; *Daniels v Brown Shoe Co Inc* (1935) 77 F 2d 899; *Queens Plaza Amusements Inc v Queens Bridge Realty Corp* (1943) 39 NYS 2d 463 at 464; *Gulbenkian v Gulbenkian* (1945) 147 F 2d 173 at 176; *Doherty v Aaron Machinery Co Inc* (1963) 238 NYS 2d 179 at 180.
176 [1981] AC 1050.
177 (1855) 7 De GM & G 722; 44 ER 280.
178 [1981] AC 1050 at 1081.
179 *Gwillim v Stone* (1807) 14 Ves 128; 33 ER 469.
180 *Connecticut Fire Insurance Co v McNeil* (1929) 35 F 2d 675 (rectification or reformation); *Jamaica Savings Bank v MS Investing Co Inc* (1937) 274 NY 215 at 220 (foreclosure).
181 JD Gordan III, '*Morse v Reid*: The First Reported Federal Copyright Case', *Law and History Review*, vol 11, 1993, p 21.
182 (1810) 17 Ves 273; 34 ER 106.
183 R P Meagher, W M C Gummow and J R F Lehane, *Equity — Doctrines and Remedies*, 2nd ed, Butterworths, Sydney, 1984, p 517 [2304]; 3rd ed, Butterworths, Sydney, 1992, p 639 [2305].

Montrose[184] where an inquiry was decreed into the loss sustained by the plaintiff for the delay in obtaining possession under an agreement for a lease. Sir John Romilly MR remarked:

> I am of opinion that the time of giving possession being of the essence of the contract and the Plaintiff, being entitled to possession on the 1st of December, is entitled to have it ascertained by this Court what, if any, loss or damage has been sustained by him by reason of possession not having been given to him until the 31st of January.[185]

Although the decree was made upon a prayer for 'compensation', it is clear that the relief actually provided was not compensation properly so called, but unliquidated damages arising out of non-delivery of possession in accordance with the contract.[186]

In cases between a vendor and purchaser the term 'compensation' is generally used to refer to the jurisdiction in equity to grant an abatement of the purchase price, for some diminution or deterioration in the value of the property contracted to be sold. An award of compensation is usually made ancillary to a decree of specific performance. In *Jenkins v Parkinson*[187] Lord Brougham LC observed that the term 'compensation' had a 'less legal and more equitable aspect' than the term 'damage'. There were also various recognised instances where the Court of Chancery would exercise its jurisdiction to award damages. These cases were those related to administration suits and those where damages were ancillary to equitable relief. Some of these cases were decided by the Vice-Chancellors.[188] This indicates that the existence of this jurisdiction by the Court of Chancery was associated with whether the court had adequate judicial resources at the time when a decision was given.

Administration suit

In an administration suit the court would assess damages rather than compel a creditor to have recourse to law. In *Sutton v Mashiter*[189] an injunction was issued to restrain an action against the executors for breaches of a covenant in a lease granted to the testator, and the master was directed to ascertain the damages of the lessor. Sir Lancelot Shadwell VC said: 'It may well be ascertained by the Master, as well as it could be by a jury, whether any breach of covenant has been committed, and what is the amount of the damage'.[190] Another administration suit was *Hervey v Audland*.[191] In that case a covenantee under a covenant for further assurance in a voluntary assignment was not allowed to prove in the estate, but was given leave to bring an action. Later in *Cox v Barnard*[192] it was

---

184 (1858) 26 Beav 45; 53 ER 813.
185 (1858) 26 Beav 45 at 49–50; 53 ER 813 at 815.
186 *King v Poggioli* (1923) 32 CLR 222 at 246.
187 (1833) 2 My & K 5 at 11; 39 ER 846 at 849.
188 See eg *Sutton v Mashiter* (1829) 2 Sim 513; 57 ER 880; *Hervey v Audland* (1845) 14 Sim 531; 60 ER 463.
189 (1829) 2 Sim 513; 57 ER 880.
190 (1829) 2 Sim 513 at 514; 57 ER 880.
191 (1845) 14 Sim 531; 60 ER 463.
192 (1850) 8 Hare 310; 68 ER 379.

held that although the court would not decree the specific performance of such a covenant, it could assess the damages of a creditor as it was the duty of the court in administering estates not to send the parties to law if it was practicable not to do so. Sir James Knight Bruce VC remarked that 'all the covenantee required was damages, and those damages the Court of Chancery could in such a case estimate and give better than a Court of law'.[193]

In an administration suit the court would not assist a claimant who did not diligently prove a claim. In *Cox v King*[194] the testator had forged a will under which he sold property. Under the covenants for title the purchaser had initially claimed from the estate the purchase price and the costs of ejectment actions. It was held that he could not subsequently claim interest some 35 years after lodging his claim.

Damages ancillary to equitable relief

A recognised category of case was where an award of damages was ancillary to specific relief. In the administration suit of *Sutton v Mashiter*[195] damages were awarded in addition to an injunction. As Pomeroy wrote: 'A court of equity occasionally grants the relief of compensatory damages in connection with some other specific relief'.[196] Similarly in *Horsley v Ramsey*[197] Owen CJ in Eq observed that prior to the enactment of *Lord Cairns' Act* 'the Court of Chancery frequently determined the amount of damages occasioned by a breach of contract, when damages were subsidiary to other equitable relief'.[198]

The Court of Chancery possessed a well-recognised jurisdiction to award damages as incidental and ancillary to a decree of specific performance.[199] In *Nelson v Bridges*[200] the plaintiff had obtained a decree for the specific performance of a licence to quarry stone. It was subsequently ascertained that there had been an abstraction by the defendant, *pendente lite*, of part of the stone. An inquiry as to damages could have been directed if the court had been aware of the abstraction when the decree was made. As Lord Langdale MR remarked:

> If that circumstance had been known at the first hearing, I cannot have the least doubt but that the Court would, in the exercise of its jurisdiction, have put in a due course of investigation the question of the amount of compensation which ought to be made to the Plaintiff.[201]

---

193 (1850) 8 Hare 310 at 313; 68 ER 379 at 380.
194 (1846) 9 Beav 530; 50 ER 448.
195 (1829) 2 Sim 513; 57 ER 880, discussed earlier.
196 J N Pomeroy, *Pomeroy's Equity Jurisprudence*, vol 1, 5th ed, Bancroft-Whitney, San Francisco, 1941, p 147, para 112(7).
197 (1889) 10 LR (NSW) Eq 41.
198 (1889) 10 LR (NSW) Eq 41 at 46–7.
199 *Wheeler v Barnes* (1848) 3 Shad 114 at 116; *King v Poggioli* (1923) 32 CLR 222 at 246–7.
200 (1839) 2 Beav 239; 48 ER 1172.
201 (1839) 2 Beav 239 at 243; 48 ER 1172 at 1173.

The terms 'compensation' and 'damages' are used indiscriminately in the judgment.[202] At that time the terms were used interchangeably. For instance, in 1856 the Chancery Commissioners recommended that the Court of Chancery 'should have jurisdiction to grant compensation in damages'.[203] It was upon their recommendation that *Lord Cairns' Act* was later passed.

In *Nelson v Bridges*[204] the Master of the Rolls declined to direct a reference upon a supplemental bill, and instead required the defendant to admit such facts as were necessary to allow the plaintiff to bring an action to ascertain his damage. The decree provided that the action should proceed on the issue of 'the amount of the loss and damage sustained by the Plaintiff in his trade or business of mason and stone delver'.[205] This was an instance of the award of damages, and not compensation or an account of profits. Lord Langdale observed:

> It appears to me that the Defendants are correct when they say that this is a case of damages and not of account, because it is to recover something which cannot be ascertained by taking an account of the profits made — it is to ascertain the amount of the loss which the Plaintiff has sustained.[206]

————◆————

1.8 Need for reform

It can be seen that prior to the enactment of *Lord Cairns' Act* the Court of Chancery exercised jurisdiction to award damages in a number of isolated instances. This supports the opinion of Spry, who observed:

> The better view, however, is that courts of equity have always had it within their power to award damages but that from a very early time they have considered it to be ordinarily undesirable to do so.[207]

This passage was referred to with approval by Dunn J in *Minter v Geraghty*[208] and Sir Robin Cooke P in *Day v Mead*.[209] Some authorities express uncertainty as to whether the Court of Chancery could award

202 C Harpum, 'Specific Performance with Compensation as a Purchaser's Remedy', *Cambridge Law Journal*, vol 40, 1981, 47 at p 71, n 49.
203 *Third Report of Her Majesty's Commissioners appointed to enquire into the Process, Practice, and System of Pleading in the Court of Chancery & c*, 1856, Command [2064], p 4.
204 (1839) 2 Beav 239; 48 ER 1172.
205 (1839) 2 Beav 239 at 244; 48 ER 1172 at 1174.
206 (1839) 2 Beav 239 at 244; 48 ER 1172 at 1174.
207 I C F Spry, *Equitable Remedies*, 4th ed, Law Book Co, Sydney, 1990, p 608. See also P W Michalik, 'The Availability of Compensatory and Exemplary Damages in Equity', *Victoria University of Wellington Law Review*, vol 21, 1991, p 391. The inherent power of the Court of Chancery to award damages was recognised by Ingman and Wakefield: see T Ingman and J Wakefield, 'Equitable Damages under *Lord Cairns' Act*', *Conveyancer and Property Lawyer*, 1981, 286 at p 287.
208 (1981) 38 ALR 68 at 80.
209 [1987] 2 NZLR 443 at 450.

damages,[210] or else assume an absence of jurisdiction.[211] This is also the case with some leading texts.[212] The cases are not easy to reconcile, perhaps because they are instances of the discretionary nature of the jurisdiction of the Court of Chancery. Although the Court of Chancery possessed jurisdiction to award damages, it was not a jurisdiction that it would generally exercise. The position prior to the enactment of *Lord Cairns' Act* was described in *Ferguson v Wilson*[213] by Turner LJ who remarked:

> ... great complaints were constantly made by the public, that when Plaintiffs came into a court of equity for specific performance the court of equity sent them to a court of law in order to recover damages, so that parties were bandied about, as it was said, from one Court to the other.[214]

Consequently there was a need for reform with the passage of *Lord Cairns' Act*. After the passage of that Act Lord St Leonards commented: 'But now courts of equity are authorised to give damages'.[215]

---

210 *Grant v Dawkins* [1973] 1 WLR 1406 at 1408.
211 *Bosaid v Andry* [1963] VR 465 at 484; *Canson Enterprises Ltd v Boughton & Co* [1991] 3 SCR 534 at 577.
212 *Chitty on Contracts*, 25th ed, Sweet & Maxwell, London, 1983, p 1007, para 1813 ('Before 1858 damages could not be awarded in the Court of Chancery'). Sir Frederick Jordan was fully cognisant of the jurisdiction of the Court of Chancery to award damages in an administration suit or as ancillary to specific performance, and yet made the following comment: 'Until *Lord Cairns' Act* it had no power to award damages': see F Jordan, *Chapters in Equity in New South Wales*, 6th ed, Sydney, p 13. As to the contribution to equity of Sir Frederick Jordan, see also W M C Gummow, 'The Equity of Sir Frederick Jordan', *Sydney Law Review*, vol 13, 1991, p 263; *Sydney Centenary Essays in Law*, Law School, University of Sydney, 1991, p 21.
213 (1866) LR 2 Ch App 77.
214 (1866) LR 2 Ch App 77 at 88.
215 E Sugden, *The Law of Vendors and Purchasers of Estates*, 14th ed, Sweet, London, 1862, p 233.

2

Reform before the Judicature Acts

---◄○►---

2.1 Reform of the courts of equity and law

Prior to the passage of the *Judicature Acts*[1] the assimilation of the courts of law and equity had progressively occurred under a succession of statutes.[2] In 1852 the Chancery Commissioners had recommended such a transfer of jurisdiction between the courts of law and equity 'as will render each Court competent to administer complete justice in the cases which fall under its cognizance'.[3] Various statutes conferred equitable jurisdiction upon the common law courts. After 1831 the common law courts could exercise jurisdiction in interpleader to the commencement proceedings.[4] Until then, such proceedings could only be taken in equity.[5] The Common Law Procedure Act 1854[6] enabled the common law courts

---

1   Supreme Court of Judicature Act 1873 (36 & 37 Vict c 66); Supreme Court of Judicature Act 1875 (38 & 39 Vict c 77).
2   See also *Raineri v Miles* [1981] AC 1050 at 1082 per Lord Edmund-Davies.
3   *First Report of Her Majesty's Commissioners appointed to inquire into the Process, Practice and System of Pleading in the Court of Chancery & c*, 1852, Command [1437], p 3.
4   Interpleader Act 1831 (1 & 2 Wm IV c 58); Common Law Procedure Act 1838 (1 & 2 Vict c 45) s 2; Common Law Procedure Act 1860 (23 & 24 Vict c 126) ss 12–18.
5   W S Holdsworth, *History of English Law*, vol XIII, Methuen, London, 1952, p 406.
6   17 & 18 Vict c 125.

to make an order for the specific delivery of chattels (s 78), grant injunctions (s 79), and give effect to an equitable defence in actions of replevin: ss 83–6.[7] The Court of Chancery was also reformed by the Chancery Procedure Act 1852[8] which discontinued the expensive practice of engrossing a bill on parchment: s 1. The Act modified the practice of taking evidence by enabling *viva voce* examination before an examiner in the presence of the parties: s 31.[9] The Act enabled a suitor to obtain equitable relief without taking preliminary proceedings in a court of law. The court could determine questions of law (s 61) and legal title (s 62) which necessarily had to be decided before equitable relief could be decreed.

2.2 Chancery Commissioners — Third Report

In 1856 the Chancery Commissioners had observed that the extension of jurisdiction of the courts of law and equity had 'to a considerable extent widened the ground common to the jurisdiction and procedure of both Courts'.[10] The Commissioners proposed a further extension of the jurisdiction of the courts of equity to enable a 'final settlement of the dispute between the parties'[11] by enabling the Court of Chancery to award damages where a suitor sought either an injunction or specific performance. It was intended that after the determination of the equity suit a suitor would have no need to institute an action in a court of law to recover damages.

Injunction

The Commissioners referred to a case where an injured party was entitled to damages at law and an injunction in equity to restrain the further continuance of a wrongful act. It was observed that: 'A Court of Equity, though granting the injunction, has at present no jurisdiction to compel the wrongdoers to make compensation for the injury committed'.[12] The Court of Chancery would not, as a general practice, award damages in a suit for an injunction. Support for a conclusion that damages could be awarded in addition to an injunction may initially appear to be found in *Smith v The London South Western Railway Co*[13] where Sir William Page

---

7   As to an equitable defence: see *Mines Royal Societies v Magnay* (1854) 10 Ex 489 at 493; 156 ER 531 at 533 per Parke B.

8   15 & 16 Vict c 86.

9   As to the previous practice of taking evidence in Chancery: see P M McDermott, 'Equitable Claims or Demands', *University of Queensland Law Journal*, vol 16, 1991, 212 at p 213–14.

10 *Third Report of Her Majesty's Commissioners appointed to enquire into the Process, Practice and System of Pleading in the Court of Chancery & c* (later cited as the *Third Report of the Chancery Commissioners)*, 1856, Command [2064], p 3.

11 *Third Report of the Chancery Commissioners*, n 10 above, p 3.

12 *Third Report of the Chancery Commissioners*, n 10 above, p 3.

13 (1854) Kay 408; 60 ER 173.

Wood VC remarked: 'Unless that primary right to an injunction exists, this Court has no jurisdiction with reference to a mere question of damages'.[14] However on closer examination it becomes clear that these remarks were directed to the jurisdiction in Chancery to direct an account of profits, as the Vice-Chancellor later remarked, 'the Plaintiff having thus obtained a right to the injunction, the right to an account would follow'.[15] There were, however, cases, such as an administration suit, where damages were awarded in addition to an injunction.[16]

The Court of Chancery had an established jurisdiction to direct an account of profits as an incident to the grant of an injunction. In *Baily v Taylor*,[17] a book piracy case, Sir John Leach MR commented: 'This Court has no jurisdiction to give to a Plaintiff a remedy for an alleged piracy, unless he can make out that he is entitled to the equitable interposition of this Court by injunction; and in such case, the Court will also give him an account, that his remedy here may be complete'.[18] The Master of the Rolls later added: 'If this Court do not interfere by injunction, then his remedy, as in the case of any other injury to his property, must be at law'.[19] The jurisdiction to direct an account was adverted to by the Commissioners when they observed that where 'it can be shown that the defendant has actually derived profit from the act complained of, the Court has power to make him refund his gains'.[20]

The Commissioners recommended that 'in all cases in which a Court of Equity interferes by injunction it should have jurisdiction to give compensation in damages for the injury done, in addition to restraining the commission of the injury for the future, and that such damages should be given although the act complained of may have produced no profit to the wrongdoer'.[21] It can thus be seen that what was proposed by the Commissioners was quite distinct from the established jurisdiction in Chancery to direct an account of profits. The Commissioners wished to avoid a multiplicity of actions by also recommending that 'a plaintiff obtaining an injunction in equity should not be entitled to proceed at law for damages'.[22] This recommendation was not enshrined in legislation, although it was reflected in actual practice. At this time a plaintiff who sought specific performance of a contract could be restrained from proceeding at law to recover damages for breach of contract, such an action being maintainable only with the leave of the court of equity.[23]

---

14   (1854) Kay 408 at 415; 69 ER 173 at 176.
15   (1854) Kay 408 at 415; 69 ER 173 at 176.
16   See eg *Sutton v Mashiter* (1829) 2 Sim 513; 57 ER 880.
17   (1829) 1 Russ & M 73; 39 ER 28.
18   (1829) 1 Russ & M 73 at 75; 39 ER 28 at 29.
19   (1829) 1 Russ & M 73 at 75; 39 ER 28 at 29.
20   *Third Report of the Chancery Commissioners*, n 10 above, p 3.
21   *Third Report of the Chancery Commissioners*, n 10 above, pp 3–4. This quotation illustrates the then interchangeable use of the terms 'compensation' and 'damages'. See also *Nelson v Bridges* (1839) 2 Beav 239 at 243; 48 ER 1172 at 1173.
22   *Third Report of the Chancery Commissioners*, n 10 above, p 4.
23   *Phelps v Prothero* (1855) 7 De GM & G 722 at 734; 44 ER 280 at 285; *Gedye v Montrose, Duke of* (1858) 26 Beav 45 at 47; 53 ER 813 at 814.

Specific performance

The Commissioners observed that 'a party entitled to the specific performance of a contract, cannot in general obtain in equity compensation for losses which he may have sustained by its non-performance'.[24] It was recommended that 'in all cases in which damages could be recovered at law for breach of a contract directed by a Court of Equity to be specifically performed, the Court should have jurisdiction to grant compensation in damages for the loss sustained up to the time of the contract being performed, in addition to decreeing its specific performance'.[25] The Commissioners envisaged the award of damages for loss occurring after the issue of process.

It was also considered that damages should be awarded where the court declined to decree specific performance by reason of the existence of a discretionary defence:

> It very frequently happens, in suits for enforcing the performance of contracts, that the Court is satisfied that a valid contract has been entered into, and that a Court of Law would give damages for breach of it, but that there are particular circumstances in the case, which prevent the Court from decreeing specific performance, and consequently it leaves the party complaining to his remedy at law. For instance, a trustee may have contracted to sell a trust estate without disclosing the trust, for an inadequate consideration, or otherwise upon terms which, as between him and his *cestuis que trust*, would be a breach of trust. To enforce such a contract against the trustee by decreeing specific execution would be contrary to the established principles of equity.[26]

The practice of the Court of Chancery where specific performance was declined for a discretionary reason was described by Kay J in *Rock Portland Cement Co Ltd v Wilson*:[27]

> Everyone who is familiar with the practice in equity knows that at the time when *Lord Cairns' Act* was passed, it was the constant practice in equity to say, when an action was brought for specific performance, This is a discretionary equity; the court does not think fit under the circumstances of this case to grant specific performance, but it dismisses the bill without prejudice to an action at law.[28]

A suitor who could not obtain specific performance because of the existence of a discretionary bar would then have to institute proceedings at law for the recovery of damages. In some cases a suitor may not have been aware of the existence of a discretionary defence at the time when a Chancery suit was commenced. It was accordingly recommended that a court of equity should be able to award damages in a case 'in which the Court, without any default on the part of the plaintiff, finds itself unable, from special circumstances, to grant him the peculiar remedy of specific performance'.[29]

————◦————

24 *Third Report of the Chancery Commissioners*, n 10 above, p 4.
25 *Third Report of the Chancery Commissioners*, n 10 above, p 4.
26 *Third Report of the Chancery Commissioners*, n 10 above, p 4.
27 (1882) 31 WR 193.
28 (1882) 31 WR 193 at 194.
29 *Third Report of the Chancery Commissioners*, n 10 above, p 4.

2.3 Enactment of Lord Cairns' Act

The Chancery Amendment Act 1858 (*Lord Cairns' Act*)[30] conferred jurisdiction upon the Court of Chancery to award damages: s 2. The sponsor of this measure was Sir Hugh Cairns (later Lord Cairns) who was then the Solicitor-General. He informed the House of Commons that the Chancery Commissioners had 'recommended that this jurisdiction should be conferred on the Court of Chancery',[31] and that the measure would 'enable the suitor to obtain in one court the complete relief to which he was entitled'.[32] He observed that the Court of Chancery 'could not give damages for the injury inflicted in time past. For these damages the suitor was obliged to go to a court of common law; and thus he got prospective relief from the Court of Chancery, and retrospective relief from the court of common law'.[33] In his first reading speech he remarked:

> Now, he proposed to remedy this state of things by empowering the Court of Chancery, upon any application for an injunction, or for the specific performance of an agreement, to award damages for the breach of the agreement up to the time when the Court gave relief. He ought to say that on this point a corresponding jurisdiction had been conferred by Parliament on the courts of common law. They could give retrospective relief by way of damages, and the Common Law Procedure Act enabled them also to exercise jurisdiction with respect to the future by way of injunction or decree for specific performance.[34] He proposed that the Court of Chancery should in the same manner complete its jurisdiction, and then every suitor would have it in his power to appeal either to the Court of Chancery or to a court of common law. In this way, if a perfect fusion of law and equity were not effected, at all events complete jurisdiction would be given to the courts of common law and equity in their several departments, so that there would be no portion of relief which any of those courts might not give to the suitor.[35]

It was commonplace at this time for a statute to be named after the sponsor of the measure.[36] Accordingly the Chancery Amendment Act became known

---

30   21 & 22 Vict c 27.

31   *Hansard's Parliamentary Debates*, 3rd series, vol 149, 15 April 1858, col 1163. (Reference was made to the Second Report of the Chancery Commissioners instead of their Third Report.)

32   *Hansard's Parliamentary Debates*, 3rd series, vol 149, 15 April 1858, col 1162.

33   *Hansard's Parliamentary Debates*, 3rd series, vol 149, 15 April 1858, col 1162.

34   The Common Law Procedure Act 1854 did not enable a common law court to decree the specific performance of a contract. It was earlier held in *Benson v Paull* (1856) 6 El & Bl 273 at 275; 119 ER 865 at 866 that s 68 of the Act only concerned duties capable of enforcement by the prerogative remedy of mandamus, and not the specific performance of contracts. Lord Campbell CJ observed that during the passage of the Act a clause that would have enabled a common law court to decree specific performance was rejected. See also E Bullen and S M Leake, *Precedents of Pleading*, 3rd ed, Stevens, London, 1868, pp 356–7. During the passage of the Chancery Amendment Bill in the House of Lords Lord Chelmsford LC observed: 'The Common Law Procedure Act gave the common law Courts power to issue a mandamus to compel the performance of a duty': see *Hansard's Parliamentary Debates*, 3rd series, vol 150, 3 June 1858, col 1441.

35   *Hansard's Parliamentary Debates*, 3rd series, vol 149, 15 April 1858, col 1162. (*Hansard* reports of speeches were at that time printed in the third person.)

36   See eg Chancery Regulation Act 1862 (*Sir John Rolt's Act*) (25 & 26 Vict c 42). See also

as *Lord Cairns' Act*.[37] Heuston has commented: 'Why it should be so known is not clear: he did not become Lord Cairns for a decade after the Act became law'.[38] The explanation is that until 1867 when Lord Cairns was elevated to the peerage the statute was known as *Sir Hugh Cairns' Act*.[39]

It is sometimes assumed that *Lord Cairns' Act* was drafted or framed by the Chancery Commissioners.[40] However, the report of the Commissioners was not accompanied by a draft Bill. There is a possibility that Lord Cairns may have had some hand in the drafting of the measure. The *Law Times* referred to 'The Chancery Amendment Bill of the Solicitor-General'.[41] It would appear from an endorsement on the Chancery Amendment Bill that Lord Cairns had the responsibility for drafting the Bill.[42] However, that endorsement may not be indicative of the actual authorship of the Bill as the endorsement is in accordance with the parliamentary practice, which still prevails today, by which leave is granted to prepare and bring in a Bill.[43] Some commentators have mentioned that s 2 of *Lord Cairns' Act* 'was not felicitously drafted'.[44] It is probable that the Bill was drafted in Lincoln's Inn by a Chancery barrister in view of the rather elaborate style of some of the clauses, which is perhaps characteristic of the equity draftsman.[45] It was quite common in those days for a parliamentary Bill to be drafted by a barrister in private practice. The office of Parliamentary Counsel was not created until 1869.

It should be appreciated that *Lord Cairns' Act* differed in various respects from the recommendations of the Chancery Commissioners. The Commissioners recommended that 'the exercise of the jurisdiction as to

---

R F V Heuston, 'Hugh McCalmont Cairns', *Northern Ireland Legal Quarterly*, vol 26, 1975, 269 at p 273.

37   An entry on Earl Cairns, by Lord Sumner of Ibstone, which was originally published in 1886 records: 'Though thus responsible for most important legal changes, the only Act which bears Cairns's name is one, now repealed, to enable the Court of Chancery to give damages in lieu of specific performance or an injunction': *Dictionary of National Biography*, vol III, Oxford University Press, Oxford, 1973, p 671. J B Atlay in his discussion of Lord Cairns in *The Victorian Chancellors*, Smith, Elder & Co, London, 1908, does not mention the Chancery Amendment Act.

38   R F V Heuston, 'Hugh McCalmont Cairns', *Northern Ireland Legal Quarterly*, vol 26 1975, 269 at p 272. See also A W B Simpson, *Biographical Dictionary of the Common Law*, Butterworths, London, 1984, p 97 (R F V Heuston).

39   *Chinnock v Sainsbury* (1860) 9 WR 7 at 8; *Howe v Hunt* (1862) 31 Beav 420; 54 ER 1201; *Bainbridge v Kinnaird* (1863) 32 Beav 346 at 347; 55 ER 135 at 136; *Johnson v Wyatt* (1863) 2 De GJ & S 18 at 27; 46 ER 281 at 284; *Durell v Pritchard* (1865) LR 1 Ch App 244 at 251; *Schotsmans v Lancashire & Yorkshire Railway Co* (1865) LR 1 Eq 349.

40   J A Jolowicz, 'Damages in Equity — A Study of *Lord Cairns' Act*', *Cambridge Law Journal*, vol 34, 1975, p 224; R F V Heuston, 'Hugh McCalmont Cairns', *Northern Ireland Legal Quarterly*, vol 26, 1975, 269 at p 273; R P Meagher, W M C Gummow and J R F Lehane, *Equity — Doctrines and Remedies*, 2nd ed, Butterworths, Sydney, 1984, p 518; 3rd ed, Butterworths, Sydney, 1992, p 640.

41   *Law Times*, vol 31, 1 May 1858, p 78.

42   The Chancery Amendment Bill, as ordered to be printed by The House of Commons, contained the following endorsement: 'Prepared and brought in by Mr Solicitor General, Mr Attorney General, and Mr Secretary Walpole' (Bill 46, 15 April 1858).

43   *House of Commons Journal*, vol 113, 15 April 1858, p 116.

44   G Jones and W Goodhart, *Specific Performance*, Butterworths, London, 1986, p 223.

45   This possibility was raised by Sir Henry de Waal, Parliamentary Counsel, Whitehall, in correspondence with the author.

damages should not be discretionary with the Court, but that the party should be entitled to require the Court to adjudicate upon his right, and if his right should be established, to have the amount of damages assessed'.[46] Clause 2 of the Chancery Amendment Bill originally provided that 'it shall also be lawful for the same Court to award Damages to the Party injured, either in addition to or in substitution for such Injunction or specific Performance'.[47] This provision could hardly be regarded as imposing a mandatory requirement to assess damages. Indeed later in *Julius v Lord Bishop of Oxford*[48] Lord Cairns LC considered that the words 'it shall be lawful' were 'according to their natural meaning permissive or enabling words only'.[49] However, it is apparent that at the time of the passage of the Bill it may have been thought that the original clause was mandatory. In his second reading speech Lord Chelmsford remarked: 'The power of giving damages would impose upon the Court of Chancery the duty of estimating the injury done, and of ascertaining all the facts relating to the case'.[50] In any event a Select Committee of the House of Lords amended cl 2 of the Chancery Amendment Bill by inserting after the word 'Court' the words 'if it shall think fit',[51] and thus emphasised the discretionary nature of the jurisdiction to award equitable damages.[52]

It has already been mentioned that the Chancery Commissioners recommended that a court of equity should be empowered to award damages in conjunction with the grant of an injunction[53] or specific performance.[54] Accordingly, s 2 of *Lord Cairns' Act* enabled the Court of Chancery to award damages 'in addition to'[55] an injunction or specific performance. What is not as clear is why s 2 also enabled the Court of Chancery to award damages 'in substitution'[56] for both of these equitable remedies. The Commissioners had only proposed that there should be jurisdiction to award damages where the remedy of specific performance was declined for discretionary reasons.[57] This was recognised by Jolowicz, who commented:

> Power to award damages *in addition* to equitable relief would obviously have been insufficient to meet such a case, and it is almost certainly for this reason that the Act as passed gave to the Court power to award damages 'either in addition to or *in substitution* for' an injunction or decree of specific performance.[58]

---

46 *Third Report of the Chancery Commissioners*, n 10 above, p 4.
47 A Bill to amend the Course of Procedure in the High Court of Chancery, Ordered, by The House of Commons, to be printed, (Bill 46, 15 April 1858). The original clause was at the time printed in the *Law Times*, vol 31, 1 May 1858, p 78.
48 (1880) 5 App Cas 214.
49 (1880) 5 App Cas 214 at 223.
50 *Hansard's Parliamentary Debates*, 3rd series, vol 150, 3 June 1858, col 1441.
51 *Journals of the House of Lords*, vol 90, 4 June 1858, p 214.
52 *Aynsley v Glover* (1874) LR 18 Eq 544 at 554.
53 *Third Report of the Chancery Commissioners*, n 10 above, pp 3–4; see n 21 above.
54 *Third Report of the Chancery Commissioners*, n 10 above, p 4.
55 Chancery Amendment Act 1858 s 2.
56 Chancery Amendment Act 1858 s 2.
57 *Third Report of the Chancery Commissioners*, n 10 above, p 4.
58 J A Jolowicz, 'Damages in Equity — A Study of *Lord Cairns' Act*', *Cambridge Law Journal*, vol 34, 1975, 224 at p 225.

However, this does not explain why the Act enabled damages to be awarded 'in substitution' for an injunction as well as 'in substitution' for specific performance. It may well have been the case that the phraseology of 'in addition to or in substitution' in s 2 was used to simplify the drafting of what is a lengthy provision. However, the provision enabled the Court of Chancery to award damages where such damages were unavailable at law. In *Price v Strange*[59] Goff LJ remarked:

> One purpose and a very important purpose of that Act was, of course, to avoid circuity of action by enabling the old Court of Chancery to award damages at law, but the Act clearly went further and enabled the court to give damages where there was no cause of action at law.[60]

At common law damages could only be awarded for actual damage sustained by a plaintiff. In enabling damages to be awarded 'in substitution' for an injunction, and therefore for prospective loss in a *quia timet* case,[61] the Act conferred a more extensive jurisdiction upon the Court of Chancery than was possessed by the courts of law. This jurisdiction was certainly not within the contemplation of the Commissioners, who had recommended that in a suit where an injunction was granted the court 'should have jurisdiction to give compensation for the injury done'.[62] The Commissioners had not considered the case where an injunction was withheld for a discretionary reason. *Lord Cairns' Act*, in enabling damages to be awarded 'in substitution' for a decree of specific performance, also conferred a more extensive jurisdiction than existed at common law. In a case where the doctrine of part performance applies, equitable damages may be awarded in substitution for specific performance where an action for damages at law is precluded by the Statute of Frauds.[63] This jurisdiction was also not contemplated by the Chancery Commissioners, who had recommended that where specific performance was withheld, the Court of Chancery should be able to award damages where 'a Court of Law would give damages'.[64]

The question has been raised whether the creation under *Lord Cairns' Act* of a jurisdiction which enabled damages to be awarded in circumstances where such damages were unavailable at law was achieved 'by accident or design'.[65] It was certainly not by design, for it appears that Sir Hugh Cairns had assumed that the measure would vest the Court of Chancery with the same jurisdiction that the courts of law possessed to 'give retrospective relief by way of damages'.[66] The result was achieved by the particular phraseology of s 2 of *Lord Cairns' Act*. It would never have occurred if s 2 had been drafted in accordance with the recommendations of the Chancery Commissioners.

---

59 [1978] Ch 337.
60 [1978] Ch 337 at 358.
61 *Leeds Industrial Co-operative Society Ltd v Slack* [1924] AC 851.
62 *Third Report of the Chancery Commissioners*, n 10 above, pp 3–4.
63 *Price v Strange* [1978] Ch 337 at 358. As to the award of equitable damages in a case of part performance: see p 172.
64 *Third Report of the Chancery Commissioners*, n 10 above, p 4.
65 A J Oakley, 'Pecuniary Compensation for Failure to Complete a Contract for the Sale of Land', *Cambridge Law Journal*, vol 39, 1980, 58 at p 74.
66 *Hansard's Parliamentary Debates*, 3rd series, vol 149, 15 April 1858, col 1162.

The Chancery Amendment Bill enabled a judge to assess damages. This was a function which was then generally within the province of a jury. This aspect of the Bill was not without some controversy. The Chancery Commissioners did not 'apprehend that there would be any difficulty in damages being assessed by a Court of Equity'.[67] However, this was a radical change to the practice of the Court of Chancery. During the passage of *Lord Cairns' Act* a contemporary report noted: 'The measure is brief, but it works a revolution in the practice of Chancery'.[68] Some judges of the era regarded it as inappropriate that questions of fact and the assessment of damages should be determined without a jury. Just before the introduction of the Chancery Amendment Bill Sir William Page Wood VC, in perhaps an oblique criticism of the measure, stated that the Court of Chancery had 'no adequate means of ascertaining the amount of damage sustained by reason of merely tortious acts, unattended with profit; for which reason such questions have always been considered by the Legislature as the province of a jury'.[69]

During the passage of *Lord Cairns' Act* in the House of Lords there was some opposition to enabling a judge to assess damages. Lord Brougham objected to 'the giving to the Court the power, without the consent of the parties, and without the intervention of a jury, to send questions of the assessment of the damages before the Masters or Chief Clerks in Chancery'.[70] Lord Cranworth riposted that: 'There was nothing in the Bill to enable the Judge to transfer the assessing of damages to the Chief Clerk'.[71] However, Lord Brougham considered that his opinion was justified by the wording of cl 2 of the Bill which provided that 'damages may be assessed in such manner as the Court may direct'.[72] Lord St Leonards remarked: 'He objected to a Judge sitting alone assessing damages, and should have divided the Committee on the point if anybody would have supported him'.[73] His Lordship later wrote in criticism of *Lord Cairns' Act* that 'another innovation which it would be difficult to defend, is vesting in the equity judge, without a jury, and without the consent of the parties, the power of assessing the damages'.[74] The attitude that judges should not assess damages prevailed for some time. In the next decade Lord Westbury observed: 'It is a settled principle of common law that questions of fact shall be tried by a jury'.[75]

The Chancery Amendment Bill as it was originally introduced only conferred jurisdiction upon the Court of Chancery.[76] The Chancery Commissioners had not proposed reform to any other court of equity. The Bill was amended in Committee to confer jurisdiction upon the Court of

---

67   *Third Report of the Chancery Commissioners*, n 10 above, p 4.

68   *Law Times*, vol 31, 1 May 1858, p 78.

69   *Powell v Aiken* (1858) 4 K & J 343 at 351; 70 ER 144 at 147.

70   *Hansard's Parliamentary Debates*, 3rd series, vol 150, 8 June 1858, col 1690.

71   *Hansard's Parliamentary Debates*, 3rd series, vol 150, 8 June 1858, col 1691.

72   *Hansard's Parliamentary Debates*, 3rd series, vol 150, 8 June 1858, col 1691.

73   *Hansard's Parliamentary Debates*, 3rd series, vol 150, 8 June 1858, col 1690.

74   E B Sugden, *A Handy Book on Property Law*, 8th ed, W Blackwood and Sons, London, 1869, p 6.

75   *Fernie v Young* (1866) LR 1 E & Ir App 63 at 78.

76   A Bill to Amend the Course of Procedure in the High Court of Chancery (Bill 46, HC, 15 April 1858).

Chancery in Ireland, and for the Lord Chancellor of Ireland to make rules and orders to take effect as General Orders.[77] It was certainly not the initial intention of Sir Hugh Cairns (as he then was) that the measure should extend to Ireland as he considered 'that it would be better to have a separate Bill for Ireland'.[78] However, J Whiteside who was the Conservative member for Enniskillen, and who later became the Lord Chief Justice of Ireland, remarked that it was certainly his wish 'to have the Bill extended to Ireland in order to avoid the necessity of another measure on the same subject'.[79] It was obvious that Sir Hugh Cairns had made a concession to a fellow Ulsterman on this issue. The Chancery Amendment Bill was amended again to confer jurisdiction upon the Court of Chancery of the County Palatine of Lancaster, and for the making of General Rules and Orders in respect of that court.[80]

2.4 Exercise of jurisdiction by the Court of Chancery

There are a number of reported instances where the Court of Chancery awarded damages under *Lord Cairns' Act*.[81] However, the Court of Chancery did not generally exercise the 'complete jurisdiction'[82] which Lord Cairns had assumed would be vested in the court. A legal historian has commented that the jurisdiction to award damages 'was little used'.[83] Indeed it was apparent soon after *Lord Cairns' Act* was enacted that the jurisdiction would only be reluctantly exercised. In *Wicks v Hunt*[84] Sir William Page Wood VC remarked that he did not consider that 'the statute extends the jurisdiction of the court to cases where there is a plain common law remedy'.[85] The Vice-Chancellor also declined to invoke *Lord*

---

77 A Bill to Amend the Course of Procedure in the High Court of Chancery cll D1 and D2 (Bill 62, HC, 26 April 1858); Chancery Amendment Act 1858, ss 8, 9. See also *House of Commons Journal*, vol 113, sess 1857–1858, 27 April 1858, p 136.
78 *Hansard's Parliamentary Debates*, 3rd series, vol 149, 3 May 1858, col 2204.
79 *Hansard's Parliamentary Debates*, 3rd series, vol 149, 3 May 1858, col 2204.
80 A Bill to Amend the Course of Procedure in the High Court of Chancery, the Court of Chancery in Ireland, and the Court of Chancery of the County Palatine of Lancaster cl D3 (Bill 87, H of C, 14 May 1858); Chancery Amendment Act 1858 s 10. See also *House of Commons Journal*, vol 113, sess 1857–1858, 11 and 15 May 1858, pp 163, 176.
81 See eg *Wedmore v Mayor of Bristol* (1862) 11 WR 136; *Cory v The Thames Iron Works and Shipbuilding Co* (1863) 8 LT (NS) 237; 11 WR 589; *Isenberg v East India House Estate Co Ltd* (1863) 3 De GJ & S 263; 46 ER 637; *Hindley v Emery* (1865) LR 1 Eq 52; *Stanley of Alderley, Lady v Shrewsbury, Earl of* (1875) LR 19 Eq 616.
82 *Hansard's Parliamentary Debates*, 3rd series, vol 150, 15 April 1858, col 1162.
83 D M Kerly, *An Historical Sketch of the Equitable Jurisdiction of the Court of Chancery*, Cambridge University Press, Cambridge, 1890, p 289. Although Pomeroy, an American commentator, perhaps somewhat eulogistically, referred to 'the readiness and completeness with which the English judges accepted the modifications made by *Lord Cairns' Act*': see J N Pomeroy and J C Mann, *Pomeroy on Specific Performance of Contracts*, 3rd ed, Banks & Co, Albany, New York, 1926, p 967, para 481.
84 (1859) Johns 372; 70 ER 466.
85 (1859) Johns 372 at 380; 70 ER 466 at 469.

Cairns' Act because the plaintiff's bill was filed before the Act was passed. However, statutes that regulate the procedure of the courts generally apply to pending actions.[86] As Sir Jonathan Pollock LCB observed 'there is a considerable difference between laws which affect vested rights and those which merely affect the proceedings of courts'.[87] The Court of Chancery would also not award damages where a plaintiff had no entitlement to equitable relief, but would dismiss a suit without prejudice to an action at law.[88] The matter was not assisted by the fact that the jurisdiction which was conferred by *Lord Cairns' Act* was discretionary in nature.[89] *Lord Cairns' Act* did not abridge the rights of suitors and a plaintiff could still maintain an action at law for damages even though such relief could be claimed in a suit in equity.[90]

The practice of the Court of Chancery of requiring undertakings originated prior to the enactment of *Lord Cairns' Act* in 1858.[91] However, quite apart from the award of damages as substantive relief, the existence of the jurisdiction under *Lord Cairns' Act* modified the practice of the court in requiring an undertaking as to damages in interlocutory proceedings.[92] Sir William Page Wood VC emphasised in *Tuck v Silver*[93] that since the enactment of *Lord Cairns' Act* the court would be more strict than ever in requiring a plaintiff, prior to his obtaining an interim injunction against the infringement of a patent, to abide by any order it may make as to damages. In *Ingram v Stiff*[94] the Vice-Chancellor stated that an undertaking would not be required in a 'clear case of fraud' by a defendant. It is also interesting to note the change of practice as to whether counsel had authority to give an undertaking on behalf of a client. At the time when *Lord Cairns' Act* was passed counsel could not give an undertaking on behalf of a corporation so that an officer of the corporation had to execute the undertaking.[95] This practice had ceased to prevail before the end of the nineteenth century.[96]

---

86 S G G Edgar, *Craies on Statute Law*, 7th ed, Sweet & Maxwell, London, 1971, pp 401–2.

87 *Wright v Hale* (1860) 30 LJ Ex 40 at 42.

88 *Collins v Stuteley* (1859) 7 WR 710; *Clarkson v Edge* (1863) 12 WR 518; *Lawrence v Austin* (1865) 13 WR 981; *Robson v Whittingham* (1866) LR 1 Ch App 442.

89 *Anglo-Danubian Co v Rogerson* (1867) LR 4 Eq 3 at 8; *Acraman v Price* (1870) 18 WR 540; 24 LT (NS) 487.

90 *Anglo-Danubian Co v Rogerson* (1867) LR 4 Eq 3.

91 *Air Express Ltd v Ansett Transport Industries (Operations) Pty Ltd* (1981) 146 CLR 249 at 267 per Aickin J.

92 For a discussion of undertakings as to damages: see I C F Spry, 'Plaintiffs' Undertakings and Equity's Power to Award Damages', *Australian Law Journal*, vol 65, 1991, p 658; P M McDermott, 'Undertakings and Lord Cairns' Act — A Comment', *Australian Law Journal*, vol 66, 1992, p 219.

93 (1859) Johns 218; 70 ER 403.

94 (1859) Johns 220n; 70 ER 404.

95 *Anglo-Danubian, etc, Co Ltd v Rogerson* (1863) 10 Jur NS 87; *Pacific Steam Navigation Co v Gibbs* (1865) 14 WR 218.

96 *Manchester & Liverpool Banking Co v Parkinson* (1888) 60 LT 47; *East Molesey Local Board v Lambeth Waterworks Co* [1892] Ch 289.

2.5 Assessment of equitable damages by the Court of Chancery

Under the authority of *Lord Cairns' Act*,[97] General Orders were made which regulated the procedure of the Court of Chancery in assessing damages.[98] *Lord Cairns' Act* provided that the Court of Chancery could assess damages without a jury.[99] The Chancery Commissioners had recognised that in many cases 'it might be expedient to have the amount of damages assessed by a jury'.[100] *Lord Cairns' Act* therefore made provision for the assessment of damages by a special or common jury before the court itself or a sheriff.[101] Lord St Leonards thought that it was 'a mistake in having a jury in a Court of Chancery, instead of sending an issue to be tried in a court of law which possessed the necessary machinery, and all the necessary experience in the ordinary working of the jury system'.[102] Where the Court of Chancery did not direct a trial as to damages before the court itself, either with or without a jury, it could under *Lord Cairns' Act* direct the issue of a writ of inquiry for the assessment of damages by a jury at *nisi prius*, at the assizes or before a sheriff.[103]

2.6 Sir John Rolt's Act

The Chancery Regulation Act 1862 (*Sir John Rolt's Act*)[104] was passed as a consequence of the Court of Chancery not having fully exercised the jurisdiction conferred by *Lord Cairns' Act*.[105] *Sir John Rolt's Act* required the Court of Chancery to determine every question of law or fact upon which a plaintiff's entitlement to equitable relief was dependent: s 1. This reform was important as it enabled the Court of Chancery to decide questions of law. In *JC Williamson Ltd v Lukey and Mulholland*[106] Sir Owen Dixon remarked:

---

97 Chancery Amendment Act 1858 s 11.
98 General Orders 1–29, Consolidated General Orders, vol 41, 4 April 1859, rr 26–52. For these General Orders: see J S Smith, *The Practice of the Court of Chancery*, vol II, 7th ed, W Maxwell, London, 1862, pp 466–71.
99 Chancery Amendment Act 1858 s 5. See *Patent Marine Inventions Co v Chadburn* (1873) LR 16 Eq 447.
100 *Third Report of the Chancery Commissioners*, n 10 above, p 4.
101 Chancery Amendment Act 1858 s 3. See *Cory v The Thames Iron Works and Shipbuilding Co* (1863) 8 LT (NS) 237; 11 WR 589.
102 *Hansard's Parliamentary Debates*, 3rd series, vol 150, 3 June 1858, cols 1443–4.
103 Chancery Amendment Act 1858 s 6; Chancery Regulation Act 1862 ss 2, 3; Consolidated General Orders, vol 41, r 40; E R Daniell, *Practice of the High Court of Chancery*, vol I, 5th ed, Stevens, London, 1871, p 948; *Yates v Kyffin-Taylor and Wark* [1899] WN 141. For the form of a writ of inquiry: see L Field, E C Dunn and J Biddle, *Forms and Precedents of Pleadings and Proceedings in the High Court of Chancery*, 2nd ed, Stevens & Sons, London, 1871, form 1092.
104 25 & 26 Vict c 42.
105 H Jarman, *The Practice of the High Court of Chancery*, 3rd ed, W Maxwell, London, 1864, p 829.
106 (1931) 45 CLR 282.

An injunction is a remedy appropriate to restrain the violation of a provision or term of a contract which is the final expression of the parties' legal relations. But, in granting an injunction for this purpose, the Courts of equity acted in aid of a legal right. Before *Sir John Rolt's Act* (25 & 26 Vict c 42) a perpetual injunction was not granted restraining breaches of such an agreement until the right had been tried at law.[107]

Sir John Rolt's Act also confirmed procedural reforms effected by *Lord Cairns' Act* for the trial of questions of fact: s 3. The Chancery Regulation (Ireland) Act 1862,[108] which was identical to *Sir John Rolt's Act*, was also passed at this time to extend the reforms to the Court of Chancery in Ireland.

It is generally acknowledged that the spirit and intention of *Sir John Rolt's Act* was to require the Court of Chancery to consider the award of damages in an appropriate case to save expense.[109] However, the Act contained a number of reservations. The court could send an issue out of Chancery to be tried at the assizes or in a superior court of common law: s 2.[110] The Act also provided that the court need not decide purely legal questions where a suit was improperly instituted in equity: s 4. Thus the court declined to consider the question of damages where the plaintiff sought a mandatory injunction to remove a building which had been completed before the bill was filed[111] or where substantial damage had not been shown to ground an injunction.[112]

In actual practice the Act did not greatly assist a suitor who sought damages in Chancery.[113] In *Swaine v Great Northern Railway Co*[114] Turner LJ observed: 'I do not think, however, that *Mr Rolt's Act* makes it compulsory upon the Court'[115] to award damages. The Lord Justice added that the court 'has been placed by *Mr Rolt's Act* in the sometimes difficult position of being compelled to decide difficult questions of fact either on insufficient statements contained in affidavits or else by examination of all the witnesses before itself'.[116] Difficulties occurred in nuisance cases where a defendant would insist upon a trial by jury, which in some cases was obviously a delaying tactic. Initially it was held that the Act did not affect the right of a defendant to have the question of nuisance or no nuisance tried by a jury,[117] although it was later held that not every such question had to be sent to a jury.[118]

---

107 (1931) 45 CLR 282 at 298.

108 25 & 26 Vict c 46. See also *Lord De Freyne v Fitzgibbon (No 2)* [1904] 1 Ir R 429.

109 *Young v Fernie* (1863) 1 De GJ & S 353 at 355; 46 ER 142 at 143; *Johnson v Wyatt* (1863) 2 De GJ & S 18 at 27; 46 ER 281 at 284–5; *Bovill v Hitchcock* (1868) LR 3 Ch App 417 at 419; *Rock Portland Cement Co Ltd v Wilson* (1882) 31 WR 193 at 194.

110 *Fernie v Young* (1866) LR 1 E & Ir App 63.

111 *Durell v Pritchard* (1865) LR 1 Ch App 224 at 251–2.

112 *Robson v Whittingham* (1866) LR 1 Ch App 442.

113 G O Morgan and C W Chute, *Practice, Pleading and Jurisdiction of the Court of Chancery*, 4th ed, Stevens & Sons, London, 1868, p 262; J A Jolowicz, 'Damages in Equity — A Study of *Lord Cairns' Act*', *Cambridge Law Journal*, vol 34, 1975, 224 at p 226.

114 (1864) 4 De GJ & S 211; 46 ER 899.

115 (1864) 4 De GJ & S 211 at 216; 46 ER 899 at 901.

116 (1864) 4 De GJ & S 211 at 216; 46 ER 899 at 901.

117 *Eaden v Firth* (1863) 1 H & M 573; 71 ER 251.

118 *Roskell v Whitworth* (1870) LR 5 Ch App 459 at 465.

3

Survival of Jurisdiction under Lord Cairns' Act[*]

3.1 Progressive repeal of the Chancery Amendment Act 1858 (Lord Cairns' Act)

In *Raineri v Miles*[1] Lord Edmund-Davies remarked that the Chancery Amendment Act 1858 (*Lord Cairns' Act*)[2] was one of the reforming statutes that 'accelerated' the 'assimilative process' which resulted in the *Judicature Acts*.[3] In discussing the Common Law Procedure Act 1854[4] and *Lord Cairns' Act*, Heuston commented: 'So taken together, the two Acts foreshadow the great reforms of the *Judicature Act* 1875, which vested all powers in one High Court of Justice'.[5] Jolowicz observed: 'The name of *Lord Cairns' Act* is familiar to every student of the English Legal System as one of the Acts which paved the way to the combined administration of law and equity in a single Supreme Court of Judicature'.[6] It is for this

---

[*] This chapter is a revised version of P M McDermott, 'Survival of Jurisdiction under the Chancery Amendment Act 1858 (*Lord Cairns' Act*)', *Civil Justice Quarterly*, vol 6, 1987, p 348.
1 [1981] AC 1050 at 1082.
2 21 & 22 Vict c 27.
3 Supreme Court of Judicature Act 1873 (36 & 37 Vict c 66); Supreme Court of Judicature Act 1875 (38 & 39 Vict c 77).
4 17 & 18 Vict c 125.
5 A W B Simpson, *Biographical Dictionary of the Common Law*, Butterworths, London, 1984, p 98.
6 J A Jolowicz, 'Damages in Equity — A Study of *Lord Cairns' Act*', *Cambridge Law Journal*, vol 34, 1975, p 224.

reason that Maitland regarded *Lord Cairns' Act* as 'a great reforming statute' and as 'prophetic'.[7] *Lord Cairns' Act* not only enabled the Court of Chancery to award damages, but the statute also effected various reforms to that court. Those reforms, however, served no useful purpose when the Court of Chancery ceased to exist upon the creation of the High Court. Consequently, *Lord Cairns' Act* was progressively repealed after the commencement of the *Judicature Acts*. Section 11 of *Lord Cairns' Act* empowered the Lord Chancellor to make General Rules and Orders to regulate the practice of the Court of Chancery.[8] This provision was repealed by the Supreme Court of Judicature (Officers) Act 1879.[9] *Lord Cairns' Act* made provision for the assessment of damages and the trial of issues of fact: ss 3, 4, 6 and 7. These procedural provisions were repealed by the Statute Law Revision and Civil Procedure Act 1881,[10] although they continued to apply to the Lancaster Chancery Court and the Court of Chancery in Ireland.[11] The Statute Law Revision and Civil Procedure Act 1883[12] repealed *Lord Cairns' Act* in its entirety.

---<o>---

3.2 Survival of jurisdiction under Lord Cairns' Act

Despite the repeal of *Lord Cairns' Act* it is generally acknowledged that the High Court continued to possess jurisdiction to award equitable damages under the Act.[13] The significance of the jurisdiction is apparent when it is realised that *Lord Cairns' Act* was not merely a procedural statute that enabled a court of equity to award damages which could be awarded in a court of law.[14] *Lord Cairns' Act* enabled damages to be awarded in circumstances where common law damages were unavailable. This was illustrated by the decision of the House of Lords in *Leeds Industrial Co-operative Society Ltd v Slack*[15] where equitable damages were awarded in lieu of a *quia timet* injunction. Another issue that was settled by the decision of the House of Lords in the *Leeds* case was the manner of survival of the jurisdiction of the High Court under *Lord Cairns' Act*. The majority of their Lordships held that the jurisdiction conferred by *Lord*

---

7   F W Maitland, *Equity*, 2nd rev ed, Cambridge University Press, Cambridge, 1949, p 14.
8   General Orders, 4 April 1859; J S Smith, *The Practice of the Court of Chancery*, vol II, 7th ed, W Maxwell, London, 1862, pp 466–71.
9   42 Vict c 78 s 29 (Second Schedule).
10 44 & 45 Vict c 59 s 3 (Schedule).
11 *Yates v Kyffin-Taylor and Wark* [1899] WN 141; *De Freyne v Fitzgibbon (No 2)* [1904] 1 Ir R 429.
12 46 & 47 Vict c 49 s 3 (Schedule).
13 *Wroth v Tyler* [1974] Ch 30 at 57–8; *Hooper v Rogers* [1975] Ch 43 at 47; *Dutton v Spink and Beeching (Sales) Ltd* [1977] 1 All ER 287 at 293; *Price v Strange* [1978] Ch 337 at 358; *Johnson v Agnew* [1980] AC 367 at 400; *Kennaway v Thompson* [1981] QB 88 at 93; *Oakacre Ltd v Claire Cleaners (Holdings) Ltd* [1982] Ch 197 at 201.
14 Contrast *Portland Cement Co v Wilson* (1882) 31 WR 193 at 194.
15 [1924] AC 851.

Cairns' Act had survived the repeal of that statute by the combined effect of s 16 of the *Judicature Act* 1873, and savings clauses which were contained in s 3 of the Statute Law Revision and Civil Procedure Act 1883 and the Schedule of the Statute Law Revision Act 1898.[16] After the *Leeds* case was decided the *Judicature Act* 1873 was repealed by the Supreme Court of Judicature (Consolidation) Act 1925,[17] but the jurisdiction of the High Court to award equitable damages was preserved by s 18 of that Act.[18]

The question of the survival of *Lord Cairns' Act* has now been rendered academic by the enactment of the Supreme Court Act 1981.[19] Section 50 of the Supreme Court Act confers jurisdiction upon the Court of Appeal and the High Court to award equitable damages. Sir Denis Dobson, in discussing the Supreme Court Act, remarked:

> ... the repeal of *Lord Cairns' Act* by a statute law revision Act in 1883 was adversely criticised by the House of Lords in *Leeds Industrial Co-operative Society v Slack* in which its provisions were treated as still being law and they are now formally restored to life.[20]

The Supreme Court Act was drafted on the assumption that *Lord Cairns' Act* may be still operative as s 52(4) of the Act repealed *Lord Cairns' Act* 'so far as unrepealed'.[21]

The *Leeds* case has been the subject of some discussion. It has even been suggested that there may have been no basis in law for the survival of the jurisdiction under *Lord Cairns' Act*. Jolowicz has commented: 'there can be no doubt that the substance of *Lord Cairns' Act* survives, if not with the authority of statute then with the authority of case law'.[22] Heuston wrote that 'the Law Lords performed prodigies of statutory interpretation to arrive at the sensible result that although the Act had been repealed the jurisdiction which it gave to the High Court had still been preserved'.[23] Bennion cited the *Leeds* case as an 'extraordinary instance' of the principle that savings clauses in statute law revision statutes may have the effect that repealed statutes are not 'altogether dead at all'.[24] Atiyah commented:

> But if no English court has ever applied an Act not yet in force, there is one remarkable decision of the House of Lords which seems to have applied an Act after it was repealed. *Lord Cairns' Act* of 1858 was repealed by the Statute Law Revision [and Civil Procedure] Act 1883, though with a savings provision which is not easy to understand, and which was itself repealed by the Statute Law Revision Act 1898 with yet further savings. In *Leeds Industrial Co-operative Society v Slack* the House of Lords applied

---

16 61 & 62 Vict c 22.
17 15 & 16 Geo V c 49.
18 *Johnson v Agnew* [1978] Ch 176 at 191.
19 1981 c 54.
20 Sir Denis Dobson, 'The Supreme Court Act 1981', *Civil Justice Quarterly*, vol 1, 1982, 1 at p 6.
21 Schedule 7.
22 J A Jolowicz, 'Damages in Equity — A Study of *Lord Cairns' Act*', *Cambridge Law Journal*, vol 34, 1975, 224 at p 229.
23 R F V Heuston, 'Hugh McCalmont Cairns', *Northern Ireland Legal Quarterly*, vol 26, 1975, 269 at p 273.
24 F A R Bennion, *Statutory Interpretation*, Butterworths, London, 1984, p 88.

Lord Cairns' Act as though it were still in force. Lord Finlay, delivering the leading judgment, attempted to penetrate the jungle of savings provisions but ended up by saying, that there had been since 1883 a general consensus of opinion that *Lord Cairns' Act* 'or something equivalent to it' was still in force. It seems almost as though the House accepted that the principle of the Act remained in force although it had been repealed; but it is not wholly clear whether this holding was in reliance on the savings' provisions or by some other alchemy. The case is so extraordinary ...[25]

In discussing the *Leeds* case it is necessary to first refer to the speech of Viscount Finlay who delivered the leading speech of the majority of their Lordships. Viscount Finlay considered that *Lord Cairns' Act* remained in force for the following reasons:

> ... it is, I think, necessary to look at the combined effect of the *Judicature Act*, 1873, and the savings clauses in the Statute Law Revision Acts; for this purpose the savings clauses in the two repealing Acts are to the same effect. The *Judicature Act* conferred the power to award damages on the Courts of the Chancery Division and in estimating the damages the principles which *Lord Cairns' Act* laid down are still applicable by virtue of the saving clause in the Statute Law Revision Act. The Court, therefore, retains the power of awarding damages on the principles which I have stated in dealing with the terms of *Lord Cairns' Act* itself. The Act itself is now repealed, but the combined effect of s 16 of the *Judicature Act* and the saving clause is that the law and practice on this point remain unaltered.[26]

Heuston has pointed out that the speech of Viscount Finlay resolved 'the vexed question whether there was jurisdiction to award damages in lieu of a *quia timet* injunction'.[27] Viscount Finlay was recognised as a distinguished Lord Chancellor with particular expertise in constitutional law and international law.[28] The speech of Viscount Finlay, which was delivered when his Lordship was over eighty years of age, was concerned with general principles, and could hardly be expected to discuss the intricacies of the *Judicature Acts*. It does not appear that their Lordships were addressed upon how the High Court assumed jurisdiction under *Lord Cairns' Act*.

Earlier in his speech Viscount Finlay remarked:

> Section 16 of the *Judicature Act*, 1873, vested in the High Court justices the jurisdiction which was vested in or capable of being exercised by the Courts of Chancery and the Courts of common law. All Courts of the Chancery Division acquired thereby the power of awarding damages, and they had, of course, the power of granting injunctions.[29]

---

25 P S Atiyah, 'Common Law and Statute Law', *Modern Law Review*, vol 48, 1985, 1 at pp 10–11.

26 [1924] AC 851 at 862–3.

27 R F V Heuston, *Lives of the Lord Chancellors 1885–1940*, Oxford University Press, Oxford, 1964, p 349.

28 R F V Heuston, *Lives of the Lord Chancellors 1885–1940*, Oxford University Press, Oxford, 1964, pp 327–8.

29 [1924] AC 851 at 861.

In all strictness what Viscount Finlay said was correct. The High Court was constituted by the *Judicature Acts,* and a court of the Chancery Division possesses jurisdiction to concurrently grant common law and equitable remedies.[30] The common law jurisdiction thereby vested in the Chancery Division would enable a court of that Division to award common law damages. What might also have been mentioned was that the equitable jurisdiction of the Chancery Division included jurisdiction under *Lord Cairns' Act.* Viscount Finlay did not distinguish between common law damages and equitable damages, although his Lordship recognised that *Lord Cairns' Act* did not confer 'merely the right of giving damages as at common law'.[31] The speech also does not contain a discussion of the relevance of the savings clauses in the statute law revision statutes.

———◄◊►———

3.3 Relevance of the Judicature Acts

The true position on the survival of the jurisdiction under *Lord Cairns' Act* was best explained by Lord Esher MR in *Chapman, Morsons & Co v Guardians of Auckland Union.*[32] Lord Esher had observed that the repeal of *Lord Cairns' Act:*

> ... was not with the intention of taking away any of the powers given by the Act in a Chancery action, but because it was considered that the *Judicature Acts* re-enacted those powers, and therefore that *Lord Cairns' Act* had become obsolete, and might be repealed.[33]

In discussing these observations Jolowicz has commented:

> This is plausible as a historical explanation of the repeal, but it does nothing to clarify the situation from the technical point of view. If and in so far as *Lord Cairns' Act* did more than anticipate the *Judicature Acts* by creating the novel jurisdiction described above, then Lord Esher says no more than the Act was repealed under a misapprehension, which is probably true but unhelpful.[34]

However, nowhere in the judgment of Lord Esher is it stated that *Lord Cairns' Act* was mistakenly repealed. This was however a view that was later expressed by Viscount Finlay in his speech in the *Leeds* case when his Lordship remarked:

> I think it unfortunate that *Lord Cairns' Act* was included in the Statute Law Revision Repeal of 1883, and suspect that it proceeded on some misapprehension, possibly the view that it conferred merely the right of giving damages as at common law.[35]

---

30 *Elmore v Pirrie* (1887) 57 LT (NS) 333 at 335.
31 [1924] AC 851 at 863.
32 (1889) 23 QBD 294.
33 (1889) 23 QBD 294 at 299.
34 J A Jolowicz, 'Damages in Equity — A Study of *Lord Cairns' Act'*, *Cambridge Law Journal*, vol 34, 1975, 224 at p 229.
35 [1924] AC 851 at 863.

It is apparent that Lord Esher considered that *Lord Cairns' Act* was obsolete, and could therefore be safely repealed. This was because, as his Lordship put it, the *Judicature Acts* had 're-enacted the powers'[36] conferred by *Lord Cairns' Act*. The analysis of Lord Esher is undoubtedly correct because s 16 of the *Judicature Act* 1873 had 'transferred to and vested in the ... High Court of Justice the jurisdiction which ... was vested in ... the High Court of Chancery'. This was recognised by Sir Robert Megarry VC who observed in *Tito v Waddell (No 2)*[37] that 'under the *Judicature Act* 1873 the jurisdiction of the Court of Chancery was transferred to the Supreme Court'.[38] This observation was made in the context of discussing the Exchequer equity jurisdiction that had been transferred to the Court of Chancery in 1841.[39]

The jurisdiction conferred upon the Court of Chancery by *Lord Cairns' Act* was accordingly included in this general transfer of Chancery jurisdiction to the High Court.[40] This was recognised in *Colls v Home and Colonial Stores Ltd*[41] by Lord Macnaghten who remarked that *Lord Cairns' Act* and the Chancery Regulation Act 1862 (*Sir John Rolt's Act*)[42] were 'superseded by the *Judicature Act*, and now the High Court has all the jurisdiction of the Court of Chancery'.[43] Similarly, in *Garden Cottage Foods Ltd v Milk Marketing Board*[44] Lord Diplock noted that 'the jurisdiction conferred upon the Court of Chancery by *Lord Cairns' Act* passed to the High Court'.[45] That is why the operation of *Lord Cairns' Act* was 'spent'[46] upon the enactment of the *Judicature Acts*. Lord Esher had therefore fully appreciated that the High Court constituted by the *Judicature Acts* had been vested with jurisdiction under *Lord Cairns' Act*. It was a consequence that Sir Owen Dixon had not adverted to when he submitted in argument in *Beswicke v Alner*[47] that 'the *Judicature Act* in itself never authorised the substitution of damages for an injunction'.[48] This aspect of the jurisdiction had been referred to by Lord Esher in his judgment in the *Auckland Union* case where his Lordship remarked:

> ... there may still be the equivalent of the old Chancery suit for an injunction, and in that action damages may be given as before the *Judicature Acts* in substitution for an injunction.[49]

---

36 (1889) 23 QBD 294 at 299.
37 [1977] Ch 106.
38 [1977] Ch 106 at 257.
39 5 Vict c 5 s 1. See also W H Bryson, *The Equity Side of the Exchequer*, Cambridge University Press, Cambridge, 1975, p 162.
40 *Chitty on Contracts*, vol 1, 24th ed, Sweet & Maxwell, London, 1977, p 729, para 565, n 89; H McGregor, *McGregor on Damages*, 14th ed, Sweet & Maxwell, London, 1980, p 214, para 295, n 69.
41 [1904] AC 179.
42 25 & 26 Vict c 42.
43 [1904] AC 179 at 188.
44 [1984] AC 130.
45 [1984] AC 130 at 144.
46 Statute Law Revision and Civil Procedure Act 1883, preamble.
47 [1926] VLR 72.
48 [1926] VLR 72 at 74.
49 (1889) 23 QBD 294 at 299.

3.4 Relevance of statute law revision statutes

In some cases it has been assumed that a statute law revision savings provision operated to preserve the operation of *Lord Cairns' Act*. It has been assumed that the jurisdiction of the High Court was preserved by s 5(b) of the Statute Law Revision and Civil Procedure Act 1883 which provided that any repeal effected by the Act shall not affect 'any jurisdiction or principle or rule of law or equity established or confirmed ... by or under any enactment repealed by this Act'.[50] In *Sayers v Collyer*[51] Baggallay J observed that the Act 'contains words preserving the jurisdiction of the Court notwithstanding the repeal'.[52] Similarly, in *Cowper v Laidler*[53] Buckley J said:

> *Lord Cairns' Act* (21 & 22 Vict c 27) was repealed by the Statute Law Revision and Civil Procedure Act, 1883, but by section 5(b) of that Act the jurisdiction of the Court under *Lord Cairns' Act* was preserved notwithstanding the repeal: *Sayers v Collyer.*[54]

In *Re R*[55] Sir Richard Collins MR commented that 'there are existing decisions which have treated the jurisdiction under *Lord Cairns' Act* as remaining in force, notwithstanding its repeal, for by some accident the repealing Act contains a saving clause'.[56] However, Cozens-Hardy LJ dissented from the Master of Rolls by remarking: 'I think the better view is expressed by Lord Esher in *Chapman, Morsons & Co v Auckland Union'.*[57]

The presence of the savings clause in the Statute Revision and Civil Procedure Act 1883 was not in fact accidental as Sir Richard Collins had suggested. Savings clauses in statute law revision statutes were inserted *ex abundanti cautela* to ensure that the law was not radically altered by reason of the inadvertent repeal of a statute. Lord Westbury LC introduced the Statute Law Revision Act 1863[58] which contained an elaborate form of savings clause which became known as the 'Westbury savings'.[59] The Bill to the 1863 Act was accompanied by the following note:

> The early statutes stand in a peculiar position with relation to modern law. Many of their provisions remain, in some sense, embodied in the existing law, notwithstanding that their immediate subject matter may no longer exist. (To mention one instance: 6 Ed 1 Stat Gloucester, c 5, respecting the Writ of Waste, forms part of the existing law as to waste, although the

---

50 G W Keeton and L A Sheridan, *Equity*, Professional Books, Milton, 1976, p 376, n 61; M P Furmston, *Cheshire, Fifoot and Furmston's Law of Contract*, 11th ed, Butterworths, London, 1986, p 617, n 5.
51 (1884) 28 Ch D 103.
52 (1884) 28 Ch D 103 at 107.
53 [1903] 2 Ch 337.
54 [1903] 2 Ch 337 at 339.
55 [1906] 1 Ch 730.
56 [1906] 1 Ch 730 at 735.
57 [1906] 1 Ch 730 at 739.
58 26 & 27 Vict c 125.
59 For a discussion of the 'Westbury Savings': see P M McDermott, 'Statute Law Revision Statutes — Westbury Savings', *Statute Law Review*, 1988, p 139.

Writ of Waste has been abolished.) This peculiarity has always been borne in mind in the compilation of the schedule and the very special terms of the saving in the repealing clause of the bill have been adopted in order to preclude any apprehension of a substantive alteration of the law being produced by the repeal of any of these early statutes.[60]

Savings clauses in successive statute law revision statutes evolved to become quite elaborate.[61] The practice of inserting savings clauses in statute law revision statutes occurred after a Joint Committee had reported on this issue in 1958.[62] C H Chorley, Parliamentary Counsel, had told the Joint Committee that s 38 of the Interpretation Act 1889[63] had rendered such clauses unnecessary. However, this provision was not as extensive in operation as the savings clause in a revision statute as it only operated to preserve rights which had vested when a statute was repealed.[64] Chorley also stated that a savings clause may 'operate, to nullify the effect of a repeal'.[65] This danger was earlier recognised in *Winfield v Boothroyd*[66] by Wills J who observed that the savings clause in s 5 of the 1883 Act 'seems almost wide enough in language to preserve everything swept away by the repealing Act'.[67]

It is sometimes assumed that *Lord Cairns' Act* vested jurisdiction in the High Court. For instance, Heuston referred to the jurisdiction which *Lord Cairns' Act* 'gave to the High Court'.[68] However in all strictness the statute had vested jurisdiction in the Court of Chancery. It is for this reason that the authorities which have held that savings clauses in statute law revision statutes operated to preserve the jurisdiction of the High Court under *Lord Cairns' Act* are unsatisfactory. No consideration appears to have been given as to how the repeal of a statute that vested jurisdiction in the Court of Chancery, which was abolished upon the creation of the High Court, could affect the jurisdiction of the High Court.

The source of jurisdiction of the High Court to award equitable damages was s 16 of the *Judicature Act*, so that the repeal of *Lord Cairns' Act* was of no consequence. It was therefore unnecessary for the House of Lords in the *Leeds* case, albeit in accordance with previous authority, to have placed reliance upon the savings clauses in the statute law revision statutes. That is why there was no basis for the apprehension that there was a 'theoretical possibility that *Lord Cairns' Act* was accidentally

---

60 New South Wales Law Reform Commission, *Report of the Law Reform Commission on the Application of Imperial Acts*, LRC 4, Parliament of New South Wales, 1967, pp 33–4.

61 Statute Law Revision Act 1892 (55 & 56 Vict c 19) s 1.

62 *Halsbury's Laws of England*, vol 44, 4th ed, Butterworths, London, 1983, p 616, para 976, n 2.

63 52 & 53 Vict c 63. See now the Interpretation Act 1978 (1978 c 30) s 16.

64 *Hamilton Gell v White* [1922] 2 KB 422 at 431. See also F A R Bennion, *Statutory Interpretation*, Butterworths, London, 1984, p 438.

65 *Seventh Report by the Joint Committee of the House of Lords and the House of Commons appointed to consider all Consolidation Bills*, 1957–1958 (HL 108, HC 209), Minutes of Evidence, p 2.

66 (1886) 54 LT 574.

67 (1886) 54 LT 574 at 577.

68 R F V Heuston, 'Hugh McCalmont Cairns', *Northern Ireland Legal Quarterly*, vol 26, 1975, 269 at p 273.

repealed in 1974'.[69] Jolowicz remarked that the Statute Law Revision and Civil Procedure Act 1883, in common with all subsequent statute law revision statutes until the Statute Law Repeals Act 1974,[70] contained a savings clause which preserved any jurisdiction that was conferred upon a court under a repealed enactment.[71] In fact no such savings clause has appeared in a statute law revision statute after the Joint Committee reported in 1958.

Lancaster Palatine Court

The Court of Chancery of the County Palatine of Lancaster formerly exercised equitable jurisdiction within the limits of the County Palatine.[72] Savings clauses in the Statute Law Revision and Civil Procedure Act 1883 preserved the jurisdiction of the Lancaster Court of Chancery under *Lord Cairns' Act*.[73] The savings clause in s 5 of the Act operated to preserve the jurisdiction of the court to award equitable damages. A savings clause in s 7 of the Act also provided that if and so far as any enactment repealed by that Act applied to the court 'such enactment shall be construed as if it were contained in a local and personal Act specially relating to such court, and shall have effect accordingly'. In *Yates v Kyffin-Taylor and Wark*[74] Hall VC remarked that the savings clause in s 7 had the consequence that any such enactment 'shall not be repealed at all, it shall be treated as if those enactments relating to this Court had been included in some special Local and Personal Act, which of course would not be repealed, because it would not be in the schedule'.[75] The continued operation of *Lord Cairns' Act* and *Sir John Rolt's Act* would therefore also have been preserved by virtue of s 7.

The Lancaster Court of Chancery was not affected by the *Judicature Acts*, so that after the enactment of those Acts *Lord Cairns' Act* remained the only statutory source of jurisdiction of the court to award damages.[76] This situation became apparent in *Proctor v Bayley*,[77] a patent infringement case, where the court could not award equitable damages as there was no case for an injunction. The court soon after acquired the jurisdiction of the Chancery Division of the High Court upon the enactment of the Chancery of Lancaster Act 1890.[78] However, even after the Chancery of Lancaster Act was passed the court continued to rely

---

69 J A Jolowicz, 'Damages in Equity — A Study of *Lord Cairns' Act*', *Cambridge Law Journal*, vol 34, 1975, 224 at p 228, n 27.

70 1974 c 22.

71 J A Jolowicz, 'Damages in Equity — A Study of *Lord Cairns' Act*', *Cambridge Law Journal*, vol 34, 1975, 224 at p 228.

72 Court of Chancery of Lancaster Act 1850 (13 & 14 Vict c 43).

73 Chancery Amendment Act 1858 s 10.

74 [1899] WN 141.

75 [1899] WN 141 at 146.

76 Contrast *Bertram v Builders' Association of North Winnipeg Ltd* (1915) 8 WWR 814 at 818; 23 DLR 534 at 538.

77 (1889) 42 Ch D 390.

78 53 & 54 Vict c 23 s 3.

upon procedural provisions in *Lord Cairns' Act*.[79] In 1972 the Lancaster Palatine Court was merged with the High Court.[80]

---

79 *Yates v Kyffin-Taylor and Wark* [1899] WN 141. See also Statute Law Revision Act 1892 (55 & 56 Vict c19) ss 1, 2 (Sch).
80 Courts Act 1971 (1971 c 23) s 41; Courts Act 1971 (Commencement) Order 1971.

4

Jurisdiction to Award Equitable Damages

4.1 *Judicature Acts*

Under the Judicature system the court possesses jurisdiction to concurrently grant legal and equitable remedies. A plaintiff may claim these remedies either concurrently or on an alternative basis. It is, of course, trite that the entitlement of a plaintiff to common law damages does not depend upon the entitlement of that person to equitable relief. The courts repeatedly emphasise the fact that common law damages for breach of contract may be awarded in a suit in which a plaintiff has no entitlement to specific performance.[1] In *Elmore v Pirrie*[2] Kay J remarked:

---

1   *Tamplin v James* (1880) 15 Ch D 215 at 223; *Sayers v Collyer* (1884) 28 Ch D 103 at 108; *Serrao v Noel* (1885) 15 QBD 549 at 559; *Ryan v Mutual Tontine Westminster Chambers Association* [1893] 1 Ch 116; *Dominion Coal Co Ltd v Dominion Iron and Steel Co Ltd* [1909] AC 293 at 311 (PC); *Dowsett v Reid* (1912) 15 CLR 695; *Robison v Sanson* (1912) 14 GLR 579 at 582; *Fullers' Theatres Ltd v Musgrove* (1923) 31 CLR 524; *King v Poggioli* (1923) 32 CLR 222 at 247; *Dell v Beasley* [1959] NZLR 89 at 97; *Bosaid v Andry* [1963] VR 465 at 484; *Headland Developments Pty Ltd v Bullen* [1975] 2 NSWLR 309 at 324; *Patel v Ali* [1984] Ch 283 at 286.

2   (1887) 57 LT (NS) 333.

... the Judicature Act of 1873 ... gave the court complete jurisdiction both in law and equity; so that, whether the court could in a particular case grant specific performance or not, it could give damages for breach of the agreement.[3]

Similarly, common law damages for actual damage sustained by a plaintiff may be awarded in a suit in which a plaintiff has no entitlement to an injunction. The jurisdiction under the Chancery Amendment Act 1858 (*Lord Cairns' Act*)[4] has significance in a case where damages are unavailable at law, where an assessment of equitable damages would be preferable to common law damages, or for procedural reasons, for example, where the pleadings are deficient in not containing a claim for damages. The jurisdiction was also of significance in the equity courts in those Commonwealth jurisdictions which had delayed in adopting the Judicature system. There are a number of decisions from New South Wales, which has a tradition of a strong equity bench and bar, on the jurisdictional aspects of *Lord Cairns' Act*.[5]

———◦———

4.2 Jurisdiction to entertain an application for an injunction or specific performance

Meagher, Gummow and Lehane point out that *Lord Cairns' Act* 'imposed some jurisdictional limitations. It clearly did not give the Court of Chancery an unfettered power to award damages whenever it wished'.[6] Section 2 of *Lord Cairns' Act* was the relevant provision which conferred jurisdiction upon the Court of Chancery to award damages. The section stated the conditions on which 'it shall be lawful' for damages to be awarded:

> In all cases in which the Court of Chancery has Jurisdiction to entertain an Application for an injunction against a Breach of any Covenant, Contract, or Agreement, or against the Commission or Continuance of any wrongful Act, or for specific Performance of any Covenant, Contract or Agreement.

Essentially, *Lord Cairns' Act* enabled the Court of Chancery to award damages only in a suit in which the court had 'jurisdiction to entertain an application' for an injunction or specific performance. This had the consequence that equitable damages could be awarded in a suit in which the court could decree specific relief in the form of an injunction or specific performance. In *JC Williamson Ltd v Lukey and Mulholland*[7] Sir Owen Dixon remarked that the requisite jurisdiction existed in:

---

3 (1887) 57 LT (NS) 333 at 335.
4 21 & 22 Vict c 27.
5 See p 237.
6 R P Meagher, W M C Gummow and J R F Lehane, *Equity — Doctrines and Remedies*, 2nd ed, Butterworths, Sydney, 1984, p 608 [2307].
7 (1931) 45 CLR 282.

... cases in which there is a title to equitable relief, cases in which there are the ingredients that enable the court, if it thought fit, to exercise its power of decreeing specific performance or of granting an injunction.[8]

The mere circumstance that in a particular case the court declines to make an order for specific performance because damages will provide an adequate remedy does not have the consequence that the court is declining jurisdiction to award equitable damages, and does not 'entertain' the claim for specific performance. In *Singh v Crafter*[9] Murray J remarked:

I rather think that such a case is one where it is proper to describe the denial of relief upon that ground as being a denial in the exercise of a discretion. And if that is the case, then it is certain jurisdiction remained in a case such as this to award equitable damages.[10]

The Court of Chancery could award equitable damages in a suit in which the court could issue a decree for an injunction or specific performance when a bill was filed.[11]

There is a considerable body of authority that jurisdiction under *Lord Cairns' Act* only exists in a suit where at the commencement of proceedings the plaintiff has an equity to an order for an injunction[12] or specific performance.[13] This jurisdictional limitation has been discussed in a number of cases. In *Ferguson v Wilson*[14] Cairns LJ commented:

---

8 (1931) 45 CLR 282 at 295.

9 Supreme Court of Western Australia, Full Court, Appeal No 8 of 1991, 28 May 1992, unreported.

10 *Singh v Crafter*, n 9 above, at 73.

11 E R Daniell, *Practice of the High Court of Chancery*, vol 1, 5th ed, Stevens, London, 1871, p 946; *Boyns v Lackey* (1958) 58 SR (NSW) 395 at 405.

12 *Wedmore v Mayor of Bristol* (1862) 11 WR 136 at 137; *Durell v Pritchard* (1865) LR 1 Ch App 244; *Lawrence v Austin, Durell v Pritchard* (1865) 13 WR 981 at 982; *Hindley v Emery* (1865) LR 1 Eq 52 at 54; *Brockington v Palmer* (1871) 18 Gr 488 at 490; *Aynsley v Glover* (1874) LR 18 Eq 544; *Stanley of Alderley, Lady v Shrewsbury, Earl of* (1875) LR 19 Eq 616; *Proctor v Bayley* (1889) 42 Ch D 390; *Wright v Carter* (1923) 23 SR (NSW) 555 at 570; *JC Williamson Ltd v Lukey and Mulholland* (1931) 45 CLR 282 at 295; *Stininato v Auckland Boxing Association Inc* [1978] 1 NZLR 1 at 23; *Beard v Baulkham Hills Shire Council* (1986) 7 NSWLR 273 at 280; *Re Children's Aid Society of Hamilton-Wentworth and Burrell* (1986) 56 OR (2d) 40 at 56; 9 CPC (2d) 298 at 300; *Surrey County Council v Bredero Homes Ltd* [1992] 3 All ER 302 at 316.

13 *Collins v Stuteley* (1859) 7 WR 710; *Rogers v Challis* (1859) 27 Beav 175 at 180; 54 ER 68 at 70; *Chinnock v Sainsbury* (1860) 9 WR 7; *Franlinski v Ball* (1864) 10 LT (NS) 447 at 448; *Lewers v Shaftesbury, Earl of* (1866) LR 2 Eq 270 at 271; *Ferguson v Wilson* (1866) LR 2 Ch App 77 at 88, 91; *Crampton v Varna Railway Co* (1872) LR 7 Ch App 562 at 567; *White v Boby* (1877) 37 LT (NS) 652; *Hipgrave v Case* (1885) 28 Ch D 356; *Elmore v Pirrie* (1887) 57 LT (NS) 333 at 335; *Wright v City of Winnipeg* (1887) 4 Man R 46; *Lavery v Pursell* (1888) 39 Ch D 508; *Allen v Fairbrother* (1907) 9 GLR 328 at 329; *Bertram v Builders' Association of North Winnipeg Ltd* (1915) 8 WWR 814 at 818; 23 DLR 534 at 538; *King v Poggioli* (1923) 32 CLR 222 at 247; *Wright v Carter* (1923) 23 SR (NSW) 555 at 570; *JC Williamson Ltd v Lukey and Mulholland* (1931) 45 CLR 282 at 295; *Cummins v Cummins* [1934] 2 DLR 228 at 230; *Conroy v Lowndes* [1958] Qd R 375; *Dobson v Winton and Robbins Ltd* [1959] SCR 775 at 778; *Craney v Bugg* [1971] 1 NSWLR 13 at 16; *Wroth v Tyler* [1974] Ch 30 at 57; *Newmont Pty Ltd v Laverton Nickel NL* [1981] 1 NSWLR 215 at 218; *McMahon v Ambrose* [1987] VR 817 at 818; *Surrey County Council v Bredero Homes Ltd* [1992] 3 All ER 302 at 316.

14 (1866) LR 2 Ch App 77.

The important words of the Act are these:– 'In all cases in which the Court of Chancery has jurisdiction to entertain an application for the specific performance of any covenant, contract, or agreement'. That, of course, means where there are, at least at the time of bill filed, all those ingredients which would enable the Court, if it thought fit, to exercise its power and decree specific performance — among other things where there is the subject matter whereon the decree of the Court can act.[15]

Similarly, Sir George Jessel MR remarked in *White v Boby*:[16]

The Act which is commonly known as *Lord Cairns' Act* does not come into operation unless there is equity in the bill. You must start with an equity, and then in certain circumstances you may get, under *Lord Cairns' Act*, damages instead of that equity.[17]

Such statements are, however, too restrictive in suggesting that the jurisdiction under *Lord Cairns' Act* can only be exercised where there is an 'equity in the bill' when a suit is commenced. *Lord Cairns' Act* did not provide such a limitation upon the jurisdiction. It should be appreciated that the jurisdiction may also exist in a case where at the commencement of proceedings a plaintiff does not possess an equity to specific relief. Provided that the plaintiff acquires such an equity before the hearing of a suit, the necessary jurisdiction will exist under *Lord Cairns' Act* to enable the award of equitable damages.[18]

Provisions which are essentially in the same terms as s 2 of *Lord Cairns' Act* appear in a number of Commonwealth statutes. It should be remembered that particular terms in these provisions may be defined in these statutes. For example the word 'jurisdiction' in the Western Australian equivalent to *Lord Cairns' Act* is defined to include 'powers and authorities'.[19] Accordingly, in Western Australia equitable damages may be awarded where a court possesses power to make an order for an injunction or specific performance.

Statutory successors to Lord Cairns' Act

The words 'jurisdiction to entertain an application' appear in some statutory provisions which have superseded *Lord Cairns' Act*. In the United Kingdom equitable damages may be awarded under s 92 of the Judicature (Northern Ireland) Act 1978 which applies in Northern Ireland, and s 50 of the Supreme Court Act 1981 which applies in England and Wales. Both of these sections provide that equitable damages may be awarded where the court has 'jurisdiction to entertain an application for an injunction or specific performance'. The word 'jurisdiction' is defined in the Judicature (Northern Ireland) Act as including 'power and authority': s 120(1). Similarly in the Supreme Court Act the word 'jurisdiction' is defined as including 'powers': s 151. These definitions make it clear that a

---

15   (1866) LR 2 Ch App 77 at 91.
16   (1877) 37 LT (NS) 652.
17   (1877) 37 LT (NS) 652.
18   See p 82.
19   Supreme Court Act 1935 (Western Australia) s 4.

court may award equitable damages in a matter in which the court has power to grant an injunction or specific performance.

Equitable damages may be awarded in New South Wales where a court possesses power to make an order for an injunction or specific performance. The provision which enables the award of equitable damages contains the word 'power'[20] instead of 'jurisdiction'; but it has been held that this change is of no consequence.[21]

Flexibility of equity

Since the jurisdiction to award equitable damages depends upon the ability of a court to decree equitable relief in the form of an injunction or specific performance, it is necessary in a particular case to examine whether such equitable relief is available. There are some statements in the cases which suggest that the circumstances in which a court of equity will decree specific performance are well-defined, and governed by 'fixed rules and principles',[22] or 'some settled rule and principle'.[23] In *Mama v Sassoon*[24] Lord Blanesburgh remarked:

> As a result of a long course of decisions by Chancellors and other equity judges, there was gradually evolved in England a body of settled principles and rules governing the exercise of that jurisdiction, so that in course of time its limits were settled almost as definitely as if they had been embodied in a statute.[25]

The doctrines of equity are, however, dynamic, and not static. They will be modified in appropriate instances to remedy any inadequacy of the common law. This after all has always been the fundamental purpose of a court of equity. At one time it was assumed that the remedy of specific performance was only available to enforce a contract for the sale of realty,[26] but this notion was later repudiated.[27] Spry, in referring to the doctrine of mutuality, has referred to the 'danger of attempting to formulate inflexible rules, such as those generally applicable in courts of law, when what is in question is in truth no more than an equitable discretionary consideration'.[28] Sir Raymond Evershed MR had earlier spoken on a similar theme:

> As an equity lawyer, let me acknowledge that I have a natural inclination to favour the undefined and undefinable in the form of principles which have never lost, by unnecessary and constricting definition, their capacity for useful growth. And I would like, here, to make the important point

---

20 Supreme Court Act 1970 (New South Wales) s 68: see Appendix at p 282.
21 *ASA Constructions Pty Ltd v Iwanov* [1975] 1 NSWLR 512 at 518.
22 *Rogers v Challis* (1859) 27 Beav 175 at 180; 54 ER 68 at 70; *Lamare v Dixon* (1873) LR 6 HL 414 at 423.
23 *Haywood v Cope* (1858) 25 Beav 140 at 151; 53 ER 589 at 594.
24 (1928) LR 55 IA 360.
25 (1928) LR 55 IA 360 at 372.
26 *Buxton v Lister* (1746) 3 Atk 383; 26 ER 1020.
27 *Adderley v Dixon* (1824) 1 Sim & St 607 at 610; 57 ER 239 at 240.
28 I C F Spry, *Equitable Remedies*, 4th ed, Law Book Co, Sydney, 1990, p 7, cited in *Price v Strange* [1978] Ch 337 at 352.

that these undefined principles of equity could never, so far as I can see (save to a very limited extent) be effectively or usefully comprehended, by codification, in the enacted law.[29]

It has been assumed that there are some limitations upon the jurisdiction which was conferred by *Lord Cairns' Act*. It has been thought that equitable damages could not be awarded in actions for the specific performance of certain classes of contract. The Law Reform Commission of British Columbia has commented:

> The use of the word 'jurisdiction' is unfortunate, and has resulted in some confusion. It is clear that 'jurisdiction' does refer to the type of contract alleged. Thus if an agreement is one of personal service, or requiring supervision by the court, then because a court of equity *could not* give specific performance, it is disabled from awarding damages. To do so is beyond its jurisdiction.[30]

It has similarly been suggested that 'equitable damages could not be awarded for breaches of a contract for personal services, a contract to sell or buy ordinary commercial goods, [or] a contract to borrow money'.[31] In cases involving these classes of contract the jurisdiction to award equitable remedies would only assume significance where common law damages were not available. However, in appropriate cases specific performance will be decreed of contracts for the loan of money, contracts for the sale of goods, and contracts for personal services.[32] Consequently, equitable damages may be awarded in such cases.

4.3 Absence of equity to an injunction or specific performance

Some decisions on the jurisdictional aspects of *Lord Cairns' Act* were decided in the era before the commencement of the *Judicature Acts*.[33] In some cases it is apparent that the primary purpose of a suitor was to obtain damages, and not specific relief. Such a case was *Betts v Gallais*[34] where a bill containing a prayer for an injunction to restrain the infringement of a patent was filed a few days prior to the expiration of the patent. In these circumstances, where the plaintiff could not have obtained even an interlocutory injunction, the court declined to award damages under *Lord*

---

29 R Evershed, 'Government Under Law in Post-War England', *Law Quarterly Review*, vol 72, 1956, 42 at pp 43–4.

30 Law Reform Commission of British Columbia, *The Statute of Frauds*, LRC 33, 1977, pp 22–3.

31 T Ingman and J Wakefield, 'Equitable Damages under Lord Cairns' Act', 1981, *Conveyancer and Property Lawyer*, 286 at p 292.

32 See p 193–6.

33 Supreme Court of Judicature Act 1873 (36 & 37 Vict c 66); Supreme Court of Judicature Act 1875 (38 & 39 Vict c 77).

34 (1870) LR 10 Eq 392.

Cairns' Act. Sir William James VC said: 'this is a mere device to transfer a plain jurisdiction to award damages from the Court to which that jurisdiction properly belongs'.[35] There are similar cases where the Court of Chancery declined to award equitable damages where a plaintiff clearly had no equity to an injunction at the time of the institution of a suit.[36] As Thomas J observed in *Barbagallo v J & F Catelan Pty Ltd*:[37]

> The experience in courts of equity of suits being brought in which there was no chance of obtaining an injunction, especially a mandatory injunction, and in which equitable damages were always the real and only remedy, was commonplace.[38]

A court will not possess jurisdiction under *Lord Cairns' Act* in a case where a plaintiff has no equity, subject to discretionary considerations, to an injunction or specific performance. In determining whether a plaintiff possesses the requisite equity it is, of course, necessary to have regard to general equitable principles. One case in which the jurisdiction clearly is not available is where specific performance of a terminated agreement is sought. As McPherson J remarked in *SJ Mackie Pty Ltd v Dalziell Medical Practice Pty Ltd*:[39]

> To decree, even notionally, specific performance of an admittedly terminated agreement is to proceed contrary to at least the tenor of what was said in *Swain v Ayres*[40].[41]

In *Gallagher v Rainbow*[42] the appellant sought interlocutory relief to prevent the registration of a plan of subdivision; this was declined except to maintain the status quo pending an appeal. At the time that the appeal was heard the plan of subdivision was approved by the local authority and lodged with the Registrar of Titles. The Court of Appeal of Queensland refused to grant any further injunction and the plan of subdivision was then registered. The appellant then sold the property, and by the time that the appeal to the High Court of Australia was argued the appellant sought an inquiry as to equitable damages in lieu of an injunction. Brennan, Dawson and Toohey JJ remarked:

> ... if an injunction was not available at any stage to the appellant, there can be no question of equitable compensation[43] or damages in lieu of an injunction.[44]

---

35 (1870) LR 10 Eq 392 at 393.
36 *City of London Brewery Co v Tennant* (1873) LR 9 Ch App 212; *Stanley of Alderley, Lady v Shrewsbury, Earl of* (1875) LR 19 Eq 616.
37 [1986] 1 Qd R 245.
38 [1986] 1 Qd R 245 at 265.
39 [1989] 2 Qd R 87.
40 (1888) 21 QBD 289.
41 [1989] 2 Qd R 87 at 96.
42 (1994) 121 ALR 129; 68 ALJR 512.
43 It is submitted that the term 'equitable compensation' is more appropriate to refer to compensation awarded in the inherent jurisdiction of a court of equity.
44 (1994) 121 ALR 129 at 136; 68 ALJR 512 at 516–17.

It can therefore be seen that unless a plaintiff possesses an equity to an injunction or specific performance when proceedings are commenced or at some later stage, that a court cannot award equitable damages. Accordingly it has been held that equitable damages cannot be awarded where:

(i) a plaintiff has 'no case for an injunction'[45] because, when a suit was commenced,[46] there was no reason to apprehend the repetition of a wrongful act;[47]

(ii) a plaintiff in a specific performance suit fails to establish, with certainty, the existence of any 'covenant, contract, or agreement' within the meaning of s 2 of *Lord Cairns' Act*;[48]

(iii) a plaintiff in an action for specific performance does not prove the requisite readiness and willingness to perform the contract;[49]

(iv) specific performance of a contract for the sale of land was impossible before the commencement of an action;[50] for example where the vendor is unable to discharge a mortgage on the land;[51]

(v) the plaintiff[52] or the defendant[53] has sold the subject matter of the contract to a third party prior to the commencement of proceedings for specific performance of the contract, or prior to the hearing of the suit;[54]

---

45 *Surrey County Council v Bredero Homes Ltd* [1992] 3 All ER 302 at 316 per Ferris J.

46 Where a plaintiff had an equity when an action was commenced: see *Fritz v Hobson* (1880) 14 Ch D 542.

47 *Brockington v Palmer* (1871) 18 Gr 488 at 490–1; *Proctor v Bayley* (1889) 42 Ch D 390; *Malone v Metropolitan Police Commissioner* [1979] Ch 344 at 360; *O'Neill v Dept of Health and Social Services (No 2)* [1986] NI 290 at 296.

48 *Darbey v Whitaker* (1857) 4 Drew 134; 62 ER 52; *Tillett v The Charing Cross Bridge Co* (1859) 26 Beav 419; 53 ER 959; *Lancaster v De Trafford* (1862) 10 WR 474; *Lewers v Shaftesbury, Earl of* (1866) LR 2 Eq 270; *Photo Art & Sound Pty Ltd v Cremorne Centre Pty Ltd* (Supreme Court of New South Wales, Powell J, Eq Div, No 3337 of 1983, 6 December 1984, unreported).

49 *King v Poggioli* (1923) 32 CLR 222 at 247 (discussed in R P Meagher, W M C Gummow and J R F Lehane, *Equity — Doctrines and Remedies*, 2nd ed, Butterworths, Sydney, 1984, p 609 [2307]); *Mines Ltd v Woodworth* [1941] 3 WWR 40 at 43; *O'Rourke v Hoeven* [1974] 1 NSWLR 622 at 626. This is also the case under the Specific Relief Acts of India and Malaysia: see *Karsandas v Chhotalal* (1923) 25 Bom LR 1037 at 1050; *Mama v Sassoon* (1928) LR 55 IA 360 at 375; *Ganam D/O Rajamany v Somoo S/O Sinnah* [1984] 2 MLJ 290 at 297.

50 *Bertram v Builders' Association of North Winnipeg Ltd* (1915) 8 WWR 814; *Norton v Angus* (1926) 38 CLR 523 at 534; *Western Electric Co (Aust) Ltd v Betts* (1935) 52 WN (NSW) 173; *Craney v Bugg* [1971] 1 NSWLR 13; *Price v Strange* [1978] Ch 337 at 358–9.

51 *Spicer v Far South Coast Regional Aboriginal Land Council* (Supreme Court of New South Wales, Needham J, Eq Div, No 1264 of 1986, 18 October 1989, unreported).

52 *Hipgrave v Case* (1885) 28 Ch D 356; *Conroy v Lowndes* [1958] Qd R 375; *Bosaid v Andry* [1963] VR 465 at 484.

53 *Ferguson v Wilson* (1866) LR 2 Ch App 77; *Miguez v Harrison* (1914) 7 Man LR 650; 7 WWR 650; *Bertram v Builders' Association of North Winnipeg Ltd* (1915) 8 WWR 814 at 818; 23 DLR 534 at 538; *Mama v Sassoon* (1928) LR 55 IA 360; *Ella v Wenham* [1971] QWN 31; *Craney v Bugg* [1971] 1 NSWLR 13 at 15; *The Millstream Pty Ltd v Schultz* [1980] 1 NSWLR 547 at 552.

54 See also *Surrey County Council v Bredero Homes Ltd* [1992] 3 All ER 302 at 316 per Ferris J.

(vi) specific performance of a covenant to develop an estate, or an injunction to restrain a breach of the covenant, could not be ordered because the defendant had sold all lots on the estate before the issue of the writ;[55]

(vii) only one joint tenant has executed a contract for the sale of jointly owned land;[56]

(viii) a contractual entitlement of the plaintiff has expired;[57]

(ix) specific performance is sought of an agreement to assign a lease which had expired prior to the commencement of proceedings;[58]

(x) an order of specific performance would compel the parties to act in breach of a statute;[59]

(xi) the plaintiff has done some act which disentitles that party to specific performance;[60]

(xii) there is an oral agreement for the purchase of a business on the assurance that a lease from a third party was obtainable;[61]

(xiii) there is an agreement for a partnership;[62] or

(xiv) there is a contract of agency.[63]

Some of these cases may be explained by reference to discretionary, as well as jurisdictional, considerations.[64] For example a vendor who seeks an order for specific performance of a contract will not be awarded equitable damages if, prior to the hearing, the subject matter of the contract is

---

55 *Surrey County Council v Bredero Homes Ltd* [1993] 1 WLR 1361 affirming *Surrey County Council v Bredero Homes Ltd* [1992] 3 All ER 302.

56 *Watts v Spence* [1976] Ch 165 at 173.

57 *Lavery v Pursell* (1888) 39 Ch D 508.

58 *McMahon v Ambrose* [1987] VR 817, reversing *Rojain Pty Ltd v Ambrose; McMahon Third Party* [1986] VR 449. However, see the dissenting judgment of McGarvie J at [1987] VR 817 at 826–32.

59 *Norton v Angus* (1926) 38 CLR 523 at 534.

60 *Collins v Stuteley* (1859) 7 WR 710; *Mama v Sassoon* (1928) LR 55 IA 360 at 376.

61 *Robinson v MacAdam* [1948] 2 WWR 425.

62 *Scott v Rayment* (1868) LR 7 Eq 112 at 115–16; *McCallum v Mackenzie* (1979) 37 NSR (2d) 328 at 347. Although a court will not ordinarily enforce an agreement for a partnership there are some instances where specific performance is available. Where the parties have carried on a business the court would order the execution of a formal deed of partnership: see *England v Curling* (1844) 8 Beav 129; 50 ER 51; *Vindachala v Ramaswami* (1863) 1 MHCR 341; *Crowley v O'Sullivan* [1900] 2 Ir R 478 at 487; *Byrne v Reid* [1902] 2 Ch 735; *Douglas v Hill* [1909] SALR 28 at 32; *Lindley on the Law of Partnership*, 14th ed, Sweet & Maxwell, London, 1979, p 537. In India the courts possess an express statutory jurisdiction to order the execution of a partnership deed: see Specific Relief Act 1963 (47 of 1963) (India) s 14(3)(b)(i). A court will also grant specific performance of a contract for the purchase of a share in a partnership: see *Dodson v Downey* [1901] 2 Ch 620; Specific Relief Act 1963 (India) s 14(3)(b)(ii). Where a partnership is in existence a partner may obtain an injunction to reinstate his rights as a partner. In one case the court awarded damages under *Lord Cairns' Act* in lieu of granting such an injunction: *Laugesen v Spensley* (1910) 12 GLR 719.

63 *Chinnock v Sainsbury* (1860) 9 WR 7.

64 Ingman and Wakefield have remarked that 'it is by no means easy to distinguish between those cases where the court has *no jurisdiction* to decree specific performance, and those where the order is refused on *discretionary* grounds': see T Ingman and J Wakefield, 'Equitable Damages under *Lord Cairns' Act*', Conveyancer and Property Lawyer, 1981, p 286.

sold.[65] In such a case the court may technically possess the requisite jurisdiction at the time when an action is commenced, but the court would understandably not be disposed to awarding equitable damages at the time of the hearing.

The mere fact that a party has consented to the grant of an interlocutory injunction does not preclude that party from later contending at the hearing that the court does not possess jurisdiction to award equitable damages.[66]

4.4 Discretionary bar to equitable relief

Meagher, Gummow and Lehane consider that:

> ... the statutory power to award damages applied in cases where the contract in question was susceptible to specific performance or the right in question is susceptible to specific performance or the right in question is susceptible to protection by injunction were it not for some discretionary defence.[67]

The Court of Chancery recognised that the requisite jurisdiction under *Lord Cairns' Act* existed if it were possible to decree equitable relief in the form of an injunction or specific performance in a particular case, notwithstanding that the court in the exercise of its discretion had decided to withhold such relief.

In *Wedmore v Mayor of Bristol*[68] Sir John Stuart VC remarked:

> The words of the Act clearly applied to the powers and jurisdiction of the Court, and not to the question whether or not the plaintiff had made out a case entitling him to an injunction. The words 'in substitution for an injunction' plainly showed that the Legislature contemplated a case in which there might be a question whether an injunction or damages were the better remedy.[69]

In *Ferguson v Wilson*[70] Cairns LJ considered that the requisite jurisdiction existed where the court could decree specific performance 'if it thought fit'.[71] Similarly in *Weily v Williams*[72] Owen CJ in Eq observed that the court:

> ... sees that the contract is one of which it could grant specific performance, but in its discretion thinks that is not the proper form of relief, but that it may enforce the contract by a decree for damages, then the court can allow damages.[73]

---

65 *Hipgrave v Case* (1885) 28 Ch D 356; *Conroy v Lowndes* [1958] Qd R 375.
66 *The Millstream Pty Ltd v Schultz* [1980] 1 NSWLR 547 at 552.
67 R P Meagher, W M C Gummow and J R F Lehane, *Equity — Doctrines and Remedies*, 2nd ed, Butterworths, Sydney, 1984, p 609 [2307]; 3rd ed, Butterworths, Sydney, 1992, p 641 [2307].
68 (1862) 11 WR 136.
69 (1862) 11 WR 136 at 137.
70 (1866) LR 2 Ch App 77.
71 (1866) LR 2 Ch App 77 at 91. See also *JC Williamson Ltd v Lukey and Mulholland* (1931) 45 CLR 282 at 295.
72 (1895) 16 LR (NSW) Eq 190.
73 (1895) 16 LR (NSW) Eq 190 at 195.

There is modern authority on the point. In *Bosaid v Andry*[74] Sholl J remarked that the court was not deprived of jurisdiction under *Lord Cairns' Act* by 'the existence of a ground entitling the court in its discretion to refuse the equitable remedy'.[75] In *Edward Street Properties Pty Ltd v Collins*[76] Douglas J agreed with Spry that the jurisdiction exists 'whether or not relief might be refused on a discretionary ground'.[77] In *Price v Strange*[78] Goff LJ recognised that the jurisdiction exists where specific performance is withheld on the discretionary ground of want of mutuality.

The position in Australia now appears to be settled. In *Wentworth v Woollahra Municipal Council*[79] the High Court of Australia considered:

> ... it conforms to the main object of the statute if damages in such a case are awarded under the section, even though the claim for equitable relief is defeated by a discretionary defence such as laches, acquiescence or hardship. We are content to assume, without finally deciding, that this is so.[80]

Subsequent Australian decisions have not departed from this ruling. In *Madden v Kevereski*[81] Helsham CJ in Eq expressed the view that the jurisdiction exists 'where a plaintiff has made out a case for equitable relief by way of injunction or specific performance, and has either got it, or for some equitable or discretionary reason, been refused it'.[82] In *Barbagallo v J & F Catelan Pty Ltd*[83] McPherson J commented:

> A related but more debateable question is whether, if there are discretionary grounds or 'bars' to refusing an injunction, the Court's jurisdiction is thereby excluded. The weight of authority favours the view that the jurisdiction to award damages persists notwithstanding that in those circumstances the injunction is or would be refused.[84]

In *McMahon v Ambrose*[85] Marks J similarly remarked that 'the weight of authority indicates' that equitable damages may be awarded 'in a case where all the ingredients empowering the court to grant specific performance are present but for discretionary reasons the court declines to do so'.[86]

The jurisdiction to award equitable damages may be accordingly exercised in a case where specific relief would otherwise issue but for the existence of personal equities between the parties.[87] There are dicta that a

---

74 [1963] VR 465.
75 [1963] VR 465 at 484.
76 [1977] Qd R 399 at 402.
77 I C F Spry, *Equitable Remedies*, 4th ed, Law Book Co, Sydney, 1990, p 611.
78 [1978] Ch 337 at 359.
79 (1982) 149 CLR 672.
80 (1982) 149 CLR 672 at 679.
81 [1983] 1 NSWLR 305.
82 [1983] 1 NSWLR 305 at 307.
83 [1986] 1 Qd R 245.
84 [1986] 1 Qd R 245 at 251.
85 [1987] VR 817.
86 [1987] VR 817 at 842.
87 *Weily v Williams* (1895) 16 LR (NSW) Eq 190 (inadequacy of consideration); *Crampton v Foster* (1897) 18 LR (NSW) Eq 136 (intoxication).

court does not possess such jurisdiction in a case in which the court would not have exercised its jurisdiction to decree an injunction or specific performance.[88] However such a view takes a restrictive interpretation of *Lord Cairns' Act*, and is not in accord with modern prevailing authority on this question. Spry observed that in some of these cases the court was probably not concerned to advert to the distinction between jurisdictional and discretionary matters.[89]

———◄o►———

4.5 Various discretionary defences

Hardship — injunction

Hardship is a discretionary ground for the refusal of an injunction.[90] This defence operates if the grant of relief would result in considerable expense to a defendant out of proportion to the injury sustained by a plaintiff. In such instances a court may award equitable damages in substitution for an injunction.[91] In *Shaw v Applegate*[92] the plaintiff sought to restrain the defendant from using a building as an amusement arcade in breach of covenant. Over a period of seven years the defendant had invested considerable capital in the installation of various machines, and built up goodwill which would be extinguished by the grant of an injunction. In these circumstances, in which there was not sufficient acquiescence to debar the plaintiffs from all remedy, the Court of Appeal awarded damages under *Lord Cairns' Act* in lieu of an injunction.[93]

Hardship — specific performance

Hardship is also a ground upon which specific performance may be resisted, and a plaintiff left to a remedy of common law damages for breach of contract.[94] The jurisdiction under *Lord Cairns' Act* may also exist in a case of hardship. Equitable damages which are awarded in

---

88   *Smith v Smith* (1875) LR 20 Eq 500 at 503 per Sir George Jessel MR ('if he had thus lost the right to a mandatory injunction, he had also lost his right to damages'); *Dillon v Macdonald* (1902) 21 NZLR 375 at 379 per Edwards J ('Nor could she have recovered damages under *Lord Cairns' Act* in substitution for specific performance, for in her prior action His Honour the Chief Justice held that the laches of the plaintiff disentitled her to any equity to specific performance').

89   I C F Spry, *Equitable Remedies*, 4th ed, Law Book Co, Sydney, 1990, p 611, n 3.

90   I C F Spry, *Equitable Remedies*, 4th ed, Law Book Co, Sydney, 1990, p 391.

91   *Haggerty v Latreille* (1913) 14 DLR 532; *Clark v McKenzie* [1930] 2 DLR 843.

92   [1977] 1 WLR 970.

93   [1977] 1 WLR 970 at 978–9, 981.

94   I C F Spry, *Equitable Remedies*, 4th ed, Law Book Co, Sydney, 1990, p 611, n 3. *Patel v Ali* [1984] Ch 283 at 286. See also *Robison v Sanson* (1912) 14 GLR 579 at 582 per Sim J ('If, however, specific performance were refused on the ground of hardship, the defendant would still be liable for damages for the breach of the contract ...'). Self-induced hardship will not operate as a defence to specific performance: *South Coast Oils (Qld and NSW) Pty Ltd v Look Enterprises Pty Ltd* [1988] 1 Qd R 680 at 692.

substitution for specific performance may be available in an appropriate case of hardship, particularly where there is part performance or equitable estoppel. The relevance of the jurisdiction has been recognised in a number of cases. In *Dell v Beasley*[95] the court declined, on the ground of hardship, to make an order for specific performance against a defendant who had formed a misconception as to the use to which the relevant property could be put. McCarthy J later remarked: 'It follows that, the decree being refused on this discretionary ground, the plaintiff is entitled to damages either under *Lord Cairns' Act* or at common law'.[96] In *Bosaid v Andry*[97] Sholl J considered that damages may be awarded in substitution for specific performance 'when the refusal of specific performance is based upon a discretionary ground, such as hardship'.[98] Equitable damages have been awarded where an order of specific performance of a contract for the sale of a home would result in personal hardship to a defendant, despite the absence of fault on the part of the plaintiff.[99] Equitable damages have also been awarded where specific performance was not granted because of factors such as inadequacy of consideration, the illiteracy of a purchaser and the lack of any independent advice.[100]

Lack of mutuality

The Court of Chancery would generally not require a party to specifically perform obligations which a contract imposed on that party if it were unable to secure the performance by the other contracting party of the conditions upon which those obligations depended. In such a case the parties would be left to their remedies at law.[101] It is now settled that the question of lack of mutuality is one of those matters that has to be considered in the exercise of a judicial discretion to make an order for specific performance.[102] Therefore lack of mutuality is a discretionary matter that does not deprive a court of jurisdiction to make an order for specific performance or to award equitable damages.[103]

---

95   [1959] NZLR 89.

96   [1959] NZLR 89 at 97.

97   [1963] VR 465.

98   [1963] VR 465 at 479. See also *Carr v McDonald's Australia Ltd* (Federal Court of Australia, Burchett, J, NSW District Registry, NG 560 of 1992, 16 February 1994, unreported).

99   *Madden v Kevereski* (1982) 2 BPR [97156] 9645; *RD McKinnon Holdings Pty Ltd v Hind* [1984] 2 NSWLR 121; *Cominos v Rekes* (Supreme Court of New South Wales, Cohen J, Eq Div, No 2065 of 1977, 27 March 1984, unreported), noted [1984] ACLD 555. See also *Zalaudek v De Boer* (1981) 33 BCLR 57.

100 *Weily v Williams* (1895) 16 LR (NSW) Eq 190.

101 *JC Williamson Ltd v Lukey and Mulholland* (1931) 45 CLR 282 at 298; *Price v Strange* [1978] Ch 337 at 363.

102 *Price v Strange* [1978] Ch 337 at 350. See also *Lyus v Prowsa Developments Ltd* [1982] 1 WLR 1044 at 1053; *Sutton v Sutton* [1984] Ch 184 at 193.

103 *Price v Strange* [1978] Ch 337 at 359, 370.

Laches and acquiescence

Laches and acquiescence are discretionary bars to the grant of equitable relief.[104] The defences of laches or acquiescence are often interrelated, but they are nonetheless separate and distinct. As Goff LJ remarked in *HP Bulmer Ltd v J Bollinger SA and Champagne Lanson Pere Et Fils*[105] 'it is important to remember that there may be a case of acquiescence which does not depend upon delay at all'.[106] Laches is more concerned with the effluxion of time. Story wrote: 'Thus, if a bar might not be good in a Court of Law by reason of the lapse of time; yet a Court of Equity might nevertheless sustain it; for it never administers to stale claims, or gross laches'.[107] In *Orr v Ford*[108] Deane J observed: 'There has, over the years been considerable criticism of the loose use of the word "acquiescence" as a broad conjunctive or disjunctive companion to "laches"'.[109]

Laches

It has long been recognised that two circumstances are important in determining the availability of the equitable defence of laches: the length of the delay, and the nature of the acts done during the interval which might affect either party and cause a balance of justice or injustice.[110]

Acquiescence

Acquiescence will in most cases involve delay, but is really concerned with whether a plaintiff has by his conduct assented to the matter under complaint. In *Archbold v Scully*[111] Lord Wensleydale commented: 'But acquiescence is a different thing; it means more than laches'.[112] In *De Bussche v Alt*[113] Thesiger LJ said that 'acquiescence ... may be defined as quiescence under such circumstances as that assent may be reasonably inferred from it, and is no more than an instance of the law of estoppel by words or conduct'.[114] Similarly in *Orr v Ford*[115] Deane J remarked: 'Strictly used, acquiescence indicates the contemporaneous and informed ("knowing") acceptance or standing by which is treated by equity as "assent" (ie consent) to what would otherwise be an infringement of rights'.[116] Deane J also observed that 'acquiescence' may be used in a number of ways:

---

104 J G Starke, 'Laches, acquiescence and delay', *Australian Law Journal*, vol 64, 1990, p 103.
105 [1977] 2 CMLR 625.
106 [1977] 2 CMLR 625 at 681.
107 J Story, *Commentaries on Equity Pleadings*, 6th ed, Little, Brown, Boston, 1857, p 463.
108 (1989) 167 CLR 316.
109 (1989) 167 CLR 316 at 337 citing *Leeds, Duke of v Amhorst, Earl of* (1846) 2 Ph 117 at 123; 41 ER 886 at 888; *De Bussche v Alt* (1878) 8 Ch D 286 at 314.
110 *Lindsay Petroleum Co v Hurd* (1874) LR 5 PC 221 at 239–41; *Hickey v Bruhns* [1977] 2 NZLR 71 at 77; *Neylon v Dickens* [1987] 1 NZLR 402 at 407.
111 (1861) 9 HLC 360; 11 ER 769.
112 (1861) 9 HLC 360 at 383; 11 ER 769 at 778.
113 (1878) 8 Ch D 286.
114 (1878) 8 Ch D 286 at 314.
115 (1989) 167 CLR 316.
116 (1989) 167 CLR 316 at 337.

First, it is sometimes used as an indefinite overlapping component of a catchall phrase also incorporating 'laches' or 'gross laches' and/or 'delay'. While such phrases may provide a convenient means of referring to a general area of equity, they tend to obscure principle rather than to assist in its identification. Secondly, acquiescence is used as a true alternative to 'laches' to divide the field between inaction in the face of 'the assertion of adverse rights', ('acquiescence') and inaction 'in prosecuting rights' ('laches'): see, eg Smith, *Manual of Equity Jurisprudence* (14th ed, 1889), at p 24. Upon analysis, that use of the word 'acquiescence' is not helpful since laches ('an old French word for slacknesse or negligence or not doing': *Co Litt* 380b; *Partridge v Partridge*[117]) comprehends silence or inaction in the face of an unwarranted assertion of adverse rights by another as well as inaction or delay in prosecuting one's own rights. Thirdly, and more commonly, acquiescence is used, in a context where laches is used to indicate either mere delay or delay with knowledge, to refer to conduct by a person, with knowledge of the acts of another person, which encourages that other person reasonably to believe that his acts are accepted (if past) or not opposed (if contemporaneous): see *eg Cashman v 7 North Golden Gate Gold Mining Co*[118]; *Glasson v Fuller*[119,120].

Laches — injunction

Equitable damages may be awarded where an injunction is denied because of laches.[121] There are some early decisions which recognised the existence of this jurisdiction. In *Eastwood v Lever*[122] the plaintiff sought to restrain the defendant from building in breach of a restrictive covenant. The Lords Justices of Appeal held that the plaintiff by his delay in instituting proceedings had lost his right to an injunction. The suit was filed after a hotel building was completed, and it was held to be unreasonable to restrain the erection of adjacent stables. Turner LJ said: '*Sir Hugh Cairns' Act*, 21 & 22 Vict c 27, has, I read it, empowered Courts of Equity to give damages in such cases'.[123] In *Senior v Pawson*[124] the plaintiff sought a mandatory injunction to demolish newly erected buildings which obstructed ancient lights. The plaintiff delayed in complaining, and had also negotiated to settle the suit for a money payment. The court directed an inquiry as to the damages sustained by the plaintiff. Sir William Page Wood VC said: 'I have no doubt as to the jurisdiction of the Court to order the buildings to be pulled down, but I question whether it would not be expedient to give relief in damages, under *Sir H Cairns' Act*'.[125] The Vice-Chancellor later added: 'the question whether a money compensation will not do substantial justice here is considerably affected by the

---

117   [1894] 1 Ch 351 at 360.
118   (1897) 7 QLJ 152 at 153.
119   [1922] SASR 148 at 161–2.
120   (1989) 167 CLR 316 at 338.
121   *Coffee v Magnus* (1892) 9 WN (NSW) 58 at 61; *Shelfer v City of London Electric Lighting Co* [1895] 1 Ch 287 at 322; *Laugesen v Spensley* (1910) 12 GLR 719; *Ramsay v Barnes* (1913) 5 OWN 322 at 324.
122   (1863) 4 De GJ & S 114; 46 ER 859.
123   (1863) 4 De GJ & S 114 at 128; 46 ER 859 at 865.
124   (1866) LR 3 Eq 330.
125   (1866) LR 3 Eq 330 at 334.

Plaintiff's readiness to accept a money compensation'.[126]

In *Bracewell v Appleby*[127] the plaintiffs sought a declaration that the defendant was not entitled to a right of way to property on which they had erected a home. The motion of the plaintiffs for an interlocutory injunction was dismissed as it was only brought when the house was finished. At trial the court ruled that it would not grant an injunction as such an order would render the home uninhabitable. Graham J remarked:

> I am unwilling in the circumstances to grant an injunction, but as, in my judgment, the plaintiffs have established their legal right, and by reason of the Chancery Amendment Act 1858 (*Lord Cairns' Act*) they can ask for, and the court can grant, damages in lieu of an injunction.[128]

Laches — specific performance

Delay in instituting proceedings for specific performance is a ground for the award of equitable damages in substitution for specific performance.[129] Equitable damages may also be awarded where there is sufficient delay in prosecuting such an action. The relevance of the jurisdiction was recognised in *Du Sautoy v Symes*[130] where there was mere delay in bringing an action to trial, and negotiation during the early stages of the action. Cross J said:

> I do not think it is sufficient to justify me in refusing to grant him specific performance and to grant damages under *Lord Cairns' Act*.[131]

Cross J added:

> I can conceive of a case where, though an action is started promptly, nevertheless by his conduct the plaintiff has lulled the defendant into a sense of false security that he is going to ask for damages only and not specific performance. But it would need a clear case to make that out, and no such case has been made out here.[132]

In *Carr v McDonald's Australia Ltd*[133] the plaintiff sought specific performance of an agreement to grant a franchise for a restaurant. It appears that there was some delay in the proceedings. The court made an order for equitable damages in lieu of specific performance in view of the lapse of time since the dispute arose. Burchett J remarked:

> But where specific performance is refused upon a discretionary ground, such as hardship, an award of equitable damages may be made: *Bosaid v*

---

126 (1863) LR 3 Eq 330 at 335.
127 [1975] Ch 408.
128 [1975] Ch 408 at 419.
129 *Edward Street Properties Pty Ltd v Collins* [1977] Qd R 399 at 401–2; *Hickey v Bruhns* [1977] 2 NZLR 71; *Bloomberg In Trust v Tricont Projects Ltd* (1980) 13 RPR 284 at 299–300.
130 [1967] Ch 1146.
131 [1967] Ch 1146 at 1168.
132 [1967] Ch 1146 at 1168.
133 Federal Court of Australia, Burchett J, NSW District Registry, NG 560 of 1992, 16 February 1994, unreported.

Andry.[134] In my opinion, in all the circumstances of this case, and having regard to the time which has inevitably elapsed since the dispute arose, I should exercise my discretion against ordering specific performance, and in favour of awarding damages in lieu of specific performance.[135]

Delay by a plaintiff in enforcing an order for specific performance may also justify an award of equitable damages. In *McKenna v Richey*[136] the plaintiff sought to enforce an order for the specific performance of a contract for the sale of an apartment. The application was made some two and a half years after the granting of the order for specific performance, and the plaintiff was partly responsible for the delay. The court held that the landlord's consent to the assignment of the lease was a prerequisite to the enforcement of the order, and in the absence of such consent the court declined to enforce the order. The delay in enforcing the order was also a subsidiary ground for declining the application as the defendant's position had changed. It was held that the court could award equitable damages under s 62(4) of the Supreme Court Act 1928 of Victoria which was derived from *Lord Cairns' Act.* O'Bryan J observed:

> ... if the case is one in which the Court can entertain an application for specific performance, it has jurisdiction to award damages in lieu thereof even though, by reason of the plaintiff's laches or delay, it has become inequitable to enforce the contract specifically.[137]

There may be cases where the delay of the plaintiff is fatal to a claim for equitable damages. In *Neylon v Dickens*[138] the purchasers of land obtained an order for the specific performance of a contract for the sale of land. The statement of claim did not include a claim for damages even though before the action the purchasers' solicitor had written a letter which itemised the specific heads of damage. The plaintiffs then unsuccessfully sought damages under *Lord Cairns' Act* some five years after the alleged loss of profits, and more than three years after the order for specific performance was made. The New Zealand Court of Appeal held that the vendors were prejudiced by this delay, both in meeting a claim for damages and in proving an oral or implied agreement with a third party who occupied the land to indemnify them against such a claim.

Acquiescence

Acquiescence by a plaintiff in a suit for an injunction may result in a court denying all equitable relief to the plaintiff. In *Sayers v Collyer*[139] a purchaser of a lot in a building estate sought to enforce mutual restrictive covenants between vendors and purchasers of lots in the estate. The plaintiff was aware that for three years the defendant, a purchaser of another lot, was using his house as a beershop in breach of covenant, and the plaintiff had bought beer at the shop. The Court of Appeal held that

---

134 [1963] VR 465.
135 *Carr v McDonald's Australia Ltd*, n 133 above, at 69.
136 [1950] VLR 360.
137 [1950] VLR 360 at 375.
138 [1987] 1 NZLR 402.
139 (1884) 28 Ch D 103.

the plaintiff had by his acquiescence lost the right to either an injunction or damages under *Lord Cairns' Act*. Similarly, in *Duchman v Oakland Dairy Co Ltd*,[140] the action of plaintiffs in signing a petition for the erection of a garage and livery stable, and their knowledge of the defendant's plans, precluded them from recovering damages in lieu of an injunction in respect of disturbances emanating from the premises.

While the conduct of a plaintiff may in a particular case disentitle the plaintiff to equitable relief in any form whether specific relief or equitable damages, common law damages may nevertheless be available for breach of contract. In *Gaunt v Fynney*[141] the court declined to grant an injunction or award equitable damages where a window had been boarded up for six years. Lord Selbourne dismissed the bill without prejudice to an action at law.

A lesser decree of acquiescence may induce a court to award equitable damages rather than decline all relief. In *Sayers v Collyer*[142] Fry LJ commented:

> Acquiescence may either be an entire bar to all relief, or it may be a ground for inducing the Court to act under the powers of *Lord Cairns' Act*.[143]

This was recognised in *HP Bulmer Ltd v J Bollinger SA and Champagne Lanson Pere Et Fils*[144] which was an unsuccessful attempt by French wine producers to restrain the use of the word 'Champagne' in connection with any beverage not being a wine produced in the Champagne district of France. A defence which did not arise for consideration was whether the French producers had lost their right to an injunction by laches and acquiescence. However, Goff LJ examined this question as the point was fully argued:

> ... acquiescence arising from delay poses two problems when one is dealing with a right at law and a continuing breach. One has to consider first, whether the right has been wholly lost, and, if not, whether the Court should withhold the equitable remedy of an injunction and award damages under *Lord Cairns' Act*, as this court did in the recent unreported case of *Shaw v Applegate*.[145]

Goff LJ later added that the right at law 'will only be wholly lost if in all the circumstances it is dishonest or unconscionable to continue to assert it'.[146]

Where a plaintiff has by acquiescence lost the right to an injunction it is clear that equitable damages may be awarded provided that the conduct of the plaintiff does not preclude such relief. In *Landau v Curton*[147] the

---

140 (1928) 63 OLR 111 at 126; [1929] 1 DLR 9 at 29.
141 (1872) LR 8 Ch App 8.
142 (1884) 28 Ch D 103.
143 (1884) 28 Ch D 103 at 110.
144 [1977] 2 CMLR 625.
145 [1977] 2 CMLR 625 at 681. *Shaw v Applegate* was later reported in [1977] 1 WLR 970.
146 [1977] 2 CMLR 625 at 681. See also *Cluett Peabody & Co Inc v McIntyre Hogg March & Co Ltd* [1958] RPC 335.
147 [1962] EGD 369. See also *Wentworth v Woollahra Municipal Council* (1982) 149 CLR 672 at 678.

plaintiff sought a mandatory injunction to demolish a building which was erected in breach of a restrictive covenant. Proceedings were commenced while the building was under construction. Cross J declined to grant an injunction by reason of the acquiescence of the plaintiff, and instead awarded damages under *Lord Cairns' Act*.

Mistake

In some cases a mistake may have resulted in no agreement having effectively been created, or a mistake may enable rescission of the agreement in equity.[148] Mistake is also a ground upon which rectification may be sought.[149] One thing is clear: specific performance will not be withheld merely because of a mistake by the defendant as to the contract. As Baggallay LJ explained in *Tamplin v James*: [150]

> If that were to be allowed, a person might always escape from completing a contract by swearing that he was mistaken as to what he bought, and great temptation to perjury would be offered.[151]

It would seem that some element of hardship must also be present before specific performance will be declined on the ground of mistake. This has been emphasised in a number of decisions.[152] One such case is *Tamplin v James*[153] where the defendant had agreed to purchase a property at an auction, and had mistakenly assumed that a garden was part of the property without examining the available plans. The Court of Appeal upheld the decree for the specific performance of the agreement. James LJ remarked:

> ... for the most part the cases where a Defendant has escaped on the ground of a mistake not contributed to by the Plaintiff, have been cases where a hardship amounting to an injustice would have been inflicted upon him by holding him to his bargain, and it was unreasonable to hold him to it.[154]

Where there is a valid agreement in existence, the effect of a mistake may be relevant in determining whether specific performance or damages is the appropriate remedy.[155] Where specific performance is declined in a case of mistake, equitable damages or common law damages are available.[156]

---

148 C J Slade, 'The Myth of Mistake in the English Law of Contract', *Law Quarterly Review*, vol 70, 1954, p 385. On equitable mistake: see *William Sindall Plc v Cambridgeshire County Council* [1994] 1 WLR 1016 at 1042 per Evans LJ.
149 *A Roberts & Co Ltd v Leicestershire County Council* [1961] Ch 555; *Riverlate Properties Ltd v Paul* [1975] Ch 133; *Johnstone v Commerce Consolidated Pty Ltd* [1976] VR 463.
150 (1880) 15 Ch D 215.
151 (1880) 15 Ch D 215 at 219.
152 *Preston v Luck* (1884) 27 Ch D 497; *Stewart v Kennedy* (1890) 15 App Cas 75 at 105; *Goldsborough, Mort & Co Ltd v Quinn* (1910) 10 CLR 674.
153 (1880) 15 Ch D 215.
154 (1880) 15 Ch D 215 at 221.
155 *Tamplin v James* (1880) 15 Ch D 215 at 221–3; *Stewart v Kennedy* (1890) 15 App Cas 75 at 105.
156 *Goldsborough, Mort & Co Ltd v Quinn* (1910) 10 CLR 674 at 701; *Dell v Beasley* [1959] NZLR 89.

4.6 Jurisdictional constraints

Section 2 of *Lord Cairns' Act* contains words such as 'injured', 'wrongful act' and 'the same court' which may arguably impose jurisdictional constraints upon a court.

'Injured'

There are strong arguments that the word 'injured' precludes the award of equitable damages in a *quia timet* case where a plaintiff has not sustained any actual damage. All members of the Court of Appeal in *Dreyfus v Peruvian Guano Co*[157] considered that equitable damages could not be awarded where no actual injury had occurred. Bowen LJ, with whom Cotton LJ agreed, commented:

> It is true the section applies in all cases in which the Court of Chancery has jurisdiction to entertain an application for an injunction, but the only weapon with which the court is armed by virtue of the section is to award damages to a party injured, which must, I think, mean damages where damages have arisen, and in a case where no damages have arisen in the ordinary sense of the term as known to lawyers, I am of the opinion the court has no power to give damages.[158]

Similarly, Fry LJ observed that 'where there has been no wrong done it appears to me that *Lord Cairns' Act* confers no power to give damages'.[159] The existence of the jurisdiction to award equitable damages under *Lord Cairns' Act* in a *quia timet* case was only confirmed by a bare majority in *Leeds Industrial Co-Operative Society Ltd v Slack*.[160] Lord Dunedin regarded the views expressed by the members of the Court of Appeal in the *Dreyfus* case as dicta.[161] Lords Sumner and Carson very cogently argued that the words 'award damages to the party injured' in s 2 of *Lord Cairns' Act* do not enable the award of damages where a person has not suffered any injury, but has merely been threatened with an injury.[162] There was existing authority that the words 'to the party injured' prima facie point to a person who has suffered an injury at the time of the institution of proceedings.[163] Lord Sumner also relied upon the statement of Cairns LJ in *Ferguson v Wilson*.[164] A contemporary note in the *Law Quarterly Review*, possibly by Sir Frederick Pollock, contained the observation that: 'There is a good deal to be said in support of Lord Sumner's view of *Lord Cairns' Act*'.[165]

---

157   (1889) 43 Ch D 316.

158   (1889) 43 Ch D 316 at 333.

159   (1889) 43 Ch D 316 at 342.

160   [1924] AC 851.

161   [1924] AC 851 at 863–4. See also *Re State of Norway's Application (No 2)* [1988] 3 WLR 603 at 620.

162   [1924] AC 851.

163   *Robinson v Currey* (1881) 7 QBD 465 discussed in *Law Quarterly Review*, vol 39, 1923, p 396.

164   (1866) LR 2 Ch App 77.

165   *Law Quarterly Review*, vol 41, 1925, p 3.

'Wrongful act'

Before the introduction of the Judicature system the jurisdiction under *Lord Cairns' Act* was held not to apply where a plaintiff sought to restrain an improper action at law. Such an action was not a 'wrongful act' within the meaning of s 2 of *Lord Cairns' Act*.[166] One issue is whether the term 'wrongful act' in *Lord Cairns' Act*, on its proper interpretation, is restricted to an act which is a tort at common law. There have been decisions that the term refers to a breach of an equitable obligation.[167] There have also been decisions that the term precludes the award of equitable damages for a breach of a town planning statute[168] or for an invalid decision of a domestic tribunal.[169] These cases are examined elsewhere in this text.[170]

'The same Court'

There are dicta that the words 'the same Court' in *Lord Cairns' Act* may preclude a court from awarding equitable damages once an order for specific performance has already been made.[171] However, it is submitted that the words should not be so narrowly construed; otherwise the court would be restricted in making an award of damages on an adjourned date, or upon the vacation of an order for specific performance. In any event, liberty to apply is often reserved.

———◇———

4.7 Reform to Lord Cairns' Act

Such jurisdictional difficulties would be obviated if the words 'injured', 'wrongful act' and 'the same court' were removed from *Lord Cairns' Act*. This was recognised by Finn who commented: 'Perhaps the solution is to amend *Lord Cairns' Act*'.[172] *Lord Cairns' Act* has been reformed in the United Kingdom and in a number of Commonwealth jurisdictions. In Northern Ireland equitable damages may be awarded under s 92 of the Judicature (Northern Ireland) Act 1978. In England and Wales equitable damages may be awarded under s 50 of the Supreme Court Act 1981. Both provisions are similar, and avoid the use of such terms as 'injured', 'the same court' and 'wrongful act'. Provisions similar to s 50 of the Supreme Court Act have also been adopted in a number of jurisdictions including

---

166 *Acraman v Price* (1870) 18 WR 540, 24 LT (NS) 487.
167 *Talbot v General Television Corp Pty Ltd* [1980] VR 224 at 241, 243; [1981] RPC 1 at 19, 21.
168 *Attorney-General v Birkenhead Borough* [1968] NZLR 383 at 393; *Neville Nitschke Caravans (Main North Road) Pty Ltd v McEntree* (1976) 15 SASR 330 at 351; *Talbot v General Television Corp Pty Ltd* [1980] VR 224 at 241, 243; [1981] RPC 1 at 19, 21; *Wentworth v Woollahra Municipal Council* (1982) 149 CLR 672.
169 *Stininato v Auckland Boxing Assn Inc* [1978] 1 NZLR 1 at 23.
170 See Chapter 8.
171 *Biggin v Minton* [1977] 1 WLR 701 at 703; *Minter v Geraghty* (1981) 38 ALR 68 at 81.
172 P D Finn, 'A Road Not Taken: The Boyce Plaintiff and *Lord Cairns' Act*, Part II', *Australian Law Journal*, vol 57, 1983, 571 at p 579.

Ontario,[173] Victoria,[174] Hong Kong,[175] Prince Edward Island,[176] Manitoba[177] and New Zealand.[178]

In those jurisdictions in which *Lord Cairns' Act* has been reformulated the courts would no longer have the jurisdictional constraints which have been mentioned. The reform of *Lord Cairns' Act* has the consequence that the requisite jurisdiction to award equitable damages exists where a court possesses jurisdiction to entertain an application for an injunction or specific performance *simpliciter*. The reformed provisions should be beneficially interpreted without any preconceptions derived from the earlier decisions upon *Lord Cairns' Act*.

---

173 Courts of Justice Act SO 1984 c 11 (Ontario) s 112.
174 Supreme Court Act (1986 No 110) (Victoria) s 38 .
175 Supreme Court Ordinance cap 4 rev ed 1987 (Hong Kong) s 17.
176 Supreme Court Act (1987 c 66) (Prince Edward Island) s 32.
177 The Court of Queen's Bench Act SM 1988 c 4 (Manitoba) s 36.
178 Judicature Act 1908 (New Zealand) s 16A.

5

Time at which a Court Possesses Jurisdiction to Award Equitable Damages

---◄○►---

5.1 Where jurisdiction to decree equitable relief exists when proceedings are commenced

It has been pointed out that 'there is some confusion as to the time at which a plaintiff seeking damages under *Lord Cairns' Act* has to demonstrate that the Court has the requisite jurisdiction'.[1] An important issue is whether it is a prerequisite to the award of equitable damages that a court should be able to make an order for an injunction or specific performance at the time that a matter is heard and determined; or whether

---

1   R P Meagher, W M C Gummow and J R F Lehane, *Equity — Doctrines and Remedies*, 2nd ed, Butterworths, Sydney, 1984, p 610 [2309]; 3rd ed, Butterworths, Sydney, 1992, p 642 [2310].

it is sufficient that a plaintiff possessed an equity at the time when proceedings were commenced. There is a considerable body of dicta that a court possesses jurisdiction to award equitable damages only if the court can make an order for an injunction or specific performance at the hearing of a matter.[2] This is an unduly narrow view of the jurisdiction and it is now settled that a court possesses the requisite jurisdiction if equitable relief could have been decreed at the time that proceedings were commenced.[3]

This jurisdictional issue arose for consideration in *Davenport v Rylands*[4] where the plaintiff sought an injunction to restrain the infringement of a patent which had expired before the hearing. The court rejected a submission that there was no jurisdiction to award damages under the Chancery Amendment Act 1858 (*Lord Cairns' Act*)[5] if equitable relief could not be decreed at the hearing. Sir William Page Wood VC said:

> Prima facie, I was somewhat impressed with the notion that in order to award damages at the hearing, the Court must have jurisdiction to grant an injunction. But I think that would be a narrow construction to put upon this beneficial Act.[6]

The actual date of the hearing of a suit is purely fortuitous, and is not ordinarily within the control of a plaintiff. This was recognised by the Vice-Chancellor who remarked that the patent in that case might have expired even 'if the Plaintiff had been as diligent as he could have been in the prosecution of his case'.[7] The Court of Exchequer in equity recognised the injustice of depriving a plaintiff of relief by reason of the state of business of the court.[8]

---

2 *Chinnock v Sainsbury* (1860) 9 WR 7 at 8 per Sir John Romilly MR ('It was admitted on both sides that *Sir Hugh Cairns' Act* only applied to the giving of damages where specific performance could be enforced'); *De Brassac v Martyn* (1863) 11 WR 1020 at 1021 per Sir William Page Wood VC ('The court would only give damages where specific performance could be decreed'); *Allen v Fairbrother* (1907) 9 GLR 328 at 329 per Cooper J ('the power of the Court of Chancery to give damages in lieu of a decree for specific performance only arose where the Court could decree specific performance, and did not extend to cases where specific performance could not be decreed'); *JC Williamson Ltd v Lukey and Mulholland* (1931) 45 CLR 282 at 294 per Starke J ('the respondents must make out that they are entitled to an equitable remedy before they can get damages'); *Boyns v Lackey* (1958) 58 SR (NSW) 395 at 405 per Hardie J ('These provisions do not, however, extend the jurisdiction of the Court; and damages will not, therefore, be given in cases where, previously to the Act, the Court would not have ordered an injunction, or decreed specific performance') adopting *Daniell's Chancery Practice*, vol 1, 5th ed, Stevens, London, 1871, p 946 (these remarks should not be taken in isolation as Hardie J later remarked (at 405) that 'the plaintiffs have failed to establish a right, as at the date of the institution of the suit to equitable relief'); *Bosaid v Andry* [1963] VR 465 at 484 per Sholl J ('... the plaintiff, in order to recover such damages from the Court of Chancery, must show that he had a right to specific performance at the hearing, or at least that he had such a right save for the existence of a ground entitling the Court in its discretion to refuse the equitable remedy').

3 See p 52.

4 (1865) LR 1 Eq 302.

5 21 & 22 Vict c 27.

6 (1865) LR 1 Eq 302 at 307.

7 (1865) LR 1 Eq 302 at 307.

8 *Wilkinson v Torkington* (1837) 2 Y & C Ex 726; 160 ER 586; *McMahon v Ambrose* [1987] VR 817 at 818.

There are many statements in the cases which acknowledge that the relevant date for the purpose of determining the existence of jurisdiction under *Lord Cairns' Act* is the date of commencement of proceedings. In *Ferguson v Wilson*[9] the plaintiff sought specific performance of a contract for the allotment of shares. The bill was filed after the shares had been allotted. In these circumstances specific performance could not be decreed, nor could damages be awarded under *Lord Cairns' Act* as relief could not be decreed when the proceedings were commenced. Turner LJ said:

> If, therefore, a Plaintiff in a suit in equity had no equitable right at the time of filing the bill — for the case would be quite different if there was an equitable right at the time of filing the bill — so that the bill was altogether improperly filed in equity, I am of opinion that the Act has no application; otherwise the consequence would necessarily be, that everybody who had a doubtful case at law would come into equity for specific performance, and when it appeared that he had no case in equity at all he would ask for damages, and so almost every action of contract would be transferred from a Court of law to a Court of equity.[10]

Similarly Cairns LJ considered that the jurisdiction existed 'where there are, at least at the time of bill filed, all those ingredients which would enable the Court, if it thought fit, to exercise its power and decree specific performance'.[11] In discussing these remarks the High Court of Australia in *Wentworth v Woollahra Municipal Council*[12] commented:

> Cairns LJ (later Lord Cairns LC) seems to have thought that the power to award damages conferred by the 1858 Act could be exercised if the plaintiff made out as at the commencement of the suit the ingredients of a case for equitable relief, notwithstanding that ultimately he failed to obtain that relief on discretionary grounds.[13]

A number of other cases have recognised that a court possesses jurisdiction under *Lord Cairns' Act* where the court could order an injunction or specific performance at the time when a suit was filed. In the Ontario case of *Brockington v Palmer*[14] Strong VC stated that 'it is now well settled that, unless the plaintiff shews himself to have been entitled to equitable relief at the date of the filing of his bill, he cannot have an assessment of damages here'.[15] In *Aynsley v Glover*[16] Sir George Jessel MR observed that the Act 'can only apply to those cases in which the court could have granted an injunction, at all events at the time of the filing of the bill'.[17] The Master of the Rolls made a similar statement in *White v Boby*:[18]

---

9   (1866) LR 2 Ch App 77.
10 (1866) LR 2 Ch App 77 at 88.
11 (1866) LR 2 Ch App 77 at 91.
12 (1982) 149 CLR 672.
13 (1982) 149 CLR 672 at 678.
14 (1871) 18 Gr 488.
15 (1871) 18 Gr 488 at 490.
16 (1874) LR 18 Eq 544.
17 (1874) LR 18 Eq 544 at 554.
18 (1877) 37 LT (NS) 652.

You must start with an equity, and then in certain circumstances you may get, under *Lord Cairns' Act*, damages instead of that equity. That rule is still in force. You must show that you had an equity at the time of the issue of the writ.[19]

In *Elmore v Pirrie*[20] Kay J stated: 'The only case under that Act where the court would give relief was where a plaintiff had an equitable right at the time of filing the bill'.[21] In *Ella v Wenham*[22] Andrews J remarked that 'where the Court could not by reason of events which had transpired prior to action, in this case the sale of the subject property, decree specific performance, it could not award damages in lieu of specific performance'.[23]

Where a defendant brings a cross-claim seeking injunctive relief the relevant time for ascertaining the existence of jurisdiction to award equitable damages is the date of filing of the cross-claim. In *Beard v Baulkham Hills Shire Council*[24] Young J considered that the jurisdiction did not exist if at 'the date of filing of the cross-claim this was not a case where an injunction could have been granted'.[25]

———◁◯▷———

5.2 Where an injunction cannot be decreed at the hearing

Equitable damages may be awarded where a plaintiff had an equity to an injunction when an action was commenced, even though an order for an injunction could not be made at the time that a suit was determined. In *Barbagallo v J & F Catelan Pty Ltd*[26] McPherson J commented upon the Queensland equivalent of *Lord Cairns' Act*:[27]

> ... the existence of jurisdiction to award damages under the statutory provision must be tested at the time the application for injunction is made. If at that time the Court has in terms of s 62 'jurisdiction to entertain an application for an injunction against ... the commission or continuance of any wrongful act', that jurisdiction is not ousted if at the trial it turns out to be impossible or inappropriate to grant an injunction.[28]

---

19 (1877) 37 LT (NS) 652.
20 (1887) 57 LT (NS) 333.
21 (1887) 57 LT (NS) 333 at 335, applied by Helsham J in *Craney v Bugg* [1971] 1 NSWLR 13 at 16.
22 [1971] QWN 31.
23 [1971] QWN 31 at 76.
24 (1986) 7 NSWLR 273.
25 (1986) 7 NSWLR 273 at 280.
26 [1986] 1 Qd R 245.
27 Equity Act of 1867 (31 Vic No 18) (Queensland) s 62.
28 [1986] 1 Qd R 245 at 251.

An early case was *Catton v Wyld*[29] where the plaintiff sought an injunction to restrain the defendant from pulling down a wall. The wall had been rebuilt by the parties prior to the hearing so that the grant of an injunction was out of the question, and the court awarded damages to the plaintiff. Sir John Romilly MR said: 'With respect to damages, *Sir Hugh Cairns' Act* (21 & 22 Vict c 27 s 2) says that the Court shall have jurisdiction to give damages in cases of this description'.[30] Another early case is *Davenport v Rylands*[31] where an injunction was sought to restrain the infringement of a patent that had expired pending litigation. Prior to the enactment of *Lord Cairns' Act* the Court of Chancery would have declined to grant relief in such a case.[32] The case of *Betts v Gallais*,[33] in which Sir William James VC declined to award equitable damages where a bill for an injunction to restrain the infringement of a patent was filed just prior to the expiry of the patent, may be explained on discretionary, and not jurisdictional, considerations.

There are various examples of the award of equitable damages where injunctive relief was no longer appropriate after a suit had been commenced. In *Fritz v Hobson*[34] damages were awarded in substitution for an injunction in respect of a nuisance that had ceased prior to the trial. In *Western Electric Co (Aust) Ltd v Betts*[35] damages were awarded in lieu of a mandatory injunction to restore sound equipment that had been removed from a cinema in breach of agreement. After the suit was commenced the lessor of the theatre had determined the plaintiff's lease. Long Innes CJ in Eq remarked:

> ... the mere fact that equitable relief has become impossible by reason other than the action of the plaintiff, does not deprive the Court of its alternative jurisdiction to grant damages in lieu of equitable relief.[36]

In *Baxter v Four Oaks Properties Ltd*[37] an injunction to enforce a restrictive covenant could not issue where the plaintiff had sold her house after the issue of the writ and prior to the hearing. The plaintiff and defendant were the successors in title of the original parties to the covenant. The parties to the action were accordingly not in privity of contract so that the plaintiff could not maintain an action for common law damages. Cross J observed: 'this is a case where I ought not to grant an injunction but should award damages instead'.[38]

———◦———

---

29 (1863) 32 Beav 266; 55 ER 105.
30 (1863) 32 Beav 266 at 267–8; 55 ER 105 at 106.
31 (1865) LR 1 Eq 302, discussed earlier.
32 *Price's Patent Candle Co Ltd v Bauwen's Patent Candle Co Ltd* (1858) 4 K & J 727 at 732; 70 ER 302 at 304.
33 (1870) LR 10 Eq 392.
34 (1880) 14 Ch D 542 at 547.
35 (1935) 52 WN (NSW) 173.
36 (1935) 52 WN (NSW) 173 at 174.
37 [1965] Ch 816.
38 [1965] Ch 816 at 830.

5.3 Where specific performance cannot be decreed at the hearing

Equitable damages may be awarded if a plaintiff had an equity to an order for specific performance at the time a suit was commenced, although an order for specific performance could not be made at the hearing.

Equitable damages may be awarded where there is a voluntary completion of a contract after proceedings for the specific performance of the contract had commenced. In *Cory v Thames Ironworks and Shipbuilding Co Ltd*[39] the plaintiff sought specific performance of an agreement for the purchase of a vessel which was delivered to the plaintiff after the institution of proceedings. The plaintiff amended his bill to pray for a declaration that at the time of the institution of the suit the plaintiff was entitled to specific performance of the agreement and to damages for the defendants' delay in performance. The court directed an inquiry into what damages the plaintiff had sustained by non-delivery of the vessel under the contract. Sir William Page Wood VC remarked:

> ... that since the original bill was, at the time of filing it, maintainable, and since it not only prayed specific performance, but also damages for non-performance of the contract, the court had jurisdiction under the statute. It did not matter that, from what happened afterwards, the former relief could no longer be asked for.[40]

Another instance of a voluntary completion is *Crockford v Pessego*.[41] In that case a contract for the sale of land was completed before the hearing of an application for the specific performance of the contract. The plaintiff sought equitable damages for the cost of bridging finance under s 68 of the Supreme Court Act 1970 of New South Wales which Helsham CJ in Eq described as 'the modern extension of *Lord Cairns' Act*'.[42] The defendant unsuccessfully contended that by reason of the doctrine of merger, no award of damages could be made.[43] Helsham CJ in Eq relied on *Cory v Thames Ironworks and Shipbuilding Co Ltd*[44] as:

> ... clear authority for what I would expect to be the law, namely, that a voluntary completion of a contract of sale notwithstanding extant proceedings for specific performance does not prejudice the innocent party's right to recover damages under *Lord Cairns' Act*.[45]

His Honour had earlier mentioned that he did not consider that an innocent party in such a case was:

---

39 (1863) 8 LT (NS) 237.
40 (1863) 8 LT (NS) 237 at 238.
41 Supreme Court of New South Wales, Helsham CJ in Eq, Eq Div, No 4399 of 1979, 6 May 1980, unreported.
42 *Crockford v Pessago*, n 41 above, at 4.
43 As to merger: see *Moretta v Western Computer Investment Corp Ltd* (1984) 3 DLR (4th) 738.
44 (1863) 8 LT (NS) 237.
45 *Crockford v Pessago*, n 41 above, at 6.

... bound to refuse to complete a purchase lest they prejudice their right in proceedings which have already been issued to recover compensation for the loss which they have suffered by the default of that party who has brought about that loss.[46]

The plaintiff had given a mortgage to secure bridging finance until the date of settlement. The award of equitable damages included the extra interest incurred by the plaintiff together with the expenses of the mortgage, including scale legal costs and stamp duty.[47] In such a case costs may be awarded to a plaintiff where there is a voluntary completion of a contract after the issue of a writ for specific performance.[48]

Equitable damages may be awarded to a plaintiff who had an entitlement to equitable relief when the action for specific performance of a contract was commenced, but was defeated by a prior purchaser who also commenced proceedings. In *ASA Constructions Pty Ltd v Iwanov*[49] a vendor had sold a property in successive contracts to two purchasers who had both commenced proceedings for specific performance. The second purchaser (Hayllar), who had conceded the priority of the first purchaser (ASA), was held entitled to equitable damages under s 68 of the Supreme Court Act 1970 of New South Wales. Needham J remarked:

> When Hayllar commenced proceedings for specific performance there was no inherent or necessary impossibility of obtaining that relief. The Court might have refused ASA's claim on some discretionary ground (laches was alleged), and then the way would have been open for the Court to grant the primary relief sought by Hayllar. I do not think that the cases relied upon should lead me to say that Hayllar's application was brought to equity without 'power' in the Court to grant him the relief primarily sought.[50]

The second purchaser, who was entitled to common law damages for breach of contract, sought damages under the equivalent of *Lord Cairns' Act* in an obvious endeavour to obtain an assessment of such damages at the date of judgment, although damages were assessed at the date of repudiation of the contract.[51]

A court may award equitable damages where an order for specific performance would be nugatory, provided that specific performance could have been decreed at the time that a suit was commenced. In *Filo v Chappuis*[52] proceedings were issued for an order of specific performance of an agreement to grant a bill of sale. While an order for specific performance could have been made at the time that the summons was issued, any bill of sale would have expired prior to the date of the hearing. In these circumstances the court would not make an order for specific performance which would be nugatory. Nevertheless the court possessed

---

46   *Crockford v Pessago*, n 41 above, at 6.
47   *Crockford v Pessago*, n 41 above, at 7.
48   *Marks v Lilley* [1959] 1 WLR 749; *Oakacre Ltd v Claire Cleaners (Holdings) Ltd* [1982] Ch 197.
49   [1975] 1 NSWLR 512.
50   [1975] 1 NSWLR 512 at 518.
51   [1975] 1 NSWLR 512 at 519.
52   Supreme Court of New South Wales, Young J, Eq Div, No 3997 of 1987, 9 June 1989, unreported.

jurisdiction to award equitable damages as the plaintiff possessed an equity to relief when proceedings were commenced. Young J explained:

> Equity does not order specific performance if at the time of trial the lease or mortgage would no longer be a current instrument because equity, like nature, does nothing in vain. That, however, does not mean that equity denies the plaintiff relief because as at the date of the commencement of the proceedings the plaintiff could have got equitable relief. He is, accordingly, entitled to damages under *Lord Cairns' Act* now, of course, embodied in s 68 of the Supreme Court Act.[53]

Questions of some difficulty arise if circumstances render performance of a contract impossible. In *Mama v Sassoon*[54] Lord Blanesburgh commented that, subject to the explanation, s 19 of the Specific Relief Act 1877 of India 'embodies the same principle as *Lord Cairns' Act*'.[55] The explanation provides: 'The circumstance that the contract has become incapable of specific performance does not preclude the Court from exercising the jurisdiction conferred by this section'. Lord Blanesburgh added that the explanation 'introduced an express divergence from *Lord Cairns' Act*, as expounded in England: see *Ferguson v Wilson*'[56].[57] It has already been mentioned that in *Ferguson v Wilson*[58] it was held that there was no jurisdiction under *Lord Cairns' Act* where the plaintiff sought specific performance of a contract for the allotment of shares, and the shares had been allotted prior to the filing of the bill. It is evident that the draftsman of the Indian provision was aware of this case, because the last illustration of the explanation is indistinguishable from the case and clarifies the fact that 'compensation' under the Specific Relief Act can be awarded in such a case.

In *Mama v Sassoon*[59] Lord Blanesburgh had also expressed the opinion that damages may not be awarded under *Lord Cairns' Act* 'as an *alternative* to specific performance — [in] a case in which that relief had become impossible'.[60] That proposition enunciated by his Lordship is perhaps expressed too widely, and fails to consider a situation where an equity is possessed by a plaintiff at the time when a suit is filed. In *Ferguson v Wilson*[61] the particular contract was impossible to perform even when the suit was commenced. There is authority that a court possesses jurisdiction under *Lord Cairns' Act* if specific performance could be decreed when the suit was filed, notwithstanding that performance has subsequently become impossible. This was recognised in *Bertram v Builders' Association of North Winnipeg Ltd*[62] by Galt J who explained that in *Miguez v Harrison:*[63]

---

53 *Filo v Chappuis*, n 52 above, at 4.
54 (1928) LR 55 IA 360 (PC).
55 (1928) LR 55 IA 360 at 376 (PC).
56 (1866) LR 2 Ch App 77.
57 (1928) LR 55 IA 360 at 376 (PC).
58 (1866) LR 2 Ch App 77.
59 (1928) LR 55 IA 360 (PC).
60 (1928) LR 55 IA 360 at 374 (PC).
61 (1866) LR 2 Ch App 77.
62 (1915) 8 WWR 814; 23 DLR 534.
63 (1914) 7 WWR 650; 20 DLR 233.

... specific performance had become impossible before the commencement of the action, the defendant having conveyed the land to a third person. In such a case a plaintiff does not possess the requisite equity, and so it is not allowable to award damages in lieu of specific performance.[64]

Difficulties arise when a vendor commences an action for specific performance of a contract for the sale of land, and then subsequently sells the relevant property to a third party. Quite apart from what remedies the vendor may have at law for damages for breach of contract, it has been held that equitable damages awarded under *Lord Cairns' Act* will not be awarded if a party has disabled himself from giving specific performance. In *Mama v Sassoon*[65] Lord Blanesburgh considered that, under *Lord Cairns' Act*, the power to give damages as an *alternative* to specific performance did not extend to a case in which the plaintiff had debarred himself by his own action from claiming that form of relief.[66] His Lordship remarked that s 19 of the Specific Relief Act:

> ... embodies the same principle as *Lord Cairns' Act*, and does not any more than did the English statute enable the Court in a specific performance suit to award 'compensation for its breach' where at the hearing the plaintiff has debarred himself from asking for a specific decree.[67]

It is clear that, in such a case, the provisions of the Indian Specific Relief Act precluded the award of compensation. Section 24(c) of the Act provides that specific performance cannot be enforced in favour of a person 'who has already chosen his remedy', and s 29 of the Act 'makes the dismissal of a suit for specific performance of a contract a bar to a right of the plaintiff to sue for compensation for breach'.[68] However, it is not apparent that the same result necessarily arises in respect of a claim for damages under *Lord Cairns' Act*.

One of the cases which the Privy Council cited in *Mama v Sassoon*[69] was *Hipgrave v Case*.[70] In *Hipgrave v Case*,[71] and a similar case *Conroy v Lowndes*,[72] it was held that vendors who had commenced proceedings for specific performance, and then sold the property, had subsequently disabled themselves not only from obtaining that remedy, but also from obtaining equitable damages. The jurisdictional issue under *Lord Cairns' Act* only arose in those cases because the alternative claims were framed as claims for equitable damages, and could not be regarded as claims for common law damages.[73] The jurisdictional issue did not receive any

---

64   (1915) 8 WWR 814 at 818; 23 DLR 534 at 538.
65   (1928) LR 55 IA 360 (PC).
66   (1928) LR 55 IA 360 at 374 (PC).
67   (1928) LR 55 IA 360 at 376 (PC).
68   (1928) LR 55 IA 360 at 377 (PC).
69   (1928) LR 55 IA 360 (PC).
70   (1885) 28 Ch D 356.
71   (1885) 28 Ch D 356.
72   [1958] Qd R 375.
73   A similar claim was made in *Oakacre Ltd v Claire Cleaners (Holdings) Ltd* [1982] Ch 197.

consideration in *Hipgrave v Case*.[74] The Earl of Selborne LC said:

> The Defendant comes to the trial to meet the case set up by the Plaintiff upon the record, viz, a case entitling the Plaintiff to specific performance or to damages in substitution for performance. I think we are regarding the substance of the case in holding the Plaintiff bound by the form of the claim which he has deliberately elected to make, and in not transforming his claim into a different claim, and the pleadings into different pleadings, at this stage of the proceedings. For these reasons I do not think we ought to give the relief that is now asked for.[75]

Sir William Brett MR (later Lord Esher) observed: 'the Plaintiff cannot now be allowed to change the whole nature of his action by turning it into an ordinary action for damages as at Common Law'.[76] Cotton LJ remarked: 'I do not think that any relief can be granted in such an action, when it appears that the Plaintiff has himself prevented specific performance by selling the property'.[77]

Spry has commented that 'special considerations applied in *Hipgrave v Case*,[78] where impossibility of performance arose from the plaintiff's own acts and a limited view was taken of the relief sought'.[79] In *McIntyre v Stockdale*[80] Clute J considered that 'there is a distinction where the plaintiff by his own act disentitles himself to specific performance, as in *Hipgrave v Case*,[81] and where, as here, the defendant commits the wrongful act which deprives the plaintiff of the rights arising under his contract'.[82] A court would accordingly not be disposed to exercise its jurisdiction to award equitable damages where a plaintiff has debarred himself or herself from the relief that is claimed in the pleadings. A case in point is *De Brassac v Martyn*[83] where the plaintiff sought specific performance of an agreement to let a house for a short term. After the bill was filed the plaintiff obtained another house, and the cause was not advanced prior to the expiration of the term. In these circumstances the court declined to award damages. The case of *Hipgrave v Case*[84] can also be explained by reference to the old rule in Chancery which precluded rescission while a suit for specific performance was on the record.[85]

———◁◦▷———

---

74 (1885) 28 Ch D 356.
75 (1885) 28 Ch D 356 at 361.
76 (1885) 28 Ch D 356 at 362.
77 (1885) 28 Ch D 356 at 362.
78 (1885) 28 Ch D 356.
79 I C F Spry, *Equitable Remedies*, 4th ed, Law Book Co, Sydney, 1990, p 617, n 2.
80 (1912) 27 OLR 460; 9 DLR 293.
81 (1885) 28 Ch D 356. (In the passage *Hipgrave v Case* is incorrectly cited as *Hargraves v Case*.)
82 (1912) 27 OLR 460 at 465; 9 DLR 293 at 297.
83 (1863) 11 WR 1020.
84 (1885) 28 Ch D 356.
85 See p 205.

5.4 Where the court acquires jurisdiction to decree equitable relief after the commencement of an action

At one time a bill was regarded as improperly filed in equity if a plaintiff had no equity to relief at the time of filing the bill. In *Durell v Pritchard*[86] Turner LJ remarked: 'I think that the Plaintiffs had not at the time of the filing of this bill any case entitling them to relief in equity'.[87] Similarly in *Ferguson v Wilson*[88] Turner LJ observed: 'If, therefore, a Plaintiff in a suit in equity had no equitable right at the time of filing the bill ... so that the bill was altogether improperly filed in equity, I am of opinion that the Act has no application'.[89] Such a case was presumably envisaged by the proviso to s 4 of the Chancery Regulation Act 1862 (*Sir John Rolt's Act*)[90] which referred to where a 'matter has been improperly brought into Equity'.

It is now accepted that the circumstance that a court was unable to decree equitable relief at the commencement of proceedings does not preclude the court from subsequently acquiring jurisdiction to decree such relief, and also jurisdiction to award equitable damages. There are statements in the cases that equitable damages may only be awarded if specific relief could be decreed at the commencement of a suit.[91] However, it is now accepted that a court possesses jurisdiction to award equitable damages if the court was able to decree equitable relief in the form of an injunction or specific performance at the hearing of a suit, even though such relief could not be decreed at the commencement of the suit. Spry considers that 'it is probable that it is also sufficient that at the time of the making of the proposed award of damages the court is able to grant specific performance or an injunction if it thinks fit'.[92] Meagher, Gummow and Lehane have similarly commented:

> It is also clear that if he (the plaintiff) commenced a suit at a time when he had the right neither to an injunction nor to specific performance he could still claim that the court had jurisdiction if such a right had accrued to him before the hearing of the suit.[93]

There are sound policy reasons why such a view is preferable. One reason is that a multiplicity of suits is avoided.[94] Another reason is that a defendant should not be able to escape the jurisdiction of a court by

---

86 (1865) LR 1 Ch App 244.
87 (1865) LR 1 Ch App 244 at 251.
88 (1866) LR 2 Ch App 77.
89 (1866) LR 2 Ch App 77 at 88.
90 25 & 26 Vict c 42.
91 *Aynsley v Glover* (1874) LR 18 Eq 544 at 554; *White v Boby* (1877) 37 LT (NS) 652; *Elmore v Pirrie* (1887) 57 LT (NS) 333 at 335.
92 I C F Spry, *Equitable Remedies*, 4th ed, Law Book Co, Sydney, 1990, p 617.
93 R P Meagher, W M C Gummow and J R F Lehane, *Equity — Doctrines and Remedies*, 2nd ed, Butterworths, Sydney, 1984, p 520 [2309], 3rd ed, Butterworths, Sydney, 1992, p 642 [2309].
94 *Roberto v Bumb* [1943] OR 299; [1943] 2 DLR 613; *Roy v Kloepfer Wholesale Hardware & Automotive Co Ltd* [1951] 3 DLR 122 at 132.

evasive conduct. One can anticipate a situation where a defendant is guilty of a nuisance when a plaintiff instructs his solicitors to seek injunctive relief, but where at the actual time of instituting the proceedings the nuisance no longer exists because of temporary remedial action taken at that time by the defendant. The subsequent resurgence of that nuisance should be subject to those proceedings. A contrary conclusion would have unfortunate consequences.

The circumstances in which proceedings for the specific performance of a contract may be instituted are not limited to cases of an actual breach or default by a defendant.[95] In *Marks v Lilley*[96] Vaisey J cited with approval the following statement by T Cyprian Williams in support of that view. Williams stated that an action for specific performance is not an action for:

> ... a breach of the contract, such as alone gives [rise] to an action at law for damages, but is the duty considered in equity to be incumbent on the defendant of actually doing what he promised by the contract to perform. It follows that a breach of the contract by one party thereto is not necessarily a condition precedent to the other party's obtaining an order for its specific performance; though a breach of the contract is usually requisite to induce the court to interfere.[97]

The Privy Council in *Hasham v Zenab*[98] emphasised: 'In equity all that is required is to show circumstances which will justify the intervention by a court of equity'.[99] In that case the defendant had repudiated a contract for the sale of land by tearing it up soon after she executed it. The plaintiff instituted proceedings for the specific performance of the contract before the last day for completion. The defendant unsuccessfully contended that the writ was issued prematurely. The Board remarked 'that the fallacy of the submission consists in equating the right to sue for specific performance with a cause of action at law'.[100] It was held that the plaintiff was entitled to an order for specific performance.

The High Court of Australia in *Turner v Bladin*[101] has held that proceedings for the specific performance of a contract can be commenced as soon as one party threatens to refuse to perform the contract, or actually refuses to perform any promise for which the time for performance has arrived. There are Canadian authorities which recognise that where a vendor under a contract of sale repudiates before the date for completion, a purchaser is entitled immediately to seek a decree for specific performance.[102] In *Leeds Industrial Co-operative Society Ltd v Slack*[103] Lord

---

95 *Olympia & York Developments Ltd v Fourth Avenue Properties Ltd* [1982] 5 WWR 88 at 91.
96 [1959] 1 WLR 749.
97 T C Williams, *Contract of Sale of Land*, Sweet & Maxwell, London, 1930, p 132 cited at [1959] 1 WLR 749 at 753.
98 [1960] AC 316.
99 [1960] AC 316 at 329.
100 [1960] AC 316 at 329.
101 (1951) 82 CLR 463 at 472.
102 *Roberto v Bumb* [1943] OR 299; [1943] 2 DLR 613; *Roy v Kloepfer Wholesale Hardware & Automotive Co Ltd* [1951] 3 DLR 122; *Olympia & York Developments Ltd v Fourth Avenue Properties Ltd* [1982] 5 WWR 88.
103 [1924] AC 851.

Sumner in his dissenting speech appeared to consider a case of anticipatory breach as satisfying the jurisdictional requirements of *Lord Cairns' Act*. His Lordship remarked: 'So far as specific performance is concerned, they must always be cases where there has been an antecedent breach'.[104]

The jurisdiction to award equitable damages may be relevant where there is delay in the completion of a contract in circumstances in which common law damages are unavailable.[105] In *Oakacre Ltd v Claire Cleaners (Holdings) Ltd*[106] a writ for the specific performance of a contract of sale, and equitable damages in addition to or in lieu of specific performance, was issued before the contractual date of completion. The subject matter of the contract was a freehold property in the occupation of tenants. The plaintiff bona fide understood the completion date to be earlier than what was, upon a true construction of the contract, the actual date. The plaintiff was awarded damages for delay in completion. The question of specific performance did not arise as the land was conveyed to the plaintiff after the issue of the writ. Judge Mervyn Davies QC observed: 'Within the framework of a specific performance action the court may, in my view, award damages for delay in completion despite the fact that the action was instituted before the contractual date of completion'.[107] The pleadings of the plaintiff contained a claim for equitable damages under *Lord Cairns' Act*. Judge Mervyn Davies QC thought that a court of equity in considering a claim for specific performance could award damages prior to *Lord Cairns' Act*.[108] Judge Mervyn Davies QC referred to *Phelps v Prothero*[109] where Turner LJ remarked: 'This Court, when it entertains jurisdiction, deals as far as it can with the whole case, and not with part of it only'.[110] Judge Mervyn Davies QC considered that in dealing with 'the whole case' the court in that case appears to have been willing to take account of damages arising after the institution of a specific performance claim. This is because Turner LJ remarked:

> It was urged, on the part of the Defendant, that the damages for which he is suing at law, in part, at least, arose after the institution of the suit; and this, no doubt, is true, but it is unimportant, for the Defendant had ample opportunity of bringing them under the consideration of the Court.[111]

There is one case which has been the subject of some criticism. In *The Millstream Pty Ltd v Schultz*[112] the plaintiff had sought specific performance of a contract for the delivery by the defendant of certain fallow deer, and damages. There was evidence that at the date of the commencement of the suit the defendant was unable to perform the contract. However, shortly prior to that date he had the deer in his

---

104 [1924] AC 851 at 866.
105 See p 187.
106 [1982] Ch 197.
107 [1982] Ch 197 at 203.
108 [1982] Ch 197 at 202.
109 (1855) 7 De GM & G 722; 44 ER 280.
110 (1855) 7 De GM & G 722 at 734; 44 ER 280 at 285.
111 (1855) 7 De GM & G 722 at 735; 44 ER 280 at 285.
112 [1980] 1 NSWLR 547.

possession and had delivered a substantial portion of them elsewhere. The plaintiff sought an award of equitable damages under s 68 of the Supreme Court Act 1970 of New South Wales. The court held that there was no jurisdiction to award equitable damages. McLelland J remarked:

> It is established that s 68(b), the branch of the section here in question, confers a power to award damages only where, at the time of the commencement of the proceedings, the facts were such that the Court could then properly have ordered specific performance.[113]

In the context of a discussion of those cases where a plaintiff acquires jurisdiction to make an order for an injunction or specific performance after a suit has commenced, it has been suggested that the 'decision of McLelland J in *The Millstream Pty Ltd v Schultz*[114] is incorrect'.[115] This is a very isolated dictum upon which to base any criticism. The court did not have to consider the case where the court subsequently acquires jurisdiction to decree specific performance. This is because at no stage in the proceedings did there exist jurisdiction to decree specific performance, and consequently equitable damages. The plaintiff was awarded common law damages for breach of contract, and the failure to award equitable damages did not disadvantage the plaintiff. Consequently the actual decision cannot be regarded as incorrect.

5.5 Award of equitable damages after equitable relief has been decreed

The Court of Chancery would apparently decline to award equitable damages upon motion in a cause, after a decree for specific performance of a covenant, where relief was sought upon facts which had arisen after the decree was made.[116] This attitude may be explained by reason of discretionary considerations, although it may have been debatable whether there was a jurisdictional barrier to such relief. There is an argument that s 2 of *Lord Cairns' Act* only enabled damages to be awarded contemporaneously with a decree of an injunction or specific performance, so that a court does not possess the requisite jurisdiction to award equitable damages after the decree of such relief. This is because *Lord Cairns' Act* provided that damages may be awarded by 'the same court'[117] that has jurisdiction to entertain an application for an injunction or specific performance.[118] This point was first raised in *Biggin v Minton*[119] by Foster J

---

113   [1980] 1 NSWLR 547 at 552.
114   [1980] 1 NSWLR 547 at 552.
115   R P Meagher, W M C Gummow and J R F Lehane, *Equity — Doctrines and Remedies*, 2nd ed, Butterworths, Sydney, 1984, p 610, n 7; 3rd ed, Butterworths, Sydney, 1992, p 642, n 7.
116   *Hythe, Corp of v East* (1866) LR 1 Eq 620 at 623.
117   Chancery Amendment Act 1858 s 2.
118   See p 70.
119   [1977] 1 WLR 701.

who remarked: 'Perhaps it was thought that once a decree of specific performance is made, *Lord Cairns' Act* no longer applies'.[120] Similarly in *Minter v Geraghty*[121] Dunn J observed: 'it seems to me that the section contemplates an award of damages made at the same time as the time at which an injunction is granted'.[122] It is arguable that, as liberty to apply is usually reserved, the words 'the same court' are apt to refer to the court that made the order for specific performance or an injunction sitting on an adjourned date. In any event the courts have awarded common law damages or equitable damages after an order for specific performance has been vacated.[123] Such difficulties do not in any event apply to the jurisdiction conferred by s 50 of the Supreme Court Act 1981, or a similar provision, which does not contain the words 'the same court'.

---

120   [1977] 1 WLR 701 at 703.
121   (1981) 38 ALR 68.
122   (1981) 38 ALR 68 at 81.
123   See p 203.

6

Discretion to Award Equitable Damages

————◦————

6.1 Discretionary nature of the jurisdiction

Once it has been established that a court possesses jurisdiction to award equitable damages, there then arises the related, but nevertheless separate, question of whether or not the jurisdiction should be exercised. Ingman and Wakefield have remarked:

> *Lord Cairns' Act* itself, however, seems clearly to postulate a distinction between jurisdiction and discretion for, on the wording of section 2, the test for the existence of the power to award damages under it appears to demand the satisfaction of those conditions which, logically, arise prior to any exercise of the court's discretion and which must be present before the court can be said to have 'jurisdiction to entertain an application for' equitable relief.[1]

Equitable damages are not awarded as a matter of right.[2] A court always retains a discretion on whether to award equitable damages in a particular case. Ingman and Wakefield have also pointed out that '*Lord Cairns' Act* gave no entitlement to damages but merely conferred a discretion on the court to award damages'.[3] This is in contradistinction to

---

1 T Ingman and J Wakefield, 'Equitable Damages under *Lord Cairns' Act*', *Conveyancer and Property Lawyer*, 1981, 286 at p 293.

2 I C F Spry, *Equitable Damages*, 4th ed, Law Book Co, Sydney, 1990, p 622.

3 T Ingman and J Wakefield, 'Equitable Damages under *Lord Cairns' Act*', *Conveyancer and Property Lawyer*, 1981, 286 at p 289.

where a plaintiff is seeking an award of common law damages. Common law damages will be awarded as a matter of course once damage has been proved and other requisite matters[4] have been established. Equitable damages are not awarded as a matter of right.[5]

The award of equitable relief in the form of an injunction or specific performance is itself a discretionary remedy. As Sir Robin Cooke P remarked in *Day v Mead*:[6] 'Equitable relief was said to be always discretionary'.[7] The Chancery Amendment Act 1858 (*Lord Cairns' Act*)[8] accordingly conferred discretionary power upon the Court of Chancery to award damages where there were circumstances which attracted jurisdiction to award an equitable remedy which is, itself, discretionary. Presumably that is why Jolowicz commented that the Act 'bases a discretion upon a discretion'.[9]

The discretionary nature of the jurisdiction can be discerned from s 2 of *Lord Cairns' Act* which conferred jurisdiction upon the Court of Chancery to award equitable damages 'if it shall think fit'.[10] These words, which clearly confer a discretionary jurisdiction, were inserted during the passage of the Act in the House of Lords.[11] In *Durell v Pritchard*[12] Turner LJ said: 'I think it clear that the Act leaves it in the discretion of the Court whether it will award damages or not'.[13] Similarly in *Aynsley v Glover*[14] Sir George Jessel MR observed that the words 'if it shall think fit' conferred a 'purely discretionary'[15] power to award damages. The Supreme Court of Canada in *McKenzie v Hiscock*[16] stated: 'While the jurisdiction conferred is discretionary the discretion must be exercised judicially'.[17] The exercise of the discretion under *Lord Cairns' Act* must, of course, depend upon the circumstances of each individual case.[18] Evidence is admissible on the issue whether the court should grant specific relief or instead award equitable damages.[19]

The discretionary nature of the jurisdiction has been continued by those statutory provisions which have replaced *Lord Cairns' Act*. Provisions such as s 92 of the Judicature (Northern Ireland) Act 1978[20]

---

4   Eg statutory formalities, Statute of Frauds.
5   I C F Spry, *Equitable Remedies*, 4th ed, Law Book Co, Sydney, 1990, p 622.
6   [1987] 2 NZLR 443.
7   [1987] 2 NZLR 443 at 451.
8   21 & 22 Vict c 27.
9   J A Jolowicz, 'Damages in Equity — A Study of *Lord Cairns' Act*', *Cambridge Law Journal*, vol 34, 1975, 224 at p 240.
10 See p 32–3.
11 *House of Lords Journal*, vol 90, 4 June 1858, p 214.
12 (1865) LR 1 Ch App 244.
13 (1865) LR 1 Ch App 244 at 252.
14 (1874) LR 18 Eq 544.
15 (1874) LR 18 Eq 544 at 554.
16 (1967) 65 DLR (2d) 123.
17 (1967) 65 DLR (2d) 123 at 130.
18 *Greenwood v Hornsey* (1886) 33 Ch D 471 at 476–7.
19 *Sydney Consumer Milk & Ice Co Ltd v Hawkesbury Dairy & Ice Society Ltd* (1931) 31 SR (NSW) 458 at 471 per Long Innes J.
20 1978 c 23.

and s 50 of the Supreme Court Act 1981[21] preserve the discretionary nature of the jurisdiction by providing that a court 'may' award damages.

————◦————

6.2 *Shelfer's case*

Central to any discussion of the discretionary nature of the jurisdiction under *Lord Cairns' Act* is the 'working rule' in *Shelfer v City of London Electric Lighting Co.*[22] In *Shelfer's* case the Court of Appeal issued an injunction to restrain a nuisance caused by the plant of an electric lighting company. The court had to consider whether it was appropriate to exercise the jurisdiction under *Lord Cairns' Act* to award damages in substitution for an injunction. A L Smith LJ formulated a 'working rule':

> In my opinion, it may be stated as a good working rule that —
>
> (1) If the injury to the plaintiff's legal rights is small,
>
> (2) And is one which is capable of being estimated in money,
>
> (3) And is one which can be adequately compensated by a small money payment,
>
> (4) And the case is one in which it would be oppressive to the defendant to grant an injunction:–
>
> then damages in substitution for an injunction may be given.[23]

A L Smith LJ also stated that where these requirements exist, the defendant by his conduct may nevertheless be disentitled from asking that damages be assessed in substitution for an injunction. The Lord Justice cited the case of where a defendant was guilty of 'hurrying up his buildings so as if possible to avoid an injunction, or otherwise acting with a reckless disregard to the plaintiff's rights'.[24]

What is sometimes not appreciated is that the 'working rule' in *Shelfer's* case was not assented to by other members of the Court of Appeal. Lord Halsbury remarked of *Lord Cairns' Act*: 'The language, of course, is general; the discretion given is necessarily wide enough in terms to authorise a Judge to award damages where formerly he would have given an injunction'.[25] Lindley LJ said: 'Without denying the jurisdiction to award damages instead of an injunction, even in cases of continuing actionable nuisances, such jurisdiction ought not to be exercised in such cases except under very exceptional circumstances'.[26] His Lordship added: 'I will not attempt to specify them or to lay down rules for the exercise of judicial discretion'.[27]

---

21   1981 c 54.
22   [1895] 1 Ch 287.
23   [1895] 1 Ch 287 at 322–3.
24   [1895] 1 Ch 287 at 323.
25   [1895] 1 Ch 287 at 311.
26   [1895] 1 Ch 287 at 316.
27   [1895] 1 Ch 287 at 316–17.

Despite the lack of consensus by the members of the Court of Appeal in *Shelfer's* case, the 'working rule' is authoritative. In *Kennaway v Thompson*[28] Lawton LJ remarked: 'The principles enunciated in *Shelfer's* case, which is binding on us, have been applied time and time again during the past 85 years'.[29] However, it may be questioned whether the rule was really binding as no other members of the Court of Appeal in *Shelfer's* case assented to the 'working rule'. Nevertheless, the *ipsissima verba* of A L Smith LJ have been construed, and applied as rigidly, as a statute.[30]

Although *Shelfer's* case concerned a nuisance, the 'working rule' has been applied in other situations. In *Snow v Willmott*[31] the court awarded equitable damages in lieu of an injunction to demolish a building erected in breach of a restrictive covenant. Clute J said:

> In the present case the injury to plaintiff's legal rights is small, and is one which is capable of being estimated in money, and which can be adequately compensated by a small money payment, and the case is one in which it would, I think, be oppressive to the defendant to grant an injunction.[32]

In a Nigerian case concerning a continuing trespass the trial judge observed that 'the conditions mentioned by A L Smith LJ ... exist in this case'.[33] The 'working rule' was also adopted by Duff J in *Canada Paper Co v Brown*[34] in an appeal from Quebec in which *Lord Cairns' Act* was not operative.

Despite such mechanical applications of the 'working rule' in *Shelfer's* case, it should be understood that the 'working rule' is not itself an inflexible rule. A L Smith LJ himself recognised that the determination of each matter in the 'four rules ... must be left to the good sense of the tribunal which deals with each case as it comes up for adjudication'.[35] In *Duchman v Oakland Dairy Co Ltd*[36] Master JA commented that 'the rule in the *Shelfer* case does not purport to be exhaustive'.[37]

It may be questioned whether it was necessary, or even desirable, to attempt to formulate a general principle in respect of a statutory discretion which must be exercised by a court having regard to the particular circumstances of each case. Earlier in *Aynsley v Glover*[38] Sir George Jessel MR said: 'I am not now going, and I do not suppose that any Judge will ever do so, to lay down a rule which, so to say, will tie the hands of the Court'.[39] Similarly in *Leader v Moody*[40] Sir George Jessel MR observed

---

28 [1981] QB 88.
29 [1981] QB 88 at 93.
30 See eg *Carpet Importing Co Ltd v Beath & Co Ltd* [1927] NZLR 37.
31 (1905) 5 OWR 361.
32 (1905) 5 OWR 361 at 363–4.
33 *Odutola v Adeyemo* (Court of Appeal, Western State, Ibadan, No I/11/66, 19 April 1974, unreported) at 3.
34 (1922) 66 DLR 287 at 292.
35 [1895] 1 Ch 287 at 323.
36 (1928) 63 OLR 111; [1929] 1 DLR 9.
37 (1928) 63 OLR 111 at 120; [1929] 1 DLR 9 at 24.
38 (1874) LR 18 Eq 544.
39 (1874) LR 18 Eq 544 at 555.
40 (1875) LR 20 Eq 145.

that he had 'on other occasions abstained from laying down, any general rule which would fetter the exercise of the discretion of the Court'.[41] Meagher, Gummow and Lehane have stated that 'it is a matter of great difficulty to lay down any principles on which courts will act in awarding damages in lieu of decreeing specific relief'.[42] Nevertheless the 'working rule' is now regarded as a matter to be considered by a court in deciding whether or not to grant an injunction or award equitable damages.

There are many examples of the application of the 'working rule' of A L Smith LJ.[43] One example is the Nova Scotia case of *Brean v Thorne*[44] where the parties were adjacent landowners. The defendants had built a house on the plaintiffs' property mistakenly believing it to be their own. In these circumstances the court did not consider that this was a case in which the 'working rule' could properly be applied. Rogers J commented:

> The facts in this case are far more serious than in the *Gallant* case. The encroachment amounts to a complete usurpation, an expropriation if you will, of the plaintiffs' rights to their property. Quite clearly, when the tests set out in the *Shelfer* case are applied, it is not difficult to reach the conclusion, and I do so, that the injury to the plaintiffs of their rights is not small, it is one that is not capable of being adequately estimated in money, and cannot be adequately compensated by a small money payment.[45]

The court granted the plaintiffs a mandatory injunction to compel the removal of the house from their property. The fact that the plaintiffs made relatively little use of their property, which was not unique, was not to the point. Rogers J said: 'But it is going too far to say that in those circumstances damages in exchange for a deed or a court-compelled exchange of deeds to Lots A-1 and A-2 is the appropriate remedy'.[46]

In *Fishenden v Higgs and Hill Ltd*[47] the plaintiff was granted an injunction to restrain the construction of a partly built building which would when erected obstruct ancient lights. Crossman J remarked:

> In order to justify me in substituting damages for an injunction, I have to find that the four rules are complied with, unless there was one of these special circumstances, none of which there is in the present case. The case must be brought within the exceptions; that is to say, all four of A L Smith, LJ's conditions must exist.[48]

The Court of Appeal considered that this was a misdirection that the court must grant an injunction if any one of the conditions was not fulfilled.

---

41 (1875) LR 20 Eq 145 at 154.
42 R P Meagher, W M C Gummow and J R F Lehane, *Equity — Doctrines and Remedies*, 2nd ed, Butterworths, Sydney, 1984, p 610 [2310].
43 *Rileys v Halifax Corp* (1907) 97 LT 278 at 279; *Appleby v Erie Tobacco Co* (1910) 22 OLR 533 at 538; *Morris v Redland Bricks Ltd* [1967] 1 WLR 967; *Kennaway v Thompson* [1981] QB 88; *Brean v Thorne* (1982) 52 NSR (2d) 241 at 246.
44 (1982) 52 NSR (2d) 241.
45 (1982) 52 NSR (2d) 241 at 246.
46 (1982) 52 NSR (2d) 241 at 246.
47 (1935) 153 LT 128.
48 (1935) 153 LT 128 at 134.

The Court of Appeal in *Fishenden* recognised that the 'working rule' was not to be inflexibly applied, and that substantial damages could be awarded under *Lord Cairns' Act* in such a case. Lord Hanworth MR pointed out that *Shelfer's* case concerned a nuisance which endangered the health of the aggrieved persons, and that the rule was not to be rigidly applied. The Master of the Rolls added:

> A L Smith LJ was only attempting to lay down some sort of canons which ought to be followed appropriately as a guide in determining whether an injunction or damages should be granted. But in the very terms he eliminates any stringency from them and indicates that the tribunal itself must consider what is the right course in any particular case.[49]

Romer LJ remarked:

> It is quite plain, therefore that in every case, even though the four conditions laid down by A L Smith LJ are not to be found, the court has, having regard to all the circumstances of the case, an exercise of its discretion in the matter.[50]

Maugham LJ considered that the 'working rule ... is not a universal or even a sound rule in all cases of injury to light'.[51] His Lordship emphasised that the 'working rule' was not a universal law, but that the guidance given by Lindley LJ should be accepted as correct. Despite the decision in *Fishenden v Higgs and Hill Ltd*,[52] some later decisions have regarded the 'working rule' as if it were a statute. However, it has been appreciated that the 'working rule' cannot be applied to all cases of breach of contract.[53]

Examples of the literal application of the 'working rule' are to be found in the judgments of the members of the Court of Appeal in *Morris v Redland Bricks Ltd*.[54] That case considered whether a mandatory injunction or damages was the appropriate remedy in relation to excavations likely to remove support from adjoining land.[55] On appeal in the House of Lords, Holland QC as counsel for the appellant submitted: 'The Court of Appeal misapplied *Shelfer's* case for it proceeded on the basis that unless the present case comes within one of the exceptions laid down by A L Smith LJ the court must perforce grant an injunction'.[56] Their Lordships recognised that *Lord Cairns' Act* was not relevant,[57] because the plaintiffs had only sought common law damages within the limited jurisdiction of the County Court.[58]

In *Kennaway v Thompson*[59] the Court of Appeal applied the 'working rule' to determine that damages should not be awarded in substitution for an injunction to restrain noisy motor boat racing. Lawton LJ remarked:

---

49 (1935) 153 LT 128 at 138.
50 (1935) 153 LT 128 at 141.
51 (1935) 153 LT 128 at 144.
52 (1935) 153 LT 128.
53 *Peacock v Leicester City Council* (Court of Appeal, 4 June 1984, unreported).
54 [1967] 1 WLR 967.
55 [1967] 1 WLR 967 at 975–6, 980, 984.
56 [1970] AC 652 at 658.
57 [1970] AC 652 at 665.
58 P H Pettit, '*Lord Cairns' Act* in the County Court: A Supplementary Note', *Cambridge Law Journal*, vol 36, 1977, p 369.
59 [1981] QB 88.

... the 'working rule' does not apply in this case. The injury to the plaintiff's legal rights is not small; it is not capable of being estimated in terms of money save in the way the judge tried to make an estimate, namely by fixing a figure for the diminution of the value of the plaintiff's house because of the prospect of a continuing nuisance — and the figure he fixed could not be described as small.[60]

In *Kennaway v Thompson*[61] the court also referred to *Miller v Jackson*,[62] where the court discharged an injunction restraining the use of a village ground for the playing of cricket and awarded damages for past and future inconvenience of a householder. The majority of the Court of Appeal in *Miller v Jackson*[63] had adjudged that the activities of the cricket club constituted a nuisance. The question that then had to be decided was whether the plaintiffs should be granted an injunction. Geoffrey Lane LJ thought that an injunction should issue, but Lord Denning MR considered that the public interest should prevail over the private interest. However, Cumming-Bruce LJ mentioned that a factor to be taken into account when exercising the judicial discretion whether to grant an injunction was that the plaintiffs had bought their house knowing that it was next to a cricket ground. In *Kennaway v Thompson*[64] Lawton LJ commented: 'Lord Denning MR's statement that the public interest should prevail over the private interest runs counter to the principles enunciated in *Shelfer's* case and does not accord with Cumming-Bruce LJ's reasons for refusing an injunction'.[65]

———◦———

6.3 Circumstances relevant to the exercise of the jurisdiction

Whether specific relief in the form of an injunction or specific performance, or an award of equitable damages is an appropriate remedy is a matter for a court to decide having regard to the facts of each case. The reported cases which have been decided on their own particular circumstances provide guidance, but are not binding precedents. There are statements that *Lord Cairns' Act* did not alter the settled principles upon which courts of equity have acted in granting injunctions.[66] However, in reality the statute enabled the court to award equitable damages where formerly an injunction was the only remedy available. In *Feinberg v Weisfeld*[67] Riddle J remarked: 'Until *Lord Cairns' Act* was passed, an

---

60   [1981] QB 88 at 93.
61   [1981] QB 88.
62   [1977] QB 966.
63   [1977] QB 966.
64   [1981] QB 88.
65   [1981] QB 88 at 93.
66   *Shelfer v City of London Electric Lighting Co* [1895] 1 Ch 287 at 311; *Sefton v Tophams Ltd* [1965] Ch 1140 at 1168–9; *Kennaway v Thompson* [1981] QB 88 at 92–3.
67   (1924) 27 OWN 363.

injunction would have been granted as a matter of right'.[68] In *Black v Scottish Temperance Assurance Co*[69] Holmes LJ said: '*Lord Cairns' Act* was a legislative declaration that in some cases the award of damages would be a more appropriate remedy'.[70]

A plaintiff may be awarded equitable damages against his will. Statements in some cases that a plaintiff must consent to an award of equitable damages are expressed too widely. Such a statement is to be found in the headnote of *Krehl v Burrell*:[71]

> Where a Plaintiff has established his right to a perpetual injunction against the Defendant the court has no power under *Lord Cairns' Act* to oblige him against his will to accept damages in lieu of the injunction.

A court, in determining whether to make an order for an injunction, may have regard to whether a plaintiff sought interlocutory relief.[72] The tendency of modern cases is to decline injunctive relief and award equitable damages where a plaintiff has not sought interim relief.[73] However, it may be legitimate for a plaintiff to apply for a permanent rather than a interim or interlocutory injunction so as not to be at risk from an undertaking to pay damages.[74] It would seem that interim relief would itself not be granted where an application is made after a building has been under construction for some time.[75]

Some general principles may be discerned from cases where an injunction has been sought. There is a general principle that an injunction will not ordinarily issue where damages are an adequate or proper remedy.[76] Special circumstances must generally be shown before the court would exercise its discretion to award damages under *Lord Cairns' Act* rather than restrain by injunction an illegal activity which infringes the rights of an individual.[77] The courts have repeatedly emphasised that the discretion under *Lord Cairns' Act* will not be exercised to award damages

---

68 (1924) 27 OWN 363. See also *Fishenden v Higgs and Hill Ltd* (1935) 153 LT 128 at 138 per Lord Hanworth MR.

69 [1908] 1 Ir R 541.

70 [1908] 1 Ir R 541 at 574.

71 (1879) 11 Ch D 146.

72 It is submitted that this is the position despite contrary dicta in an Irish Appeal: see *Black v Scottish Temperance Assurance Co* [1908] 1 Ir R 541 at 577 per Lord Loreburn LC (HL). ('He did not apply for an interim injunction, very sensibly, I think, because he would have been obliged to give an undertaking as to damages which might have proved ruinous if his case failed.') See also *Snell & Prideaux Ltd v Dutton Mirrors Ltd* (Court of Appeal, Stuart-Smith, Hoffmann and Seville LJJ, 22 April 1994, unreported) where the plaintiff was given an opportunity to apply for interlocutory relief.

73 *Landau v Curton* [1962] EGD 369; *Wrotham Park Estate Co Ltd v Parkside Homes Ltd* [1974] 1 WLR 798 at 810; *Shaw v Applegate* [1977] 1 WLR 970 at 981.

74 *Black v Scottish Temperance Life Assurance Co* [1908] 1 Ir R 541 at 577 per Lord Loreburn LC; *Oxy Electric Ltd v Zainuddin* [1990] 2 All ER 902.

75 *Bracewell v Appleby* [1975] Ch 408 at 415.

76 *London & Blackwall Railway Co v Cross* (1886) 31 Ch D 354 at 369; *Kennard v Cory Bros & Co* [1922] 2 Ch 1; *Gross v Wright* [1923] 2 DLR 171 at 176; *Masai Minerals Ltd v Heritage Resources Ltd* [1979] 2 WWR 352.

77 *Shelfer v City of London Electric Lighting Co* [1895] 1 Ch 287 at 316; *Sefton v Tophams Ltd* [1965] Ch 1140 at 1169. See also *New Brunswick Power Co v Maritime Transit Ltd* (1937) 12 MPR 152.

in lieu of an injunction so that the statute is regarded as a charter to license the commission of future wrongs by a defendant who is willing and able to pay damages.[78] On the other hand any argument that an award of damages would license the commission of future torts has little weight when invoked by a defendant.[79]

It would not be appropriate to award equitable damages in lieu of an injunction where a defendant has acted in an oppressive or high-handed manner as an injunction may be necessary to do justice to the plaintiff and deter others.[80] Consequently an award of equitable damages would be an inappropriate remedy where a defendant had showed a total or unreasonable disregard for the rights of a plaintiff.[81] In *Elliott v London Borough of Islington*[82] Lord Donaldson of Lymington MR, in discussing *Shelfer's* case, emphasised that *Lord Cairns' Act* would not be used 'to license breaches of the rights of the citizens'.[83]

The jurisdiction will not be exercised to facilitate the compulsory purchase of property of the plaintiff by the defendant at a price fixed by the court.[84] In *Shelfer's* case Lindley LJ remarked:

> Expropriation, even for a money consideration, is only justifiable when Parliament has sanctioned it. Courts of Justice are not like Parliament, which considers whether proposed works will be so beneficial to the public as to justify exceptional legislation, and the deprivation of people of their rights with or without compensation. *Lord Cairns' Act* was not passed to supersede legislation for public purposes, but to enable the Court of Chancery to administer justice between litigants more effectively than it could before the Act.[85]

This principle was applied in *Biogen Inc v Medeva Plc*[86] where a suit was brought against the defendant for the infringement of a patent for a

---

78 *Smith v Smith* (1875) LR 20 Eq 500 at 505; *Krehl v Burrell* (1879) 11 Ch D 146 at 148; *Shelfer v City of London Electric Lighting Co* [1895] 1 Ch 287 at 315–16; *Cowper v Laidler* [1903] 2 Ch 337 at 341; *Black v Scottish Temperance Life Assurance Co* [1908] 1 Ir R 541 at 560; *Gross v Wright* [1923] 2 DLR 171 at 188; *Leeds Industrial Co-operative Society Ltd v Slack* [1924] AC 851 at 860; *KVP Co Ltd v McKie* [1949] 4 DLR 497 at 500–1; *Sefton v Tophams Ltd* [1965] Ch 1140 at 1169; *Kennaway v Thompson* [1981] QB 88 at 92.

79 *Sampson v Hodson-Pressinger* [1981] 3 All ER 710 at 715.

80 *Colls v Home and Colonial Stores Ltd* [1904] AC 179 at 193; *Black v Scottish Temperance Assurance Co* [1908] 1 Ir R 541 at 567, 568, 575.

81 *Economy Shipping Pty Ltd v ADC Buildings Pty Ltd* [1969] 2 NSWR 97; *Post Investments Pty Ltd v Wilson* (Supreme Court of New South Wales, Powell J, Eq Div, No 5019 of 1987, 9 May 1990, unreported).

82 [1991] 1 EGLR 167.

83 [1991] 1 EGLR 167 at 168.

84 *Dent v Auction Mart Co* (1866) LR 2 Eq 238 at 246; *Aynsley v Glover* (1874) LR 18 Eq 544 at 552; *Krehl v Burrell* (1878) 7 Ch D 551 at 554–7; (1879) 11 Ch D 146 at 148; *Holland v Worley* (1884) 26 Ch D 578 at 587; *Shelfer v City of London Electric Lighting Co* [1895] 1 Ch 287 at 316; *Cowper v Laidler* [1903] 2 Ch 337 at 341; *Black v Scottish Temperance Life Assurance Co* [1908] 1 Ir R 541 at 567; *Moore v Corrigan* [1949] Tas SR 34 at 73; *Brean v Thorne* (1982) 52 NSR (2d) 241 at 246; *Elliott v London Borough of Islington* [1991] 1 EGLR 167 (CA).

85 [1895] 1 Ch 287 at 315.

86 [1993] RPC 476.

vaccine against the hepatitis B virus. The defendant pleaded in its defence that if there was an infringement of the patent, the court should decline to exercise its discretion to grant an injunction to prevent the manufacture and sale of the vaccine because the vaccine would be superior to any vaccine likely to be available from the plaintiff and an injunction would lead to loss of human life or avoidable damage to human health. The court declined in interlocutory proceedings to strike out this part of the defence as this could fetter the exercise of a discretion to be exercised after judgment, when the background facts might have changed. It was held that, applying the principles enunciated by Lindley LJ in *Shelfer's* case, it would be inappropriate to award damages under *Lord Cairns' Act*. Aldous J observed:

> If those principles are applied to the facts that appear likely in this case, I do not envisage that the court could award damages in lieu of an injunction, that would amount to expropriation of Biogen's property as I do not think that it would be possible to quantify the damages. Further, as Lindley LJ pointed out, it is not the task of the court to legalise wrongful acts even if though in this case Medeva could be considered to be a public benefactor because it was producing a life-saving vaccine. Further, the refusal to grant an injunction would be likely to cause considerable damage to Biogen.[87]

Equitable damages will be awarded where a court considers that an award of damages would better meet the circumstances of a case than an order for specific performance.[88] It is submitted that a court would be inclined to compel the performance of a statutory contract rather than consider an award of damages.[89] This is because parliament has provided for the contract to be executed.

The Supreme Court of Canada has held that it would be inappropriate to award damages under *Lord Cairns' Act* rather than issue an order for contempt for failure to comply with an injunction. This is because civil damages are not part of the weaponry of a court in ensuring compliance with its injunctions.[90]

There may be some cases where it is appropriate to award equitable damages. Where a plaintiff has not suffered substantial injury, a court may award equitable damages rather than grant a mandatory injunction.[91] However, a court will also ensure that solemn obligations freely undertaken are not lightly disregarded, and damages will not be awarded merely because an injunction will be of no benefit to a plaintiff.[92] A court would

---

87 [1993] RPC 476 at 486–7.
88 *Wilson v Northampton and Banbury Junction Railway Co* (1874) LR 9 Ch App 279.
89 Compare *Scottish Australian Coal Mining Co v Redhead Coal Mining Co* (1891) 12 LR (NSW) Eq 111. (This particular case did not concern equitable damages, but the availability of compensation under a statute which sanctioned a contract.)
90 *St Anne-Nackawic Pulp & Paper Co Ltd v Canadian Paper Workers' Union, Local 219* [1986] 1 SCR 704 at 728; 28 DLR (4th) 1 at 19.
91 *Bowes v Law* (1870) LR 9 Eq 636 at 642; *Holland v Worley* (1884) 26 Ch D 578 at 587; *Sharp v Harrison* [1922] 1 Ch 502 at 516; *Port Adelaide, Corp of the City of v South Australian Railways Commissioner* [1927] SASR 197 at 211.
92 *Sefton v Tophams Ltd* [1965] Ch 1140 at 1168–9.

be inclined to award equitable damages where a plaintiff is prepared to accept payment as compensation, and where the grant of a mandatory injunction would cause disproportionate damage.[93] It would be appropriate to award equitable damages in lieu of an injunction where the grant of an injunction would cause extreme hardship, and where the damage to the plaintiff is nominal.[94] The court would be more ready to award equitable damages in lieu of an injunction where a plaintiff made an offer to decline to apply for an injunction only on unreasonable or extortionate terms.[95] The fact that a plaintiff has, upon legal advice, compromised in respect of past events does not debar the plaintiff from obtaining injunctive relief.[96]

The jurisdiction may also be exercised where discretionary defences to a claim for an injunction or specific performance are established. These discretionary defences include hardship to a defendant[97] and laches or acquiescence.[98] A court may be inclined to award equitable damages in lieu of an injunction where there is a real question as to whether a defendant is within his rights, or where a defendant has acted fairly.[99] There may, however, be cases where actual damage occurs and equitable damages would not be a sufficient or adequate remedy.[100]

———◦———

6.4 Policy considerations

There may be circumstances where a court would, for reasons of policy, exercise its discretion to award equitable damages rather than decree specific relief. A court would be reluctant to order the destruction of machinery. In *Saltman Engineering Co Ltd v Campbell Engineering Co Ltd*[101] the defendant, in breach of an obligation of confidence, used drawings of the plaintiff to make a large number of leather punches. The court awarded equitable damages under *Lord Cairns' Act* rather than order the sterilisation of tools which might serve a useful purpose.[102] An

---

93 *Senior v Pawson* (1866) LR 3 Eq 330 at 336.
94 *Pettey v Parsons* [1914] 1 Ch 704 at 723.
95 *Isenberg v East India House Estate Co Ltd* (1863) 3 De GJ & S 263 at 273; 46 ER 637 at 641; *Senior v Pawson* (1866) LR 3 Eq 330; *Aynsley v Glover* (1874) LR 18 Eq 544 at 555; *Krehl v Burrell* (1878) 7 Ch D 551 at 554; *Holland v Worley* (1884) 26 Ch D 578 at 585; *Colls v Home and Colonial Stores Ltd* [1904] AC 179 at 193.
96 *McKinnon Industries Ltd v Walker* [1951] 3 DLR 577 at 580 (PC).
97 *Haggerty v Latreille* (1913) 14 DLR 532; *Sharp v Harrison* [1922] 1 Ch 502; *Clark v McKenzie* [1930] 2 DLR 843; *Dell v Beasley* [1959] NZLR 89; *Bosaid v Andry* [1963] VR 465; *Shaw v Applegate* [1977] 1 WLR 970; *Bloomberg in Trust v Tricont Projects Ltd* (1980) 13 RPR 284 at 300; *Madden v Kevereski* (1982) 2 BPR [97156] 9645; *RD McKinnon Holdings Pty Ltd v Hind* [1984] 2 NSWLR 121.
98 *Sayers v Collyer* (1884) 28 Ch D 103 at 110; *Bracewell v Appleby* [1975] Ch 408 at 419.
99 *Colls v Home and Colonial Stores Ltd* [1904] AC 179 at 193; *Kine v Jolly* [1905] 1 Ch 480 at 504; *Feinberg v Weisfeld* (1924) 27 OWN 363.
100 *Redland Bricks Ltd v Morris* [1970] AC 652 at 665–6; *Belgrave Nominees Pty Ltd v Barlin-Scott Airconditioning (Aust) Pty Ltd* [1984] VR 947 at 954.
101 (1948) 65 RPC 203.
102 (1948) 65 RPC 203 at 219.

important consideration in that case would have been the fact that judgment was given at a time of post-war reconstruction.

A court would also not readily order the demolition of a building which has already been constructed. There is an old precedent in which the Court of Chancery declined to order the specific performance of a building lease which would involve the destruction of housing, and instead directed a trial upon a *quantum damnifactus*.[103] There are a number of cases where a court awarded damages under *Lord Cairns' Act* rather than order the demolition of housing.[104] In *Wrotham Park Estate Co Ltd v Parkside Homes Ltd*[105] the court awarded damages instead of ordering the demolition of houses erected in breach of a restrictive covenant. The defendant suffered no damage of a financial nature arising from the breach and it was totally unnecessary to demolish the houses to preserve the integrity of the scheme. Brightman J remarked:

> It would, in my opinion, be an unpardonable waste of much needed houses to direct that they now be pulled down and I never had a moment's doubt during the hearing of this case that such an order ought to be refused.[106]

The policy reasons underlying the award of equitable damages in the *Wrotham Park* case were mentioned in *Stoke-on-Trent City Council v W & J Wass Ltd*[107] by Nourse LJ:

> Injunctions could therefore and would have been granted in that case but for the social and economic reasons against ordering the demolition of 14 houses.[108]

A court would also not readily order the demolition of any works, especially public works. In one South Australian case the court declined to order the removal of a railway line that was erected on a road without the requisite consent of a municipality. Both parties were corporations established in the public interest. The railways commissioner had given due notice of the intended construction, there had been delay in instituting proceedings, the expense of restoring the road would be great and the advantage to the plaintiff would be 'infinitesimal'. The court held that an award of equitable damages was the appropriate remedy.[109]

The use of solar energy is increasing because of concern as to the damage to the environment caused by the mining and use of fossil fuels. Debate has centred upon issues such as the conservation of resources and global warming. There are also economic benefits in the use of solar energy. The question of public policy is relevant in protecting access to

---

103 *City of London v Nash* (1747) 3 Atk 512; 26 ER 1095.
104 *Kilbey v Haviland* (1871) 24 LT 353 at 356; *Martin v Price* [1894] 1 Ch 276; *Wrotham Park Estate Co Ltd v Parkside Homes Ltd* [1974] 1 WLR 798 at 811; *Bracewell v Appleby* [1975] Ch 408 at 419.
105 [1974] 1 WLR 798.
106 [1974] 1 WLR 798 at 811.
107 [1988] 1 WLR 1406.
108 [1988] 1 WLR 1406 at 1414.
109 *Port Adelaide, Corp of the City of v South Australian Railways Commissioner* [1927] SASR 197 at 211–12.

solar energy. There is an obvious public interest in the conservation of resources. It has been argued that the public interest is sufficient justification for awarding an injunction rather than equitable damages if nuisance is held to lie in a case of obstruction to solar access.[110]

---

110 A J Bradbrook, 'Nuisance and the Right of Solar Access', *University of Western Australia Law Review*, vol 15, 1983, 148 at p 173; A J Bradbrook, *Solar Energy and the Law*, Law Book Co, Sydney, 1984, p 104; A J Bradbrook, 'The Role of the Courts in Advancing the Use of Solar Energy', *Journal of Energy Law and Policy*, vol 9, 1989, 135 at p 168. See also p 142.

7

Assessment of Equitable Damages

7.1 Introduction

At issue in a number of cases has been whether equitable damages should be assessed in the same manner as common law damages, or according to different principles.[1] Section 2 of the Chancery Amendment Act 1858 (*Lord Cairns' Act*)[2] concludes with the words: 'Damages may be assessed in such manner as the court shall direct'. One issue is whether these concluding words are relevant in assessing the quantum of equitable damages. In *Edward Street Properties Pty Ltd v Collins*[3] it was obviously thought that these words had procedural significance as Douglas J examined the rules of court determining which judicial officer would

---

1   *Dobson v Winton and Robbins Ltd* [1959] SCR 775 at 780; 20 DLR (2d) 164 at 167; *Bosaid v Andry* [1963] VR 465 at 483; *Ansdell v Crowther* (1984) 55 BCLR 216; 11 DLR (4th) 614; *Kemp v Lee* (1983) 44 BCLR 172 at 182; 28 RPR 141 at 158–9.

2   21 & 22 Vict c 27.

3   [1977] Qd R 399.

assess damages. Later in *Johnson v Agnew*[4] Lord Wilberforce remarked that this concluding phrase 'clearly refers only to procedure'.[5] This is undoubtedly correct for *Lord Cairns' Act* provided for the assessment of damages by different tribunals.[6] In any event, these concluding words are not to be found in modern provisions which confer jurisdiction to award equitable damages such as s 50 of the English Supreme Court Act 1981.

7.2 Necessity for proof of actual damage or impending damage

A court will award equitable damages if it is satisfied that a plaintiff has suffered damage, or is likely to suffer damage as in a *quia timet* action. As a general principle a court will only direct an inquiry into equitable damages if there is some evidence of more than nominal damage.[7] Where there is no evidence that a party who seeks an inquiry has suffered any damage, a court may order an inquiry at the risk of that party as to costs.[8]

7.3 Distinction between common law damages and equitable damages

It is important to appreciate that equitable damages which are awarded under *Lord Cairns' Act* (or its statutory successors), are quite distinct from common law damages. After the Act was passed, Lord St Leonards wrote:

> This was not a blending of the powers of the two courts, but the creation of a new power to grant at once specific performance and damages, or damages in substitution of specific performance.[9]

Early authority established that *Lord Cairns' Act* was not merely a procedural statute which enabled the Court of Chancery to award common law damages. In *Eastwood v Lever*[10] Turner LJ observed that the Act 'is

---

4 [1980] AC 367.
5 [1980] AC 367 at 400.
6 Chancery Amendment Act 1858 s 3 (Court of Chancery with a jury), s 5 (Court of Chancery without jury), s 6 (common law judge or sheriff).
7 *Griffin v Mercantile Bank* (1890) 11 LR (NSW) Eq 231 at 258; *Union Bank v Downes* (1896) 12 WN (NSW) 131; *Edward Street Properties Pty Ltd v Collins* [1977] Qd R 399 at 403. See also *Foster v Wheeler* (1887) 36 Ch D 695; *Bonham-Carter v Hyde Park Hotel Ltd* (1948) 64 TLR 177 at 178; *Lee Sau Kong v Leow Cheng Chiang* (1961) 27 MLJ 17 at 20; *Enkelmann v Glissan* (1982) 2 BPR [97155].
8 *Rosser v Maritime Services Board of New South Wales (No 2)* (Supreme Court of New South Wales, Young J, Eq Div, No 1624 of 1993, 30 August 1993, unreported).
9 E B Sugden, *Property Law*, 8th ed, W Blackwood & Sons, London, 1869, p 6.
10 (1863) 4 De GJ & S 114; 46 ER 859.

not as I think confined to cases in which the Plaintiffs could recover damages at law'.[11] This has been confirmed by subsequent authority. A century later in *Crabb v Arun District Council (No 2)*[12] Lord Denning MR remarked:

> The power to give compensation or damages in respect of an equitable interest was not limited to where damages could be awarded at law.[13]

The High Court of Australia in *Wentworth v Woollahra Municipal Council*[14] observed that 'it has been said that neither *Lord Cairns' Act* nor its statutory successors gave power to award common law damages as such'.[15] The decision of the House of Lords in *Johnson v Agnew*[16] did not abolish the distinction between equitable damages and common law damages. In *Re Claridge House Ltd; Mount v Tomlinson*[17] Williams J considered that 'the House did not say that therefore damages awarded under *Lord Cairns' Act* were to be treated as common law damages or that there was no distinction between common law damages and equitable damages'.[18] A contrary suggestion has come from Anderson JA in *Ansdell v Crowther*:[19]

> ... the judgments of the House of Lords in *Johnson v Agnew* make it clear that there is no distinction between damages at common law and so-called 'equitable damages'.[20]

There are thus conflicting authorities, and a need for some clarification of the relevant principles.

In *Madden v Kevereski*[21] Helsham CJ in Eq said while commenting upon the New South Wales equivalent of *Lord Cairns' Act*:[22]

> In my view the law in this area is in such a mess that it is time some court gave an authoritative decision about s 68. I take the view that the damages which the court has power to award under s 68 have nothing to do with common law damages. Since the Supreme Court Act, the court sitting in the Equity Division has power to award damages for breach of contract quite independently of s 68.[23]

His Honour added:

> The damages which the court may award under s 68 are *sui generis*; the power to award them is a power to enable the court to do complete justice so far as equity considers it ought to be done, by supplementing with money the equitable remedy, or attempting with money to substitute a remedy.[24]

---

11   (1863) 4 De GJ & S 114 at 128; 46 ER 859 at 865.

12   (1976) 121 SJ 86.

13   (1976) 121 SJ 86.

14   (1982) 149 CLR 672.

15   (1982) 149 CLR 672 at 677.

16   [1980] AC 367, discussed below.

17   (1981) 28 SASR 481.

18   (1981) 28 SASR 481 at 487–8.

19   (1984) 55 BCLR 216; 11 DLR (4th) 614.

20   (1984) 55 BCLR 216 at 221; 11 DLR (4th) 614 at 619.

21   [1983] 1 NSWLR 305.

22   Supreme Court Act 1970 (New South Wales) s 68.

23   [1983] 1 NSWLR 305 at 306–7.

24   [1983] 1 NSWLR 305 at 307, cited by Einfeld J in *Vanmeld Pty Ltd v Cussen* (1994) 121 ALR 619 at 621.

The High Court of Australia has also provided some guidance. In *Wentworth v Woollahra Municipal Council*[25] it was observed that 'damages under s 68 are not common law damages'.[26] In *Chatfield v Jones*[27] Sir Robin Cooke P, in discussing *Lord Cairns' Act*, said: 'The damages recoverable are not limited to such as could have been awarded at common law, but I think that they certainly include common law damages'.[28]

Academic commentators have recognised the distinction between equitable damages and common law damages. Barber wrote: 'that equitable damages are not meant necessarily to take the place of common law damages, but are intended to put the plaintiff into a position equivalent to that which he would have been in if the contract had been specifically performed'.[29] The view that equitable damages may be an attempt to do complete justice by granting total as opposed to reasonable compensation has also been expressed.[30]

A number of important differences exist between common law damages and equitable damages. Equitable damages may be awarded for prospective loss occurring after the date of issue of a writ, and even after judgment.[31] Common law damages are not available if, at the time when a claim for specific performance of a contract was instituted, the plaintiff had not accepted the defendant's repudiation nor put an end to the contract. In contrast, equitable damages which are awarded in substitution for specific performance may be awarded in such a case.[32] Another important distinction is that equitable damages are awarded at the discretion of the court, whereas common law damages are not discretionary and will generally be awarded once damage and other necessary formalities have been proved.[33]

An award of equitable damages, like any other equitable remedy, is subject to equitable considerations. A discretionary bar to a claim for equitable relief will not operate as a bar or defence to a claim for damages at common law.[34] This aspect of *Lord Cairns' Act* was not mentioned by Lord Wilberforce in *Johnson v Agnew*.[35] Spry has commented that 'the

---

25 (1982) 149 CLR 672.
26 (1982) 149 CLR 672 at 678.
27 [1990] 3 NZLR 285.
28 [1990] 3 NZLR 285 at 290.
29 R N Barber, 'The Operation of the Doctrine of Part Performance, in Particular to Actions for Damages', *University of Queensland Law Journal*, vol 8, 1973, 79 at pp 83–4.
30 E Veitch, 'An Equitable Export — *Lord Cairns' Act* in Canada', *Ottawa Law Review*, vol 12, 1980, p 227.
31 See p 122.
32 *Bosaid v Andry* [1963] VR 465 at 484 per Sholl J; *Corpers (No 664) Pty Ltd v NZI Securities Australia Ltd* [1989] ASC 55–714 at 58,419 (Supreme Court of New South Wales, Young J); *Rosser v Maritime Services Board of New South Wales (No 2)* (Supreme Court of New South Wales, Young J, Eq Div, No 1624 of 1993, 30 August 1993, unreported).
33 See Chapter 6.
34 *Williamson v Bors* (1900) 21 LR (NSW) Eq 302 at 309; *Wentworth v Woollahra Municipal Council* (1982) 149 CLR 672 at 679. See also *Legal & General Life of Australia Ltd v A Hudson Pty Ltd* (1985) 1 NSWLR 314 at 336.
35 [1980] AC 367.

observations of Lord Wilberforce can hardly have been intended to exclude equitable considerations in cases where equitable damages are sought'.[36] Gareth Jones postulated that 'if the only claim is under *Lord Cairns' Act*, the courts should retain a large discretion to refuse to award or to reduce the amount'.[37] Thus, any claim for equitable damages is subject to the usual equitable defences such as delay, mistake, acquiescence and unconscionable conduct.

The relevance of an equitable defence to a claim for equitable damages was recognised by the Supreme Court of Canada. In *Elsley v JG Collins Insurance Agencies Ltd*[38] Dickson J remarked:

> The award is still governed, however, by special equitable considerations which would not apply if the plaintiff were seeking damages at law rather than in equity. These considerations might serve, for example, to reduce the amount, due to such factors as delay or acquiescence. In addition, if the parties have agreed on a set amount of damages at law, or a maximum amount, it would be unconscionable, in my opinion, to allow recovery of a greater amount of damages in equity.[39]

If an equitable defence is made out, a court may either reduce equitable relief or deny relief altogether.[40] Damages may be reduced where there has been delay by a plaintiff.[41] The court may deny all relief to a plaintiff who is guilty of unconscionable conduct[42] or to a volunteer.[43]

The conduct of the plaintiff is not the only relevant consideration; the conduct of the defendant is also relevant. If a defendant were guilty of inequitable conduct, a court would be justified in awarding equitable damages without regard to any common law limitations, such as remoteness, so that the plaintiff would receive full compensation for any loss. A court of equity also has an inherent jurisdiction to award punitive damages in an appropriate case.[44]

The distinction between common law relief and equitable relief has survived the introduction of the Judicature system. In *Legal & General Life of Australia Ltd v A Hudson Pty Ltd*[45] McHugh JA stated:

> Furthermore, when a party seeks the assistance of equitable remedies to enforce an agreement to abide by the valuation of a third party, mistake, fraud or collusion can be a defence to the action in certain circumstances: *Collier v Mason; Weekes v Gallard*.[46] But those equitable defences are not

---

36 I C F Spry, *Equitable Remedies*, 4th ed, Law Book Co, Sydney, 1990, p 632.
37 G Jones, *Modern Law Review*, vol 45, 1982, p 240.
38 [1978] 2 SCR 916; 83 DLR (3d) 1.
39 [1978] 2 SCR 916 at 935; 83 DLR (3d) 1 at 13.
40 See Chapter 4.
41 See n 164 below.
42 *Weily v Williams* (1895) 16 LR (NSW) Eq 190 at 196.
43 See p 199.
44 *Tideway Oil Programs Inc v Serio* (1983) 431 So 2d 454. See also J G Arnold, 'Equity Jurisdiction — Punitive Damages — Mississippi Chancery Courts are empowered to award punitive damages', *Mississippi Law Journal*, vol 53, 1983, p 521; P W Michalik, 'The Availability of Compensatory and Exemplary Damages in Equity', *Victoria University of Wellington Law Review*, vol 21, 1991, p 391.
45 (1985) 1 NSWLR 314.
46 (1858) 25 Beav 200; 53 ER 613.

available when the plaintiff seeks a common law remedy. To hold otherwise is to become a victim of "the fusion fallacy" which Messrs Meagher QC, Gummow and Lehane so roundly condemn: *Equity, Doctrines and Remedies*, 2nd ed (1984) at 44–58. Of course, defences of fraud, collusion or mistake may be available when a common law remedy is sought. But that is because the express or implied terms of the contract permit them. The defences of which Sir John Romilly MR spoke in *Collier v Mason* were equitable defences to an equitable remedy. They are not available in a common law action.[47]

This raises for consideration what are the consequences of the introduction of the Judicature system. There are various statements in the cases that the systems of the common law and equity were 'fused', 'merged', or 'mingled' upon the introduction of the Judicature system.[48] However, the Judicature system was introduced on the assumption that both systems (law and equity) would continue. As Baker has observed: 'The Bill which ultimately became the *Judicature Act* of 1873 did not attempt to provide for the absorption of the doctrines of equity into the common law, but contemplated their continued co-existence'.[49] As Sir Anthony Mason has observed:

> ... the *Judicature Acts*, by providing for the administration by the same court of the two bodies of law, naturally encouraged that kind of development and, in particular, convergence of the two bodies of law.[50]

The harmonious development of common law and equitable rules can occur without attributing any substantive effect to the *Judicature Acts*.[51]

The fact that there is a statutory injunction that the rules of equity shall prevail in the event of a conflict between the rules of equity and the rules of common law with reference to the same matter,[52] is evidence that it was intended that the rules of equity and common law would continue as separate systems. Other provisions in the *Judicature Act*, by referring to such terms as 'equitable estate or right or relief', 'legal estate right or title' or 'equitable duties and liabilities', make it quite clear that it was not intended that the rules of equity should be coalesced into the rules of law. Nor was it intended that the distinction between equitable and legal interests would disappear, although in a number of instances there has been a clear departure from the original scheme of the *Judicature Acts*

---

47 (1985) 1 NSWLR 314 at 336.

48 *United Scientific Holdings Ltd v Burnley Borough Council* [1978] AC 904 at 924–7; *Kemp v Lee* (1983) 44 BCLR 172 at 184; *Day v Mead* [1987] 2 NZLR 443; *Attorney-General for the United Kingdom v Wellington Newspapers Ltd* [1988] 1 NZLR 129 at 172.

49 P V Baker, 'The Future of Equity', *Law Quarterly Review*, vol 93, 1977, 529 at p 531. For a comprehensive discussion of fusion: see P H Pettit, *Equity and the Law of Trusts*, 7th ed, Butterworths, London, 1993, pp 7–11.

50 A Mason, 'The Place of Equity and Equitable Remedies in the Contemporary Common Law World', *Law Quarterly Review*, vol 110, 1994, 238 at p 240.

51 J Martin, 'Fusion, Fallacy and Confusion; A Comparative Study', *Conveyancer and Property Lawyer*, 1994, 13 at p 26.

52 *England*: Supreme Court of Judicature Act 1873 (36 & 37 Vict c 66) s 25; Supreme Court of Judicature (Consolidation) Act 1925 (15 & 16 Geo V c 49) s 44; Supreme Court Act 1981 (1981 c 54) s 49.

without any statutory warrant. In *LeMesurier v Andrus*[53] Grange JA said: 'Whatever the original intention of the Legislature, the fusion of law and equity is now real and total'.[54]

It has even been suggested that 'fusion' has now removed the distinction between common law damages and equitable damages. Such a suggestion was recently made by Tipping J in *New Zealand Land Development Co Ltd v Porter*:[55]

> Incidentally there is in my respectful view no longer any value, except for historical purposes, in seeking to distinguish or keep conceptually separate common law damages and damages in equity whether under *Lord Cairns' Act* or otherwise. The Court should award such damages as are a proper and fair reflection of what the plaintiff has lost by reason of the failure of the defendant to perform the contract. It no longer matters whether the damages are called common law or equitable damages. Any residual distinction has now gone and perhaps serves more to confuse than to assist. Let us carry the fusion of law and equity into the area of damages.[56]

7.4 Principles of assessment

The traditional method of assessment of damages where a vendor has failed to complete a contract for the sale of land is to subtract the contract price from the market value of the property at the contractual time for completion.[57] This was established by the Exchequer Chamber in *Engell v Fitch*.[58] In that case the mortgagees of a house with a power of sale had contracted to deliver possession of a piece of land on a particular date, but without having ensured that the mortgagor would give up his possession of the house. Kelly CB remarked that 'the measure of damages is the difference between the contract price and the value at the time when the contract was broken'.[59] This decision has been followed in a line of subsequent cases.[60]

However, as Oliver J observed in *Radford v De Froberville*:[61] 'The older authorities in this area of the law were decided in times of relative financial stability in which the date of assessment made relatively little, if any, difference and the passage of time could be adequately compensated for

---

53 (1986) 54 OR (2d) 1; 25 DLR (4th) 424.
54 (1986) 54 OR (2d) 1 at 9; 25 DLR (4th) 424 at 432.
55 [1992] 2 NZLR 462.
56 [1992] 2 NZLR 462 at 468-9.
57 H McGregor, *McGregor on Damages*, 14th ed, Sweet & Maxwell, London, 1980, p 508. See also *Wenham v Ella* (1972) 127 CLR 454 at 473; *Turner v Superannuation & Mutual Savings Ltd* [1987] 1 NZLR 218 at 226.
58 (1869) LR 4 QB 659.
59 (1869) LR 4 QB 659 at 669.
60 *Hoffman v Cali* [1985] 1 Qd R 253 at 263 per McPherson J.
61 [1977] 1 WLR 1262.

by an award of interest'.[62] This traditional method of assessment is clearly inadequate in times of inflation where property values escalate rapidly. It is also inappropriate where there has been fraud.[63]

Lord Cairns' Act assumed significance after the decision in *Wroth v Tyler*.[64] In that case a purchaser sought specific performance of a contract for the sale of a house which had substantially increased in value between the dates of completion and judgment. The spouse of the vendor had a statutory right not to be evicted.[65] The plaintiff was awarded equitable damages which were assessed as at the date of judgment. This manner of assessment of damages was innovative at the time.[66] Megarry J considered that damages which are awarded in substitution for specific performance should 'constitute a true substitute for specific performance'.[67] His Lordship remarked:

> ... if under *Lord Cairns' Act* damages are awarded in substitution for specific performance, the court has jurisdiction to award such damages as will put the plaintiffs into as good a position as if the contract had been performed, even if to do so means awarding damages assessed by reference to a period subsequent to the date of the breach. This seems to me to be consonant with the nature of specific performance which is a continuing remedy, designed to secure (inter alia) that the purchaser receives in fact what is his in equity as soon as the contract is made, subject to the vendor's right to the money, and so on.[68]

Megarry J relied upon decisions recognising that damages awarded under *Lord Cairns' Act* are awarded on a different basis to that of common law damages.[69]

The decision in *Wroth v Tyler*[70] illustrates an important principle. Equitable damages which are awarded in substitution for an injunction or specific performance should be a true substitute for specific relief. A similar approach was taken in the nineteenth century. In *Dreyfus v Peruvian Guano Co*[71] Fry LJ commented:

---

62 [1977] 1 WLR 1262 at 1286.
63 In an action for deceit, damages are not limited to the difference between the purchase price and the actual value of land. A plaintiff in such an action is entitled to be compensated for all losses suffered or expenses incurred as a result of being misled by the deceit of the defendant: see *Doyle v Olby (Ironmongers) Ltd* [1969] 2 QB 158.
64 [1974] Ch 30.
65 Matrimonial Homes Act 1967 (1967 c 75); compare Wife's Protection Act RSBC 1960 c 407 (British Columbia); *AVG Management Ltd v Barwell Development Ltd* [1976] 6 WWR 289; (1976) 69 DLR (3d) 741.
66 There were earlier precedents on *Lord Cairns' Act* for this method of assessment: see *Horsnail v Shute* [1921] 3 WWR 270; 62 DLR 199; *Bosaid v Andry* [1963] VR 465.
67 [1974] Ch 30 at 58.
68 [1974] Ch 30 at 60.
69 *Fritz v Hobson* (1880) 14 Ch D 542 at 556–7; *Dreyfus v Peruvian Guano Co* (1889) 43 Ch D 316 at 342; *Leeds Industrial Co-operative Society Ltd v Slack* [1924] AC 851 at 859–60, 865.
70 [1974] Ch 30.
71 (1889) 43 Ch D 316.

... it often enables the Court, where a wrong has been done, to give damages upon a different scale from what was done by the Courts of Common Law, because it may give them in substitution for an injunction.[72]

In *Leeds Industrial Co-operative Society Ltd v Slack*[73] Viscount Finlay remarked:

... the power to give damages in lieu of an injunction must in all reason import the power to give an equivalent for what is lost by the refusal of the injunction.[74]

In *Johnson v Agnew*[75] Lord Wilberforce took the view that *Lord Cairns' Act* enabled the Court of Chancery to exercise the same power as a court of law in awarding damages, although his Lordship mentioned instances where the jurisdiction could be invoked where damages were not available at law.[76] His Lordship said:

But apart from these, and similar cases where damages could not be claimed at all at common law, there is sound authority for the proposition that the Act did not provide for the assessment of damages on any new basis.[77]

Placing reliance upon statements in cases such as *Ferguson v Wilson*,[78] and *Rock Portland Cement Co Ltd v Wilson*,[79] Lord Wilberforce concluded:

On the balance of these authorities and also on principle, I find in the Act no warrant for the court awarding damages differently from common law damages.[80]

Hence, as a consequence of the decision in *Johnson v Agnew*,[81] it is generally accepted that the assessment of damages will be governed by the same principles whether damages are awarded at law or under *Lord Cairns' Act* in equity.[82] It is however submitted that the reasoning in this case is unsatisfactory. Either a statute is or is not a procedural statute. It is submitted that there is some difficulty in *Lord Cairns' Act* being a

---

72 (1889) 43 Ch D 316 at 342.

73 [1924] AC 851.

74 [1924] AC 851 at 859.

75 [1980] AC 367.

76 Eg damages in lieu of a *quia timet* injunction, and damages for the breach of a restrictive covenant to which a plaintiff was not a party.

77 [1980] AC 367 at 400.

78 (1866) LR 2 Ch App 77 at 88 ('The object, therefore, of that Act of Parliament was to prevent parties from being so sent from one Court to the other.')

79 (1882) 52 LJ Ch 214 at 216; 31 WR 193 at 194 ('It does not seem to me that *Lord Cairns' Act* was intended to manufacture a new right to damages which a man had not before; but that it was intended, as I have said, to prevent the mischief of his having to work out his rights by another action in another Court.')

80 [1980] AC 367 at 400.

81 [1980] AC 367.

82 G H Treitel, *The Law of Contract*, 7th ed, Stevens, Sweet & Maxwell, London, 1987, p 806; *Chitty on Contracts*, vol I, 25th ed, Law Book Co, Sydney, 1983, p 1009.

procedural statute in the case of a breach of contract, but not being a procedural statute in the case of a *quia timet* injunction, a restrictive covenant to which a plaintiff was not a party, or part performance.

As *Lord Cairns' Act* enables equitable damages to be awarded in substitution for an injunction, the statute clearly envisages the assessment of damages by a method quite different from that applied in the common law.[83] It is submitted that the cases cited by Lord Wilberforce are unsatisfactory authorities. In *Ferguson v Wilson*[84] and *Rock Portland Cement Co Ltd v Wilson*[85] it was assumed that *Lord Cairns' Act* was a procedural statute. One case which was not mentioned was *Dreyfus v Peruvian Guano Co*[86] in which it was recognised that damages in substitution for an injunction are awarded 'upon a different scale from what was done by the Courts of Common Law'.[87] Nor did Lord Wilberforce consider the cases on part performance. No other Law Lord delivered judgment. It appears that Lord Wilberforce insisted on a single judgment being given in this case.[88]

The decision in *Johnson v Agnew*[89] may perhaps be explained on policy grounds that the mode of recovery should not advantage a litigant.[90] Gareth Jones has remarked that: '[i]t is proper to measure damages in the same way if the same set of facts gives rise to a claim for damages both at law and in equity'.[91] Similar views may be found in numerous judgments. In *Jegon v Vivian*[92] Lord Hatherley LC observed: 'I do not feel called upon to give, in the nature of damages, that which in accordance with the decisions would apparently not have been given at law by way of damages'.[93] In *Souster v Epsom Plumbing Contractors Ltd*[94] a purchaser limited his claim to damages where the vendor had resold. McMullin J commented:

> There is much to be said in such cases for the measure of damages at common law to be the same as would be made under *Lord Cairns' Act*.[95]

In *306793 Ontario Ltd in Trust v Rimes*[96] Mackinnon ACJO expressed the view that 'equating the measure of damages at common law and equity, subject to the exceptions noted by Lord Wilberforce, is an eminently sensible and rational approach and I adopt it'.[97] Similarly, in

---

83 M Evans, *Outline of Equity and Trusts*, 2nd ed, Butterworths, Sydney, 1993, p 433.

84 (1866) LR 2 Ch App 77.

85 (1882) 52 LJ Ch 214; 31 WR 193.

86 (1889) 43 Ch D 316.

87 (1889) 43 Ch D 316 at 342.

88 A Paterson, *The Law Lords*, Macmillan, England, 1983, p 186, n h.

89 [1980] AC 367.

90 H A J Ford and W A Lee, *Principles of the Law of Trusts*, 2nd ed, Law Book Co, Sydney, 1990, p 144.

91 *Modern Law Review*, vol 45, 1982, p 240.

92 (1871) LR 6 Ch App 742.

93 (1871) LR 6 Ch App 742 at 762.

94 [1974] 2 NZLR 515.

95 [1974] 2 NZLR 515 at 522.

96 (1979) 25 OR (2d) 79; 100 DLR (3d) 350. See also *EJH Holdings Ltd v Bougie* (1977) 3 Alta LR (2d) 244.

97 (1979) 25 OR (2d) 79 at 83; 100 DLR (3d) 350 at 354.

ASA Constructions Pty Ltd v Iwanov[98] Needham J considered that a court 'should not adopt a different standard, if the breach of the contract which caused the institution of proceedings for specific performance was a breach which would have sounded in damages at common law'.[99]

Despite such statements, it should be appreciated that a court is not obliged to award equitable damages on the same basis as common law damages. *Lord Cairns' Act* contained no direction requiring the Court of Chancery to award damages on the same basis as the common law courts at Westminster. Where equitable damages are assessed on the same basis as common law damages, this is not because of any statutory obligation, but because the court regards such a result as just and equitable. This was recognised in *JG Collins Insurance Agencies Ltd v Elsley*[100] by Dickson J:

> This is so not because the Court is obliged to apply analogous legal criteria, but because the amount of compensation which would satisfy the loss suffered, and which the Court considers it just and equitable be paid, usually happens to be equivalent to the amount of legal damages which would be appropriate.[101]

It should be appreciated that in *Johnson v Agnew*[102] counsel for both the appellant[103] and respondent[104] made submissions that *Lord Cairns' Act* did not enable damages to be assessed on a different basis from common law damages. Thus alternative arguments were not ventilated. There was consequently no reason why the issue of whether *Lord Cairns' Act* enabled damages to be assessed on a different basis to common law damages had to be determined. As McGregor has mentioned: 'Resort to *Lord Cairns' Act* was unnecessary'.[105] In all strictness, the remarks of Lord Wilberforce, who delivered the judgment of the court, were obiter. Once it was clear that common law damages were available, there was no reason for claiming equitable damages. It is submitted that it was open on the pleadings, without any amendment, to award the plaintiffs common law damages. The statement of claim of the plaintiffs included a claim for 'damages for breach of contract in lieu of or in addition to specific performance'.[106] This was not a conventional prayer for equitable damages, but was appropriate to encompass a claim for common law damages for breach of contract. In any event the pleadings may have been amended to make such a claim.

It might also be mentioned that Lord Wilberforce stated that in *Wroth v Tyler*[107] Megarry J placed reliance upon the words 'in lieu of specific

---

98   [1975] 1 NSWLR 512.
99   [1975] 1 NSWLR 512 at 516–17.
100 [1978] 2 SCR 916; (1978) 83 DLR (3d) 1.
101 [1978] 2 SCR 916 at 935; (1978) 83 DLR (3d) 1 at 13.
102 [1980] AC 367.
103 [1980] AC 367 at 379 per J H Hames QC ('Till 1974 there is no authority to suggest that damages under *Lord Cairns' Act* should be assessed otherwise than in the same manner as common law damages').
104 [1980] AC 367 at 387 per P J Millett QC ('As to the measure of damages, it is the same both at common law and under *Lord Cairns' Act*').
105 H McGregor, *McGregor on Damages*, 15th ed, Sweet & Maxwell, London, 1988, p 590.
106 [1978] Ch 176 at 179.
107 [1974] Ch 30.

performance'.[108] However, in *Wroth v Tyler*[109] Megarry J had not used those words. Instead his Lordship had mentioned that *Lord Cairns' Act* enabled damages to be awarded 'in substitution for specific performance'.[110] The words 'in lieu of specific performance', which while commonly found in a prayer for equitable damages, do not suggest an award of damages which are a true substitute for specific performance.

Despite the observations of Lord Wilberforce in *Johnson v Agnew*,[111] there will be cases where both remedies are available but where common law damages and equitable damages will not be assessed on the same basis. This has been recognised in a number of cases.

In *Wenham v Ella*[112] specific performance of an agreement to procure the transfer of a part interest in an income-yielding property was not possible because by the date of the commencement of the action the third party had disposed of all its shares in the property. Barwick CJ observed:

> However, by the date of hearing of the action, specific performance could not have been ordered. The remedy of the respondent then was damages for breach of the promise to cause delivery of the transfer of the described interest in land at the agreed time. There is no need to discuss whether the inability in the circumstances to order specific performance deprived the court of equitable jurisdiction to order damages in lieu of specific performance because the measure of damages which could be awarded at common law for breach of contract between these parties is, in my opinion, the same as a court of equity would employ in this case in ordering damages in lieu of specific performance. In some circumstances, damages in the latter case may exceed those which would be awarded at law: but circumstances which might justify a larger amount of damages in lieu of specific performance than would be given at law are not present in this case.[113]

The Chief Justice, who had extensive experience at the equity bar of New South Wales, obviously considered that there were circumstances in which a plaintiff might be awarded damages in equity which would exceed an award of common law damages to which the plaintiff was entitled.

In *Surrey County Council v Bredero Homes Ltd*[114] two municipal councils each owned adjoining parcels of land. Each council subsequently transferred its land to a developer. Each transfer contained a covenant by the developer to commence a specified scheme of development within six months of the date of the transfer. The developer completed the development, although not in accordance with the covenants in the transfers. The developer built more houses than were specified in the covenants, and then sold the developed land. Neither council at any time sought injunctive relief to compel the developer to develop the estate in accordance with the covenants, however they sought to recover common law damages for breach of the covenants. Such damages are assessed in

---

108   See [1980] AC 367 at 400.
109   [1974] Ch 30.
110   [1974] Ch 30 at 60 (quoted earlier at p 107).
111   [1980] AC 367.
112   (1972) 127 CLR 454.
113   *Wenham v Ella* (1972) 127 CLR 454 at 460.
114   [1992] 3 All ER 302.

accordance with the ordinary principles for breach of contract, as set out in *Robinson v Harman*.[115] Thus a party is to be placed in the same position, as far as money can do it, as if the contract had been performed. However, an obstacle to a substantial award of damages was that neither council had suffered any actual loss which flowed from the breach of covenants. In assessing common law damages the court is concerned with a plaintiff's loss and not with a defendant's profit. It has been pointed out that the plaintiffs were, in effect, seeking substantial damages for the breach of a contract that had never been made, namely, a contract which provided for a cash payment if the defendant built more than the specified number of houses.[116] Had the contract contained an express provision which required the developer to account for the profits of the breach, the plaintiff could have recovered those profits.[117]

At first instance the plaintiffs were given judgment for nominal damages. Ferris J ruled that 'substantial, as distinct from nominal, damages are not recoverable by the plaintiffs at common law'.[118] This ruling was undoubtedly correct, but Ferris J realised that it was quite unsatisfactory 'as the plaintiffs will receive no compensation and the defendant will be left in undisturbed possession of the fruits of its wrongdoing'.[119] While the original statement of claim disclosed a claim for damages for breach of the covenants, the plaintiffs were given leave to amend their prayer for relief by adding a claim for an injunction; and to amend the simple claim for damages so that it became a claim for 'damages at common law or alternatively in equity'. The purpose of the amendment was not to pursue the claim for mandatory relief, but merely in case it was necessary to advance a claim for equitable damages under s 50 of the Supreme Court Act 1981.[120] It was held that as there was no case for an injunction or specific performance at the date of issue of the writ, there was no jurisdiction to award equitable damages under s 50 of the Supreme Court Act 1981. Ferris J commented:

> In the present case, as I have already said, Bredero had disposed of all the houses on the estate before the writ in this action was issued. Bredero could not, therefore, comply with a mandatory injunction requiring the estate to be redeveloped in accordance with planning permission 1214 even if the court would otherwise have been prepared to grant an injunction ... In truth, therefore, there never was a case for an injunction or specific performance at the date of the writ or probably for a substantial period of time before that.[121]

---

115 (1848) 1 Ex 850; 154 ER 363.
116 T Ingham, 'Damages in Equity — A Step in the Wrong Direction', *Conveyancer and Property Lawyer*, 1994, 110 at p 111.
117 P Birks, 'Profits of Breach of Contract', *Law Quarterly Review*, vol 109, 1993, p 518.
118 [1992] 3 All ER 302 at 315.
119 [1992] 3 All ER 302 at 316.
120 It is submitted that equitable damages may be awarded where the statement of claim does not disclose a prayer for equitable damages or equitable relief providing that the facts as pleaded disclose an equity to such relief: see pp 209, 211.
121 [1992] 3 All ER 302 at 316.

It was clear that had the councils in the *Surrey County Council* case commenced proceedings for an injunction before the developer had sold the land, then equitable damages would have been awarded on the principle of *Wrotham Park Estate Co Ltd v Parkside Homes Ltd.*[122] The assessment of equitable damages would be based upon a hypothetical price for the relaxation of a covenant which reflected a small percentage of anticipated profit from a development. Ferris J remarked:

> Had relief by way of injunction still been available, as it was in the *Wrotham Park* case, I am practically certain that I would have refused injunctive relief. But I am equally certain that I would have followed the course taken in the *Wrotham Park* case and directed an inquiry as to damages on the basis that they should be the amount which the two councils might reasonably have charged for a variation of the covenants.[123]

The decision of Ferris J exposed an instance where the remedies of common law damages and equitable damages will not be assessed on the same basis. Ferris J did not regard the observations by Lord Wilberforce in *Johnson v Agnew*[124] as overruling the decision in *Wrotham Park Estate Co Ltd v Parkside Homes Ltd.*[125] As Ferris J had observed:

> In my view *Wrotham Park* was a decision on the award of damages under *Lord Cairns' Act* and nothing else and has not been transmuted into a decision on common law damages by virtue of the observations of Lord Wilberforce in *Johnson v Agnew.*[126]

The decision of Ferris J in the *Surrey County Council* case has been criticised by some scholars essentially on the ground that the decision is irreconcilable with the decision of the House of Lords in *Johnson v Agnew.*[127] This criticism of the *Surrey County Council* case is based upon the assumption that the decision in *Johnson v Agnew*[128] is binding authority for the proposition that equitable and common law damages should be assessed in the same way where both remedies are available. However, earlier in this chapter it has been submitted that in *Johnson v Agnew*[129] it was not necessary to make any observations about *Lord Cairns' Act* as common law damages were available in that case. It is also submitted that *Lord Cairns' Act* was not a procedural statute. In any event one comes back to the fundamental principle that common law damages are only awarded for the actual loss sustained by a plaintiff.

It is accordingly submitted that the decision of Ferris J was correct in awarding the plaintiffs only nominal damages. If any remedy was available to the plaintiffs in the *Surrey County Council* case it could only have been of a restitutionary character as contractual remedies are inadequate if a

---

122 [1974] 1 WLR 798; 27 P & CR 296, discussed later in this chapter.
123 [1992] 3 All ER 302 at 316.
124 [1980] AC 367.
125 [1974] 1 WLR 798; 27 P & CR 296, discussed later in this chapter.
126 [1992] 3 All ER 302 at 314.
127 R Goff and G Jones, *The Law of Restitution*, 4th ed, Sweet & Maxwell, 1993, p 60, n 415; A Burrows, *The Law of Restitution*, Butterworths, London, 1993, p 400.
128 [1980] AC 367.
129 [1980] AC 367.

defendant can evade a 'carefully constructed contractual bargain'.[130]

The decision of Ferris J was affirmed by the Court of Appeal which held that an award of nominal damages was the appropriate common law damages award for a breach of contract which had occasioned no actual loss to a plaintiff.[131] In this case the plaintiffs conceded that they had not suffered any loss. Dillon LJ remarked that 'the established basis of an award of damages in contract is compensation for the plaintiff's loss'.[132] His Lordship referred to the statement in *Chitty*:

> Damages for a breach of contract committed by the defendant are a compensation to the plaintiff for the damage, loss or injury he has suffered through that breach.[133]

Dillon LJ observed:

> The plaintiffs have merely sought damages which have been described as 'damages at common law', as opposed to damages in equity under the Chancery Amendment Act 1858. They accepted that they have not suffered any damage at all of the nature of damage to adjoining property owned or occupied by them.[134]

The *Surrey County Council* case can be sharply distinguished from the *Wrotham Park* case in which the court possessed jurisdiction under *Lord Cairns' Act*. Nevertheless the members of the Court of Appeal in the *Surrey County Council* case made some observations about the *Wrotham Park* case. Dillon LJ remarked that the *Wrotham Park* case was decided 'under *Lord Cairns' Act* and stands or falls by that; whereas, the present case is not, and makes no pretence of being, under that Act'.[135] His Lordship also recognised that the decision of Brightman J in the *Wrotham Park* case 'involves a conclusion by the judge that *Lord Cairns' Act* effected a substantive change in the law of damages and was not a merely procedural statute as *Johnson v Agnew* has held'.[136] Steyn LJ and Rose LJ regarded the *Wrotham Park* case as being correctly decided, although for different reasons. Steyn LJ regarded the *Wrotham Park* as 'only defensible' on a 'restitutionary principle',[137] whereas Rose LJ stated that 'Brightman J correctly answered the particular question which confronted him'.[138] In *Wrotham Park Settled Estates v Hertsmere Borough Council*[139] Sir Thomas Bingham MR in discussing the *Wrotham Park* case expressed the view that 'the ratio of the case may well be open to serious question and deserves consideration in a suitable case'.[140] It is submitted that the *Wrotham Park* case was correctly decided as the

---

130 R O'Dair, 'Damages for Breach of Contract: A Wrong Turn', *Restitution Law Review*, 1993, 31 at p 41.
131 *Surrey County Council v Bredero Homes Ltd* [1993] 1 WLR 1361.
132 [1993] 1 WLR 1361 at 1367.
133 *Chitty on Contracts*, vol 1, 26th ed, Sweet & Maxwell, 1989, p 1116 cited at [1993] 1 WLR 1361 at 1364.
134 [1993] 1 WLR 1361 at 1364.
135 [1993] 1 WLR 1361 at 1364.
136 [1993] 1 WLR 1361 at 1367.
137 [1993] 1 WLR 1361 at 1369.
138 [1993] 1 WLR 1361 at 1371.
139 [1993] 2 EGLR 15.
140 [1993] 2 EGLR 15 at 18.

damages were assessed on the basis of what the plaintiff could reasonably demand of the defendant as the price of releasing the restrictive covenant.[141]

In *Dyer v Barnard*[142] the defendant sold a boat to the plaintiff but also later sold it to a third party. The plaintiff's claim to specific performance was abandoned because of the equities which had been acquired by the third party, and the plaintiff was content to claim damages. Damages were assessed at the difference between the market value and the sale price, together with a sum for loss of use of the boat. Stuart-Smith LJ considered that this assessment of damages was justifiable:

> ... on the basis of *Lord Cairns' Act* where the court is empowered to grant damages in lieu of specific performance, and it seems to me that a different measure of damages may apply in those circumstances from that which is applicable at common law for damages for breach of contract.

In this case whilst *Lord Cairns' Act* provided a convenient jurisdictional basis for an award of damages, other members of the Court of Appeal had not agreed with this aspect of the judgment. The award of damages for loss of use of the boat would in any event be justifiable at common law, as it would be a foreseeable loss which flows from a breach of contract.

The House of Lords in *Johnson v Agnew*[143] also emphasised the compensatory function of damages. Lord Wilberforce said:

> The general principle for the assessment of damages is compensatory, ie, that the innocent party is to be placed, so far as money can do so, in the same position as if the contract had been performed.[144]

This general principle was a restatement of existing principle.[145] Lord Wilberforce remarked that damages for the breach of a contract of sale are normally assessed as at the date of breach,[146] but this was not an absolute rule as 'the court has power to fix such other date as may be appropriate in the circumstances'.[147] It might be mentioned that in *Wroth v Tyler*,[148] and later in *Horsler v Zorro*,[149] Megarry J recognised that the common law rule that damages be assessed as at the date of breach was not an inflexible rule. There was a relevant precedent where a plaintiff had sought specific restitution of a chattel by an action in detinue. In *General and Finance Facilities Ltd v Cooks Cars (Romford) Ltd*[150] Diplock LJ had explained that a plaintiff had always been entitled to claim the value of the chattel assessed as at the date

---

141 J A Jolowicz, 'Damages in Equity — A Study of *Lord Cairns' Act*', *Cambridge Law Journal*, 1975, 224 at p 237; G Jones, 'The Recovery of Benefits Gained from a Breach of Contract', *Law Quarterly Review*, vol 99, 1983, 443 at p 450. See also *Tito v Waddell (No 2)* [1977] Ch 106 at 335–6 per Sir Robert Megarry VC.

142 Court of Appeal, Civil Division, Lord Donaldson MR, Stuart-Smith LJ, 16 April 1991, unreported.

143 [1980] AC 367.

144 [1980] AC 367 at 400.

145 *Robinson v Harman* (1848) 1 Ex 850 at 855; 154 ER 363 at 365; *Wertheim v Chicoutimi Pulp Co* [1911] AC 301 at 307 (PC).

146 Sale of Goods Act 1893 s 51.

147 [1980] AC 367 at 401.

148 [1974] Ch 30 at 57.

149 [1975] Ch 302 at 316.

150 [1963] 1 WLR 644 at 648–9. See also *Malhotra v Choudhury* [1980] Ch 52 at 79.

of judgment. This method of assessment is analogous to where the court awards equitable damages in substitution for specific performance, and where such damages are assessed as at the date of judgment.

Lord Wilberforce considered that where an innocent party reasonably seeks the completion of a contract it would be just 'to assess damages as at the date when (otherwise than by his default) the contract is lost'.[151] His Lordship stated that 'the date on which that remedy [of specific performance] became aborted (not by the vendor's fault) should logically be fixed as the date on which damages should be assessed'.[152] In the particular case the mortgagees contracted to sell a portion of the property thereby rendering the decree for specific performance abortive. Lord Wilberforce relied upon common law decisions.[153] His Lordship also relied upon s 2 of *Lord Cairns' Act* enabling damages to be awarded 'in substitution for ... specific performance'. This was a case where the value of the property had declined after the breach had occurred. There are a number of similar cases where a vendor has sought the dissolution of an order for specific performance and damages in a falling market.[154]

This principle enunciated by Lord Wilberforce was applied in *Madden v Kevereski*[155] where a purchaser was awarded equitable damages, specific performance being denied because of hardship. It was held that the Master should assess damages as at the date of the judgment in which specific performance was refused. Helsham CJ in Eq observed that 'the contract was lost as at the date of my judgment'.[156] Similarly, in *Bosaid v Andry*[157] it was recognised that equitable damages could be assessed as at a date later than the date of breach. Sholl J concluded that the relevant date for assessing equitable damages under the then Victorian equivalent of *Lord Cairns' Act* was when 'the contract came to an end by the act of the Court itself in withholding specific performance'.[158]

---

151 [1980] AC 367 at 401. For difficulties in applying this formulation: see R P Meagher, W M C Gummow and J R F Lehane, *Equity — Doctrines and Remedies*, 2nd ed, Butterworths, Sydney, 1984, p 614 [2313].

152 [1980] AC 367 at 401.

153 *Ogle v Vane, Earl* (1867) LR 2 QB 275; (1868) LR 3 QB 272 (date when innocent party acting reasonably went into the market); *Hickman v Haynes* (1875) LR 10 CP 598 (at a reasonable time after the last request of buyers to withhold delivery); *Radford v De Froberville* [1977] 1 WLR 1262 (where defendant had covenanted to build a wall, damages were held measurable at the date of hearing unless the plaintiff ought reasonably to have mitigated his damage earlier).

154 In *Gaspari v Creighton Holdings Ltd* (1984) 13 DLR (4th) 570 at 582; 52 BCLR 30 Bouck J held that the relevant date, for the purposes of assessment, was when the purchaser first refused to obey the order which on that date 'became aborted'. In *New Horizon Investments Ltd v Montroyal Estates Ltd* (1982) 26 RPR 268 the vendor breached the contract for sale on a rising market, and the market subsequently fell. Nemetz CJBC held that damages were to be assessed taking into account both the chance that the plaintiff would have had to have sold some lots, and the subsequent fall. Matters that were considered included the intention of the plaintiff to proceed to resell quickly, the likelihood of defaults and of there being unsold lots after the market had fallen.

155 [1983] 1 NSWLR 305.

156 [1983] 1 NSWLR 305 at 306.

157 [1963] VR 465.

158 [1963] VR 465 at 484.

In a number of cases equitable damages that have been awarded to a purchaser have been assessed as at the date of judgment.[159] In some cases there has been a rejection of any attempt to postpone the relevant date to when damages would actually be assessed.[160] Equitable damages, like common law damages, may be assessed as at any date in order to do justice in the circumstances of a particular case.[161] For instance, where property was sold which was subject to mortgages exceeding the purchase price, damages were assessed as at the date appointed by the court for the discharge of the mortgages.[162]

The assessment of equitable damages is linked with the availability of specific performance. Where a purchaser has a basis for commencing proceedings for specific performance and later abandons a claim, equitable damages may be assessed as at the date of abandonment of the claim.[163] Where a purchaser without justification delays in seeking specific performance, damages (equitable or common law) may be assessed as at a date prior to judgment, reflecting the inexcusable delay.[164] Where there is delay in commencing and prosecuting an action, a court may be disposed to make an assessment of equitable damages as at the date of breach.[165] Where a court declines to order specific performance because to do so would result in hardship and the plaintiff is without fault, it may be appropriate that an award of equitable damages be assessed as at the date that the court declines specific performance.[166]

Ordinarily a vendor will be awarded damages assessed as at the date of breach, though a court may select another date for assessment to do justice between the parties.[167] In *Johnson v Perez*[168] Mason CJ confirmed that:

---

159 *Bosaid v Andry* [1963] VR 465 at 490; *Wroth v Tyler* [1974] Ch 30; *Souster v Epsom Plumbing Contractors Ltd* [1974] 2 NZLR 515 at 521; *Metropolitan Trust Co v Pressure Concrete Services Ltd* (1975) 9 OR (2d) 375 at 651; 60 DLR (3d) 431; *Hechter v Thurston* [1978] 1 WWR 695; (1977) 80 DLR (3d) 685; *306793 Ontario Ltd in Trust v Rimes* (1979) 25 OR (2d) 79 at 84; 100 DLR (3d) 350 at 355; *O'Connor v McCarthy* [1982] 1 ILRM 201 at 203; *Madden v Kevereski* [1983] 1 NSWLR 305; *Kemp v Lee* (1983) 44 BCLR 172; 28 RPR 141; *Kopec v Pyret* [1987] 3 WWR 449; (1987) 36 DLR (4th) 1. See also *Stewart v Ambrosino* (1975) 63 DLR (3d) 595 at 607.

160 *Hechter v Thurston* (1977) 80 DLR (3d) 685 at 690; *Madden v Kevereski* [1983] 1 NSWLR 305 at 306 (value of property decreased after judgment and prior to actual assessment).

161 *Horsler v Zorro* [1975] Ch 302; *Kemp v Lee* (1983) 44 BCLR 172; 20 RPR 141.

162 *Grant v Dawkins* [1973] 1 WLR 1406 at 1411.

163 *Horsnail v Shute* [1921] 3 WWR 270; 62 DLR 199; *Domb v Isoz* [1980] Ch 548 at 559–60; *The Millstream Pty Ltd v Schultz* [1980] 1 NSWLR 547 at 555–6; *Emeness Pty Ltd v Rigg* [1984] 1 Qd R 172 at 177.

164 *Hickey v Bruhns* [1977] 2 NZLR 71 at 79; *Asamera Oil Corp Ltd v Sea Oil & General Corp* [1979] 1 SCR 633 at 667–8; [1978] 6 WWR 301 at 328; 89 DLR (3d) 1 at 25; *Malhotra v Choudhury* [1980] Ch 52 at 81; *Cominos v Rekes* (Supreme Court of New South Wales, Cohen J, Eq Div, No 2065 of 1977, 27 March 1984, unreported), noted [1984] ACLD 555; *New Zealand Land Development Co Ltd v Porter* [1992] 2 NZLR 462.

165 Compare *Zalaudek v De Boer* (1981) 33 BCLR 57.

166 *Cominos v Rekes* (Supreme Court of New South Wales, Cohen J, Eq Div, No 2065 of 1977, 27 March 1984, unreported), noted [1984] ACLD 555.

167 H McGregor, *McGregor on Damages*, 15th ed, Sweet & Maxwell, London, 1988, p 575; *Johnson v Agnew* [1980] AC 367 at 400; *New Horizon Investments Ltd v Montroyal Estates Ltd* (1982) 26 RPR 268.

168 (1989) 166 CLR 351.

The general rule that damages are assessed as at the date of breach or when the cause of action arose has been applied more uniformly in contract than in tort and for good reason. But even in contract cases courts depart from the general rule whenever it is necessary to do so in the interests of justice.[169]

There are instances where a vendor who has sought specific performance has been awarded equitable damages assessed as at the date of judgment.[170] However, this approach was disapproved by the Court of Appeal of British Columbia in *Ansdell v Crowther*.[171] It was held that only in exceptional circumstances should a vendor be able to obtain an assessment of damages as at the date of judgment. The court rejected a submission that the measure of damages in an action for specific performance is always the difference between the contract price and the market value as at the date of trial. Anderson JA stated:

> ... there ... is no fixed rule as to the date when damages ought to be assessed and, in order to do justice, the courts are empowered to fix damages as of the date found to be appropriate in the circumstances.[172]

The court held that damages would be assessed as at the date a sale would have occurred if the property had continued to be listed for sale.[173]

The view has been expressed that there is no justification for allowing a vendor to speculate at the purchaser's expense by maintaining an action for specific performance should property values decline, but later abandoning the action if prices increase.[174] However the vendor has a duty to take reasonable steps to mitigate damage, such as relisting the property for sale.[175]

It seems clear then, that in an action between a vendor and purchaser, special circumstances must exist before damages would be assessed as at the date of judgment. Such circumstances may include the inability of a purchaser to make an equivalent purchase because the vendor has retained the deposit[176] and where a purchaser is duly prosecuting a claim for specific performance.[177] There is authority that a purchaser who has agreed to purchase land as a speculative investment would not be granted specific performance as damages would be an adequate remedy.[178] Damages would be assessed as at the date of breach.[179]

---

169 (1989) 166 CLR 351 at 356.
170 *Simpson v Kondra* (1982) 42 BCLR 13 at 21–2; *Fraser Valley Little Search Ltd v Gallagher* (1983) 45 BCLR 381 at 385–7.
171 (1984) 55 BCLR 216; 11 DLR (4th) 614.
172 (1984) 55 BCLR 216 at 221; 11 DLR (4th) 614 at 619.
173 See also *Shuper v Noble* (1982) 38 OR (2d) 64 (damages in a vendor action assessed as at six months after breach at time of resale).
174 B J Reiter and R J Sharpe, '*Wroth v Tyler*: Must Equity Remedy Contract Damages', *Canadian Business Law Journal*, vol 3, 1979, 146 at p 155.
175 *Shuper v Noble* (1982) 38 OR (2d) 64 at 69.
176 Compare *Wroth v Tyler* [1974] Ch 30; *Madden v Kevereski* [1983] 1 NSWLR 305.
177 *Radford v De Froberville* [1977] 1 WLR 1262 at 1285–6. See also H McGregor, *McGregor on Damages*, 15th ed, Sweet & Maxwell, London, 1988, p 578; G H Treitel, *The Law of Contract*, 7th ed, Stevens, Sweet & Maxwell, London, 1987, p 741, n 7.
178 See p 51.
179 *ASA Constructions Pty Ltd v Iwanov* [1975] 1 NSWLR 512 at 519; *AVG Management Science Ltd v Barwell Developments Ltd* [1976] 6 WWR 289 at 302; 69 DLR (3d) 741 at 753; affirmed *AVG Management Science Ltd v Barwell Developments Ltd* [1979] 2 SCR 43 at 62.

The decision of the House of Lords in *Johnson v Agnew*[180] did not affect the duty of an innocent party to act reasonably to mitigate against loss. The victim of a breach of contract cannot cut short this duty by merely commencing an action for specific performance or damages.[181] If a purchaser could have purchased an equivalent property after the vendor's breach then he would need to show good reason why he did not do so before prices escalated in value.[182] Mitigation is obviously not an issue where there was no comparable property for sale at the date of the breach or before the market changed adversely.[183]

The claim of a plaintiff to be relieved from the obligation to mitigate is directly linked to the strength of the plaintiff's case for specific performance.[184] A purchaser with no reasonable prospect in an action for specific performance would be under a duty to mitigate where that was possible.[185] Damages would be assessed as if the plaintiff had exercised a suitable avenue for mitigation.[186] It has been argued that the remedy of equitable damages should not be available where a commercial purchaser is able to mitigate loss, and has no special interest requiring equitable protection.[187]

Legislation may be relevant in some jurisdictions because a statute may prescribe a method of assessment of damages. Lord Wilberforce's formulation in *Johnson v Agnew*[188] differs from that in s 68 of the Property Law Act 1974 of Queensland. This provision is based upon the second rule in *Hadley v Baxendale*.[189] Section 68(1) provides that a vendor who in breach of contract fails to perform a contract for the sale of land is liable in damages 'for the loss sustained by the purchaser in such sum as at the time the contract was made was reasonably foreseeable as the loss liable to result, and which does in fact result, from the failure of the vendor to perform the contract'.[190] Where there is such a statutory limitation on the award of common law damages, it may be advantageous for a plaintiff to claim equitable damages so as to receive proper compensation for any loss.

If a court decides to award equitable damages it is not necessary for it to have regard to common law considerations such as foreseeability and remoteness. These considerations do not limit a court of equity,

---

180 [1980] AC 367.
181 *Asamera Oil Corp Ltd v Sea Oil & General Corp* [1979] 1 SCR 633 at 667–8. See also *Techno Land Improvements Ltd v British Leyland (UK) Ltd* (1979) 252 EG 805 at 809.
182 H McGregor, *McGregor on Damages*, 15th ed, Sweet & Maxwell, London, 1988, p 578.
183 *New Horizon Investments Ltd v Montroyal Estates Ltd* (1982) 26 RPR 268 at 271; *Kopec v Pyret* (1983) 146 DLR (3d) 242.
184 E Veitch, 'An Equitable Export — Lord Cairns' Act in Canada', *Ottawa Law Review*, vol 12, 1980, 227 at p 232.
185 *Richter v Simpson* (1982) 37 BCLR 325 at 327; 24 RPR 37 at 40; *Waspe v Lydia Court Pty Ltd* [1985] Q ConvR 54–165.
186 *Asamera Oil Corp Ltd v Sea Oil & General Corp* [1978] 6 WWR 301; 89 DLR (3d) 1; *Kopec v Pyret* (1983) 146 DLR (3d) 242 at 258.
187 M H Ogilvie, 'Sale of Land — Defect in Title — Limitation and Measure of Damages — Common Law or Equity?', *Canadian Bar Review*, vol 58, 1980, 394 at p 410–11.
188 [1980] AC 367 at 401.
189 (1854) 9 Exch 341; 156 ER 145.
190 See also *Waspe v Lydia Court Pty Ltd* [1985] Q ConvR 54–165 at 57,096 (Supreme Court of Queensland, Derrington J).

particularly not where a court considers that a plaintiff should receive full compensation for the loss sustained. They are not relevant where an award of compensation is made to restore a loss caused by breach of an equitable obligation.[191] They are also not always relevant to a statutory remedy of damages. In *Elna Australia Pty Ltd v International Computers (Australia) Pty Ltd*[192] Gummow J observed that common law analogies of causation, remoteness, and measure of damages will not necessarily provide sufficient guidance in assessing damages under s 82 of the Australian Trade Practices Act, particularly as that 'statute evinces an intention to supplement the common law or, further, to travel into new fields'.[193] Similarly, as *Lord Cairns' Act* enables damages to be awarded in situations where no common law remedy exists, an assessment of equitable damages cannot be constrained by common law concepts.

A more appropriate analogy for the assessment of equitable damages is the method of assessing equitable compensation. The courts of common law and equity have traditionally applied different principles when assessing damages and equitable compensation. In *United States Surgical Corp v Hospital Products International Pty Ltd*[194] McLelland J remarked: 'The principles of assessment of equitable compensation do not necessarily coincide with those applicable to common law damages'.[195] In assessing equitable compensation a court of equity recognises the need for restitution for any loss suffered.[196] A court will assess equitable compensation at a date that will maximise the compensation that an innocent beneficiary will be awarded.[197] Any assessment made will have regard to the date when recoupment of the loss is to be effected.[198]

The relevance of equitable principles in assessing equitable damages was recognised in *Postle v Sengstock*[199] where a contract for the sale of a business provided for immediate vendor finance of the purchase price and for the retention of the legal title in the business assets as security. It was held that the transaction was a mortgage. The failure by the purchasers to repay the loan on the stipulated date did not entitle the vendor to terminate the contract. The equity of redemption of the purchasers/mortgagors could only be extinguished by foreclosure proceedings. The

---

191 I E Davidson, 'The Equitable Remedy of Compensation', *Melbourne University Law Review*, vol 13, 1982, 349 at p 352. See also *Re Dawson; Union Fidelity Trustee Co Ltd v Perpetual Trustee Co Ltd* [1966] 2 NSWR 211; *Bartlett v Barclays Bank Trust Co Ltd (No 2)* [1980] Ch 515 at 543; *Guerin v R* (1985) 13 DLR (4th) 321 at 362–7; *Elna Australia Pty Ltd v International Computers (Australia) Pty Ltd* (1987) 16 FLR 410 at 421; 75 ALR 271 at 282.

192 (1987) 16 FLR 410; 75 ALR 271.

193 (1987) 16 FLR 410 at 419; 75 ALR 271 at 280.

194 [1982] 2 NSWLR 766.

195 [1982] 2 NSWLR 766 at 816. See also *Kimberley Mineral Holdings Ltd v Triguboff* [1978] 1 NSWLR 364 at 369; *Re Claridge House Ltd* (1981) 28 SASR 481 at 487.

196 *Canson Enterprises Ltd v Boughton & Co* [1991] 3 SCR 534 at 548 per McLachlin J.

197 *Jaffray v Marshall* [1993] 1 WLR 1285; [1994] 1 All ER 143.

198 A G Nevill and A W Ashe, *Equity Proceedings With Precedents (New South Wales)* Butterworths, Sydney, 1981, p 41.

199 Court of Appeal, Queensland, Macrossan CJ, McPherson JA and Derrington J, Appeal No 151 of 1992, 3 February 1993; *Queensland Law Reporter*, 30 April 1994; to be reported in [1994] 2 Qd R.

purchasers were awarded equitable damages in lieu of the re-transfer of the title by the mortgagee. The Court of Appeal of Queensland remarked:

> ... it is acceptable to allow the judgment to stand upon the basis that it reasonably equates the value of the property and reasonable profits less the amount due in respect of the sum secured. This is most permissible in these special circumstances despite the fact that the amount involved exceeds the measure of damages usually granted in lieu of a specific relief: *Shelfer v City of London Electric Lighting Co;*[200] *Kennaway v Thompson.*[201] The method of calculation used by the learned trial judge in assessing damages in lieu of specific performance has similar application to the case, as here, of a trustee who is permitted to retain the trust property.[202]

7.5 Infringement of property rights

The courts have considered the principles for assessing damages where a property right such as a restrictive covenant or easement has been infringed. In *Wrotham Park Estate Co Ltd v Parkside Homes Ltd*[203] damages were awarded in lieu of a mandatory injunction for the demolition of houses erected in violation of a restrictive covenant. The restrictive covenant was entered into between successors in title to the parties and was for the benefit of the estate. If damages were assessed on a common law basis then the plaintiff could not recover more than nominal damages as the plaintiff conceded that the value of the estate had not diminished because of the breach of covenant. Damages were assessed as the sum that the plaintiffs might reasonably have charged for relaxation of the covenant: 5% of anticipated profits arising from the development.[204] This principle has been applied in England by the Lands Tribunal in awarding compensation for the modification of a restrictive covenant under s 84 of the Law of Property Act 1925.[205] The jurisdiction under s 84 is regarded as analogous to the jurisdiction which is conferred by *Lord Cairns' Act.*[206] Interestingly, the Lands Tribunal does not calculate compensation payable for injurious affection by considering the amount likely to be obtained by a claimant in free negotiation for relaxation of a covenant. It is required by statute to consider the actual damage caused to land or the loss of value of land attributable to works executed on the servient land.[207]

---

200 [1895] 1 Ch 287.
201 [1981] QB 88.
202 *Postle v Sengstock*, n 199 above, at 15.
203 [1974] 1 WLR 798.
204 [1974] 1 WLR 798 at 815–16. See also *Stoke-on-Trent City Council v W & J Wass Ltd* [1988] 1 WLR 1406.
205 1925 c 20. *SJC Construction Co Ltd v Sutton London Borough Council* (1975) 29 P & CR 322. However, in *Re Vaizey* (1974) 28 P & CR 517 at 525 it was considered unjust to award the objector a share of the development value.
206 *Re Bass Ltd* (1973) 26 P & CR 156 at 157.
207 *Wrotham Park Settled Estates v Hertsmere Borough Council* (1991) 62 P & CR 652.

In *Bracewell v Appleby*[208] damages were awarded in lieu of an injunction denying access to a house other than as permitted under a right of way. The plaintiffs delayed enforcing their rights until the house was almost completed. The owner resided in the house and had acquired it for speculative purposes. Graham J declined to award damages as a proportion of the notional profit of the defendant. Instead, they were assessed at a fair sum to compensate the plaintiffs for loss of amenity and increased user, but at a value which would not have deterred the building of the house.[209]

In *Carr-Saunders v McNiel (Dick) Associates*[210] the plaintiff sued in respect of obstruction to his right to·light and was awarded damages in lieu of an injunction. Millett J followed the method of assessing damages used in *Wrotham Park Estate Co Ltd v Parkside Homes Ltd*[211] and *Bracewell v Appleby*.[212] While there was no evidence of the profits by the defendant from the development, there was evidence of a general loss of amenity due to infringement of the right to light. From this evidence an assessment of damages could be made.[213]

———<o>———

7.6 Damage sustained after the commencement of an action

A special aspect of the jurisdiction conferred by *Lord Cairns' Act* is that equitable damages may be awarded for damage sustained after the issue of the writ,[214] or even for prospective loss after judgment.[215] This is because *Lord Cairns' Act* and its statutory successors enables equitable damages to be awarded 'in substitution' for an injunction or specific performance.

At common law, damages may in some cases be awarded for prospective loss which is reasonably anticipated to flow from a defendant's wrong.[216] However, it is clear that at common law damages for such loss will only be awarded where a cause of action is completely constituted. In *ASA Constructions Pty Ltd v Iwanov*[217] Needham J remarked:

> Common law damages, unlike equitable damages, cannot generally take account of events which transpire after proceedings have commenced.[218]

---

208 [1975] Ch 408.
209 [1975] Ch 408 at 420.
210 [1986] 1 WLR 922; 53 P & CR 14.
211 [1974] 1 WLR 798.
212 [1975] Ch 408.
213 *Wrotham Park Settled Estates v Hertsmere Borough Council* (1991) 62 P & CR 652 at 669.
214 *Davenport v Rylands* (1865) LR 1 Eq 302 at 308; *Fritz v Hobson* (1880) 14 Ch D 542 at 557; *Saltman Engineering Co Ltd v Campbell Engineering Co Ltd* (1948) 65 RPC 203 at 219.
215 *Leeds Industrial Co-operative Society Ltd v Slack* [1924] AC 851; *Saltman Engineering Co Ltd v Campbell Engineering Co Ltd* (1948) 65 RPC 203 at 219.
216 H McGregor, *McGregor on Damages*, 15th ed, Stevens, Sweet & Maxwell, London, 1988, p 240.
217 [1975] 1 NSWLR 512.
218 [1975] 1 NSWLR 512 at 517.

The recovery of damages for prospective loss may be barred by rulings that a cause of action is not complete or that the damage is too remote. The continuing conduct of a defendant causes some difficulties. For instance, in *Pearson v Arcadia Stores, Guyra, Ltd*[219] the High Court of Australia mentioned that the continual breach by a person of a covenant in restraint of trade 'exposes him day by day to repeated actions for damages'.[220]

The common law position has been ameliorated in some jurisdictions by rules of court which enable damages in respect of a continuing cause of action to be assessed up to the date of assessment.[221] However, this procedural reform falls short of allowing damages to be awarded for prospective loss after judgment. This was recognised by Macrossan J in *Minter v Geraghty:*[222]

> This remedial extension to the scope of the damages which may be awarded still falls short of what may be awarded in the equity jurisdiction in *quia timet* actions and, in any event, it is subject to the restriction of applying only in respect of causes of action which can properly be categorised as 'continuing'.[223]

7.7 Rule in Bain v Fothergill

The rule in *Bain v Fothergill*[224] precludes the recovery of damages from a vendor who without default or bad faith is unable to make a good title.[225] The rationale for this rule was the difficulty of making title to land under English law. This rationale is no longer valid with the establishment of title by registration,[226] and is anomalous.[227] The Law Commission recommended

---

219 (1935) 53 CLR 571.
220 (1935) 53 CLR 571 at 583.
221 *England*: RSC 1965 O 37 r 6; *New South Wales*: Supreme Court Rules 1970 Pt 35 r 3, *Ritchie's Supreme Court Procedure — New South Wales*, Butterworths, Sydney, 1989 to date (looseleaf), p 2746 [3532]; *Victoria*: General Rules of Procedure in Civil Proceedings 1986 O 51 r 6; *Queensland*: RSC O 39 r 54. See also *Hole v Chard Union* [1894] 1 Ch 293; *National Coal Board v Galley* [1958] 1 WLR 16 (noted *Law Quarterly Review*, vol 74, 1958, p 161); *Aden Port Trustees v Ishi* [1964] EA 49; *Minter v Geraghty* (1981) 38 ALR 68.
222 (1981) 38 ALR 68.
223 (1981) 38 ALR 68 at 85–6.
224 (1874) LR 7 HL 158. This rule originated in *Flureau v Thornhill* (1776) 2 Black W 1078; 96 ER 635.
225 *Day v Singleton* [1899] 2 Ch 320 at 328–9; *Kelly v Duffy* [1922] 1 Ir R 62; *ASA Constructions Pty Ltd v Iwanov* [1975] 1 NSWLR 512 at 516; *AVG Management Service Ltd v Barwell Developments Ltd* [1979] 2 SCR 43; (1978) 92 DLR (3d) 289; *Malhotra v Choudhury* [1980] Ch 52; *Westward Farms Ltd v Cadieux* [1981] 3 WWR 673 at 700; *Sharneyford Supplies Ltd v Edge* [1987] Ch 305; *Seven Seas Properties Ltd v Al-Essa* [1988] 1 WLR 1272; See also R P Austin, 'Contract for Sale of Land ... Two Recent English Cases', *Australian Law Journal*, vol 48, 1974, p 273; C T Emery, 'In Defence of the Rule in *Bain v Fothergill*', *Conveyancer and Property Lawyer*, 1978, p 338; A J Oakley, 'Pecuniary Compensation for Failure to Complete a Contract for the Sale of Land', *Cambridge Law Journal*, vol 39, 1980, p 58. The rule in *Bain v Fothergill* has been comprehensively analysed by the Law Reform Commission of New South Wales: see New South Wales Law Reform Commission, *Damages for Vendor's Inability to Convey Good Title: The Rule in Bain v Fothergill*, LRC 64, 1990.
226 *Sharneyford Supplies Ltd v Edge* [1987] Ch 305 at 318.
227 *Day v Singleton* [1899] 2 Ch 320 at 329; *Wroth v Tyler* [1974] Ch 30 at 56; *Malhotra v Choudhury* [1980] Ch 52 at 68.

the abolition of the rule subject to a right of vendors to include an express term in the contract to limit their liability for a defect in title.[228] Similar recommendations have been made: in Australia by the Law Reform Commissions of Queensland and New South Wales;[229] in Canada by the Law Reform Commission of British Columbia;[230] and in New Zealand by the Law Commission.[231] There was thus a common consensus about the need for this reform.

In England the rule was abolished by s 3 of the Law of Property (Miscellaneous Provisions) Act 1989:

Abolition of rule in *Bain v Fothergill*
The rule of law known as the rule in *Bain v Fothergill* is abolished in relation to contracts made after this section comes into force.[232]

The rule was also abolished in other jurisdictions by statute,[233] or even by judicial decision.[234] It is in any event subject to recognised exceptions.[235] Now that the rule has been abrogated in England it would seem that the Misrepresentation Act 1967 would allow damages to be recovered for a misrepresentation of good title.[236]

The New South Wales Law Reform Commission had suggested that *Lord Cairns' Act* could be used to circumvent the rule:

Under the successor legislation to *Lord Cairns' Act*, where the Supreme Court has power to order specific performance of a contract it may award damages in addition to or in substitution for the order. The court will not make such an order where it would be futile, as when the Vendor has no title at all, and of course cannot award damages in equity, where it has no power to order specific performance. But as the Court has wide powers to award damages in equity so as to do complete justice particularly when

---

228 Law Commission, *Transfer of land: the rule in Bain v Fothergill*, Law Com No 166 [Cm 192], 1987.

229 Queensland Law Reform Commission, *The Law Relating to Conveyancing, Property, and Contract and to terminate the application of certain Imperial Statutes*, QLRC 16, 1973; New South Wales Law Reform Commission, *Damages for Vendor's Inability to Convey Good Title: The Rule in Bain v Fothergill*, LRC 64, 1990.

230 Law Reform Commission of British Columbia, *Report on the Rule in Bain v Fothergill*, LRC 38, 1976.

231 New Zealand Law Commission, *Aspects of Damages: The Rules in Bain v Fothergill and Joyner v Weeks*, Report No 19, 1991. In *Clasper v Lawrence* [1990] 3 NZLR 231 the rule was held inapplicable where there was no inherent defect in a vendor's title.

232 1989 c 34.

233 *New South Wales*: Conveyancing Act 1919 s 54A (proposed amendment); *Queensland*: Property Law Act 1974 s 68; *British Columbia*: Conveyancing and Law of Property Act 1978 s 33.

234 In *AVG Management Science Ltd v Barwell Developments Ltd* [1979] 2 SCR 43; (1978) 92 DLR (3d) 289 the Canadian Supreme Court considered that the rule was inapplicable to the Torrens system of land title registration. See also *Kopec v Pyret* [1987] 3 WWR 449 at 461; (1987) 36 DLR (4th) 1 at 11. There was contrary Australian authority which assumed that the rule applied to land under the Torrens system: see *Merry v Australian Mutual Provident Society (No 3)* (1872) 3 QSCR 40; *Boardman v McGrath* [1925] QWN 8.

235 Eg covenants for right to convey: see *Turner v Moon* [1901] 2 Ch 825.

236 Compare *Sharneyford Supplies Ltd v Edge* [1987] Ch 305 at 323 approving the criticism of *Watts v Spence* [1976] Ch 165 in H McGregor, *McGregor on Damages*, 14th ed, Sweet & Maxwell, London, 1980, paras 1486–9.

common law damages would be an inadequate remedy, it is conceivable that this power could be used to circumvent the Rule.[237]

However, there would be no jurisdiction to award equitable damages where there is a defect in title because an order for specific performance could not be made. There was one case which held that the rule applies equally to damages under *Lord Cairns' Act* and at common law,[238] although it is submitted that the case is unsatisfactory because it was assumed that the Act was a mere procedural statute. There are also discretionary considerations which may preclude an award of equitable damages. In *Wroth v Tyler*[239] Megarry J emphasised: 'No doubt in exercising the jurisdiction conferred by the Act a court with equitable jurisdiction will remember that equity follows the law'.[240]

------◦------

7.8 Interest

In a number of cases equitable damages, together with pre-judgment interest at the statutory rate, have been awarded.[241] However, a court of equity has an inherent jurisdiction to award interest at an appropriate rate to compensate a plaintiff for loss, and is not constrained by interest rates prescribed by statute.[242]

Difficulties occur where the rate of inflation exceeds prescribed interest rates. It has been recognised that one consequence of *Wroth v Tyler*[243] is to transfer to the defendant the risk of particularly high inflationary increases. In some cases an award of interest would have the same effect, unless the rate of inflation is much higher than the interest rate allowed by the court.[244]

In a vendor and purchaser action, a court of equity can make an order for the payment of interest as part of the process of adjustment of the rights of the parties. In *Davies v Littlejohn*[245] Isaacs J noted that the 'mutual rights to interest on the one hand and the rents and profits on the other' of vendor and purchaser are part of the 'scheme of equitable adjustment of mutual rights and obligations applying, unless negatived, to every ordinary contract of the sale of land'.[246] Where a purchaser has been

---

237 New South Wales Law Reform Commission, *Damages for Vendor's Inability to Convey Good Title: The Rule in Bain v Fothergill*, LRC 64, 1990, p 21, para 3.9.
238 *Rock Portland Cement Co Ltd v Wilson* (1882) 52 LJ Ch 214 as explained by P J Millett QC *arguendo* in *Johnson v Agnew* [1980] AC 367 at 380.
239 [1974] Ch 30.
240 [1974] Ch 30 at 60.
241 *Coleman v Myers* [1977] 2 NZLR 225; *Day v Mead* [1987] 2 NZLR 443; *Talbot v General Television Corp Pty Ltd* [1980] VR 224.
242 J R L Davis, 'Interest as Compensation' in P D Finn (ed), *Essays on Damages*, Law Book Co, Sydney, 1992, 129 at pp 139–41. For instances of equitable interest: see *Wallersteiner v Moir (No 2)* [1975] 1 QB 373; *Hieber v Hieber* [1991] 1 NZLR 315.
243 [1974] Ch 30.
244 *Tominski v Headway Builders (Sault) Ltd* (1980) 12 RPR 290 at 291. See also J Swan, 'Damages, Specific Performance, Inflation and Interest', *Real Property Reports*, vol 10, 1980, p 267.
245 (1923) 34 CLR 174.
246 (1923) 34 CLR 174 at 185–6, cited by Einfeld J in *Vanmeld Pty Ltd v Cussen* (1994) 121 ALR 619 at 623.

let into possession of premises before paying the purchase moneys, that purchaser will, in the absence of any agreement to the contrary, be liable to pay interest on the outstanding purchase moneys.[247] This is because in equity a vendor is entitled to interest on the purchase moneys where a purchaser is enjoying the fruits of the contract before payment.

Where there is a delay in the completion of a contract of sale, a vendor is generally entitled to interest on the purchase moneys in equity in the absence of evidence that the delay was caused by the fault of the vendor.[248] In *Vanmeld Pty Ltd v Cussen*[249] the court ordered the specific performance of agreements which related to a land swap between the parties. Einfeld J later made an order for the payment of interest in the form of equitable damages, under s 68 of the Supreme Court Act 1970 of New South Wales, on the balance of purchase moneys owing.[250]

---

247 *Brake v Boote* [1991] 2 NZLR 757 at 766 per Holland J.
248 *Vanmeld Pty Ltd v Cussen* (1994) 121 ALR 619.
249 (1994) 121 ALR 619.
250 (1994) 121 ALR 619 at 621.

8

Injunction

———◦———

8.1 *Award of equitable damages in an action for an injunction*

Section 2 of the Chancery Amendment Act 1858 (*Lord Cairns' Act*)[1] enabled the Court of Chancery to award equitable damages where there was:

> ... jurisdiction to entertain an application for an injunction against a breach of any covenant, contract, or agreement, or against the commission or continuance of any wrongful act.

---

1   21 & 22 Vict c 27.

Modern statutory provisions that confer jurisdiction to award equitable damages in the United Kingdom are not as elaborate as *Lord Cairns' Act*. In the United Kingdom the legislation provides that the requisite jurisdiction exists where the court 'has jurisdiction to entertain an application for an injunction'.[2] Similar provisions are in force in Victoria,[3] Hong Kong[4] and Manitoba.[5] In Ontario the requisite jurisdiction to award equitable damages exists where a court 'has jurisdiction to grant an injunction'.[6] This difference in language is not significant as a court would not have jurisdiction to entertain an application for an injunction where an order for an injunction could not be made.

Lord Cairns' Act enables damages to be awarded in addition to or in substitution for an injunction. It is accordingly clear that this jurisdiction can be invoked in an action where a plaintiff has an equity to an injunction.

8.2 Equitable damages in addition to an injunction

Lord Cairns' Act confers jurisdiction upon a court to award damages 'in addition to ... [an] injunction'.[7] Thus damages can be sought in addition to an injunction in an action. *Lord Cairns' Act* provides a convenient jurisdictional basis for an award of common law damages. In *Leeds Industrial Co-operative Society Ltd v Slack*[8] Viscount Finlay commented:

> If the damages are given in addition to the injunction they are to compensate for the injury which has been done and the injunction will prevent its continuance or repetition.[9]

There may be an advantage in claiming equitable damages 'in addition to' an injunction where it is sought to recover damages for loss incurred after the date of issue of the writ, but before the hearing of a matter. In some cases an award of equitable damages 'in addition to' an injunction may be made where there is no claim for monetary relief in the pleadings.

There have been a number of cases in which *Lord Cairns' Act* was relied upon, or appeared to have been relied upon. In one case the court made an award of equitable damages in addition to an injunction where the plaintiff sought to enforce an option to take an easement to construct a pipeline. Damages were awarded for the increased cost of constructing the

---

2 Judicature (Northern Ireland) Act 1978 (1978 c 23) s 92: Supreme Court Act 1981 (1981 c 54) s 50.
3 Supreme Court Act 1986 (1986 No 110) (Victoria) s 38.
4 Supreme Court Ordinance cap 4 rev ed 1987 (Hong Kong) s 17.
5 The Court of Queen's Bench Act SM 1988–9 c 4 (Manitoba) s 36.
6 Courts of Justice Act SO 1984 c 11 RSO 1990 c C 43 (Ontario) s 112.
7 Chancery Amendment Act 1858 s 2.
8 [1924] AC 851.
9 [1924] AC 851 at 857.

pipeline.[10] In a passing off action in which a *quia timet* injunction was granted the court made an order for an inquiry into 'equitable damages'.[11]

————◄○►————

8.3 Equitable damages in substitution for an injunction

Lord Cairns' Act confers jurisdiction upon a court to award damages 'in substitution for ... [an] injunction'.[12] This enables damages to be awarded for future or prospective loss. In *Leeds Industrial Co-operative Society Ltd v Slack*[13] Viscount Finlay remarked:

> But if damages are given in substitution for an injunction they must necessarily cover not only injury already sustained but also injury that would be inflicted in the future by the commission of the act threatened.[14]

His Lordship later remarked:

> Injunctions are given to prevent wrongs which are threatened, and the power to give damages in lieu of an injunction must in all reason import the power to give an equivalent for what is lost by the refusal of the injunction; for this purpose compensation for what has passed would be futile.[15]

The Supreme Court of Canada has emphasised that damages may not be awarded 'in substitution' for an injunction where an injunction has already issued.[16] However, once an order for an injunction has been vacated, there can be no objection to an award of equitable damages in substitution for an injunction.

————◄○►————

8.4 Nuisance

Formerly a nuisance was enforced in the courts of law by an action on the case for nuisance.[17] An action for nuisance was quite distinct from an

---

10 *Gas & Fuel Corp v Barba* [1976] VR 755 at 766. The High Court of Australia, on appeal, held that the option was a contingent equitable interest which did not become vested in possession until the option was exercised. Accordingly, there was no jurisdiction to award damages until the exercise of the option: see *Barba v Gas & Fuel Corp* (1976) 136 CLR 120 at 137–9 per Gibbs J, 143 per Jacobs J.

11 *Noel Leeming Television Ltd v Noel's Appliance Centre Ltd* (1985) 5 IPR 249.

12 Chancery Amendment Act 1858 s 2.

13 [1924] AC 851 at 857.

14 [1924] AC 851 at 857.

15 [1924] AC 851 at 859.

16 *St Anne Nackawic Pulp & Paper Co Ltd v Canadian Paper Workers' Union, Local 219* [1986] 1 SCR 704 at 727–8; 28 DLR (4th) 1 at 19.

17 F H Newark, 'The Boundaries of Nuisance', *Law Quarterly Review*, vol 65, 1949, 480 at p 484.

action for trespass.[18] Procedural reforms were effected by the abolition of the writ of assize[19] and by the Common Law Procedure Act 1852.[20] The Court of Chancery would not generally determine the existence of a legal right upon which equitable relief was sought to protect the legal right. In such circumstances it was necessary for the legal right to be initially established before an injunction would be granted. In *Broadbent v Imperial Gas Co*[21] Lord Cranworth LC observed:

> I take it to be clear — at least according to the old practice of this Court — that a person making such a complaint ... is bound first of all to establish that it is a nuisance by a trial at law; or if he has not done so, this Court will, not necessarily, but in the ordinary course, put the matter in the train of a legal inquiry.[22]

At this time the Court of Chancery was empowered under the Chancery Procedure Act 1852[23] to try the legal right itself. As Lord Brougham LC remarked, the Court of Chancery could also: 'stay irreparable mischief, without waiting for the result of a trial'.[24] Once a right at law had been established, a court of equity would enjoin a nuisance which infringed that legal right.[25] Statutory reforms enabled the courts of law and equity to grant complete relief in cases of nuisance. The Common Law Procedure Act 1854[26] enabled a court of law to grant an injunction. *Lord Cairns' Act* enabled the Court of Chancery to award equitable damages in addition to or in lieu of an injunction. Now, under the Judicature system, a superior court has jurisdiction to determine all legal and equitable claims and defences.

Where a nuisance is of a continuing nature a court may grant a mandatory injunction ordering the cessation of the nuisance, or award of equitable damages in lieu of an injunction. A court may also enjoin the more offensive aspects of a nuisance *and* award equitable damages in lieu of an injunction for prospective damage caused by a residual nuisance. A court may accordingly decree equitable relief in a more limited form than originally sought, and award equitable damages for any prospective loss and common law damages for any actual damage sustained.

Thus, where a plaintiff seeks the abatement of a nuisance the court may grant a more limited injunction to lessen the effect of the nuisance, and may additionally award common law damages for actual injury sustained and equitable damages for prospective loss caused by the residual nuisance.[27] Whether this jurisdiction will be invoked will depend upon the circumstances of each case.

---

18 *Kine v Jolly* [1905] 1 Ch 480 at 487.
19 3 & 4 Will IV c 27 (1833) s 36.
20 15 & 16 Vict c 76 s 3.
21 (1857) 7 De GM & G 436; 44 ER 170.
22 (1857) 7 De GM & G 436 at 443; 44 ER 170 at 173.
23 15 & 16 Vict c 86 s 62.
24 *Ripon, Earl v Hobart* (1834) 3 My & K 169 at 179; 40 ER 65 at 69.
25 *Imperial Gas Light & Coke Co v Broadbent* (1859) 7 HLC 600 at 612; 11 ER 239 at 244.
26 17 & 18 Vict c 125 ss 81, 82.
27 *Rombough v Crestbrook Timber Ltd* (1966) 55 WWR 577; 57 DLR (2d) 49 (BCCA).

It should also be appreciated that a plaintiff who is awarded equitable damages in lieu of an injunction will necessarily lose the right to abate the nuisance.[28] This is because an award of equitable damages in such a case is given for prospective loss.

There are a number of cases where a court declined to make an award of equitable damages in lieu of an injunction. In the leading case, *Shelfer v City of London Electric Lighting Co*,[29] the Court of Appeal declined to withhold an injunction where vibrating machinery generating power was injurious to health. In a case where contaminated debris was piled against a wall that would in time be destroyed, the court considered that an injunction rather than damages was the appropriate remedy.[30] Similarly, an injunction rather than damages was regarded as the appropriate remedy where a tree belonging to a local authority and not subject to a tree preservation order was damaging a wall.[31] A court would be reluctant to award damages in lieu of an injunction where a nuisance is intolerable,[32] where there is a real difficulty in assessing damages[33] or where there is an increase in the disturbance caused by a business after a plaintiff has moved to a neighbourhood.[34] It would not be appropriate to withhold an injunction, and award equitable damages in lieu of an injunction, on the ground that a plaintiff came to the nuisance.[35]

There have been a number of instances where the jurisdiction to award equitable damages in lieu of an injunction has been exercised. It is said that exceptional circumstances must exist before a court will award damages under *Lord Cairns' Act* in substitution for an injunction to restrain a nuisance.[36] Where a defendant erected a house, believing in good faith that it had purchased a good title to the land on which it was built, an award of damages was considered the appropriate remedy, particularly as the plaintiff's loss was small.[37] Similarly, damages, rather than a mandatory injunction, were appropriate where the defendants had submitted their plans to the plaintiff for approval prior to commencing building.[38] Circumstances that incline a court to award damages are where the damage of the plaintiff is

---

28 R A Buckley, *The Law of Nuisance*, Butterworths, London, 1981, pp 129, 147.
29 [1895] 1 Ch 287.
30 *Maberley v Henry W Peacock & Co of London Ltd* [1946] 2 All ER 192 at 195.
31 *Elliott v London Borough of Islington* [1991] 10 EG 145; [1991] 1 EGLR 167 (CA).
32 *Pennington v Brinsop Hall Coal Co* (1877) 5 Ch D 769; *Gilling v Gray* (1910) 27 TLR 39 at 40; *Wood v Conway Corp* [1914] 2 Ch 47.
33 *McKenzie v Kayler* (1905) 1 WLR 290; 15 Man Rep 660 at 665; *Wood v Conway Corp* [1914] 2 Ch 47 at 57.
34 *Duchman v Oakland Dairy Co Ltd* (1928) 63 OLR 111; [1929] 1 DLR 9.
35 Compare R A Buckley, *The Law of Nuisance*, Butterworths, London, 1981, p 97.
36 *Shelfer v City of London Electric Lighting Co* [1895] 1 Ch 287 at 316; *Kennaway v Thompson* [1981] QB 88; *Allen v Gulf Oil Refining Ltd* [1981] AC 1001 at 1013, *semble*, per Lord Wilberforce; *Elliott v London Borough of Islington* [1991] 10 EG 145; [1991] 1 EGLR 167 (CA). The operation of an injunction may be stayed for a reasonable period to enable the defendant to abate a nuisance: see *Appleby v Erie Tobacco Co* (1910) 22 OLR 533 (Ont CA); *KVP Co Ltd v McKie* [1949] 4 DLR 497; [1948] OWN 812.
37 *Owen v O'Connor* [1964] NSWR 1312 at 1335.
38 *Fishenden v Higgs and Hill Ltd* (1935) 153 LT 128.

small,[39] where the conduct of the plaintiff is such as to disentitle that plaintiff to an injunction[40] or where the plaintiff has not pressed for an injunction.[41] Any damages awarded under *Lord Cairns' Act* may include components for diminution of the market value of the affected premises and discomfort.[42]

In exercising a discretion to grant injunctive relief it would seem that a court will now more readily consider the issue of public benefit.[43] The fact that a wrongdoer is a public utility does not provide a sufficient justification for awarding damages rather than granting an injunction to protect an individual whose rights are being infringed.[44] Statutory powers are sometimes conferred upon public utilities with an express proviso that they do not exonerate an undertaking from liability for nuisance.[45] However, in the absence of negligence, there may be no right of action if a nuisance is the inevitable consequence of an operation authorised by statute.[46] This is based upon the principle enunciated by Lord Blackburn in *Geddis v Proprietors of Bann Reservoir*[47] that 'no action will lie for what the legislature has authorised, if it be done without negligence'.[48] Sometimes a statute will only exempt a public authority from liability where it acts in good faith and without negligence.[49] It is always a matter of construction of the particular statute.

A court will not decline to enjoin a nuisance merely because the nuisance provides some public benefit.[50] In Canada the economic consequences to the community of restraining a nuisance have generally been regarded as relevant by the courts, although in some instances the legislature has overridden the courts on economic grounds.[51] There have been some cases

---

39 *Haggerty v Latreille* (1913) 29 OLR 300; 14 DLR 532; *Duchman v Oakland Dairy Co* (1928) 63 OLR 111; [1929] 1 DLR 9; *Owen v O'Connor* [1964] NSWR 1312 at 1335.

40 *Duchman v Oakland Dairy Co Ltd* (1928) 63 OLR 111; [1929] 1 DLR 9.

41 *Smyth v Dublin Theatre Co Ltd* [1936] Ir R 692; *McGrath v Munster and Leinster Bank Ltd* [1959] Ir R 313.

42 *Rombough v Crestbrook Timber Ltd* (1966) 55 WWR 577; 57 DLR (2d) 49 (BCCA).

43 R A Buckley, *The Law of Nuisance*, Butterworths, London, 1981, pp 121–4.

44 *Shelfer v City of London Electric Lighting Co* [1895] 1 Ch 287 at 316; *Wood v Conway Corp* [1914] 2 Ch 47. See also *Imperial Gas Light & Coke Co v Broadbent* (1859) 7 HLC 600; 11 ER 239; *Manchester Corp v Farnworth* [1930] AC 171 at 194–5.

45 *Shelfer v City of London Electric Lighting Co* [1895] 1 Ch 287 at 310; *Midwood & Co Ltd v Manchester Corp* [1905] 2 KB 597; *Charing Cross Electricity Supply Co v Hydraulic Power Co* [1914] 3 KB 772; *Clerk & Lindsell on Torts*, 15th ed, Sweet & Maxwell, London, 1982, p 1199, para 23–84.

46 *Manchester Corp v Farnworth* [1930] AC 171 at 183; *Allen v Gulf Oil Refining Ltd* [1981] AC 1001 at 1011.

47 (1878) 3 App Cas 430.

48 (1878) 3 App Cas 430 at 455–6. See also R A Buckley, *The Law of Nuisance*, Butterworths, London, 1981, pp 87–8.

49 *Evans v Port of Brisbane Authority* (1992) 78 LGERA 174; (1992) Aust Torts Reports 81–181.

50 *Pennington v Brinsop Hall Coal Co* (1877) 5 Ch D 769; *Canada Paper Co v Brown* (1922) 63 SCR 243; 66 DLR 287; *Bellew v Cement Ltd* [1948] Ir R 62; *Kennaway v Thompson* [1981] QB 88 at 93. Compare *Miller v Jackson* [1977] QB 966; *Allen v Gulf Oil Refining Ltd* [1980] QB 156 at 169.

51 P Anisman, 'Water Pollution Control in Ontario', *Ottawa Law Review*, vol 5, 1972, p 342; P S Elder, 'Environmental Protection through the Common Law', *Western Ontario Law Review*, vol 12, 1973, p 107.

where equitable damages have been awarded in lieu of an injunction to restrain a nuisance created by a public utility. Early this century the jurisdiction under *Lord Cairns' Act* was exercised to award damages in lieu of an injunction to restrain a nuisance where the pumping of water was necessary for municipal purposes[52] and in respect of a railway embankment that was illegally constructed.[53] These cases have been explained on the basis that *Lord Cairns' Act* has been more liberally applied in Canada than in England,[54] although that explanation has been doubted.[55] More realistically, these Canadian cases were decided during wartime when the courts would not prejudice the war effort by rendering public works inoperable.

In examining the jurisdiction to award equitable damages in a case of nuisance it is important to understand the general principles upon which a plaintiff possesses an equity to an injunction. This is particularly important when considering the liability of a landlord in respect of a nuisance which exists on a tenancy. Injunctive relief is available against a landlord in respect of a nuisance emanating from a tenancy. In most cases a landlord cannot escape liability by reason that there is a tenancy over the property because a right in the landlord to enter and carry out repairs will be implied as a term of the tenancy.[56] Accordingly, in such circumstances, a court may award injunctive relief.[57] A landlord is also liable for effectively authorising an act from which a nuisance will result. This principle was established in *Harris v James*,[58] where a landlord was held liable for a nuisance caused by a tenant burning lime because the landlord had let the land for that purpose. This principle was applied in *Sampson v Hodson-Pressinger*[59] where a demised flat was close to a terrace which had been constructed in such a way that whenever it was used the plaintiff was disturbed. The plaintiff was awarded damages, which included a component for prospective loss. Everleigh LJ remarked:

> ... it is possible to award damages for prospective nuisance in exercise of the court's power first introduced by *Lord Cairns' Act* (the Chancery Amendment Act 1858).[60]

In the circumstances the tenant, a defendant, was entitled to a complete indemnity from the original landlord who was responsible for the offending construction.

——◁○▷——

52 *Chadwick v City of Toronto* (1914) 32 OLR 111 at 113.
53 *Cadwell & Fleming v Canadian Pacific Railway Co* (1916) 37 OLR 412; 28 DLR 190.
54 *Duchman v Oakland Dairy Co Ltd* (1928) 63 OLR 111 at 127; [1929] 1 DLR 9 at 10.
55 *Duchman v Oakland Dairy Co Ltd* (1928) 63 OLR 111 at 134; [1929] 1 DLR 9 at 17.
56 *Heap v Ind Coope and Allsopp Ltd* [1940] 2 KB 476; *Mint v Good* [1951] 1 KB 517; *Carter v Murray* [1981] 2 NSWLR 77.
57 *Carter v Murray* [1981] 2 NSWLR 77.
58 (1876) 45 LJ QB 545; 35 LT 240; [1874–80] All ER Rep 1142. See also R A Buckley, *The Law of Nuisance*, Butterworths, London, 1981, p 77.
59 [1981] 3 All ER 710. See also M Owen, 'Authorised Nuisances', *Cambridge Law Journal*, vol 41, 1982, p 38.
60 [1981] 3 All ER 710 at 715.

8.5 Trespass

An injunction will not be granted as a matter of course in all cases of trespass. An injunction is a formidable legal weapon which will not be granted in cases of trivial trespass.[61] It is an appropriate remedy in the case of a flagrant continuing trespass.[62] The courts will also not grant injunctive relief where persons are unreasonably standing on their rights, *de minimus non curat lex* ('the law does not concern itself with trifles').[63]

Common law damages in trespass actions do not merely serve a compensatory function. In cases of trespass, damages are awarded not merely to compensate the plaintiff for damage to the land of the plaintiff, but also to vindicate the right of the plaintiff to the exclusive use and occupation of the land.[64] In some cases an award of exemplary damages, and an order for solicitor and client costs, may be justified where there has been contumelious conduct by a defendant.[65]

Where a plaintiff is granted an injunction damages can be awarded in addition to an injunction for past loss.[66] *Lord Cairns' Act* assumes relevance in those cases where a plaintiff possesses an equity to an injunction and where damages will be awarded for an injunction for prospective loss. *Lord Cairns' Act* was a clear source of jurisdiction to award damages where an injunction was sought prior to the introduction of the Judicature system.[67] It would seem that a plaintiff would prima facie be entitled to recover damages, whether common law damages or equitable damages, in the case of refusal of a mandatory injunction.[68]

The jurisdiction under *Lord Cairns' Act* is more extensive than the jurisdiction of a court of law. The position at law in respect of a continuing trespass was discussed in *Aden Port Trustees v Ishi*[69] by Newbold JA who remarked that 'a fresh cause of action arises *de die in diem* ['from day to day'] as the trespass continues'.[70] It was recognised that *Lord Cairns' Act* enables damages to be awarded in respect of loss subsequent to the time of assessment. Newbold JA added:

> In England, by virtue of provisions originally introduced by *Lord Cairns' Act*, 1858, the court may, in the case of a continuing cause of action as in this case, instead of granting an injunction make an award of damages. Such an award would be in respect of damage from causes of action which

---

61 *Llandudno Urban District Council v Woods* [1899] 2 Ch 705 at 710.
62 *London & Manchester Assurance Co Ltd v O & H Construction Ltd* [1989] 2 EGLR 185 (order for removal of crane made on motion without trial).
63 S Tromans, 'Nuisance — Prevention or Payment', *Cambridge Law Journal*, vol 41, 1982, 87 at p 92.
64 *Plenty v Dillon* (1991) 171 CLR 635 at 654–5 per Gaudron and McHugh JJ.
65 *LJP Investments Pty Ltd v Howard Chia Investments Pty Ltd* (1990) 24 NSWLR 490.
66 See eg *Moore v Dunn* [1927] GLR 361.
67 See eg *Phillips v Homfray* (1871) 6 Ch App 770; *Want v Moss* (1891) 12 LR (NSW) Eq 101 at 103.
68 *Burton v Winters* [1993] 1 WLR 1077 at 1081.
69 [1964] EA 49.
70 [1964] EA 49 at 51. See also *Konskier v B Goodman Ltd* [1928] 1 KB 421.

would arise subsequent to the institution of the suit and thus, in effect, the purchase price of the right to commit the tort *in perpetuo*.[71]

It can therefore be seen that an important aspect of the jurisdiction under *Lord Cairns' Act* is that damages may be awarded for prospective loss. The jurisdiction may be invoked where a court declines to enjoin a continuous trespass. In *Phillips v Homfray*[72] the customary tenants, by a cross-suit, had unsuccessfully sought injunctive relief to restrain unlawful underground mining; instead, the court directed an inquiry into what minerals had been removed and the amount which should be paid for a way-leave for carriage of the minerals and royalties for the use of the passages. Lord Hatherley LC remarked:

> ... but this Court now has the power to grant compensation in respect of a continuously accruing damage *de die in diem*, arising from a continuous trespass underground, which can only be stopped by injunction restraining any further conveyance of coal through the Repondent's property. These damages cannot be better assessed than by an inquiry what is fit and proper to be paid for wayleave for the coals carried through the property.[73]

Gummow J has pointed out that this was an instance where *Lord Cairns' Act* was invoked.[74]

Equitable damages may be awarded in lieu of a mandatory injunction to restrain a continuing trespass. In *Healey v Hawkins*[75] Goff J recognised that in a trespass case a court has a discretion to grant an injunction or 'at least to have granted under *Lord Cairns' Act* some sum of damages more than nominal for the future trespasses'.[76] Before the jurisdiction is exercised there must be some exceptional reason to justify the withholding of an injunction. In *Tollemache & Cobbold Breweries Ltd v Reynolds*[77] Fox J remarked that 'the court is in general not justified in awarding damages and refusing a mandatory injunction to compel the owners of the land in effect to grant the right to the trespasser'.[78] Damages must also be an adequate remedy.[79]

The jurisdiction to award equitable damages in lieu of a mandatory injunction has been exercised in a number of cases of continuing trespass. In *Leader v Moody*[80] the lease of a theatre provided that the demised premises could not be used for other than theatrical purposes. The underlease of the stalls contained a covenant for the quiet enjoyment of the demised premises, but no covenant by the grantor of the underlease to perform the covenants of the original lease. The lessee agreed to let the

---

71   [1964] EA 49 at 51.
72   (1871) 6 Ch App 770.
73   (1871) 6 Ch App 770 at 780–1.
74   W M C Gummow, 'Unjust Enrichment, Restitution and Proprietary Remedies' in *Essays on Restitution* (ed P D Finn), Law Book Co, Sydney, 1990, 47 at p 61.
75   [1968] 1 WLR 1967.
76   [1968] 1 WLR 1967 at 1976.
77   (1983) 268 EG 52.
78   (1983) 268 EG 52 at 56. See also *Regional Properties Ltd v City of London Real Property Co Ltd* (1979) 257 EG 64 at 70.
79   *Gross v Wright* [1923] 2 DLR 171.
80   (1875) LR 20 Eq 145.

theatre for a term of three months for the purpose of holding religious meetings. It was held that without the consent of the plaintiff, who held the underlease, the theatre could not be converted to other than theatrical purposes, but that, under the circumstances, the proper remedy was in damages and not an injunction. Sir George Jessel MR relied upon 'the power which has been given me by the Act commonly called *Lord Cairns' Act*, of substituting damages for injunction in a case where it appears to the Court that all the circumstances of the case justify such a course'.[81]

There has been some difference of opinion as to whether the *Shelfer* case is relevant to a trespass action. In *Rileys v Halifax Corp*[82] a municipal council during its construction of a reservoir had inadvertently carried its underground workings below the surface of the plaintiff's lands. Any actual damage was minor and would be considerably less than the cost of removing the works. Joyce J applied the 'working rule' in the *Shelfer* case to award damages in substitution for an injunction to compel removal of the reservoir. However, in *Woolerton and Wilson Ltd v Rochard Costain Ltd*[83] Stamp J considered that the 'working rule' had no application to a case of a trespass in which nominal damages can be recovered. In *LJP Investments Pty Ltd v Howard Chia Investments Pty Ltd*,[84] where the defendant's scaffolding projected into the airspace of the plaintiff, Hodgson J observed:

> In *Kelsen v Imperial Tobacco Co (of Great Britain and Ireland) Ltd*,[85] McNair J treated as applicable the principles stated by Smith LJ in *Shelfer v City of London Electric Lighting Co*,[86] to the following effect. The plaintiff is prima facie entitled to an injunction. However, there may be cases where damages is the appropriate remedy, for example where the plaintiff is disentitled by his acts or by laches. Furthermore, if the injury to the plaintiff's rights is small, capable of being estimated in money and adequately compensated by a money payment, and if the grant of an injunction would be oppressive to the defendant, then an injunction may be refused. However, the defendant may be disentitled to this approach, for example by reckless disregard of the plaintiff's rights.[87]

The jurisdiction under *Lord Cairns' Act* is appropriate where there is a minor encroachment, such as where the encroachment causes nominal damage.[88] In *Behrens v Richards*[89] the court made an award of nominal damages and refused to grant an injunction where a landowner was not injured by the public use of rights of way. The jurisdiction has been exercised in a number of Canadian cases which involved minor encroachments. In *Clark v McKenzie*[90] Macdonald J applied the 'working

---

81 (1875) LR 20 Eq 145 at 154.
82 (1907) 97 LT 278.
83 [1970] 1 WLR 411 at 414.
84 (1989) 24 NSWLR 490.
85 [1957] 1 QB 224 at 345.
86 [1895] 1 Ch 287 at 322.
87 (1989) 24 NSWLR 490 at 496.
88 See eg *Pettey v Parsons* [1914] 1 Ch 704; *Algie v Leaning* [1927] GLR 284.
89 [1905] 2 Ch 614.
90 [1930] 1 WWR 67 at 72; [1930] 1 DLR 226 at 231; affirmed [1930] 1 WWR 785; [1930] 2 DLR 843.

rule' in the *Shelfer* case to award damages in respect of a minor encroachment by the defendant's building on a few inches of the plaintiff's land. In *Mayo v Hefferton*[91] damages were awarded for the market value of the land encroached upon by the defendant's motel complex as well as exemplary damages. The plaintiff was ordered to execute a conveyance of the land upon which the building was erected.

In England the Court of Appeal has considered two cases where landowners had built garages which encroached onto neighbouring land. In *Barker v O'Mahony*[92] the garage encroached on neighbouring land by up to two feet. During the completion of the garage the owner of the neighbouring land did not make any protest about the construction of the garage. In the circumstances the Court of Appeal held that an award of equitable damages was more appropriate than an injunction. Parker LJ remarked:

> I have no hesitation whatever in concluding that this is not a case for an injunction and that the court can and should exercise its power under *Lord Cairns' Act* to award damages, notwithstanding that so to do will have the effect of forming upon the respondent a sale of a small, that is to say some 25 square feet, wedge shaped piece of land at the very far end of her land.

In *Harrow London Borough Council v Donohue*[93] the garage was constructed after the plaintiff had declined an offer made by the defendant to purchase the land upon which he later erected the garage. In such a case where the defendant had acted in total disregard of the plaintiff's rights it was held that a mandatory injunction requiring the demolition of the garage was inevitable. Waite LJ observed that 'there was no authority which provided a precedent for a court allowing total dispossession to be achieved by means of an award of damages in lieu of an injunction'.

The courts can grant interlocutory relief to restrain the publication by the media of a film that was made during a trespass.[94] In such cases it would be inappropriate to contemplate an award of equitable damages in lieu of an injunction where irreparable damage would result.

In *Tipler v Fraser*[95] the plaintiffs were granted an injunction to restrain the owners of adjoining land, who had a street frontage, from using an easement for access to their residence. The easement was created to provide access to other lands which did not have a street frontage. The defendant unsuccessfully sought the imposition of a statutory right of user over the land under s 180 of the Queensland Property Law Act 1974, and the exercise of the jurisdiction under *Lord Cairns' Act*. Matthews J remarked:

---

91 (1972) 3 Nfld & PEIR 236. See also *Luedee v Nova Construction Co Ltd* (1973) 4 Nfld & PEIR 361; *Tucker v Gosse* (1984) 48 Nfld & PEIR 163.
92 Court of Appeal, Lord Donaldson MR, Parker and Stuart-Smith LJJ, 12 July 1990, unreported.
93 [1993] NPC 49.
94 *Lincoln Hunt Australia Pty Ltd v Willesee* (1986) 4 NSWLR 457; *Emcorp Pty Ltd v Australian Broadcasting Corp* [1988] 2 Qd R 169.
95 [1976] Qd R 272.

... in cases of continuing wrongs courts may and will in very exceptional circumstances exercise jurisdiction conferred by *Lord Cairns' Act* to award damages. The cases to which reference is made deal generally with nuisances and not trespass and, without accepting that very exceptional circumstances present themselves in the instant case, I think that the answer to the submission emerges from a statement of what is proposed by it. If the submission be accepted it is that the Court should, despite the provisions of the *Real Property Acts* and as a substitute for the circumscribed rights conferred by s 180 of the Property Law Act, grant to the defendants, upon payment by them of some guessed amount of damages, a right, without limit as to time, to use the land of the plaintiffs in the same way as if they were entitled to an easement of access and right of way over it.[96]

8.6 Restrictive covenants

In most cases involving restrictive covenants affecting land the plaintiff is not in a contractual relationship with the defendant, and could not maintain an action for common law damages for breach of covenant.[97] An award of damages where the parties have not mutually executed a covenant can only be made under *Lord Cairns' Act*. This was recognised in *Shaw v Dalbridge Finance Co Ltd*[98] by Plowman J who remarked:

> ... the defendants were successors in title of the original covenantors. They were therefore not liable at law on the covenant, and the claim for damages was brought under *Lord Cairns' Act*.[99]

Even where the parties are in a contractual relationship and there is a breach of a covenant (including a restrictive covenant), a plaintiff has the option of recovering common law damages or seeking equitable relief (in the form of an injunction or equitable damages).[100]

In practice an injunction is an appropriate remedy for cases involving a negative covenant. The jurisdiction under *Lord Cairns' Act* can be exercised to award equitable damages in lieu of an injunction where a plaintiff has established a case for an injunction.[101] The courts have had no difficulty in exercising the jurisdiction in cases of a breach of a restrictive covenant.[102]

---

96 [1976] Qd R 272 at 275.
97 G L Newsom, *Preston & Newsom's Restrictive Covenants*, 8th ed, Sweet & Maxwell, London, 1991, p 188.
98 (1970) 213 EG 885.
99 (1970) 213 EG 885.
100 *Snow v Willmott* (1905) 5 OWR 361 at 363.
101 R E Megarry and H W R Wade, *The Law of Real Property*, 5th ed, Sweet & Maxwell, London, 1984, p 778.
102 *Landau v Curton* [1962] EGD 369 at 374–5 ; *Baxter v Four Oaks Properties Ltd* [1965] Ch 816 at 830.

The jurisdiction to award equitable damages under *Lord Cairns' Act* appears to have been first exercised in *Eastwood v Lever*[103] where the plaintiff had lost a right to enforce a restrictive covenant by reason of delay. The offending building had been in the course of construction for some months before the suit. Turner LJ said:

> But although the Plaintiffs are not ... entitled to the relief by way of injunction sought by this bill, it does not follow that they may not be entitled to damages for such injury (if any) as may have been done to their property by the Defendant having built otherwise than in conformity with the covenant. *Sir Hugh Cairns' Act*, 21 & 22 Vict c 27, has, as I read it, empowered Courts of Equity to give damages in such cases.[104]

There was no discussion in the judgment of the basis for the exercise of jurisdiction, although it is evident that the court did not consider that there was any difficulty in exercising the jurisdiction in respect of an equitable right. Turner LJ recognised that *Lord Cairns' Act* was not confined to 'cases in which the Plaintiffs could recover damages at law'.[105] There was also no consideration of whether the infringement of a restrictive covenant was either 'a breach of any covenant',[106] or 'a wrongful act' within the meaning of s 2 of *Lord Cairns' Act*. Such questions would not now arise where *Lord Cairns' Act* has been replaced by a provision which does not contain such terms which may arguably impose jurisdictional constraints.

The manner in which the jurisdiction will be exercised has been discussed in a number of cases. In *Elliston v Reacher*[107] the jurisdiction was not exercised as the court decreed an injunction. However, Parker J observed: 'that if the plaintiff's right be equitable only, as in the present case, the Court will more readily award damages instead of an injunction'.[108] It may be inferred from these remarks that a plaintiff having a legal right would be more readily granted an injunction. This is consistent with the approach later taken in *Sefton v Tophams Ltd*[109] of not exercising the jurisdiction under *Lord Cairns' Act*. In that case an injunction was issued to enforce a covenant by the purchaser of land not to use the land during the lifetime of the vendor, otherwise than for the purposes of horseracing or agriculture. It was recognised that if the jurisdiction was invoked the plaintiff would be awarded no more than nominal damages. Stamp J commented that 'solemn obligations freely undertaken are not to be lightly disregarded'.[110] An injunction is the more appropriate remedy where it is necessary to preserve the integrity of a

---

103 (1863) 4 De GJ & S 114; 46 ER 859.

104 (1863) 4 De GJ & S 114 at 128; 46 ER 859 at 865.

105 (1863) 4 De GJ & S 114 at 128; 46 ER 859 at 865.

106 It has been pointed out that such an action really arises on the general equities and not the covenant: see R P Meagher, W M C Gummow and J R F Lehane, *Equity — Doctrines and Remedies*, 2nd ed, Butterworths, Sydney, 1984, p 617 [2320]; 3rd ed, Butterworths, Sydney, 1992, p 649 [2321].

107 [1908] 2 Ch 374.

108 [1908] 2 Ch 374 at 395.

109 [1965] Ch 1140.

110 [1965] Ch 1140 at 1162.

building scheme.[111] There have been cases where an injunction was issued where a plaintiff had not suffered any damage.[112]

The jurisdiction under *Lord Cairns' Act* may be appropriately exercised in a case of minor damage.[113] An award of nominal damages was made in *Sharp v Harrison*[114] where the court declined to order the destruction of a window which was erected in breach of covenant. The plaintiff had delayed in instituting proceedings, and could prove no depreciation of his property resulting from the breach of covenant. A mandatory injunction would also have prejudiced the interests of a third party. Astbury J remarked: 'The flat in which this window is situated has been let on a lease to a person not a party to this action for a term of five years. It is absolutely impossible to disregard that fact'.[115] The defendant had also given appropriate undertakings to protect the interests of the plaintiff.

The jurisdiction may be exercised where, even in a case of actual damage, the court is obviously reluctant to grant an injunction ordering demolition of a building.[116] In *Shaw v Applegate*[117] the jurisdiction was exercised where the court declined to enjoin a business that was being undertaken in breach of a covenant, and thereby destroy goodwill.

There may be cases where the court will decline to award damages under *Lord Cairns' Act*, and will instead, to quote Sir James Bacon VC, 'exercise that authority, which the court unquestionably possesses'[118] to order the removal of a building. This course of action may be justified where the rights of a plaintiff have been flagrantly disregarded. In one case it was held that a mandatory injunction to remove building alterations, rather than an award of equitable damages, was the appropriate remedy where a plaintiff had for 33 years a view of the sea protected by a restrictive covenant, and where the building alterations which blocked the view were erected in disregard of the objections of the plaintiff.[119]

The tendency of modern cases is to decline injunctive relief where interim relief is not obtained.[120] Where a building has not been erected a plaintiff may seek a permanent injunction rather than an interlocutory injunction because of the risk attached to an undertaking as to damages.[121]

Where a breach of a restrictive covenant causes substantial damage the court may have no discretion to award equitable damages in lieu of a

---

111 Compare *Oxy Electric Ltd v Zainuddin* [1990] 2 All ER 902 at 907.

112 *Manners v Johnson* (1875) 1 Ch D 673; *Stevens v Willing & Co Ltd* [1929] WN 53 (advertising hoarding).

113 *Bowes v Law* (1870) LR 9 Eq 636.

114 [1922] 1 Ch 502.

115 [1922] 1 Ch 502 at 515.

116 *Snow v Willmott* (1905) 5 OWR 361; *Wrotham Park Estate Co Ltd v Parkside Homes Ltd* [1974] 1 WLR 798 at 811; *Arbutus Park Estates Ltd v Fuller* [1977] 1 WWR 729; (1977) 74 DLR (3d) 257.

117 [1977] 1 WLR 970.

118 *Kilbey v Haviland* (1871) 24 LT 353 at 356.

119 *Post Investments Pty Ltd v Wilson* (Supreme Court of New South Wales, Powell J, Eq Div, No 5019 of 1987, 9 May 1990, unreported).

120 *Landau v Curton* [1962] EGD 369; *Wrotham Park Estate Co Ltd v Parkside Homes Ltd* [1974] 1 WLR 798 at 810; *Shaw v Applegate* [1977] 1 WLR 970 at 981.

121 *Oxy Electric Ltd v Zainuddin* [1990] 2 All ER 902.

mandatory injunction.[122] However the question of whether or not a breach causes substantial damage is not in itself a satisfactory test. In *Tipping v Eckersley*[123] Sir William Page Wood VC remarked:

> ... if the construction of the instrument be clear and the breach clear, then it is not a question of damage, but the mere circumstance of the breach of covenant affords sufficient ground for the Court to interfere by injunction.[124]

These remarks were made prior to the enactment of *Lord Cairns' Act* which conferred a discretion upon the court as to what remedy would be appropriate.[125] In determining the appropriate remedy the court will have regard to the conduct of the defendant which is always a relevant consideration.

———<o>———

8.7 Easements

The jurisdiction to award equitable damages may be exercised where an injunction is sought to restrain infringement of an easement.[126] In *Krehl v Burrell*[127] the plaintiff commenced an action to restrain the erection of a building over a right of way. The defendant completed the erection of the building after receiving notice of the plaintiff's rights and the action. In these circumstances the court held that a mandatory injunction was appropriate and declined to award damages under *Lord Cairns' Act*.

A court will be reluctant to grant a mandatory injunction in a case of delay by a plaintiff. In *Bracewell v Appleby*[128] equitable damages were awarded where the plaintiffs had not commenced proceedings until a building was almost complete. Graham J remarked:

> I am unwilling in the circumstances to grant an injunction, but as, in my judgment, the plaintiffs have established their legal right, and by reason of the Chancery Amendment Act 1858 (*Lord Cairns' Act*) they can ask for, and the court can grant, damages in lieu of an injunction.[129]

When an award of equitable damages is made in substitution for an injunction, the award includes compensation for prospective loss. Consequentially, once a judgment for such an award of equitable damages is made, any future action for such loss will be barred unless the judgment is vacated by the court. Sara says:

---

122 *Achilli v Tovell* [1927] 2 Ch 243.
123 (1855) 2 K & J 264; 69 ER 779.
124 (1855) 2 K & J 264 at 270; 69 ER 779 at 782.
125 Compare *Snow v Willmott* (1905) 5 OWR 361 at 363; *Black v Scottish Temperance Life Assurance Co* [1908] 1 Ir R 541 at 574.
126 C J Gale, *Gale on Easements*, 14th ed, Sweet & Maxwell, London, 1972, p 388; P Jackson, *The Law of Easements and Profits*, Butterworths, London, 1978, p 215. See also *Carpet Importing Co Ltd v Beath & Co Ltd* [1927] NZLR 37.
127 (1878) 7 Ch D 551; (1879) 11 Ch D 146.
128 [1975] Ch 408.
129 [1975] Ch 408 at 419.

Although this point has not been judicially resolved, presumably if once an award of damages in lieu of an injunction has been made representing the value of the right seized, then a person bringing a subsequent action for damages would be estopped in equity from pursuing his claim.[130]

—◁▷—

8.8 Light

The question of impairment of access to light is closely associated with the law relating to nuisance. Originally a wronged party would have an action on the case for nuisance where an interference with light was also an infringement of a legal right.[131] Courts of equity had no original jurisdiction, their province being simply to grant an injunction in aid of the legal right where there was danger of irreparable mischief or to prevent a multiplicity of actions.[132] Even after procedural reform to the law of nuisance, the law for the protection of access to light is still reliant on the law of nuisance. In *Colls v Home and Colonial Stores Ltd*[133] Lord Lindley remarked that 'the right to light is in truth no more than a right to be protected against a particular form of nuisance'.[134] The question of access to light often arises in a case of a nuisance, and it follows that the cutting off of sunlight is a matter that may be relevant in the assessment of equitable damages.[135]

There is a public interest in ensuring the use of solar energy. Consequently it would be inappropriate to award equitable damages in lieu of an injunction if nuisance is held to lie where solar access is blocked.[136] In Wisconsin it has been held that an owner of a solar-heated residence has a cause of action in nuisance for an unreasonable obstruction of access to sunlight.[137] In the United States, legislation declares that the shading of solar panels constitutes a public nuisance.[138]

The jurisdiction under *Lord Cairns' Act* has been exercised in a number of cases where a mandatory injunction was sought to remove a building which obstructed ancient lights. The law relating to easements is also relevant in cases of interference with light. At common law a landowner has no inherent right to the passage of natural light over his land. Such a right can only exist as an easement and has to be acquired.[139] The cases are accordingly

---

130 C Sara, *Boundaries and Easements*, Sweet & Maxwell, London, 1991, p 414.
131 R G N Combe, *A Treatise on the Law of Light*, Butterworths, London, 1911, p 275.
132 *Colls v Home and Colonial Stores Ltd* [1904] AC 179 at 188.
133 [1904] AC 179.
134 [1904] AC 179 at 212.
135 *Owen v O'Connor* [1964] NSWR 1312 at 1335.
136 A J Bradbrook, 'Nuisance and the Right of Solar Access', *University of Western Australia Law Review*, vol 15, 1983, 148 at p 173; A J Bradbrook, *Solar Energy and the Law*, Law Book Co, Sydney, 1984, p 104. See also A J Bradbrook, 'The Role of the Courts in Advancing the Use of Solar Energy', *Journal of Energy Law and Policy*, vol 9, 1989, p 135.
137 *Prah v Maretti* (1982) 108 Wis 2d 223; 321 NW 2d 182; noted M A Bedree, *University of Cincinnati Law Review*, vol 52, 1983, p 208.
138 A J Bradbrook, 'The Role of the Courts in Advancing the Use of Solar Energy', *Journal of Energy Law and Policy*, vol 9, 1989, 135 at p 138.
139 R A Buckley, *The Law of Nuisance*, Butterworths, London, 1981, pp 30–1.

concerned with easements of light.[140] In *Isenberg v East India House Estate Co Ltd*[141] Lord Westbury LC emphasised that a mandatory injunction should issue only where damages would be an inadequate remedy. A mandatory injunction will generally only issue where there is substantial interference, including discomfort, with the rights of a plaintiff.[142] In one instance the defendant gave an undertaking as to damages during the trial,[143] but the jurisdiction of the court to order the demolition of a building where it interferes with an easement of light does not depend upon the existence of any such undertaking.[144] There is no doubt that the court may order the demolition of a building which is completed before a suit is instituted.[145] However, a court would be reluctant to exercise its jurisdiction to demolish a building if there has been a failure to obtain interim relief.

Ancient light cases where the jurisdiction to award equitable damages has been exercised include: where the injury to a plaintiff is small and would be adequately compensated by damages;[146] where a plaintiff has delayed in commencing proceedings;[147] where a plaintiff is not an occupant complaining of personal inconvenience;[148] where a plaintiff has not pressed a claim for an injunction;[149] and where the defendant had acted reasonably in giving the plaintiff adequate notice of an intended building even though the damage to the plaintiff could not be regarded as small.[150]

---<o>---

8.9 Quia timet[151] relief

In an appropriate case an injunction may issue where there is a threat of damage to the property of a plaintiff.[152] There is some divergence in the authorities as to the degree of likelihood of injury which will warrant the exercise of the jurisdiction. In *Fletcher v Bealey*[153] Pearson J spoke of 'proof

---

140 The nature of an easement of light was discussed by Lord Macnaghten in *Colls v Home and Colonial Stores Ltd* [1904] AC 179 at 185–6.
141 (1863) 3 De GJ & S 263; 46 ER 637. See also *National Provincial Plate Glass Insurance Co v Prudential Assurance Co* (1877) 6 Ch D 757 at 769.
142 *Jackson v Newcastle, Duke of* (1863) 3 De GJ & S 275; 46 ER 642; *Dyers Co v King* (1870) 9 Eq 438 at 442; *Robson v Whittingham* (1866) LR 1 Ch App 442; *Aynsley v Glover* (1874) LR 18 Eq 544 at 553; *Smith v Smith* (1875) LR 20 Eq 500; *Greenwood v Hornsey* (1886) 33 Ch D 471.
143 *Greenwood v Hornsey* (1886) 33 Ch D 471.
144 *Smith v Day* (1880) 13 Ch D 651.
145 *City of London Brewery Co v Tennant* (1873) LR 9 Ch App 212.
146 *Holland v Worley* (1884) 26 Ch D 578 at 587; *Leeds Industrial Co-operative Society Ltd v Slack* [1924] AC 851.
147 *Senior v Pawson* (1866) LR 3 Eq 330; *Stanley of Alderley, Lady v Shrewsbury, Earl of* (1875) LR 19 Eq 616; *Allen v Seckham* (1879) 11 Ch D 790.
148 *Curriers Co v Corbett* (1865) 2 Dr & Sm 355; 62 ER 656 (plaintiff company, a reversioner, complaining of the deterioration in value of the reversion).
149 *Smyth v Dublin Theatre Co Ltd* [1936] Ir R 692; *Carr-Saunders v Dick McNeil Associates Ltd* [1986] 1 WLR 922.
150 *Fishenden v Higgs and Hill Ltd* (1935) 153 LT 128.
151 'Because he fears.'
152 *Carter v Murray* [1981] 2 NSWLR 77.
153 (1885) 28 Ch D 688.

of imminent danger'.[154] In *Hooper v Rogers*[155] Russell LJ observed that the use of the word 'imminent' in the context of the *quia timet* jurisdiction means that an injunction must not be granted prematurely, and that the degree of probability of future injury is not an absolute standard.[156] Spry has mentioned that the criterion by which the degree of probability of future injury must be established is not fixed or invariable but rather depends upon various other relevant circumstances of the case.[157]

Interlocutory and *quia timet* injunctions are granted for different reasons: an interlocutory injunction will be granted to preserve the status quo until a hearing on the merits, a *quia timet* injunction will be granted after a trial on the merits.[158]

The *quia timet* injunction is available in cases of nuisance, including environmental pollution.[159]

After the turn of this century it was still unsettled whether damages in lieu of an injunction could be awarded under *Lord Cairns' Act* for injury not actually committed, but only threatened or intended.[160] The jurisdiction of the court to award equitable damages for prospective loss was confirmed by a majority of the House of Lords in *Leeds Industrial Co-operative Society Ltd v Slack*.[161]

In the *Leeds* case the defendant was about to erect buildings which would in time have obstructed the ancient lights of the plaintiff. The plaintiff had not sustained any actual injury as the buildings had not been erected. The plaintiff could not therefore commence an action for common law damages because damages may be recovered only in respect of an actual injury sustained by a plaintiff.[162] This rule was described long ago by Blackstone who remarked that 'damages [are] given to a man by a jury, as a compensation and satisfaction of some injury sustained'.[163] The only recourse available to the plaintiff in these circumstances was injunctive relief. Indeed it is apparent that the plaintiff sought only to maintain the injunction that he was granted. However, the House of Lords held that in a *quia timet* action, equitable damages under *Lord Cairns' Act* could be awarded in substitution for an injunction to restrain a threatened obstruction of ancient lights. Viscount Finlay remarked:

---

154 (1885) 28 Ch D 688 at 698.

155 [1975] Ch 43.

156 [1975] Ch 43 at 49.

157 I C F Spry, *Equitable Remedies*, 4th ed, Law Book Co, Sydney, 1990, p 371.

158 P S Elder, 'Environmental Protection through the Common Law', *Western Ontario Law Review*, vol 12, 1973, 107 at p 164.

159 P S Elder, 'Environmental Protection through the Common Law', *Western Ontario Law Review*, vol 12, 1973, 107 at pp 163–70.

160 *Daniell's Chancery Practice*, 7th ed, vol 1, Stevens & Sons, London, 1901, pp 601–2; *Dreyfus v Peruvian Guano Co* (1889) 43 Ch D 316; *Chapman, Morsons & Co v Guardians of Auckland Union* (1889) 23 QBD 294; *Martin v Price* [1894] 1 Ch 276 at 284; *Shelfer v City of London Electric Lighting Co* [1895] 1 Ch 287; *Cowper v Laidler* [1903] 2 Ch 337 at 340; *Canadian Pacific Railway Co v Canadian Northern Railway Co* (1912) 3 WWR 4; 5 Alta LR 407; 7 DLR 120.

161 [1924] AC 851.

162 *Backhouse v Bonomi* (1861) 9 HLC 503; 11 ER 825; *Darley Main Colliery Co v Mitchell* (1886) 11 App Cas 127; *Barbagallo v J & F Catelan Pty Ltd* [1986] 1 Qd R 245 at 248.

163 Blackstone, *Commentaries*, vol 2, 1766, p 438.

... if damages are given in substitution for an injunction they must necessarily cover not only injury already sustained but also injury that would be inflicted in the future by the commission of the act threatened.[164]

In allowing the award of equitable damages in the *Leeds* case their Lordships confirmed that equitable damages could be awarded in a case where common law damages were not available. This judgment resolved the uncertainty which until then had existed as to whether equitable damages could be awarded for a merely threatened injury. One commentator has stated that 'the affirmative answer of the House of Lords (by a bare majority) has provoked abundant doubt and debate'.[165] The decision was controversial in view of the fact that the plaintiff had only sought injunctive relief to protect his proprietary rights. The House of Lords effectively sanctioned the award of damages to a plaintiff who did not seek such relief. In some respects it was extraordinary for a court to award relief to a plaintiff which had not been sought in the pleadings.

The jurisdiction to award equitable damages in a case of *quia timet* relief exists in all jurisdictions in which *Lord Cairns' Act* has been adopted, excepting Tasmania. In Tasmania the court does not have jurisdiction 'to award damages in substitution for an injunction in any case in which ... no wrongful act ... has been committed'.[166] Accordingly the decision of the House of Lords in *Leeds Industrial Co-Operative Society Ltd v Slack*[167] cannot be followed in Tasmania.

There is one case in which there was no recognition of the jurisdiction to award equitable damages in a *quia timet* case. In *York Bros (Trading) Pty Ltd v Commissioner of Main Roads*[168] Powell J remarked:

Such authorities as there are on the application of *Lord Cairns' Act* (*Dreyfus v Peruvian Guano Co*;[169] *Shelfer v City of London Electric Lighting Co*[170]) lay down the principle that where, as here, what is sought is a *quia timet* injunction, the court has no jurisdiction to award damages in respect of the injury not yet committed but only threatened.[171]

This passage from the judgment may have been based upon the 1982 Australian reprint of the seventh edition of *Daniell's Chancery Practice* which was published prior to the *Leeds* case.[172]

The jurisdiction under *Lord Cairns' Act* has been exercised to award damages in respect of excavations that would in time lead to a loss of support to land. This may be contrasted with the position at common law where no cause of action arises for loss of support until a plaintiff has actually sustained damage to land.[173] In *Barbagallo v J & F Catelan Pty*

---

164 [1924] AC 851 at 857.
165 *Stephen's Commentaries on the Laws of England*, vol II, 21st ed, Butterworth & Co, London, 1950, p 353.
166 Supreme Court Civil Procedure Act 1932 (Tasmania) s 11(13)(b).
167 [1924] AC 851.
168 [1983] 1 NSWLR 391.
169 (1889) 43 Ch D 316.
170 [1895] 1 Ch 287.
171 [1983] 1 NSWLR 391 at 399.
172 E R Daniell, *Practice of the High Court of Chancery*, vol 1, 7th ed, 1901, pp 601–2.
173 *Backhouse v Bonomi* (1861) 9 HLC 503; 11 ER 825; *Darley Main Colliery Co v Mitchell* (1886) 11 App Cas 127 at 141; *Barbagallo v J & F Catelan Pty Ltd* [1986] 1 Qd R 245 at 248–9.

Ltd[174] McPherson J referred to 'the well established rule of the common law that the landowner's right of action accrues not at the date of the excavation but at the date of the damage, whether it be physical, as by subsidence, or merely pecuniary'.[175] Therefore common law damages are not available to a plaintiff who is seeking relief in respect of a mere threatened loss of support. Equitable damages may however be awarded in substitution for an injunction that is issued to prevent injury whether the injunction is of a prohibitory or mandatory nature. In *Barbagallo v J & F Catelan Pty Ltd*[176] McPherson J commented that the Queensland equivalent of *Lord Cairns' Act* 'enables equitable damages to be awarded in substitution for an injunction to restrain ... a threatened interference'.[177]

There are early Canadian instances of the exercise of the jurisdiction under *Lord Cairns' Act* in excavation cases. *Ramsay v Barnes*[178] was an action for injury to the plaintiff's land by excavations made by the defendant upon his adjoining land, thereby depriving the plaintiff's land of lateral support. Some injury to the plaintiff's land had occurred, but further injury would occur in the future. An award of equitable damages was made in substitution for an injunction. Middleton J remarked:

> I have come to the conclusion that the case is one in which I should not award an injunction, but damages, and that the damages awarded should be in the nature of compensation, and should not be confined to the damages already sustained.[179]

This case was followed in *Gage v Barnes*[180] where the defendants had by reason of their excavations caused the plaintiff's land to subside, and there was the probability of a future subsidence from this cause. Lennox J gave judgment which included not only past damage but also 'future damage by reason of excavations'.[181]

The leading case which establishes that equitable damages may be awarded for a threatened loss of support is *Hooper v Rogers*.[182] In that case the defendant had excavated soil from property adjacent to the plaintiff's farmhouse. The excavation would eventually cause the farmhouse to collapse. The plaintiff was awarded damages in lieu of a mandatory injunction which required the defendant to reinstate the excavated site to which both parties had rights of occupation. Russell LJ observed:

> ... this is a case in which a mandatory order was sought upon the defendant to take such steps as were necessary to reinstate the excavated track to its former condition so as to restore to the slope the angle of repose of the soil and thus avert the threat of future removal of support to the farmhouse. The award of damages could only be supported as equitable

---

174 [1986] 1 Qd R 245.
175 [1986] 1 Qd R 245 at 249.
176 [1986] 1 Qd R 245.
177 [1986] 1 Qd R 245 at 252.
178 (1913) 5 OWN 322.
179 (1913) 5 OWN 322 at 324.
180 [1914] 26 OWR 225.
181 [1914] 26 OWR 225 at 229.
182 [1975] Ch 43.

damages under the Chancery Amendment Act 1858 (*Lord Cairns' Act*) in lieu of such an injunction .[183]

In *Gur v Burton*[184] Dillon LJ considered that the decision in *Hooper v Rogers*[185] 'remains good law'. The decision has been followed in a number of *quia timet* cases where equitable damages have been awarded for the cost of stabilising land.[186] In some cases an award of equitable damages may be made to a plaintiff to cover the cost of remedial works. An award of equitable damages must not be disproportionate to the value of the property affected, and must do justice between the parties.[187]

————◄O►————

8.10 Breach of statutory public duty

There is considerable debate on whether a breach of a statute which imposes a public duty creates a correlative private right of action.[188] The courts have held that industrial legislation is one area where a breach of statute creates a private right of action. The courts have been reluctant to regard town planning legislation as conferring a private right of action. There is authority that damages will not be awarded under *Lord Cairns' Act* where an injunction is sought for the breach of a statutory duty which does not create a civil right of action to an aggrieved individual. The cases have concerned town planning legislation in which it was held that there was no jurisdiction to award equitable damages for the breach of a statute imposing a public duty. This will be so irrespective of whether an individual has locus standi to seek an injunction[189] or whether a relator action is brought.[190]

---

183 [1975] Ch 43 at 47.
184 Court of Appeal, England, 29 July 1993, unreported.
185 [1975] Ch 43.
186 *Grocott v Ayson* [1975] 2 NZLR 586 at 590; *Barbagallo v J & F Catelan Pty Ltd* [1986] 1 Qd R 245.
187 *Barbagallo v J & F Catelan Pty Ltd* [1986] 1 Qd R 245 at 258, 270. As to the general principles of assessment of damages for a loss of a right of support: see *Minter v Eacott* (1952) 69 WN (NSW) 93.
188 E R Thayer, 'Public Wrong and Private Action', *Harvard Law Review*, vol 27, 1914, p 317; C Morris, 'The Relation of Criminal Statutes to Tort Liability', *Harvard Law Review*, vol 46, 1933, p 453; C Morris, 'The Role of Criminal Statutes in Negligence Actions', *Columbia Law Review*, vol 49, 1949, p 21; G Williams, 'The Effect of Penal Legislation in the Law of Tort', *Modern Law Review*, vol 23, 1960, p 233; G M Fricke, 'The Juridical Nature of the Action upon the Statute', *Law Quarterly Review*, vol 76, 1960, p 240; A M Linden, 'Tort Liability for Criminal Non-feasance', *Canadian Bar Review*, vol 44, 1966, p 25; C S Phegan, 'Breach of Statutory Duty as a Remedy against Public Authorities', *University of Queensland Law Journal*, vol 8, 1974, p 158.
189 *Neville Nitschke Caravans (Main North Road) Pty Ltd v McEntree* (1976) 15 SASR 330; *Wentworth v Woollahra Municipal Council* (1982) 149 CLR 672; 56 ALJR 745; *Thorne v Doug Wade Consultants Pty Ltd* [1985] VR 433.
190 *Attorney-General v Birkenhead Borough* [1968] NZLR 383.

It has been assumed that *Lord Cairns' Act* was only intended to award damages for the infringement of a private right. This was the conclusion of Richmond J in the *Birkenhead Borough*[191] case in New Zealand where the plaintiff unsuccessfully sought to invoke *Lord Cairns' Act* in a relator action to enforce town planning legislation. The question of damage in such an action was immaterial. The plaintiff argued that the infringement of the legislation was a 'wrongful act' within the meaning of *Lord Cairns' Act*. Richmond J remarked that the Act 'contemplates the exercise of a jurisdiction in which there will always be a party injured — this is implicit in the case of the phrase "to *the* party injured"'.[192]

In the *Neville Nitschke*[193] case the Full Court of South Australia, by a majority, held that the South Australian equivalent of *Lord Cairns' Act* did not enable the award of damages in lieu of an injunction to a plaintiff suing in respect of a public general duty as distinct from an infringement of a private right. The plaintiff sought to restrain a nuisance on land used in infringement of town planning legislation. The case was concerned with the preliminary question of whether the statement of claim could include a claim for damages. King J, with whom Jacobs J concurred, expressed agreement with the judgment of Richmond J in the *Birkenhead Borough*[194] case. King J remarked:

> A plaintiff who sues for breach of a public general duty without the intervention of the Attorney-General, relying for locus standi on particular damage suffered in consequence of such breach, is not, in my opinion the 'party injured' by such breach within the meaning of s 30.[195]

One criticism can be made of the decisions in the *Birkenhead Borough* and *Neville Nitschke* cases. It is submitted that the term 'party injured' in *Lord Cairns' Act* should have been beneficially interpreted. In *Leeds Industrial Co-Operative Society Ltd v Slack*[196] a majority of the House of Lords considered that *Lord Cairns' Act* conferred jurisdiction in *quia timet* proceedings in which a plaintiff had not sustained any actual injury. In the *Neville Nitschke* case the question of the jurisdiction under *Lord Cairns' Act* was really academic as the statement of claim did not allege any particular damage. This was recognised by Bray CJ who considered that the plaintiff in the *Birkenhead Borough* case was entitled to damages in substitution for an injunction under the second limb of *Boyce v Paddington Borough Council*.[197] The Chief Justice said:

---

191 [1968] NZLR 383.
192 [1968] NZLR 383 at 393.
193 (1976) 15 SASR 330.
194 [1968] NZLR 383.
195 (1976) 15 SASR 330 at 351.
196 [1924] AC 851.
197 [1903] 1 Ch 109. The principle in the *Boyce* decision was summarised in the *Birkenhead Borough* case by Richmond J as follows: 'It means that the equitable remedy of injunction is available at the suit of private individuals where there is no common law action for damages for breach of statutory duty or for the interference with any private right': [1968] NZLR 383 at 390.

I find difficulty in seeing why the cause of action in its new generalised setting should not continue to possess the incidents it had when it was simply an action for damages in tort for particular damage arising out of a public nuisance.[198]

The High Court of Australia in *Wentworth v Woollahra Municipal Council*[199] held that the New South Wales equivalent of *Lord Cairns' Act* did not authorise the award of damages for the erection of a dwelling house built in breach of a planning ordinance that manifested no intention to create a private cause of action. The High Court observed:

> In 1858 it would not have occurred to anyone that, apart from public nuisance, damages might be awarded to an individual on violation of a public right or for non-performance of a public duty.[200]

Finn has pointed out that this assumption is questionable because there are cases where damages have been awarded to a plaintiff who sustained injury resulting from a failure to provide or maintain a service or facility required by statute.[201] The leading case, which was decided some four years prior to the passage of *Lord Cairns' Act*, is *Couch v Steel*[202] where a shipowner was held liable to a seaman for having neglected to carry medicines on board a vessel, as required by merchant shipping legislation.[203] It was held that the fact that the legislation provided a penalty did not preclude an action. Lord Campbell CJ said:

> ... the plaintiff's right, by the common law, to maintain an action on the case for special damage sustained by the breach of a public duty is not taken away by reason of the statute which creates the duty imposing a penalty recoverable by a common informer.[204]

The decision of the High Court in the *Wentworth* case was followed in *Thorne v Doug Wade Consultants Pty Ltd*[205] in which it was held that equitable damages under *Lord Cairns' Act* could not be awarded where town planning legislation was contravened. Kaye and Marks JJ (with whom McGarvie J agreed) remarked:

> Damages were not and are not available to the appellants for breach of their right as members of the public. This was decided by the High Court in *Wentworth v Woollahra Municipal Council*[206] and reaffirmed in *Wentworth v Woollahra Municipal Council (No 3)*,[207] where it was also held that the provisions of *Lord Cairns' Act* (enacted in respectively s 62 of the

---

198 (1976) 15 SASR 330 at 341.
199 (1982) 149 CLR 672.
200 (1982) 149 CLR 672 at 682; 56 ALJR 745 at 749.
201 P D Finn, 'A Road Not Taken: The Boyce Plaintiff and *Lord Cairns' Act*', *Australian Law Journal*, vol 57, 1983, 493 at p 496.
202 (1854) 3 El & Bl 412; 118 ER 1193 discussed in R A Buckley, 'Liability in Tort for Breach of Statutory Duty', *Law Quarterly Review*, vol 100, 1984, 204 at p 205.
203 7 & 8 Vict c 112 s 18.
204 (1854) 3 El & Bl 412 at 415; 118 ER 1193 at 1198.
205 [1985] VR 433.
206 (1982) 149 CLR 672.
207 (1984) 154 CLR 518 at 523.

Supreme Court Act (Vic) and s 68 of the Supreme Court Act (NSW)) do not authorise an award of damages for breach of a statutory provision which shows no intention to create a private right to an action for damages.[208]

However, in *Thorne's* case the plaintiffs did not pursue their claim for damages. It is submitted that the case is no longer authority in Victoria because s 36 of the Supreme Court Act 1986, which enables equitable damages to be awarded, does not contain the words 'wrongful act'.

The decisions in the *Birkenhead Borough* and *Neville Nitschke* cases raise philosophical questions relating to the development of the law in this area. In the *Birkenhead Borough* case Richmond J recognised that 'the common law has developed in a restricted way as regards acknowledging the existence of any private right of action for breach of a statutory duty'.[209] In the *Neville Nitschke* case King J considered that 'the authorities do not justify an extension of the right which exists to recover particular damage sustained as a consequence of infringements of public rights or of public law generally'.[210] It has already been mentioned that there is old, but respectable authority on this question. Glanville Williams regarded the decision in *Couch v Steel*[211] as establishing that where a statute has been passed for the benefit of the public at large, a plaintiff could sue for breach of statutory duty if that plaintiff suffered particular damage over and above that suffered by the rest of the public. He recognised that later decisions have rejected this criterion of particular damage.[212] The law in this area is developing to provide a remedy to a plaintiff who has suffered particular damage. In *Booth & Co (International) v National Enterprise Board*[213] Forbes J held that it was arguable that a plaintiff had a right of action where a breach of statutory duty causes peculiar and special injury greater than 'that suffered by the generality of Her Majesty's subjects'.[214] It has been recognised that this decision may well evidence a 'reversion to the old orthodoxy for actions on the statute'.[215]

The law will undoubtedly develop in such a way as to extend the remedies available to a plaintiff injured by a breach of statutory duty. An indication of this development is to be found in *Rickless v United Artists Corp*[216] where the executors of Peter Sellers sought, inter alia, to restrain the use of 'out-takes' from five *Pink Panther* films. The use of these films was in breach of s 2 of the Dramatic and Musical Performers Protection

---

208 [1985] VR 433 at 492.
209 [1968] NZLR 383 at 391.
210 (1976) 15 SASR 330 at 351.
211 (1854) 3 El & Bl 402; 118 ER 1193.
212 G Williams, 'The Effect of Penal Legislation in the Law of Tort', *Modern Law Review*, vol 23, 1960, 233 at p 245.
213 [1978] 3 All ER 624.
214 [1978] 3 All ER 624 at 631.
215 P D Finn, 'A Road Not Taken: The Boyce Plaintiff and *Lord Cairns' Act*', *Australian Law Journal*, vol 57, 1983, 493 at p 571.
216 (1985) 135 NLJ 656; *Times LR*, 17 June 1985.

Act 1958.[217] The court held that the Act conferred civil remedies as well as imposing criminal sanctions. Hobhouse J awarded equitable damages of one million dollars (US) under s 50 of the Supreme Court Act 1981 rather than restrain performance of the films. The decision of Hobhouse J was affirmed by the Court of Appeal.[218]

One case inhibits the evolution of just principles. In *CBS Songs Ltd v Amstrad Consumer Electronics Plc*[219] the Court of Appeal held in an interlocutory appeal that inciting members of the public to commit a breach of copyright legislation did not confer on copyright owners a right to sue in equity for an injunction and damages under *Lord Cairns' Act*. The claim for damages was appended to the claim for an injunction. The majority of the Court of Appeal held that, in the absence of an express statutory provision, a person other than the Attorney-General acting *ex officio* or *ex relatione* had no standing to enforce the observance of the criminal law through the civil courts. It is submitted that the dissenting judgment of Sir Denys Buckley in that case is correct in stating that an injunction can issue to protect private property rights on the authority of *Emperor of Austria v Day and Kossuth*.[220] Where an injunction is available to restrain a breach of a statutory prohibition, the fact that damages could not be recovered at law was appreciated by Sir Denys Buckley to be a discretionary rather than a jurisdictional matter. There is much force in the following observations of Sir Denys Buckley:

> I do not think the claim to damages under *Lord Cairns' Act* presents any difficulty. The award of such damages would be discretionary. If no damages could be recovered at common law, a court of equity might well regard this as a proper circumstance to take into account.[221]

It may be argued that there would be an incongruity if *Lord Cairns' Act* is construed so as to permit the award of damages in circumstances where no private right of action for damages for breach of statutory duty is available. In the *Birkenhead Borough* case Richmond J said:

> It would be a curious result if *Lord Cairns' Act* were so construed as to permit a private award of compensatory damages where no such award would be permitted by these settled principles of law ... The notion of compensation to an individual as an alternative to enforced compliance with a duty owed to the public at large is to my mind incongruous and illogical.[222]

However, the fact is that *Lord Cairns' Act* enables damages to be awarded where no such damages may be awarded at law, for example *quia timet* relief and restrictive covenants.

---

217 1958 c 44.
218 *Rickless v United Artists Corp* [1988] QB 40.
219 [1988] Ch 61, affirmed *CBS Songs Ltd v Amstrad Consumer Electronics Plc* [1988] AC 1013.
220 (1861) 3 De GF & J 217; 45 ER 861.
221 [1988] Ch 61 at 84.
222 [1968] NZLR 383 at 393.

There are Canadian authorities which recognise that damages may be awarded under *Lord Cairns' Act* in the case of the breach of a public statutory duty. It has been held that equitable damages can be awarded in respect of a breach of a statute which enables an informer to recover a penalty. In *Lounsbury v Sutherland Motor Bus Co*[223] it was held that the jurisdiction to award damages under the New Brunswick equivalent of *Lord Cairns' Act* was not limited by a statute which imposed a penalty which was not recoverable by an aggrieved person. In *Tenning v Manitoba*[224] it was held that the Manitoba Human Rights Act[225] was a complete code for dealing with discrimination, and that no civil right of action could be maintained for a breach of the statute. However, it was appreciated that an award of equitable damages could be made. Where an injunction to restrain discrimination was sought under s 34 of the Human Rights Act, Deniset J envisaged the possibility of an award of equitable damages in commenting that the plaintiff 'could possibly have been awarded damages pursuant to s 60 of the Queen's Bench Act, RSM 1970, c 280'.[226]

In the *Birkenhead Borough* and *Neville Nitschke* cases jurisdictional constraints were imposed because of the terminology of *Lord Cairns' Act*. It has been recognised that the answer may be to reform *Lord Cairns' Act*.[227] This is because *Lord Cairns' Act* contains terms such as 'wrongful act' and 'party injured' which may arguably preclude relief. In those jurisdictions such as Victoria and Manitoba which have adopted provisions derived from s 50 of the Supreme Court Act, the courts do not have the jurisdictional constraints which have been mentioned. This is because now the sole criterion of jurisdiction is whether the court has jurisdiction to entertain an application for an injunction, or, as in Ontario, has jurisdiction to grant an injunction. In those jurisdictions in which *Lord Cairns' Act* has been reformulated, it is submitted that the question of whether or not a penal statute evidences an intention to permit a private right of action is no longer a matter which affects the jurisdiction of a court to award equitable damages. That is because under the reformulated provisions, the sole criterion of jurisdiction is whether a plaintiff has a case for an injunction. Accordingly whether a statute confers a private right of action is really a discretionary, and not a jurisdictional, consideration. The question of whether the statute permits a right of action is now a matter which a court may consider in determining whether it will exercise its discretion to award equitable damages.

---

223 (1928) 54 NBR 7.
224 (1983) 23 Man R (2d) 227.
225 SM 1974 c 65.
226 (1983) 23 Man R (2d) 227 at 228.
227 P D Finn, 'A Road Not Taken: The Boyce Plaintiff and *Lord Cairns' Act*', *Australian Law Journal*, vol 57, 1983, 493 at p 579.

8.11 Equitable obligations or interests

Since the decision in *Eastwood v Lever*[228] it is now settled that equitable damages can be awarded under *Lord Cairns' Act* in aid of an equitable right.[229] Gurry[230] states that this view explains the decision in the *Saltman Engineering* case.[231] In *Crabb v Arun District Council (No 2)*,[232] Lord Denning MR relied upon the decision in *Eastwood v Lever*[233] in remarking: 'The power to award compensation or damages in respect of an equitable interest is not limited to where damages could be awarded at law'.[234] Similarly in *Price v Strange*[235] Goff LJ observed:

> One purpose and a very important purpose of that Act was, of course, to avoid circuity of action by enabling the old Court of Chancery to award damages at law, but the Act clearly went further and enabled the court to give damages where there was no cause of action at law.[236]

In *Wentworth v Woollahra Municipal Council*[237] the justices of the High Court of Australia commented:

> An incidental object of the Act was to enable the court to award damages in lieu of an injunction or specific performance, even in the case of a purely equitable claim.[238]

It has been suggested that these remarks are best regarded as being uttered *per incuriam*.[239] However, it is submitted that the High Court meant to state that an 'incidental result'[240] of *Lord Cairns' Act* was to enable the court to grant damages in the case of a purely equitable claim. In *Attorney-General v Guardian Newspapers Ltd (No 2)*[241] the potential of the jurisdiction under *Lord Cairns' Act* was recognised for cases of a breach of an equitable obligation. Lord Goff of Chieveley remarked that equitable damages could be awarded 'despite the equitable nature of the wrong, through a beneficent interpretation of the Chancery Amendment Act 1858 (*Lord Cairns' Act*)'.[242]

There has been some debate as to whether *Lord Cairns' Act* enabled equitable damages to be awarded for the breach of a purely equitable obligation. Some leading Australian commentators have recognised that

---

228 (1863) 4 De GJ & S 114; 46 ER 859 discussed earlier at p 138.
229 N Ashburner, *Principles of Equity*, 2nd ed, Butterworths, London, 1933, p 352.
230 F Gurry, *Breach of Confidence*, Oxford University Press, Oxford, 1984, p 430.
231 (1948) 65 RPC 203.
232 (1976) 121 SJ 86.
233 (1863) 4 De GJ & S 114; 46 ER 859.
234 (1976) 121 SJ 86.
235 [1978] Ch 337.
236 [1978] Ch 337 at 358.
237 (1982) 149 CLR 672.
238 (1982) 149 CLR 672 at 676.
239 R P Meagher, W M C Gummow and J R F Lehane, *Equity — Doctrines and Remedies*, 2nd ed, Butterworths, Sydney, 1984, p 618 [2320]; 3rd ed, Butterworths, Sydney, 1992, p 650 [2321].
240 *Landau v Curton* [1962] EGD 369 at 375 per Cross J (cited at 149 CLR 672 at 676).
241 [1990] AC 109.
242 [1990] AC 109 at 286.

'this applies an interpretation of the legislation which may be open',[243] although they[244] obviously prefer the view that the term 'wrongful act' in s 2 of *Lord Cairns' Act* bears the same meaning in s 82 of the Common Law Procedure Act 1854.[245] Section 82 of the Common Law Procedure Act provided:

> ... it shall be lawful for the plaintiff at any time after the commencement of the action ... to apply ... for a writ of injunction to restrain the defendant in such action from the repetition or continuance of the wrongful act or breach of contract complained of.

Section 99 of the Common Law Practice Act provided that the word 'action' shall be understood to mean any personal action in any of the superior courts of common law at Westminster. The term 'wrongful act' when used in the Common Law Procedure Act certainly could not be regarded as including any violation of any equitable right. This is because such a right would not be the subject of an action at law. However, it does not necessarily follow that the term 'wrongful act' in *Lord Cairns' Act* bears the same meaning. There is a danger if the term 'wrongful act' in *Lord Cairns' Act* is restrictively interpreted to accord with the meaning ascribed to that term in another statute. In *Macbeth & Co v Chislett*[246] Lord Loreburn LC warned:

> ... it would be a new terror in the construction of Acts of Parliament if we were required to limit a word to an unnatural sense because in some Act which is not incorporated or referred to such an interpretation is given to it for the purposes of that Act alone.[247]

These Australian commentators have placed reliance upon the recommendations of the Chancery Commissioners who considered that the Court of Chancery should have jurisdiction to award damages to 'a person injured by a wrongful act, which would entitle him to damages in a Court of Law'.[248] However, it has earlier been mentioned that *Lord Cairns' Act* differed in significant respects from the recommendations of the Chancery Commissioners.[249] *Lord Cairns' Act* enabled damages to be awarded in substitution for an injunction and this jurisdiction had not been envisaged by the Commissioners. *Lord Cairns' Act* therefore enabled the award of damages in substitution for an injunction in respect of an equitable obligation which could not be the subject of an action at law for damages. It is *Lord Cairns' Act* which must be construed, and not the report of the Commissioners who did not draft *Lord Cairns' Act*.

---

243 R P Meagher, W M C Gummow and J R F Lehane, *Equity — Doctrines and Remedies*, 2nd ed, Butterworths, Sydney, 1984, p 52 [231]; 3rd ed, Butterworths, Sydney, 1992, p 52 [231].

244 Meagher, Gummow and Lehane, n 243 above, 2nd ed, p 618 [2320]; 3rd ed, p 649 [2321].

245 17 & 18 Vict c 125.

246 [1910] AC 220.

247 [1910] AC 220 at 223.

248 *Third Report of Her Majesty's Commissioners appointed to inquire into the Process, Practice and System of Pleading in the Court of Chancery & c*, 1856, Command [2064], p 3.

249 See p 31.

Lord Cairns' Act does not evidence any limitation that damages could only be awarded for legal wrongs. The term 'wrongful act' in *Lord Cairns' Act* is quite capable of referring to an infringement of a legal or an equitable right. This is because both classes of right may be vindicated and protected by injunctive relief. It has been held that the expression 'wrongful act' in the Fatal Accidents Act 1846 (*Lord Campbell's Act*)[250] was not restricted to tortious acts, and included a breach of contract. In *Woolworths Ltd v Crotty*[251] Sir John Latham CJ remarked:

> The words are very general. 'Wrongful act' is a term which in a perfectly natural meaning can be applied to breaches of contract as well as to torts.[252]

The Chief Justice added that the House of Lords in *South Wales Miners' Federation v Glamorgan Coal Co Ltd*[253] regarded a breach of contract as a legal wrong.

In *Talbot v General Television Corp Pty Ltd*[254] Harris J rejected a submission that the term 'wrongful act' in the then Victorian equivalent of *Lord Cairns' Act*[255] was restricted to acts which are torts at common law. This ruling was not challenged on appeal.[256] Earlier in *Gas & Fuel Corp v Barba*[257] Crocket J had assumed that damages for the infringement of a purely equitable right under an easement could be awarded under the then Victorian equivalent to *Lord Cairns' Act*. In those jurisdictions which have reformed *Lord Cairns' Act* provisions such as s 50 of the Supreme Court Act pose no jurisdictional barriers as the term 'wrongful act' does not appear in the reformulated provision. Accordingly, in those jurisdictions, equitable damages may be awarded where a plaintiff has an equity to an injunction to prevent the infringement of an equitable obligation.

———<o>———

8.12 Fiduciary duties

The inherent jurisdiction of a court of equity to grant compensation for a breach of a fiduciary duty was reaffirmed by Viscount Haldane LC in *Nocton v Lord Ashburton*.[258] The scope of the compensatory jurisdiction of equity has been subject to comprehensive analysis recently and is still developing.[259] It has been recognised in a number of decisions that this

---

250 9 & 10 Vict c 93.
251 (1942) 66 CLR 603.
252 (1942) 66 CLR 603 at 619.
253 [1905] AC 239 at 253.
254 [1980] VR 224 at 241; [1981] RPC 1 at 19, discussed at p 156.
255 Supreme Court Act 1958 (Victoria) s 62(3).
256 [1980] VR 224 at 243; [1981] RPC 1 at 21.
257 [1976] VR 755 at 766.
258 [1914] AC 932.
259 P D Finn, *Fiduciary Obligations*, Law Book Co, Sydney, 1977; J C Shepherd, *The Law of Fiduciaries*, Carswell, Toronto, 1981; P D Finn, 'Fiduciary Obligations of Operators and Co-venturers in Natural Resources Joint Ventures', *Australian Mining and Petroleum Law*

jurisdiction is inherent and is not dependent upon *Lord Cairns' Act*. In *United States Surgical Corp v Hospital Products International Pty Ltd*[260] McLelland J commented:

> Apart from the limited power to award damages in addition to or in substitution for equitable relief, conferred by the Supreme Court Act, 1970, s 68 (following *Lord Cairns' Act*), which is of no present relevance, the court has an inherent power to grant relief by way of monetary compensation for breach of a fiduciary or other equitable obligation.[261]

Presumably, one reason why *Lord Cairns' Act* was not relevant in the *Hospital Products* case was that there was no basis for injunctive relief as there were no continuing breaches of duty.[262]

In *Markwell Bros Pty Ltd v CPN Diesels Queensland Pty Ltd*[263] Thomas J remarked:

> In my opinion, the origin of the power is not in *Lord Cairns' Act*, it is part of the long established power of a court of equity to award compensation for breach of a trust, and a manifestation of the court's power over a fiduciary.[264]

In *Day v Mead*[265] Sir Robin Cooke P observed:

> In this Court it has been accepted that, independently of *Lord Cairns' Act*, damages or equitable compensation can be awarded for part breaches of a duty deriving historically from equity.[266]

Ordinarily, in a case of breach of a fiduciary duty where an account of profits is not appropriate, the appropriate remedy sought would be compensation.[267] Where a plaintiff has an equity to an injunction the jurisdiction to award equitable damages may also be invoked.

8.13 Breach of confidence

The jurisdictional basis of the action for breach of confidence is not settled. The Law Commission recognised the 'uncertainty as to the nature and scope of the remedy owing to its somewhat obscure legal basis',[268] and commented that 'it would seem more realistic to regard the modern action

---

    Assn Yearbook, 1974, p 160. See also *United States Surgical Corp v Hospital Products International Pty Ltd* [1982] 2 NSWLR 766 at 809.

260 [1982] 2 NSWLR 766.
261 [1982] 2 NSWLR 766 at 816.
262 [1982] 2 NSWLR 766 at 819.
263 [1983] 2 Qd R 508; 7 ACLR 425.
264 [1983] 2 Qd R 508 at 523.
265 [1987] 2 NZLR 443.
266 [1987] 2 NZLR 443 at 450. See also *Coleman v Myers* [1977] 2 NZLR 225 at 359–62 ; *Van Camp Chocolates Ltd v Aulsebrooks Ltd* [1984] 1 NZLR 354 at 361.
267 *Dominion Insurance Co of Australia Ltd v Finn* (Supreme Court of New South Wales, Hodgson J, Eq Div, No 1308 of 1984, 18 December 1987, unreported).
268 Law Commission, *Breach of Confidence*, Law Com No 110, 1981, p 10.

simply as *sui generis*.[269] The various jurisdictional grounds for imposing liability upon a recipient of confidential information have been discussed and liability has been imposed on the basis of contract, property or equity.[270] In New Zealand there is appellate authority that liability is imposed irrespective of whether the duty is equitable or not.[271] It has also been recognised that there may be tortious liability for a breach of confidence.[272]

The scope of the equitable jurisdiction to grant relief in an action for breach of confidence was considered by the High Court of Australia in *Moorgate Tobacco Co Ltd v Philip Morris Ltd (No 2)*.[273] Deane J has summarised the essential principles:

> It is unnecessary, for the purposes of the present appeal, to attempt to define the precise scope of the equitable jurisdiction to grant relief against an actual or threatened abuse of confidential information not involving any tort or any breach of some express or implied contractual provision, some wider fiduciary duty or some copyright or trade mark right. A general equitable jurisdiction to grant such relief has long been asserted and should, in my view, now be accepted: see *The Commonwealth v John Fairfax & Sons Ltd*.[274] Like most heads of exclusive equitable jurisdiction, its rational basis does not lie in proprietary right. It lies in the notion of an obligation of conscience arising from the circumstances in or through which the information was communicated or obtained. Relief under the jurisdiction is not available, however, unless it appears that the information in question has "the necessary quality of confidence about it" (per Lord Greene MR, *Saltman*)[275] and that it is significant, not necessarily in the sense of commercially valuable (see *Argyll v Argyll*)[276] but in the sense that the preservation of its confidentiality or secrecy is of substantial concern to the plaintiff.[277]

This is an important restatement that the fundamental basis for the intervention of equity is the 'obligation of conscience' reflecting the clerical origins of the Chancery jurisdiction. In *Smith Kline & French Laboratories (Australia) Ltd v Secretary, Dept of Community Services and Health*[278] Gummow J, in approving the views of a number of commentators,[279]

---

269 Law Commission, *Breach of Confidence*, Law Com No 110, 1981 p 11.

270 P D Finn, *Fiduciary Obligations*, Law Book Co, Sydney, 1977, ch 19; J C Shepherd, *The Law of Fiduciaries*, Carswell, Toronto, 1981, p 325; F Gurry, *Breach of Confidence*, Oxford University Press, Oxford, 1984, p 25. See also *LAC Minerals v International Corona Resources Ltd* (1989) 61 DLR (4th) 14.

271 *Attorney-General v Wellington Newspapers Ltd* [1988] 1 NZLR 129; *Aquaculture Corp v New Zealand Green Mussel Co Ltd* [1990] 3 NZLR 299.

272 R Goff and G Jones, *The Law of Restitution*, 2nd ed, Sweet & Maxwell, London, 1978, p 518, n 59; P M North, 'Breach of Confidence: Is There a New Tort?', *Journal of the Society of Public Teachers of Law*, 1972, p 141.

273 (1984) 156 CLR 414.

274 (1980) 147 CLR 39 at 50–2.

275 (1947) 65 RPC 203 at 215.

276 [1967] Ch 302 at 329.

277 (1984) 156 CLR 414 at 437–8.

278 (1990) 17 IPR 545.

279 F Gurry, *Breach of Confidence*, Oxford University Press, Oxford, 1984, pp 407–8; P Birks, 'A Lifelong Obligation of Confidence', *Law Quarterly Review*, vol 105, 1989, p 501; R Dean, *The Law of Trade Secrets*, Law Book Co, Sydney, 1990, pp 177–8.

emphasised 'that equity intervenes to uphold an obligation and not necessarily to prevent or to recover loss'.[280]

In a case involving a breach of confidence the existence of jurisdiction under *Lord Cairns' Act* is itself dependent on whether there is a basis for injunctive relief. Therefore in some cases *Lord Cairns' Act* would provide an obvious source of jurisdiction to award damages. Birks has commented: 'The interest in privacy is best defended by means of injunctions'.[281]

There are a number of authorities which recognise that confidential information may be protected by injunction. In *Coco v AN Clark (Engineers) Ltd*[282] Megarry J remarked:

> The equitable jurisdiction in cases of breach of confidence is ancient; confidence is the cousin of trust. The Statute of Uses, 1535, is framed in terms of 'use, confidence or trust;' and a couplet attributed to Sir Thomas More, Lord Chancellor avers that
> > Three things are to be helpt in Conscience;
> > Fraud, Accident and things of Confidence.[283]

In *Ashburton (Lord) v Pape*[284] Swinfen Eady LJ observed:

> The principle upon which the Court of Chancery has acted for many years has been to restrain the publication of confidential information improperly or surreptitiously obtained or of information imparted in confidence which ought not to be divulged.[285]

This principle was cited by Sir Anthony Mason in *Commonwealth of Australia v John Fairfax & Sons Ltd*[286] as a 'fundamental principle of Equity'.[287]

The courts will protect confidential information which Lord Greene MR in *Saltman Engineering Co Ltd v Campbell Engineering Co Ltd*[288] described as not 'public property and public knowledge'.[289] Equity will therefore only enjoin the disclosure of information which is not in the public domain. This important limitation upon the jurisdiction of a court of equity has been emphasised in a number of decisions. In *Malone v Metropolitan Police Commissioner*[290] Sir Robert Megarry VC observed that there would be 'no case for the grant of an injunction, as when the disclosure has already been made'.[291]

The jurisdiction under *Lord Cairns' Act* may even have relevance against third parties, provided that an injunction is properly available. In interlocutory proceedings it has been held that an injunction lies against a

---

280 (1990) 17 IPR 545 at 584.
281 P Birks, *An Introduction to the Law of Restitution*, Clarendon Press, Oxford, 1985, p 343.
282 [1969] RPC 41.
283 [1969] RPC 41 at 46.
284 [1913] 2 Ch 469.
285 [1913] 2 Ch 469 at 475.
286 (1980) 147 CLR 39.
287 (1980) 147 CLR 39 at 50.
288 (1948) 65 RPC 203.
289 (1948) 65 RPC 203 at 215.
290 [1979] Ch 344.
291 [1979] Ch 344 at 360.

person who obtains confidential information innocently, once that person gets to know that it was originally given in confidence. It was also held that there are no property rights associated with an equity to restrain a person from acting in breach of confidence which is owed to another, so that the equitable defence of a bona fide purchaser for value which is directed towards the resolution of priorities in relation to property rights does not apply.[292] Whether or not confidential information is property has been the subject of some discussion.[293]

The significance of the jurisdiction under *Lord Cairns' Act* to breach of confidence cases lies in those cases where there is a breach of an equitable duty of confidence. Common law damages may be awarded where there is a breach of a contract, such as a licence agreement.[294] *Lord Cairns' Act* may be relied upon where there is doubt as to the existence of a contract between the parties; although the jurisdiction under the Act will be invoked for other reasons, such as where damages for prospective loss are sought, or for procedural reasons.

The relevance of *Lord Cairns' Act* has been recognised in a number of cases.[295] In *Malone v Metropolitan Police Commissioner*[296] Sir Robert Megarry VC observed in relation to the right of confidentiality:

> This is an equitable right which is still in course of development, and is usually protected by the grant of an injunction to prevent disclosure of the confidence. Under *Lord Cairns' Act* 1858 damages may be granted in substitution for an injunction; yet if there is no case for the grant of an injunction, as when the disclosure has already been made, the unsatisfactory result seems to be that no damages can be awarded under this head: see *Proctor v Bayley*[297].[298]

In *Attorney-General v Guardian Newspapers Ltd (No 2)*[299] Lord Goff of Chieveley referred to:

> ... the remedy of damages, which in cases of breach of confidence is now available, despite the equitable nature of the wrong, through a beneficent interpretation of the Chancery Amendment Act 1858 (*Lord Cairns' Act*).[300]

In *Johns v Australian Securities Commission*[301] Brennan J remarked, in considering an equitable obligation of confidence:

---

292 *Wheatley v Bell* [1982] 2 NSWLR 544.
293 J E Stuckey, 'The Equitable Action for Breach of Confidence', *Sydney Law Review*, vol 9, 1981, p 406.
294 *National Broach & Machine Co v Churchill Gear Machines Ltd* [1965] RPC 516; *Fraser v Thames Television Ltd* [1984] QB 44.
295 In *Talbot v General Television Corp Pty Ltd* [1980] VR 224 at 243; [1981] RPC 1 at 21 Marks J considered that the observations of Pennycuick J in *Peter Pan Manufacturing Corp v Corsets Silhouette Ltd* [1967] RPC 45; [1963] 3 All ER 402 at 411 imply that there was an award of damages in addition to the injunctions. Presumably such damages were equitable damages. See also *O'Neill v Dept of Health and Social Services (No 2)* [1986] NI 290.
296 [1979] Ch 344.
297 (1889) 42 Ch D 390.
298 [1979] Ch 344 at 360.
299 [1990] AC 109.
300 [1990] AC 109 at 286.
301 (1993) 116 ALR 567.

The condition may be enforced by injunction or perhaps, in the event of breach, by damages in lieu of injunction under *Lord Cairns' Act*.[302]

There have been a number of decisions in which equitable damages have been awarded for a breach of confidence. In *Saltman Engineering Co Ltd v Campbell Engineering Co Ltd*[303] tools were manufactured in breach of an obligation of confidence. There was some argument as to whether the parties were in a contractual relationship. The Court of Appeal held that there was a contract, contrary to the findings of the trial judge. However, the Court of Appeal emphasised that liability would arise irrespective of whether there was a contractual obligation of confidence. The report of the case records that:

> ... their Lordships expressed reluctance to make any order which would involve the destruction or sterilisation of tools which might serve a useful purpose, since under *Lord Cairns' Act* the court could award damages, to cover both past and future acts, in lieu of an injunction.[304]

The form of order that was settled provided for 'An inquiry as to what damages have been and may be suffered ... by reason of the Defendant's breaches of confidence'.[305] This case was clearly an instance of the exercise of the jurisdiction under *Lord Cairns' Act* to award damages in substitution for an injunction which would have otherwise issued to restrain a continuing breach of confidence.[306]

There is one case in which the basis for an inquiry into damages is not apparent. In *Nichrotherm Electrical Co Ltd v Percy*[307] the plaintiffs sought relief in respect of the breach of confidence of the defendant in using the design of a machine for feeding piglets. Harman J held that there was no contractual relationship between the parties. Nevertheless, on the authority of the *Saltman Engineering* case[308] it was held that liability for breach of confidence arises whether or not the parties were in a contractual relationship, and an order was made for an inquiry into damages. The Court of Appeal held that it was sufficient to found the claim on a breach of an implied contractual term.[309] Lord Evershed MR made the following remarks:

> If the confidence, breach of which is alleged or proved, is imposed by or arises out of contract, express or implied, then the remedy would, I assume, be by way of damages at law as upon a breach of contract. If, on the other hand, the confidence infringed is one imposed by the rules of equity, then the remedy would be, prima facie, by way of injunction or damages in lieu of an injunction under *Lord Cairns' Act*.[310]

---

302 (1993) 116 ALR 567 at 578.
303 (1948) 65 RPC 203.
304 (1948) 65 RPC 203 at 219.
305 (1948) 65 RPC 203 at 219.
306 F Gurry, *Breach of Confidence*, Oxford University Press, Oxford, 1984, p 434.
307 [1956] RPC 272 at 281.
308 (1948) 65 RPC 203.
309 [1957] RPC 207.
310 [1957] RPC 207 at 213.

Lord Evershed MR accordingly recognised that damages under *Lord Cairns' Act* may be awarded where there is an equitable obligation of confidence. In the *Nichrotherm* case Harman J did not expressly state the basis for the order directing an inquiry into damages. Lord Evershed MR said: 'it does not appear that the learned Judge, in holding that the Plaintiffs were entitled to such enquiry, was invoking *Lord Cairns' Act*'.[311]

The basis of the order in the *Nichrotherm* case has been the subject of some discussion. Gareth Jones has commented:

> It is trite law that, under *Lord Cairns' Act*, a plaintiff may sue for damages instead of equitable relief. But Harman J's suggestion is mildly revolutionary in that, by implying that a damages claim can succeed independently of any prayer for equitable relief, it presupposes a fusion of law and equity.[312]

Gurry has observed that in a number of cases the courts have granted damages in addition to an injunction against defendants held liable in equity for breach of confidence,[313] and that the decision of Havers J in *Ackroyds (London) Ltd v Islington Plastics Ltd*[314] seems to assume that damages were available in addition to an injunction for breach of an equitable duty.[315] Gurry remarked:

> It is probably on this basis that the decision of Harman J in the *Nichrotherm* case is to be understood. The judge ordered an inquiry as to damages in addition to an injunction for breach of an equitable duty of confidence.[316]

It is submitted that the jurisdiction under *Lord Cairns' Act* was available in the *Nichrotherm* case. The claim of the plaintiff did not, as Gareth Jones has observed, contain a prayer for equitable relief. However, it is submitted that a prayer for equitable relief was not essential in these circumstances. It should be mentioned that Harman J did not order the issue of an injunction. All that was ordered was that the plaintiff was granted leave to apply for injunctions. In these circumstances where the pleadings disclose a basis for equitable relief, the jurisdiction under *Lord Cairns' Act* is available despite the absence of any prayer for equitable relief.[317]

Another case in which the basis of an award of damages was not apparent is *Seager v Copydex Ltd*.[318] In this case the defendant had unconsciously made use of an idea for an invention that was communicated to him in confidence by the plaintiff. The plaintiff's claim

---

311 [1957] RPC 207 at 214.
312 G Jones, 'Restitution of Benefits Obtained in Breach of Another's Confidence', *Law Quarterly Review*, vol 86, 1970, 463 at p 491.
313 *Interfirm Comparison (Australia) Pty Ltd v Law Society of New South Wales* [1977] RPC 137 (damages and an undertaking in lieu of an injunction); *Talbot v General Television Corp Pty Ltd* [1981] RPC 1 (damages and injunction).
314 [1962] RPC 97.
315 F Gurry, *Breach of Confidence*, Oxford University Press, Oxford, 1984, p 438.
316 F Gurry, *Breach of Confidence*, Oxford University Press, Oxford, 1984, p 438.
317 See p 211.
318 [1967] RPC 349.

was not founded on contract. The Court of Appeal, in allowing the appeal of the plaintiff, awarded damages to the plaintiff. Lord Denning MR remarked:

> It may not be a case for injunction or even for an account, but only for damages, depending on the worth of the confidential information to him [ie, the defendant] in saving him time and trouble.[319]

Their Lordships in awarding damages did not state the jurisdictional basis of their award. There are only two possible alternatives: either the award was made under *Lord Cairns' Act*, or it is an instance of the exercise of the inherent compensatory jurisdiction possessed by a court of equity.

In *English v Dedham Vale Properties Ltd*[320] Slade J considered that the jurisdiction under *Lord Cairns' Act* was invoked in the *Seager* case which his Lordship regarded 'as being an instance where the court granted damages in lieu of an injunction'.[321] Similarly in *Talbot v General Television Corp Pty Ltd*[322] Harris J appears to have regarded the *Seager* case as an instance of the exercise of the jurisdiction under *Lord Cairns' Act*. The case was cited in the context of his discussion on the meaning of the expression 'wrongful act' in *Lord Cairns' Act*.[323]

Certainly, the plaintiff in the *Seager* case claimed an injunction, as well as damages or an account. Gurry has taken the view that it would seem plausible to regard the award of damages as being in substitution for an injunction under the jurisdiction conferred by *Lord Cairns' Act*.[324] However, Lord Denning's remarks do not indicate whether the plaintiff possessed the requisite equity for an injunction which would have attracted jurisdiction to grant equitable damages; they may have been directed to the question of the appropriateness of the remedy. In the *Seager* case the plaintiff was awarded damages by reference to the value of what the defendant took from him. Different principles apply where the plaintiff is a manufacturer and would be entitled to loss of profits.[325]

There is no doubt that the jurisdiction under *Lord Cairns' Act* may be exercised, as in the *Saltman Engineering* case, where there is no contractual foundation for an action for breach of confidence. In *Talbot v General Television Corp Pty Ltd*[326] a television network had made unauthorised use of a concept communicated to the network in confidence. The plaintiff claimed, inter alia, damages for equitable compensation for breach of confidence. The plaintiff was granted a restraining injunction and an inquiry as to damages sustained by reason of the unauthorised use of the confidential information. Harris J relied upon the then Victorian

---

319 [1967] RPC 349 at 368. See also *Conveyor Co of Australia Pty Ltd v Cameron Bros Engineering Co Ltd* [1973] 2 NZLR 30 at 44.
320 [1978] 1 All ER 382.
321 [1978] 1 All ER 382 at 399.
322 [1980] VR 224; [1981] RPC 1.
323 [1980] VR 224 at 241; [1981] RPC 1 at 19.
324 F Gurry, *Breach of Confidence*, Oxford University Press, Oxford, 1984, p 435.
325 *Dowson & Mason Ltd v Potter* [1986] 1 WLR 1419.
326 [1980] VR 224; [1981] RPC 1.

equivalent of *Lord Cairns' Act*[327] describing it as 'the most obvious source, and perhaps the only source, of a power to award such damages'.[328] Harris J rejected a submission that the expression 'wrongful act' in *Lord Cairns' Act* was restricted to acts which are torts. Cornish has commented that in the *Talbot* case the court held that *Lord Cairns' Act* was 'a provision which applied not only to common law torts but also to equitable wrongs such as a breach of confidence'.[329]

The decision in the *Talbot* case was also concerned with the assessment of damages. The defendant, on appeal to the Full Court of Victoria, did not challenge the relevance of *Lord Cairns' Act*, and damages were assessed on the basis that the breach of confidence was a 'wrongful act' within the meaning of the Act. Marks J acceded to the submission of the plaintiff that in assessing damages the court 'should inquire into what money compensation would represent the restitution to the plaintiff of the value by which his right, which equity recognised, has been depreciated by the defendant's breach of confidence'.[330] Marks J later remarked:

> In my view some guidance can be derived from the authorities concerned with the assessment of damages both in breach of copyright and confidence cases. However, I do not think that the method prescribed in any particular one of those cases can be said to provide an exclusive method by which I must be rigidly guided.[331]

In *Whimp v Kawakawa Engineering Ltd*[332] a plaintiff sought an injunction to restrain the defendant manufacturer from using confidential information in their manufacture of mowers. While the court accepted that the information had the necessary quality of confidence, the court considered that in the particular circumstances of this case there were no grounds for an injunction. The defendant had expended capital in developing the mowers and this expenditure had in fact assisted the plaintiff. It was considered that the 'springboard principle' applied to the case which envisaged that the defendant would not have the use of the plaintiff's confidential information for a period of twelve months but would have the use of it thereafter. Chilwell J remarked:

> The next problem is to translate a twelve month starter's handicap into the framework of *Lord Cairns' Act* 1858 — damages in *substitution* for an injunction. In my view the issue is simply what is the price for not being enjoined? See *Leeds Industrial Co-op Society Ltd v Slack*.[333] That must be examined from the viewpoint of the plaintiff and the defendants. There should be an inquiry into the loss which the defendants would have suffered if enjoined for a period of twelve months from 4 September 1975

---

327 Supreme Court Act 1958 (Victoria) s 62(3).
328 [1980] VR 224 at 241; [1981] RPC 1 at 19.
329 W R Cornish, 'Confidence in Ideas', *Intellectual Property Journal*, vol 1, 1990, 3 at p 5.
330 [1980] VR 224 at 243; [1981] RPC 1 at 22.
331 [1980] VR 224 at 245; [1981] RPC 1 at 23. As to assessment of damages: see also *Interfirm Comparison (Australia) Pty Ltd v Law Society of New South Wales* [1975] 2 NSWLR 104; [1977] RPC 137.
332 [1979] 1 NZIPR 144.
333 [1924] AC 851.

and the loss to the plaintiff in the reverse situation ie of the defendants not being enjoined for that period.[334]

It may be arguable that the term 'wrongful act' in *Lord Cairns' Act* may have been a jurisdictional limitation to the award of equitable damages in respect of a breach of equitable obligation. There is, however, contrary authority on this issue. It has already been mentioned that in the *Guardian Newspaper* case[335] Lord Goff remarked that *Lord Cairns' Act* has been beneficially interpreted. An instance of this beneficial interpretation is *Talbot v General Television Corp Pty Ltd*[336] in which the term 'wrongful act' in *Lord Cairns' Act* was held appropriate to apply to the unauthorised use of a concept communicated in confidence.

In those countries in which *Lord Cairns' Act* has been reformed, such jurisdictional constraints no longer arise. Section 50 of the English Supreme Court Act enables damages to be awarded in any case in which the court has jurisdiction to order the issue of an injunction. This provision does not contain words such as 'injured party' and 'wrongful act'. Gurry has appreciated that there has been the removal of any such jurisdictional constraints in England:

> It will be noticed that the power to award damages in the combined administration of law and equity now exists whenever the court has jurisdiction simply 'to entertain an application for an injunction ...'. Any circumstances in which such jurisdiction arises — such as an injunction against 'the commission or continuance of any wrongful act' — is now omitted. On a literal construction of the new provision, therefore, the court can award damages whenever it has jurisdiction to entertain an injunction, which it certainly has in breach of confidence cases, whether exercising the auxiliary or the exclusive equitable jurisdiction.[337]

There has been some criticism of a failure to acknowledge the inherent jurisdiction possessed by a court of equity. In *Concept Television Productions Pty Ltd v Australian Broadcasting Corp*[338] Gummow J remarked:

> I would not, even at this interlocutory level, accept what was said in *Talbot v General Television Corporation Ltd*[339] as to the source of this jurisdiction lying in *Lord Cairns' Act* and its Australian representatives. What was said in the Victorian decision seems to have overlooked the inherent jurisdiction of equity and the fundamental principles that are explained in *Re Dawson (dec'd)*;[340] *Bartlett v Barclays Bank Trust Co Ltd (No 2)*[341] and *United States Surgical Corp v Hospital Products International*[342].[343]

In *Smith Kline & French Laboratories (Australia) Ltd v Secretary, Dept of Community Services and Health*[344] the applicants wished to reserve for a

334 [1979] 1 NZIPR 144 at 168.
335 [1990] AC 109.
336 [1980] VR 224; [1981] RPC 1.
337 F Gurry, *Breach of Confidence*, Oxford University Press, Oxford, 1984, p 432.
338 (1988) 12 IPR 129.
339 [1980] VR 224.
340 [1966] 2 NSWR 211.
341 [1980] Ch 515 at 543.
342 [1982] 2 NSWLR 766 at 816.
343 (1988) 12 IPR 129 at 136.
344 (1990) 17 IPR 545.

later stage of the proceedings an inquiry as to any pecuniary loss suffered by the alleged breach of an equitable obligation of confidence owed to them by a government department. The applicants relied upon s 68 of the Supreme Court Act 1970 (New South Wales) (*Lord Cairns' Act*) as providing the basis of this liability. Gummow J observed:

> If it transpires that the applicants are entitled to an inquiry, it would, in my view, be on this basis in the inherent equitable jurisdiction and s 68 of the Supreme Court Act would not enter into consideration.[345]

There may be situations where a plaintiff in a breach of confidence action may have no basis for an award of equitable damages under *Lord Cairns' Act*. An obvious case where the inherent jurisdiction of equity should be relied upon is where there has already been public disclosure of the confidential material. There may, however, be some cases where an award of equitable damages may be preferred by a plaintiff. Such cases would be where a plaintiff did not press a claim for an injunction, and was content to obtain an award of equitable damages which included a component for prospective loss, or where no claim for monetary relief is made in the pleadings.

It is submitted, in agreement with Dean, that 'it is now certain that the courts have at their disposal both *Lord Cairns' Act* damages and equity's inherent indemnification powers of "restitutory compensation" as a basis of awarding damages'.[346]

———◦———

8.14 Domestic tribunals

There is authority that the jurisdiction under *Lord Cairns' Act* is not available where an invalid decision has been made by a domestic tribunal. In *Stininato v Auckland Boxing Assn Inc*[347] a boxing association had declined to renew a professional boxer's licence in circumstances where the boxer was alleged to have been denied natural justice. The boxer appealed against the dismissal of an action in which he claimed damages, and a declaration that the association had wrongfully refused to grant his application for a licence. The New Zealand Court of Appeal found no grounds for interfering with the judge's exercise of his discretion to refuse any relief to the plaintiff. The plaintiff did not seek an injunction so that there was no question of an award of damages under *Lord Cairns' Act*. However, Cooke J observed that an invalid decision of a domestic tribunal is not a 'wrongful act' within the meaning of s 2 of *Lord Cairns' Act*:

> If, however, the action of members of a domestic tribunal were held to be sufficiently 'wrongful' to justify an award of damages, there is no reason why this evolution should not be brought about directly by development of the law of tort. It would be neither necessary nor desirable to fall back

---

345 (1990) 17 IPR 545 at 556.
346 R Dean, *The Law of Trade Secrets*, Law Book Co, Sydney, 1990, p 320.
347 [1978] 1 NZLR 1.

on the old statutory jurisdiction of the Court of Chancery, especially as this sort of problem in the borderland between tort and administrative law, must be remote from anything that the Chancery Commissioners or Parliament could have had in mind in 1856 or 1858.[348]

The Court of Appeal declined leave to appeal to the Privy Council on this issue. In *Stininato v Auckland Boxing Assn Inc (No 2)*[349] Richardson J remarked '... we are satisfied that the interpretation and application of *Lord Cairns' Act* in this class of case does not raise a question of great general or public importance'.[350]

Modern statutory provisions[351] that confer jurisdiction to award equitable damages do not contain the term 'wrongful act'. There is accordingly no jurisdictional barrier under these provisions to an award of equitable damages in domestic tribunal cases. Whether or not equitable damages will be awarded in such cases is now a matter of discretion. There is now less force in the observation of Sir Robin Cooke that a plaintiff will not be awarded equitable damages by the 'side wind of a discretion under *Lord Cairns' Act*'.[352] Quite apart from the jurisdiction under *Lord Cairns' Act*, damages for a wrongful domestic judgment may be awarded against an incorporated society.[353] Such claims are founded on contract.[354]

———◁◦▷———

8.15 Criminal law

Although the courts will exercise restraint in providing injunctive relief where criminal sanctions attend the conduct complained of, an injunction may be granted if there is a deliberate flouting of the law.[355] The jurisdiction of the courts to grant an injunction in such cases is not restricted to cases of public health and safety, although that may be a factor which influences the grant of the relief.[356] The jurisdiction to award equitable damages may be invoked in some situations where injunctive relief is sought in respect of a breach of the criminal law.

Several cases on this question have concerned the Dramatic and Musical Performers' Protection Act 1958.[357] It is now settled that although the Act created criminal sanctions, parliament intended that under the Act performers should have a private right to give or withhold consent to their

348 [1978] 1 NZLR 1 at 23.

349 [1978] 1 NZLR 609.

350 [1978] 1 NZLR 609 at 612.

351 See eg Supreme Court Act 1981 (England) s 50.

352 [1978] 1 NZLR 1 at 23.

353 J R S Forbes, *The Law of Domestic or Private Tribunals*, Law Book Co, Sydney, 1982, p 218, n 67.

354 *Bonsor v Musicians Union* [1956] AC 104; *Byrne v Auckland Irish Society Inc* [1979] 1 NZLR 351.

355 *Peek v New South Wales Egg Corp* (1980) 6 NSWLR 1.

356 *Attorney-General of the Commonwealth of Australia v Legal Research Pty Ltd* (Court of Appeal, Queensland, 5 June 1992, unreported).

357 6 & 7 Eliz II c 44.

performances and to enforce that right by action in the civil courts.[358]

This issue first appears to have been raised in *Ex parte Island Records Ltd*[359] which concerned the availability of an Anton Pillar order[360] where there was a contravention of the Dramatic and Musical Performers' Protection Act. The case was an ex parte application by performers and recording companies for injunctive relief to restrain unauthorised recordings of live performances. The possibility of an award of equitable damages was mentioned in argument by counsel who submitted that:

> ... the question is whether the court has jurisdiction where the plaintiffs claim (1) damages for breach of statutory duty and (2) an injunction in equity (to which damages could be added under *Lord Cairns' Act*).[361]

A majority of the Court of Appeal (Shaw and Waller LJJ) held that no civil action could be brought for a breach of the statute. Lord Denning MR was of a contrary view, and considered that the jurisdiction under *Lord Cairns' Act* was available. Lord Denning MR adopted the submission of the *amicus* in relation to the jurisdiction of a Court of Equity:

> It intervened to protect a private individual in his rights of property, and in aid of this would grant an injunction to restrain a defendant from committing an unlawful act, even though it was a crime punishable by the criminal court: and would supplement its jurisdiction in this regard by its power under *Lord Cairns' Act* to award damages in lieu of or in addition to an injunction.[362]

The view of Lord Denning has ultimately prevailed, for an award of equitable damages has been made for a breach of the Dramatic and Musical Performers' Protection Act. In *Rickless v United Artists Corp*[363] the executors of Peter Sellers sought an injunction to restrain the use of 'out-takes' from five *Pink Panther* films. Hobhouse J held that the legislation was passed to protect the economic interests of performers. In the absence of civil remedies, as well as criminal sanctions, the performer had inadequate protection. The plaintiff was awarded equitable damages in lieu of an injunction. Hobhouse J said:

> Under section 50 of the Supreme Court Act 1981 and the law as stated in *Leeds Industrial Co-operative Society Ltd v Slack*,[364] the court has a power to award damages in lieu of an injunction. The Plaintiffs before me have not contended that damages would be an inadequate remedy in the present case. The court is able fully to compensate the Plaintiffs for both past and

---

358 *Rickless v United Artists Corp* [1988] QB 40. Compare *RCA Corp v Pollard* [1983] Ch 135; *Shelly v Cunane* [1983] FSR 390.

359 [1978] Ch 122.

360 This form of order was first made by Templeman J in *EMI Ltd v Pandit* [1975] 1 WLR 302. The use of the order was sanctioned by the Court of Appeal in *Anton Pillar KG v Manufacturing Processes Ltd* [1976] Ch 55.

361 [1978] Ch 122 at 128–9.

362 [1978] Ch 122 at 135. The court was referred to cases where an injunction was granted to prevent a crime that would affect property rights: see *Austria, Emperor of v Day and Kossuth* (1861) 3 De GF & J 217; 45 ER 861. It was submitted that the jurisdiction under *Lord Cairns' Act* was available in these circumstances.

363 (1985) 135 NLJ 656; *Times LR*, 17 June 1985.

364 [1924] AC 851.

future losses by an award of damages. I therefore consider that the present case is not a case where injunctions ought to be granted; the Plaintiffs should be compensated by a full award of damages.[365]

This decision was affirmed on appeal.[366] On appeal, argument was primarily directed to whether a breach of the Dramatic and Musical Performers Protection Act conferred a civil action on performers. The award of equitable damages under s 50 of the Supreme Court Act was not challenged.

---◄○►---

8.16 Intellectual property

Before the commencement of the *Judicature Acts* a plaintiff who sought an injunction to restrain the infringement of a patent would rely upon *Lord Cairns' Act* for the award of damages.[367] Now legislation provides for the award of damages.[368] Ordinarily a plaintiff would not need to rely on *Lord Cairns' Act* for an award of damages, as an express statutory basis for an award of damages is available. However, the jurisdiction may be appropriate where intellectual property is unregistered or where a plaintiff seeks an award of damages to obtain a full indemnity. It would not be appropriate to make an award of equitable damages in lieu of an injunction to restrain an infringement of intellectual property which would amount to an expropriation of property against the will of the proprietor of the property.[369]

---

365 LEXIS.
366 *Rickless v United Artists Corp* [1988] QB 40.
367 *Penn v Jack* (1867) LR 5 Eq 81.
368 *Australia*: Circuit Layouts Act 1989 (Cth) (1989 No 28) s 27; Copyright Act 1968 (Cth) (1968 No 63) s 115(2); Patents Act 1990 (Cth) (1990 No 83) s 122(1); Plant Variety Rights Act 1987 (Cth) (1987 No 2) s 27; Trade Marks Act 1955 (Cth) (1955 No 20) s 65; *England*: Copyright Act 1956 (4 & 5 Eliz II) s 17; Copyright, Designs & Patents Act 1988 (1988 c 48) ss 96(1), 229(1); Patents and Designs Act 1949 (12, 13 & 14 Geo VI c 87) s 60; Patents Act 1977 s 61.
369 *Biogen Inc v Medeva Plc* [1993] RPC 476.

9

Specific Performance

9.1 Award of equitable damages in an action for specific performance

The jurisdiction to award equitable damages can be invoked where a plaintiff possesses an equity to specific performance. Section 2 of the Chancery Amendment Act 1858 (*Lord Cairns' Act*)[1] provides that

---

1   21 & 22 Vict c 27.

equitable damages may be awarded in a case where there is 'jurisdiction to entertain an application ... for the specific performance of any covenant, contract, or agreement'. Modern statutory provisions that confer jurisdiction to award equitable damages are not as elaborate as *Lord Cairns' Act*. In the United Kingdom the relevant legislation provides that jurisdiction to award equitable damages exists where the court 'has jurisdiction to entertain an application for ... specific performance'.[2] Similar provisions are in force in Victoria,[3] Hong Kong[4] and Manitoba.[5] In Ontario the relevant provision provides that the jurisdiction exists where a court 'has jurisdiction to ... order specific performance'.[6] This difference in language is not significant; if a court could not order specific performance, it would not have jurisdiction to entertain an application for specific performance.

9.2 Equitable damages in addition to specific performance

Lord Cairns' Act confers jurisdiction upon a court to award damages 'in addition to ... specific performance'.[7] *Lord Cairns' Act* therefore enables the award of damages in addition to specific performance. In some cases *Lord Cairns' Act* may provide a convenient jurisdictional basis for an award of common law or exemplary damages. It would be necessary for a plaintiff to prove loss before damages could be awarded under *Lord Cairns' Act* in addition to such relief.[8]

9.3 Equitable damages in substitution for specific performance

Lord Cairns' Act confers jurisdiction upon a court to award damages 'in substitution for ... specific performance'.[9] In *Wroth v Tyler*[10] Megarry J remarked:

---

2   Judicature (Northern Ireland) Act 1978 (1978 c 23) s 92; Supreme Court Act 1981 (1981 c 54) s 50.
3   Supreme Court Act 1986 (1986 No 110) (Victoria) s 38.
4   Supreme Court Ordinance 1987 cap 4 (rev ed) (Hong Kong) s 17.
5   The Court of Queen's Bench Act SM 1988 c 4 (Manitoba) s 36.
6   Courts of Justice Act 1984 (Ontario) c 11 s 112. For the text of s 112 of the Courts of Justice Act 1984: see Appendix at p 289.
7   Chancery Amendment Act 1858 s 2.
8   *Cowan v Cavanagh* [1978] VR 665 at 667.
9   Chancery Amendment Act 1858 s 2.
10 [1974] Ch 30.

... if under *Lord Cairns' Act* damages are given in substitution for specific performance, the court has jurisdiction to award such damages as will put the plaintiffs into as good a position as if the contract had been performed.[11]

Equitable damages may not be awarded 'in substitution' for specific performance where an order for specific performance has already been made.[12] There may well be cases in which an order for specific performance may have to be dissolved. In such a case there could be no objection to an award of equitable damages in lieu of specific relief being made after the dissolution of the order.

9.4 Partial specific performance

A court may decree specific performance of part of a contract and award damages for that part of the contract that will not be specifically enforced. Owen J in *Wright v Carter*[13] stated:

> In England, before the passing of the *Judicature Acts*, the Court of Chancery in a number of cases where it had jurisdiction to grant equitable relief with regard to part of an agreement between the parties, granted damages for breaches of other parts of the same agreement in respect of which it had no power to grant equitable relief.[14]

The cases, although decided before the *Judicature Acts* commenced operation, illustrate how partial specific performance together with equitable damages may be awarded in an appropriate case. One such case was *Soames v Edge*[15] where the plaintiff sought specific performance of an agreement under which he would grant a lease to the defendant when the defendant built a new house on the land. When the bill was filed the defendant had merely demolished the old house. The court held that *Lord Cairns' Act* applied so that the plaintiff was entitled to damages for the failure of the defendant to build the house, and to specific performance of the contract to accept the lease. Sir William Page Wood VC observed that the court would not decree specific performance of a building contract. However, the Vice-Chancellor remarked:

> But there is a distinct agreement here, not only to build the house but to accept the lease. The Court having therefore acquired jurisdiction, may give damages, either in addition to or in substitution for specific performance.[16]

Lord St Leonards doubted whether *Lord Cairns' Act* enabled damages to be awarded in *Soames v Edge*:[17]

---

11   [1974] Ch 30 at 60.
12   *Hyder v Edgar* (1979) 10 Alta LR (2d) 17 at 23.
13   (1923) 23 SR (NSW) 555.
14   (1923) 23 SR (NSW) 555 at 568.
15   (1860) Johns 669; 70 ER 588.
16   (1860) Johns 669 at 673; 70 ER 588 at 590.
17   (1860) Johns 669; 70 ER 588.

As a court of equity does not execute a part only of a contract specifically, it may be considered doubtful whether this case fell within the Act.[18]

However, the principle established in *Soames v Edge*[19] was applied in other cases.

In *Middleton v Greenwood*[20] the defendant agreed to grant the plaintiff a lease of a public house, to construct certain works, including a spirit vault, and to undertake repairs to the public house. The court granted specific performance of the agreement to grant the lease and an inquiry as to damages for the non-performance of the agreement with respect to the works and repairs. Turner LJ commented that these matters were 'mere incidents of the agreement, not affecting its substance'.[21] The Lord Justice added: 'there being jurisdiction for specific performance, it was in the power of the Court to direct the inquiry as to damages, under the provisions of the Act'.[22] Equitable damages were also awarded in *Mayor of London v Southgate*[23] which also concerned a contract to lease and build. Damages would not be awarded where there was some uncertainty as to repairs.[24]

Difficulties occur where a contract is divisible into parts, and where a court will not make an order for the specific performance of part of the contract. It has been held that where an agreement for personal services is part of a larger agreement, that will prevent a court from decreeing specific performance of the larger agreement.[25] In one Canadian case involving an agreement for personal services and for conveyance of land, it was held that damages could not be awarded under *Lord Cairns' Act*.[26] Later in this chapter it is submitted that there is no reason in principle why a court cannot make an order for the specific performance of a contract, or alternatively an award of equitable damages in substitution for such relief.

———◁◦▷———

9.5 Part performance

Section 4 of the Statute of Frauds 1677[27] provided that contracts 'to charge any Person ... upon any Contract or Sale of Land, Tenements or Hereditaments, or any Interest in or concerning them' were unenforceable in the absence of a sufficient memorandum of their terms. This provision was the ancestor of s 40(1) of the Law of Property Act 1925[28] which has been adopted in some jurisdictions, and which provided:

---

18 E B Sugden, *The New Statutes Relating to Property,* 2nd ed, H Sweet, London, 1862, p 327.
19 (1860) Johns 669; 70 ER 588.
20 (1864) 2 De GJ & S 142; 46 ER 329.
21 (1864) 2 De GJ & S 142 at 145; 46 ER 329 at 330.
22 (1864) 2 De GJ & S 142 at 145–6; 46 ER 329 at 330.
23 (1868) 20 LT 107.
24 *Norris v Jackson* (1860) 1 John & Hem 319; 70 ER 769.
25 *Ogden v Fossick* (1862) 4 De GF & J 426.
26 *Rushton v McPherson* (1939) 14 MPR 235.
27 29 Cha II c 3.
28 15 & 16 Geo V c 20 s 207.

No action may be brought upon any contract for the sale or other disposition of land or any interest in land, unless the agreement upon which such action is brought, or some memorandum or note thereof, is in writing, and signed by the party to be charged or by some other person thereunto by him lawfully authorised.

Despite the Statute of Frauds, it has long been the case that a court of equity may decree specific performance of a contract for the sale of land which has been partly performed by the plaintiff, notwithstanding the absence of a sufficient memorandum. The doctrine of part performance is nearly as old as the Statute of Frauds.[29] The statute was passed in 1677, and one of the earliest cases of part performance dates from 1685.[30]

At one time there was some controversy as to whether part performance would enable a plaintiff to recover common law damages. During the eighteenth century there were suggestions that part performance would take an action out of the Statute of Frauds, enabling a plaintiff to recover damages at law. In *Whitbread v Brockhurst*[31] Lord Thurlow LC said:

There certainly are cases which have considered an agreement which has been partly executed as never having been within the original view of the statute; and this has been a ground to induce the Court of King's Bench, as I am told, to determine this case to be entirely out of the statute.[32]

Similarly in *Brodie v St Paul*[33] Buller J remarked:

As to the part-performance; Courts of law have lately adopted the same sort of reasoning, that prevails in this Court; that there can be but one true construction upon the Statute of Frauds. Whatever it is, it ought to hold equally both in Courts of Law and of Equity; and that, as it is settled in Equity, that a part-performance takes it out of the statute, the same rule shall hold at law.[34]

Despite these statements, it was decided by Sir Jonathan Pollock LCB in *Massey v Johnson*[35] that there was 'no legal foundation' for any doctrine that damages may be awarded at law in a case of part performance. It is now settled that part performance will not support an action for common law damages which the Statute of Frauds would otherwise defeat.[36] In the United States, damages have been awarded where there was reliance on estoppel,[37] and where there was a high standard of proof of the existence of a contract and it was considered that relief should be granted to discourage fraud.[38]

---

29 P A Ridge, 'The Equitable Doctrines of Part Performance and Equitable Estoppel', *Melbourne University Law Review*, vol 16, 1988, 725 at p 730.
30 *Butcher v Stapely* (1685) 1 Vern 363; 23 ER 524.
31 (1784) 1 Bro CC 404; 28 ER 1205.
32 (1784) 1 Bro CC 404 at 417; 28 ER 1205 at 1211.
33 (1791) 1 Ves 326; 30 ER 368.
34 (1791) 1 Ves 326 at 333; 30 ER 368 at 372.
35 (1847) 1 Ex 241 at 252; 154 ER 102 at 107.
36 *McLean v Cooper* (1862) 1 SCR (NSW) 186; *Wi Rangi Rangi v Sutton* (1878) 3 NZ Jur (NS) SC 139; *Lavery v Pursell* (1888) 39 Ch D 508; *JC Williamson Ltd v Lukey and Mulholland* (1931) 45 CLR 282 at 293, 297; *Dillon v Nash* [1950] VLR 293 at 300; *Ellul v Oakes* (1972) 3 SASR 377 at 382–3; *O'Rourke v Hoeven* [1974] 1 NSWLR 622 at 626; *Price v Strange* [1978] Ch 337 at 358.
37 *Wolfe v Wallingford Bank & Trust Co* (1938) 124 Conn 507.
38 *Miller v McCamish* (1971) 78 Wash 2d 821.

While common law damages are not available on the ground of part performance, it is now clear that equitable damages may be awarded in addition to, or in substitution for, specific performance where the entitlement of a plaintiff to relief is dependent upon part performance.[39] In such a case equitable damages can only be awarded where a plaintiff has an equity to an order for specific performance.[40] As is stated in a New Zealand text:

> ... part performance, being an equitable doctrine, can be pleaded only in support of a claim for specific performance, including actions where damages are given in lieu of specific performance under *Lord Cairns' Act* 1858, and is so limited to contracts which are specifically enforceable.[41]

There have been a number of cases in which the plaintiff should have claimed equitable damages. One such case was *O'Rourke v Hoeven*[42] where a lessor sued the lessee for damages for the breach of certain covenants in the lease, including the failure to yield up possession of the premises at the expiration of the term of the lease. The lessee brought a cross-action for damages for breach of contract and deceit. The lessee alleged that the lessor had orally agreed to renew the lease for five years in return for certain improvements made to property by the lessee. The lessor defended the cross-action on the ground of an absence in writing of the agreement to renew. The lessee relied on part performance of the agreement. The Court of Appeal of New South Wales held that the cross-action for damages was barred for want of writing by s 54A of the Conveyancing Act 1919 (New South Wales), and that part performance did not enable the recovery of damages in an action for common law damages. Glass JA recognised
that the lessee should have sought an award of equitable damages. His Honour remarked:

> Of course, the defendant was at liberty to claim by way of defence to the action the specific performance of the oral agreement for a lease and an award of damages in addition to or in lieu of specific performance.[43]

However, in this case the evidence of the defendant did not support reliance on the doctrine.

---

39 *Chitty on Contracts*, 25th ed, vol 1, 1983, p 172, para 292. See also H Mayo, 'Statute of Frauds — Part Performance in Relation to Damages', *Australian Law Journal*, vol 6, 1932, p 283; R A Brewer, 'A Comparison of *Lavery v Pursell*, and *McIntyre v Stockdale*', *University of New Brunswick Law School Journal*, vol 1(1), 1947, p 25; J M MacIntyre, 'Equity — Damages in Place of Specific Performance', *Canadian Bar Review*, vol 47, 1969, p 644; M G Bridge, 'The Statute of Frauds and Sale of Land Contracts', *Canadian Bar Review*, vol 64, 1986, 58 at p 87; P M McDermott, 'Equitable Damages in Nova Scotia', *Dalhousie Law Journal*, vol 12, 1989, p 131.

40 *Allen v Fairbrother* (1907) 9 GLR 328; *Treadgold v Rost* (1912) 12 WWR 300; 7 DLR 741; *Robinson v MacAdam* [1948] 2 WWR 425; *Dillon v Nash* [1950] VLR 293.

41 G W Hinde, D W McMorland and P B A Sim, *Land Law*, vol 2, Butterworths, Wellington, 1979, para 10.039 cited by Robertson J in *Mahoe Buildings v Fair Investments Ltd* [1994] 1 NZLR 281 at 284.

42 [1974] 1 NSWLR 622.

43 [1974] 1 NSWLR 622 at 626.

The potential of *Lord Cairns' Act* in a case of part performance was adverted to by Chitty J in two cases. In *Re Northumberland Avenue Hotel Co*[44] an agreement with a company for a building lease was executed before the company was incorporated, and was thus incapable of ratification.[45] The company failed to complete the building in accordance with the agreement, and the Metropolitan Board re-entered the land. The Board claimed damages for the breach of contract by the company. This claim was dismissed on the ground that there was no valid agreement in existence. Chitty J commented:

> ... that if there had been an agreement of which specific performance could have been originally decreed on the ground of part performance, there would not be any jurisdiction to give damages after specific performance had become impossible.[46]

In *Lavery v Pursell*[47] the plaintiff sought specific performance of a parol agreement for the sale of building materials on a site. The action was commenced after the contractual entitlement of the plaintiff to remove the materials had expired. Specific performance was therefore impossible when the writ was issued. The court dismissed any claim for specific performance or damages. Chitty J said:

> It was suggested that after *Lord Cairns' Act* the Court of Equity could give damages in lieu of specific performance. Yes, but it must be in a case where specific performance could have been given.[48]

The jurisdiction to award equitable damages in a case of part performance was also recognised in *Price v Strange*[49] where specific performance of a partly performed oral agreement was decreed. The Court of Appeal held that lack of mutuality did not deprive the court of jurisdiction to decree such relief or equitable damages. Goff LJ remarked that s 40 of the Law of Property Act 1925 'would not prevent an award of damages in equity under *Lord Cairns' Act'*.[50] In the New Zealand case of *Ward v Metcalfe*[51] an oral contract for the sale of a home unit was unenforceable in an action for common law damages because of the lack of a memorandum in writing under s 2 of the Contracts Enforcement Act 1956. An order for specific performance could not be made as the property was sold to a third party after the commencement of proceedings. However, Fisher J held that the plaintiff could be awarded equitable damages under *Lord Cairns' Act* as the acts of part performance of the plaintiff warranted enforcement of the contract in equity.

---

44 (1886) 33 Ch D 16.
45 *Kelner v Baxter* (1866) LR 2 CP 174.
46 (1886) 33 Ch D 16 at 18.
47 (1888) 39 Ch D 508.
48 (1888) 39 Ch D 508 at 519.
49 [1978] Ch 337.
50 [1978] Ch 337 at 358.
51 [1990] BCL 1422. See also R D Mulholland, 'Part performance and common law damages', *New Zealand Law Journal*, 1991, p 211.

Colonial cases

The potential of *Lord Cairns' Act* in a case of part performance appears to have been first appreciated in the outposts of the British Empire. In the Queensland case of *Noagues v Hope*,[52] the claim of the plaintiff was essentially one of damages for the breach of an unexecuted agreement of lease. The case was decided before the Judicature system was introduced into Queensland. The plaintiff relied upon s 1 of the Equity Procedure Act 1873[53] which enabled the Supreme Court at law and a District Court to entertain an action for a monetary equitable claim or demand. The defendant had not formally executed a lease to the plaintiff in accordance with the agreement for a lease. This was emphasised by G R Harding, counsel for the defendant, who stated in argument: 'The foundation for this action is the refusal to grant a lease'.[54] Although the plaintiff had taken possession of the relevant land, the absence of an executed memorandum of lease would have precluded the plaintiff from recovering damages at law. It was also clear that it would not have been open to the plaintiff to have recovered damages for a breach of the agreement to lease because such an action could only be maintained where all the essential terms of the lease were to be found in the agreement.[55] The actual portion of the land could not be identified from the agreement, though it was afterwards shown to the plaintiff by the defendant. Therefore the only relief which was at all available to the plaintiff was equitable relief.

The plaintiff relied upon the doctrine of part performance, and the jury found that the agreement had been partly performed by the plaintiff.[56] This doctrine was relevant because equitable damages may be awarded in substitution for a decree of specific performance. Section 62 of the Queensland Equity Act of 1867,[57] derived from *Lord Cairns' Act*, conferred jurisdiction upon the Supreme Court in equity to award equitable damages 'in substitution' for the specific performance of an agreement. Cockle CJ had remarked that the case 'was partially connected with s 62 of the Equity Act of 1867'.[58] It was held on demurrer that s 1 of the Equity Procedure Act conferred jurisdiction to award damages in these circumstances.

Another colonial decision which recognised the relevance of *Lord Cairns' Act* in a case of part performance was that of the Supreme Court of the Straits Settlement at Penang in *Tan Seng Qui v Palmer*.[59] The court could award damages under *Lord Cairns' Act* as it was vested with the same jurisdiction as the High Court of Chancery.[60] Pellereau J remarked:

---

52 (1874) 4 QSCR 57.
53 37 Vict No 3 (Queensland).
54 (1874) 4 QSCR 57 at 59.
55 *Chapman v Towner* (1840) 6 M & W 100 at 104; 151 ER 338 at 340.
56 *Noaques v Hope (No 3)* (14 May 1874, unreported (Queensland State Archives)). *Questions put to jury and answers thereto*, Q 2 ('Was it partly performed by Plaintiff Noughes to the Knowledge of Dept Hope? — Yes'). (In the papers the name of the plaintiff is spelt variously.)
57 31 Vict No 18 (Queensland).
58 (1874) 4 QSCR 57 at 59. See also *Barbagallo v J & F Catelan Pty Ltd* [1986] 1 Qd R 245 at 255–6 per McPherson J.
59 (1887) 4 Ky 251.
60 R St J Braddell, *The Law of the Straits Settlements: A Commentary*, Oxford University

It will be noticed that I have not alluded to the legal point which was argued in the case, as to whether the Statute of Frauds was a bar to the plaintiff's claim for damages. I incline to think that it was not as the part performance took the case out of the Statute. I incline to think that the damages that this court can award are the same in England under *Lord Cairns' Act* where it was provided that in every case where specific performance could have been granted the Court of Chancery could in addition to, or in substitution for, decreeing specific performance, award damages for any breach of the contract.[61]

In a number of Victorian decisions in the late nineteenth century part performance was relied upon to award damages for breach of a parol agreement for lease.[62] The jurisdictional basis of these awards was not clear, as *Lord Cairns' Act* had not been adopted in Victoria at that time.

In the New South Wales case of *Williamson v Bors*[63] the court rejected a submission that equitable damages under *Lord Cairns' Act* could be awarded in a case of part performance. The court regarded *Lord Cairns' Act* as a statute enabling a court of equity to award common law damages to avoid a multiplicity of proceedings. Walker J said:

> The power, given by the 32nd section to this Court to award damages in lieu of specific performance, is given only to avoid circuity of action, so that if it should be found that, under the circumstances of the case, specific performance should not be granted, but that the plaintiff ought to be left to his legal remedy, the Court of Equity, having seisin of the case, might give that remedy without putting the plaintiff to the delay and expense of instituting fresh proceedings in another jurisdiction. It was not intended that the Court of Equity should give damages when an action would not lie at law.[64]

It is submitted that this dictum is based upon a restrictive interpretation of the decision of Chitty J in *Lavery v Pursell*[65] in which his Lordship recognised that the Court of Chancery could award damages 'in a case in which specific performance could be given'.[66]

Academic writings

A number of misconceptions have arisen through the omission in the literature of any discussion of the relevance of *Lord Cairns' Act* in a case of part performance. In *Dillon v Nash*[67] Sholl J observed that 'the statements in *Anson*, and in *Fry* ... are too wide inasmuch as they would incorrectly exclude s 62(4) of the Supreme Court Act [*Lord Cairns' Act*] in a case where part performance is relied on'.[68] Sholl J referred to a passage from *Anson* which then stated:

Press, New York, 1982, p 67.
61 (1887) 4 Ky 251 at 257.
62 *M'Bean v Brown* (1887) 13 VLR 726; *Kaufman v Michael* (1892) 18 VLR 375.
63 (1900) 21 LR (NSW) Eq 302.
64 (1900) 21 LR (NSW) Eq 302 at 309.
65 (1888) 39 Ch D 508.
66 (1888) 39 Ch D 508 at 519.
67 [1950] VLR 293.
68 [1950] VLR 293 at 301.

As the Chancery could not have given damages in lieu of specific performance before the Acts [ie the *Judicature Acts*], so damages can still not be obtained where parol evidence is admitted under the doctrine.[69]

Sholl J also referred to a passage from *Fry* which then stated that the doctrine rendered a parol contract 'capable of being enforced by specific performance, though not by way of damages, even since the *Judicature Acts*'.[70] Not only do these texts not advert to the jurisdiction under *Lord Cairns' Act*, but one edition of *Fry* contains the following passage:

It has been held that the doctrine of part performance does not extend to enable the Court to award damages on a parol contract.[71]

In *Rushton v McPherson*[72] Harrison J relied upon a similar passage in a later edition of *Fry*[73] to deny jurisdiction under *Lord Cairns' Act*.[74] Some Australian commentators have remarked:

There have been various attempts to argue there where (a) a contract is unenforceable at law because of for example non-compliance with the Statute of Frauds, (b) there were acts of part performance but (c) equity would not decree part performance because of delay or the character of the contract, the acts of part performance could now be relied upon at law to overcome the Statute and give a remedy in damages. If this were so, the plaintiff would be asserting a right which before 1873 existed neither at law nor in equity: *Marsh v Mackay*[75].[76]

Such an account does not advert to the jurisdiction that was vested in the Court of Chancery in 1858 by *Lord Cairns' Act* which enabled equitable damages to be awarded. The decision in *Marsh v Mackay*[77] is not really of general application. The court was concerned with the issue of whether the Magistrates' Court in Queensland could award damages for breach of an unexecuted agreement of lease by reason of the doctrine of part performance. In denying any such jurisdiction the Full Court relied upon authorities concerning the jurisdiction of the County Courts of England.[78] A basis for the award of damages was, however, to be found in the statutory jurisdiction to determine an equitable claim or demand.[79] Such provisions have been regarded as 'curious'[80] and have their origin in

---

69 *Anson's Principles of the Law of Contracts*, 19th ed, Clarendon Press, Oxford, 1945, p 80.
70 E Fry, *Specific Performance of Contracts*, 6th ed, Stevens, London, 1921, p 276.
71 E Fry, *Specific Performance of Contracts*, 5th ed, Stevens, London, 1911, p 298.
72 (1939) 14 MPR 235.
73 E Fry, *Specific Performance of Contracts*, 6th ed, Stevens, London, 1921, p 283.
74 (1939) 14 MPR 235 at 245.
75 [1948] St R Qd 113.
76 R P Meagher, W M C Gummow and J R F Lehane, *Equity — Doctrines and Remedies*, 2nd ed, Butterworths, Sydney, 1984, p 53 [233]; 3rd ed, Butterworths, Sydney, 1992, p 54 [233].
77 [1948] St R Qd 113.
78 *Foster v Reeves* [1892] 2 QB 255.
79 *Magistrates' Courts Act 1921* (Queensland) s 4(1)(c). See also T J Lehane, 'Equitable Jurisdiction of Magistrates' Courts', *Queensland Justice of the Peace*, vol 42, 1948, p 133.
80 See S Owen-Conway, 'The Equitable Jurisdiction of the Inferior Courts in Western Australia', *University of Western Australia Law Review*, vol 14, 1979, 150 at p 163; R P Meagher, W M C Gummow and J R F Lehane, *Equity — Doctrines and Remedies*, 2nd ed, Butterworths, Sydney, 1984, p 62.

s 1 of the Queensland Equity Procedure Act 1873 which enables equitable damages to be awarded.[81] This statutory jurisdiction may be exercised by a court which does not have jurisdiction to award equitable relief in the form of an injunction or specific performance provided that a plaintiff has a notional entitlement to such relief.[82] The jurisdiction is still of relevance in Queensland and Western Australia.[83]

Judicature Acts

There has been some discussion of the effect of the *Judicature Acts*. The Court of Appeal in *Britain v Rossiter*[84] held that the *Judicature Acts* did not alter the rights of parties to a suit, but only changed procedure. Consequently part performance cannot be invoked in a common law action for damages for the breach of a contract of service.[85] In *Ellul v Oakes*[86] the purchasers of a house succeeded in an action for damages for breach of warranty in respect of a representation that the house was sewered. The purchasers succeeded because it was held that there was a sufficient memorandum in writing. The argument was canvassed that part performance could have provided the plaintiff with a method of defeating the Statute of Frauds. One obstacle to an award of equitable damages was that, at the time the action had commenced, everything possible had been done by both parties.[87] However, Wells J considered that equitable relief may still have been available had 'anything remained to be done by the vendor that was not done'.[88]

Wells J also remarked:

> It seems to me, on principle, that, since the passing of the *Judicature Acts*, if a contract is enforceable in equity, in particular, if it is sufficiently proved to meet the demands of equity so that a claim for specific performance would succeed, that contract is also proved for the purpose of founding an action for damages.[89]

However, as Macdonald J observed in *Carter v Irving Oil Co Ltd*[90] the enactment of the *Judicature Acts* did not affect the operation of the doctrine of part performance. The jurisdiction to award equitable damages in substitution for specific performance, where the availability of that remedy is dependent upon the doctrine, has been available since *Lord*

---

81   *Noagues v Hope* (1874) 4 QSCR 57.
82   *Barbagallo v J & F Catelan Pty Ltd* [1986] 1 Qd R 245; *Dunlop Olympic Ltd v Ellis* [1986] WAR 8.
83   P M McDermott, 'Equitable Claims and Demands — Queensland District and Magistrates Courts and the Western Australian Local Courts', *University of Queensland Law Journal*, vol 16, 1991, p 212.
84   (1879) 11 QBD 123.
85   J Williams, *The Statute of Frauds*, Cambridge University Press, Cambridge, 1932, pp 237–8; *O'Rourke v Hoeven* [1974] 1 NSWLR 622 at 626.
86   (1972) 3 SASR 377.
87   R N Barber, 'The Operation of the Doctrine of Part Performance, in Particular to Actions for Damages', *University of Queensland Law Journal*, vol 8, 1973, p 79.
88   (1972) 3 SASR 377 at 395.
89   (1972) 3 SASR 377 at 395.
90   [1952] 4 DLR 128 at 133.

Cairns' Act. This was recognised by Palles CB who remarked in *Crowley v O'Sullivan*[91] that:

> ... part performance can be relied upon whether the relief which a Court of Equity would have thought proper to have given before the *Judicature Acts* or this Court may now think proper to give, is specific performance or damages.[92]

In *Ellul v Oakes*[93] Bray CJ regarded the doctrine of part performance as providing 'an equitable defence only and [which] is only relevant in actions of specific performance'.[94] It is, with respect, difficult to regard the doctrine as an equitable defence as that concept would defeat a claim for equitable relief.

Partnership agreements

The Statute of Frauds has relevance where a partnership agreement includes an agreement to acquire premises where a partnership is to be undertaken. Damages in lieu of specific performance may be awarded where a party has failed to execute a partnership deed, but there have been sufficient acts of part performance in carrying on a partnership. In these circumstances the court may grant specific performance to compel the parties to execute a formal deed of partnership.[95] In *Crowley v O'Sullivan*[96] the Queen's Bench Division of the High Court of Ireland dismissed an appeal against a verdict for damages obtained by a partner who had unsuccessfully sought the execution of the partnership deed by the defendant. Sufficient acts of part performance were constituted by the parties carrying on business for several months. It was held that the doctrine of part performance was not restricted to contracts for the sale of land. Palles CB accepted the argument of the plaintiff that 'part performance can be relied upon whether the relief which a Court of Equity would have thought proper to have given before the *Judicature Acts* or this Court may now think proper to give, is specific performance or damages'.[97]

In *Douglas v Hill*[98] damages were awarded by a Local Court in respect of an unexecuted partnership agreement for a dental practice which could be specifically enforced by virtue of part performance. The case has been explained on the basis that once the court decreed specific performance, the Statute of Frauds would not have provided a defence.[99] However, a Local Court could not then decree specific performance, nor award equitable damages under *Lord Cairns' Act*. The award of damages was justified under a provision which was derived from s 25(11) of the

---

91 [1900] 2 Ir R 478 at 485–6.
92 [1900] 2 Ir R 478 at 485–6.
93 (1972) 3 SASR 377.
94 (1972) 3 SASR 377 at 382–3.
95 *England v Curling* (1844) 8 Beav 129; 50 ER 51.
96 [1900] 2 Ir R 478 at 485–6.
97 [1900] 2 Ir R 478 at 485–6.
98 [1909] SALR 28.
99 R N Barber, 'The Operation of the Doctrine of Part Performance in Particular to Actions for Damages', *University of Queensland Law Journal*, vol 8, 1973, 79 at p 88.

Judicature Act 1873 which provided that where there is any conflict or variance between the rules of equity and the rules of common law with reference to the same matter the rules of equity shall prevail. It is, however, doubtful whether that provision of itself enabled the award of damages in that case.[100] Courts of inferior jurisdiction do not, in the absence of statute, possess jurisdiction to entertain money claims which are dependent upon the grant of equitable relief.[101]

Where a partnership is in existence, a partner can claim an injunction to reinstate his rights as a partner and damages at law or under *Lord Cairns' Act* whether in substitution for an injunction or specific performance.[102]

Canada

The principle enunciated by Chitty J in *Lavery v Pursell*[103] is generally accepted in Canada.[104] Initially, in Ontario the principle was disregarded by Clute J in *McIntyre v Stockdale*[105] on the basis that Chitty J had ignored that after the *Judicature Acts* the court could award common law damages irrespective of whether or not the court could decree specific performance. However, as Meredith CJCP pointed out in *Bennett v Stodgell*[106] 'there were the best of reasons for not referring to common law rights, because the case was one in which common law courts never could have any jurisdiction — a case for specific performance on the ground of part performance'.[107] In cases of part performance damages have been awarded in Alberta,[108] Newfoundland,[109] Nova Scotia[110] and Ontario.[111] In New Brunswick the court has disclaimed jurisdiction to award damages in the case of an agreement for personal services and for the conveyance of land.[112]

---

100 *Moore v Dimond* [1929] SASR 274 at 279–80; H Mayo, 'Statute of Frauds — Part Performance in Relation to Damages', *Australian Law Journal*, vol 6, 1932, p 283. See also *Foster v Reeves* [1892] 2 QB 255; *New Zealand Express Co Ltd v Kettle* (1903) 6 GLR 160.

101 *New Zealand Express Co Ltd v Kettle* (1903) 6 GLR 160; *Taylor v Holmes* [1919] QWN 25; *Taranaki Hospital Board v Woodward* [1941] GLR 330; *Barbagallo v J & F Catelan Pty Ltd* [1986] 1 Qd R 245 at 266 per Thomas J; P M McDermott, 'Equitable Claims and Demands — Queensland District and Magistrates Courts and the Western Australian Local Courts', *University of Queensland Law Journal*, vol 16, 1991, p 212.

102 *Laugesen v Spensley* (1910) 12 GLR 719 (damages in lieu of an injunction, delay).

103 (1888) 39 Ch D 508.

104 The decision was not applied in *Treadgold v Rost* (1912) 7 DLR 741 at 753 where it was found that acts of payment by the plaintiff were not such a part performance of the contract as would entitle him to specific performance. The jurisdiction under *Lord Cairns' Act* was not adverted to in one case where it was held that damages could be awarded where specific performance of an agreement could be decreed because of part performance: see *Calgary Hardwood & Veneer Ltd v Canadian National Railway Co* [1977] 4 WWR 18; (1977) 74 DLR (3d) 284.

105 (1912) 27 OLR 460; 9 DLR 293 followed in *Tozer v Berry* [1955] OWN 399.

106 (1916) 36 OLR 45; 28 DLR 639.

107 (1916) 36 OLR 45 at 57; 28 DLR 639 at 644–5.

108 *Brownscombe v Public Trustee of Alberta* [1969] SCR 658; 68 WWR 483.

109 *Arns v Halliday* (1982) 36 Nfld & PEIR 337; 101 APR 337.

110 *Carter v Irving Oil Co Ltd* [1952] 4 DLR 128 at 133; *McCallum v Mackenzie* (1979) 37 NSR (2d) 328 at 347. Compare *Dominion Supply & Construction Co v Foley Bros* (1919) 53 NSR 333 at 348. See also P M McDermott, 'Equitable Damages in Nova Scotia', *Dalhousie Law Journal*, vol 12, 1989, 131 at pp 140–3.

111 *Pearson v Skinner School Bus Lines (St Thomas) Ltd* (1968) 69 DLR (2d) 283 at 289.

112 *Rushton v McPherson* (1939) 14 MPR 235.

Law of Property (Miscellaneous Provisions) Act 1989 (England)

The doctrine of part performance in relation to contracts for the sale of realty has been abrogated by statute in England and Wales. Section 2(1) of the Law of Property (Miscellaneous Provisions) Act 1989[113] provides:

> A contract for the sale or other disposition of an interest in land can only be made in writing and only by incorporating all the terms which the parties have expressly agreed in one document or, where contracts are exchanged, in each.

This provision replaced the statutory requirement for writing in s 40 of the Law of Property Act 1925[114] which has ceased to have effect by virtue of s 2 of the Law of Property (Miscellaneous Provisions) Act 1989. The Law of Property Act 1925 contained a savings clause which preserved the operation of the doctrine of part performance. Section 40(2) of the Law of Property Act 1925 provided that the section 'does not affect the law relating to part performance'.[115] Such a provision removed the objection that the doctrine of part performance enables the courts to disregard a statute.[116] Section 2 of the Law of Property (Miscellaneous Provisions) Act 1989 does not, unlike the former s 40 of the Law of Property Act 1925, preserve the law relating to part performance. However, whether or not the doctrine of part performance survives is not dependent upon the existence of an express savings clause. The Law Commission recognised that merely repealing s 40(2) of the Law of Property Act 1925 would not abolish the doctrine of part performance as the subsection was merely there for the avoidance of doubt.[117] The Law of Property (Miscellaneous Provisions) Act 1989 has effectively abrogated the doctrine by providing in s 2(1) that 'a contract for the sale or other disposition of an interest in land can only be made in writing'. In contrast provisions derived from the Statute of Frauds effectively provide that a contract not in writing is unenforceable. The Law Commission considered that the courts would use doctrines of equitable estoppel to achieve very similar results, where appropriate, to those of part performance.[118] In some cases relief could be given on the basis of part performance and equitable estoppel.[119]

It may be questioned whether the abolition of the doctrine of part performance, albeit introducing certainty, was on balance the best alternative available, and whether it may have had unintended consequences. The recommendations of the Law Commission have inadvertently

---

113 1989 c 34.

114 15 & 16 Geo V c 20.

115 Provisions which preserve the law relating to part performance are also in force in various Commonwealth jurisdictions: see eg Property Law Act 1974 (Queensland) s 6(d).

116 M P Thompson, 'The Role of Evidence in Part Performance', *The Conveyancer and Property Lawyer*, 1979, 402 at p 413.

117 Law Commission (UK), *Transfer of Land — Formalities for Contracts for the Sale etc of Land*, Working Paper No 92, 1985, p 26, para 4.3.

118 Law Commission (UK), *Transfer of Land — Formalities for Contracts for Sale etc of Land*, Law Com No 164, HC 2, 1987, p 18.

119 *Raffaele v Raffaele* [1962] WAR 29; *Jackson v Crosby (No 2)* (1979) 21 SASR 280.

abrogated the established law relating to equitable mortgages. Since the eighteenth century it has been established that a deposit of title deeds by way of security has been taken to show a contract to create a mortgage and an act of part performance of that contract.[120] The acceptance and discounting of bills by a bank may be sufficient acts of part performance of an agreement to grant a mortgage enforceable in equity and thereby create an equitable mortgage.[121] It would now appear to be the case in England that a deposit of title deeds, unaccompanied by a written memorandum, can no longer create an equitable mortgage.[122] Where an agreement to execute a legal mortgage is in writing so as to satisfy the Statute of Frauds, an equitable mortgage is created.[123]

Prior to the enactment of the Law of Property (Miscellaneous Provisions) Act 1989, Finn had warned that part performance should not be absorbed into equitable estoppel:

> Part performance in its present form should be abandoned. But it should not, without qualifications, be absorbed into equitable estoppel. Whatever may be its shortcomings, in its remedy it secures the maintenance and the enforcement of the contract itself. Though equitable estoppel commonly protects the expectation interest of the relying party, it is not a doctrine which today requires this outcome. To introduce the discretionary element of its remedies into the contract/Statute of Frauds context would, in the writer's view, be less than helpful given, as noted below, that the law of quasi-contract/restitution already has a role to play where a contract is unenforceable for want of writing.[124]

Finn considered that the referability test was inappropriate where a contract is admitted by the defendant or is proved by means other than the contested oral testimony of the plaintiff. Finn mentioned that:

> ... substantial justice can be done to the plaintiff, not by protecting his expectation interest through specific enforcement, but by protecting his restitution/reliance interests through quasi-contractual or restitutionary remedies.[125]

The doctrines of equitable estoppel and part performance also have distinct functions. The former doctrine is concerned with representations created or encouraged by the defendant, whereas the latter doctrine is concerned with the enforcement of an actual agreement which lacks the formality required by the Statute of Frauds.[126]

--------◄○►--------

120 R E Megarry and H W R Wade, *The Law of Real Property*, 5th ed, Stevens, London, 1984, pp 927–8.

121 *Australia and New Zealand Banking Group Ltd v Widin* (1990) 102 ALR 289.

122 E F Cousins, *The Law of Mortgages*, Sweet & Maxwell, London, 1989, p vi.

123 *Re Collens* (1982) 140 DLR (3d) 755.

124 P D Finn, 'Equity and Contract' in *Essays on Contract* (ed P D Finn), Law Book Co, Sydney, 1987, p 124.

125 Finn, n 124 above, p 125.

126 C N H Bagot, 'Equitable Estoppel and Contractual Obligations in the Light of *Waltons v Maher*', *Australian Law Journal*, vol 62, 1988, 926 at p 929.

9.6 Equitable estoppel

It is only in relatively recent times that cases have been categorised as being instances of 'equitable estoppel'. Formerly such cases would have been regarded as instances of acquiescence, waiver or estoppel by representation. A number of decisions of the High Court of Australia and other superior courts in Australia concerning equitable estoppel[127] have prompted some considerable academic discussion on the relevant principles concerning the application of this long-standing equity jurisdiction.[128] The relevant principles relating to the existence of an equitable estoppel were comprehensively summarised by Brennan J in *Waltons Stores (Interstate) Ltd v Maher*:[129]

> In my opinion, to establish an equitable estoppel, it is necessary for a plaintiff to prove that (1) the plaintiff assumed that a particular legal relationship then existed between the plaintiff and the defendant or expected that a particular legal relationship would exist between them and, in the latter case, that the defendant would not be free to withdraw from the expected legal relationship; (2) the defendant has induced the plaintiff to adopt that assumption or expectation; (3) the plaintiff acts or abstains from acting in reliance on the assumption or expectation; (4) the defendant knew or intended him to do so; (5) the plaintiff's action or inaction will occasion detriment if the assumption or expectation is not fulfilled; and (6) the defendant has failed to act to avoid that detriment whether by fulfilling the assumption or expectation or otherwise. For the purposes of the second element, a defendant who has not actively induced the plaintiff to adopt an assumption or expectation will nevertheless be held to have done so if the assumption or expectation can be fulfilled only by a transfer of the defendant's property, a diminution of his rights or an increase in his obligations and he, knowing that the plaintiff's reliance on the assumption or expectation may cause detriment to the plaintiff if it is not fulfilled, fails to deny to the plaintiff the correctness of the assumption or expectation on which the plaintiff is conducting his affairs.[130]

The High Court of Australia has also changed some assumptions regarding the nature of common law estoppel and equitable estoppel.

---

127 *Legione v Hateley* (1983) 152 CLR 406; *Waltons Stores (Interstate) Ltd v Maher* (1988) 164 CLR 387; *Foran v Wight* (1989) 168 CLR 385; *Commonwealth of Australia v Verwayen* (1990) 170 CLR 394. See also *Riches v Hogben* [1985] 2 Qd R 292; *Riches v Hogben* [1986] 1 Qd R 315; *Beaton v McDivitt* (1985) 13 NSWLR 134; *Silvovi Pty Ltd v Barbaro* (1988) 13 NSWLR 466.

128 P D Finn 'Equitable Estoppel' in *Essays in Equity* (ed P D Finn), Law Book Co, Sydney, 1985, p 59; K G Nicholson, '*Riches v Hogben*: Part Performance and the Doctrines of Equitable and Proprietary Estoppel', *Australian Law Journal*, vol 60, 1986, p 345; D M J Bennett, 'Equitable Estoppel and Related Estoppels', *Australian Law Journal*, vol 61, 1987, p 540; P A Ridge, 'The Equitable Doctrines of Part Performance and Proprietary Estoppel', *Melbourne University Law Review*, vol 16, 1988, p 725; C N H Bagot, 'Equitable Estoppel and Contractual Obligations in the Light of *Waltons v Maher*', *Australian Law Journal*, vol 62, 1988, p 926; G Jones, 'A Topography of the Law of Restitution', in *Essays in Restitution* (ed P Finn), vol 1, Law Book Co, Sydney, 1990, 1 at p 5; P A Butler, 'Mistaken Payments, Change of Position and Restitution' in *Essays in Restitution* (ed P Finn), Law Book Co, Sydney, 1990, 87 at pp 125–31.

129 (1988) 164 CLR 387.

130 (1988) 164 CLR 387 at 428–9.

Common law estoppel has sometimes been regarded as an evidentiary doctrine which did not extend to a future state of facts, whereas equitable estoppel was available in those circumstances. Common law estoppel was regarded as a shield and not a sword. This orthodoxy was overthrown by the High Court in *Waltons Stores (Interstate) Ltd v Maher*.[131] In that case Deane J considered that even before the fusion of law and equity there was general consistency between common law and equitable principle in relation to estoppel by conduct. His Honour concluded:

> Upon analysis, there is no acceptable reason why the doctrine of promissory estoppel should be seen, in a fused system, as exclusively equitable or as raising some new or heightened conflict between law and equity.[132]

This theme was taken up in *Commonwealth of Australia v Verwayen*[133] by Sir Anthony Mason CJ who remarked:

> In these circumstances, it would confound principle and common sense to maintain that estoppel by conduct occupies a special field which has as its hallmark function the making good of assumptions. There is no longer any purpose to be served in recognizing an evidentiary form of estoppel operating in the same circumstances as the emergent rules of substantive estoppel. The result is that it should be accepted that there is but one doctrine of estoppel, which provides that a court of common law or equity may do what is required, but not more, to prevent a person who has relied upon an assumption as to a present, past or future state of affairs (including a legal state of affairs), which assumption the party estopped has induced him to hold, from suffering detriment in reliance upon the assumption as a result of the denial of its correctness.[134]

However, there is not yet unanimity on this issue for in *Verwayen's* case McHugh J observed:

> But more importantly, in the present state of authority, the common law doctrine of estoppel does not, but the equitable doctrine of promissory estoppel does, extend to representations or assumptions concerning the future: *Legione v Hateley*;[135] *Waltons*.[136] Hence any representations or assumptions concerning the future can be dealt with, and on the traditional view can be dealt with only, by equitable estoppel. Even if 'there is no acceptable reason why the doctrine of promissory estoppel should be seen, in a fused system, as exclusively equitable', as Deane J asserted in *Waltons*,[137] the equitable rules must prevail over the common law rules 'concerning the same matter': Supreme Court Act 1986 (Victoria), s 29.[138]

This statement of principle was in accordance with a previous judgment of his Honour in which he rejected the 'fusion fallacy'.[139] It has been pointed

---

131   (1988) 164 CLR 387.
132   (1988) 164 CLR 387 at 448.
133   (1990) 170 CLR 394.
134   (1990) 170 CLR 394 at 413.
135   (1983) 152 CLR 406 at 432–5.
136   (1988) 164 CLR 387 at 398–9, 459.
137   (1988) 164 CLR 387 at 448.
138   (1990) 170 CLR 394 at 499–500.
139   *A Hudson Pty Ltd v Legal & General Life of Australia Ltd* (1985) 1 NSWLR 314 at 336.

out that the English cases on estoppel[140] do not discard their common law or equitable origins.[141]

In the context of a discussion on equitable damages the subject of equitable estoppel has increasing relevance, particularly in view of the abrogation in England of the doctrine of part performance by the Law of Property (Miscellaneous Provisions) Act 1989. A court in enforcing an equitable estoppel has jurisdiction to award equitable damages.[142] The jurisdiction was exercised in *Jackson v Crosby (No 2)*[143] where there was an arrangement between a man and woman, in expectation of marriage, that the man would build a house on land owned by the woman. Under the arrangement the parties were to have an equality of interest in the property. The man was awarded equitable damages under the South Australian equivalent to *Lord Cairns' Act*.[144] The plaintiff was content with an award of damages rather than an order for specific performance. The damages were assessed by reference to half the value of the property rather than on a *quantum meruit* basis of the value of his labour in building the house.

In some cases of proprietary estoppel a plaintiff would seek an award of equitable compensation, rather than damages under *Lord Cairns' Act*. In *Stiles v Tod Mountain Development Ltd*,[145] a purchaser of an unregistrable interest in a lot took possession of the lot and improved the lot with the encouragement of the owner. Huddart J awarded the purchaser 'equitable damages' against a subsequent purchaser who took with notice of his interest in circumstances regarded as fraudulent in equity. This award was undoubtedly an instance of the inherent jurisdiction in equity. In this particular case an order for specific performance was out of the question as the subdivisional plan creating the lot was unlikely ever to be approved. Accordingly there would not be the jurisdictional basis in that case to support an award of equitable damages under *Lord Cairns' Act*.

————◁○▷————

9.7 Vendor and purchaser

In a number of vendor and purchaser cases equitable damages have been sought either in addition to, or in substitution for, specific performance. These cases were discussed earlier in the context of the assessment of equitable damages.[146] Some cases were decided before the decision in

---

140 *Crabb v Arun District Council* [1976] Ch 179; *Amalgamated Investment and Property Co Ltd v Texas Commerce International Bank Ltd* [1982] QB 84; *Taylors Fashions Ltd v Liverpool Victoria Trustees Co Ltd* [1982] QB 133.

141 J Martin, 'Fusion, Fallacy and Confusion: A Comparative Study', *Conveyancer and Property Lawyer*, 1994, 13 at p 24.

142 G Jones and W Goodhart, *Specific Performance*, Butterworths, London, 1986, p 18; *Raffaele v Raffaele* [1962] WAR 29; *Crabb v Arun District Council (No 2)* (1976) 121 SJ 86; *Jackson v Crosby (No 2)* (1979) 21 SASR 280.

143 (1979) 21 SASR 280 at 290, 302.

144 Supreme Court Act 1935 (South Australia) s 30.

145 (1992) 88 DLR (4th) 735.

146 See Chapter 7.

Johnson v Agnew[147] where it was held that an assessment of equitable damages would equal an assessment of common law damages where both remedies are available.[148] It is submitted that the jurisdiction to award equitable damages will be relevant where common law damages are unavailable for procedural reasons, or where common law principles prevent the assessment of damages on a basis where complete justice can be given to a plaintiff.

————◇————

9.8 Delay in performance of contracts

The Chancery Commissioners had recommended that the Court of Chancery, in a specific performance suit, should have jurisdiction to 'grant compensation in damages for the loss sustained up to the time of the contract being performed'.[149] *Lord Cairns' Act* certainly conferred jurisdiction upon the Court of Chancery to award damages, in addition to specific relief, for delay in performance of a contract. This was recognised by Sholl J who remarked in *Dillon v Nash*[150] that 'since *Lord Cairns' Act* the typical case in which damages are given in addition to specific performance is the case of delay by the defendant in fulfilling the contract'.[151] Lord St Leonards commented upon this aspect of the jurisdiction:

> I tried in vain to prevent it, as it was not called for, and would lead, in every case, to a contest for damages — on account of delay, for example — which would be conducted with more pertinacity, and with greater expense, than the real question between the vendor and the purchaser.[152]

Equitable damages have been awarded for delay in performance of a contract in a number of cases prior to the introduction of the Judicature system in various jurisdictions.[153] It is necessary to examine the relevance of this jurisdiction since the fusion of law and equity.

In considering the delay in the performance of a contract it is relevant to advert to s 24(7) of the *Judicature Act* 1873 which provides:

> Stipulations in contracts, as to time or otherwise, which would not before the passing of this Act have been deemed to be or to have become of the essence of such contracts in a Court of Equity, shall receive in all Courts the same construction and effect as they would have heretofore received in equity.[154]

---

147 [1980] AC 367.
148 *Wroth v Tyler* [1974] Ch 30.
149 *Third Report of Her Majesty's Commissioners appointed to enquire into the Process, Practice and System of Pleading in the Court of Chancery & c*, 1856, Command [2064], p 4.
150 [1950] VLR 293.
151 [1950] VLR 293 at 301. See also *Bosaid v Andry* [1963] VR 465 at 485.
152 E B Sugden, *Handy Book on Property Law*, 8th ed, Blackwood & Sons, London, 1869, p 6.
153 *Cory v Thames Ironworks and Shipbuilding Co Ltd* (1863) 8 LT (NS) 237; 11 WR 589; *Griffin v Mercantile Bank* (1890) 11 LR (NSW) Eq 231 at 258.
154 Supreme Court of Judicature Act 1873 (36 & 37 Vict c 66) s 24(7).

This provision was superseded by s 41 of the Law of Property Act 1925[155] which provides:

> Stipulations in a contract, as to time or otherwise, which according to rules of equity are not deemed to be or to have become of the essence of the contract, are also construed and have effect at law in accordance with the same rules.

Similar provisions are in force in other Commonwealth jurisdictions.[156] They are an attempt to reconcile the rigidity of the common law and the flexibility of equity. Maitland considered that this reform removed the anomaly where 'a man could enforce a contract in equity though he could no longer enforce it at law'.[157] Although Spry has observed that: 'The traditional view has been that special provisions of this kind have a limited operation'.[158] In *Stickney v Keeble*[159] Lord Parker of Waddington commented that the provision did not have the consequence that the rules of equity 'shall be applied generally and without inquiry whether the particular case, purpose, or circumstances are such that equity would have applied the rules'.[160] It was earlier mentioned that the equitable maxim that the time fixed for completion is not of the essence of the contract, never applied where 'the parties, for reasons best known to themselves, had stipulated that the time fixed should be essential'.[161] Most contracts of sale expressly provide that the condition as to time is essential, although it is clear since the decision in *Raineri v Miles*[162] that the fact that a contract has not declared time to be of the essence does not enable a court to disregard an express date for completion.

Ordinarily a court can award common law damages for a breach of contract for a delay in completion. In *CSS Investments Pty Ltd v Lopiron Pty Ltd*[163] Davies J remarked: 'A purchaser may in an appropriate case obtain an order for specific performance and in addition an order for damages for breach of a contractual term as to time'.[164] In such a case there is no need to place any reliance on *Lord Cairns' Act*. In *Gloucester House Ltd v Peskin*[165] the Federal Supreme Court rejected a submission that the English cases since 1873, where damages for unreasonable delay have been given in addition to specific performance, are to be supported by reason of *Lord Cairns' Act* rather than by virtue of the *Judicature Acts*. In *Raineri v*

---

155 15 & 16 Geo V c 20.
156 *Australia: New South Wales:* Conveyancing Act 1919 (1919 No 6) s 13; *Queensland:* Property Law Act 1974 (1974 No 76) s 62; *South Australia:* Law of Property Act 1936 (1936 No 2328) s 16; *Tasmania:* Supreme Court Civil Procedure Act 1932 (23 Geo V No 58) s 11(7); *Victoria:* Property Law Act 1958 (No 6344) s 41; *Western Australia:* Property Law Act 1969 (1969 No 32) s 21; *British Columbia:* Law and Equity Act RSBC 1979 c 224 s 27; *New Zealand:* Judicature Act 1908 (1908 No 89) s 90.
157 F W Maitland, *Equity,* 2nd rev ed, Cambridge University Press, Cambridge, 1949, p 308.
158 I C F Spry, *Equitable Remedies,* 4th ed, Law Book Co, Sydney, 1990, pp 212–3.
159 [1915] AC 386.
160 [1915] AC 386 at 417.
161 [1915] AC 386 at 416.
162 [1981] AC 1050.
163 (1987) 76 ALR 463.
164 (1987) 76 ALR 463 at 483.
165 (1961) 3 WIR 375.

Miles[166] Viscount Dilhorne referred to some decisions[167] where a contract had been construed as containing a term that completion would take place on a date fixed in the contract.[168] In each case damages were awarded for loss of profits or income arising from the breach of contract resulting from the failure of a vendor to complete on the appointed date. These cases were also cited in *Gloucester House Ltd v Peskin*.[169]

The leading case is *Jaques v Millar*[170] where damages were awarded for loss of profits where there was a refusal to grant a lease for a trade. In that case the pleader might appear to be using the language of *Lord Cairns' Act* in making a claim for damages 'in addition to'[171] specific performance. However, such a claim is equally appropriate to refer to a claim for common law damages, and no significance can be placed upon this claim. In formulating the relevant principle for the assessment of damages Fry J observed:

> I shall not attempt to explain in detail the motives which operate on my mind. But I am entitled to have regard to the damages which may reasonably be said to have naturally arisen from the delay, or which may be reasonably supposed to have been in the contemplation of the parties as likely to arise from the partial breach of contract.[172]

This was clearly an application of the second rule in *Hadley v Baxendale*[173] which was cited in argument. In *Hadley v Baxendale*[174] Alderson B remarked:

> ... if the special circumstances under which the contract was actually made were communicated by the plaintiffs to the defendants, and thus known to both parties, the damages resulting from the breach of such a contract, which they would reasonably contemplate, would be the amount of injury which would ordinarily follow from a breach of contract under these special circumstances so known and communicated.[175]

This rule concerning special circumstances known by the defaulting party was also the basis on which damages were awarded to the purchaser for loss of profits in *Gloucester House Ltd v Peskin*.[176] The rule was formulated prior to *Lord Cairns' Act* and is a basic principle for the assessment of damages for breach of contract.[177]

---

166 [1981] AC 1050.
167 *Jaques v Millar* (1877) 6 Ch D 153; *Royal Bristol Permanent Building Society v Bomash* (1887) 35 Ch D 390; *Jones v Gardiner* [1902] 1 Ch 191; *Phillips v Lamdin* [1949] 2 KB 33. In the first three cases the purchaser was awarded specific performance, and damages. In the last case there was a voluntary completion after a writ for specific performance was issued.
168 [1981] AC 1050 at 1075.
169 (1961) 3 WIR 375.
170 (1877) 6 Ch D 153.
171 (1877) 6 Ch D 153 at 159.
172 (1877) 6 Ch D 153 at 160.
173 (1854) 9 Ex 341; 156 ER 145.
174 (1854) 9 Ex 341; 156 ER 145.
175 (1854) 9 Ex 341 at 354–5; 156 ER 145 at 151.
176 (1961) 3 WIR 375 at 377.
177 A W B Simpson, 'Innovation in Nineteenth Century Contract Law', *Law Quarterly Review*, vol 91, 1975, 247 at pp 274–6.

The jurisdiction under *Lord Cairns' Act* has relevance in some instances where there is a delay in the performance of a contract. The statute provides a convenient jurisdictional base for an award of damages. The jurisdiction has been exercised where proceedings for specific performance were commenced before there was a completely constituted cause of action at law,[178] where there was an open contract for the sale of property which was subject to encumbrances which secured an amount greater than the purchase price,[179] where there was a voluntary completion after proceedings for specific performance had been commenced[180] and to award interest upon purchase moneys that were due in a matter in which orders for specific performance had already been made.[181] The jurisdiction has relevance in a case of part performance[182] or equitable estoppel. It is also relevant where a plaintiff has not accepted a repudiation of a contract, or has put an end to a contract in circumstances where common law damages are unavailable.[183]

——◁○▷——

9.9 'Benefit and burden' transactions

The jurisdiction to award equitable damages may arise in 'benefit and burden'[184] transactions where there is typically no privity of contract between the parties. In *Tito v Waddell (No 2)*,[185] the *Ocean Island* case, Sir Robert Megarry VC enunciated the 'basic principle' relating to 'benefit and burden':

> ... he who takes the benefit of a transaction must also bear the burden.[186]

The 'basic principle' is justified by reasons of fairness. One form of this principle is the old rule relating to deeds:

> ... it is ancient law that a man cannot take benefit under a deed without subscribing to the obligations thereunder.[187]

---

178   *Oakacre Ltd v Claire Cleaners (Holdings) Ltd* [1982] Ch 197.
179   *Grant v Dawkins* [1973] 1 WLR 1406.
180   *Crockford v Pessago* (Supreme Court of New South Wales, Helsham CJ in Eq, Eq Div, No 4399 of 1979, 6 May 1980, unreported). See also *Ford-Hunt v Raghbir Singh* [1973] 1 WLR 738 at 742.
181   *Vanmeld Pty Ltd v Cussen* (1994) 121 ALR 619.
182   *Dillon v Nash* [1950] VLR 293.
183   *Corpers (No 664) Pty Ltd v NZI Securities Australia Ltd* (1989) ASC 55–714.
184   D Gordon, 'The Benefit and Burden of the Rules of Assignment', *Conveyancer and Property Lawyer*, 1987, p 103; E P Aughterson, 'In Defence of the Benefit and Burden Principle', *Australian Law Journal*, vol 65, 1991, p 319.
185   [1977] Ch 106.
186   [1977] Ch 106 at 289.
187   *Halsall v Brizell* [1957] Ch 169 at 182 per Upjohn J as cited in R E Megarry and H W R Wade, *The Law of Real Property*, 5th ed, Stevens, London, 1984, p 769. On the application of this principle: see *Rhone v Stephens* [1994] 2 WLR 429 at 437 per Lord Templeman; *Gallagher v Rainbow* (1994) 121 ALR 129 at 146 per McHugh J.

In the *Ocean Island* case native landowners by deeds gave a mining company permission to mine phosphate and the company covenanted to replant the land with native trees. The British Phosphate Commissioners, the successors to the company, were held liable to replant the land because having taken the benefit of the land, they were subject to the normal remedies for the breach of these obligations. The Vice-Chancellor remarked:

> My conclusion on the benefit and burden point is that the British Phosphate Commissioners are liable at law on the replanting obligations in the A and C deeds, and so are subject to the normal remedies (including damages) for any breach of that obligation. That, of course, is subject to other matters dealt with in this judgment. This liability could be supported, if necessary, by the liability to pay damages in substitution for specific performance under the Chancery Amendment Act 1858 (*Lord Cairns' Act*) if this is a case in which specific performance could be decreed.[188]

Accordingly it is clear that an award of equitable damages can be made in such a case providing that a plaintiff has an equity to specific performance.

In *Lyus v Prowsa Developments Ltd*[189] a vendor agreed to sell a plot on an estate to the plaintiffs and erect a house on it. The plaintiffs paid a deposit and contracted to sell their existing house and arranged for a mortgage to recover the excess required to complete the contract. Before the completion of the house the vendor went into liquidation. The vendor's bank sold the plot to the first defendant in the exercise of the mortgagee's power of sale. A clause in the contract of sale provided that the sale was subject to the plaintiffs' contract with the vendor. The first defendant then sold the plot to the second defendant, the contract of sale provided that the plot was sold subject to the plaintiffs' contract. The plaintiffs claimed, inter alia, damages for breach of contract, specific performance and damages in addition to or in lieu of specific performance. It was held that the defendants, having accepted the plot under the contracts, held the plot under a constructive trust in favour of the plaintiffs. The plaintiffs obtained specific performance of the original building contract against the second defendant. Dillon J observed:

> ... there are well established authorities, such as *Halsall v Brizell*,[190] to the effect that any person who takes the benefit of a contract must assume the burden. In so far, therefore, as the plaintiffs have sought to assert the benefits of their contract with the vendor company ... they must submit to the burden of that contract.[191]

In *Lyus v Prowsa Developments Ltd*[192] it was submitted that an order for specific performance should not be made as there was a lack of mutuality between the parties. It was held that lack of mutuality is merely a discretionary, and not a jurisdictional, barrier to relief. Dillon J remarked:

---

188 [1977] Ch 106 at 309. See also *Government Insurance Office (NSW) v KA Reed Services Pty Ltd* [1988] VR 829 at 833 per Brooking J.
189 [1982] 1 WLR 1044.
190 [1957] Ch 169.
191 [1982] 1 WLR 1044 at 1053–4.
192 [1982] 1 WLR 1044.

It has been submitted for the defendants that such a conclusion would involve a want of mutuality which is offensive to the traditional approach of the courts of equity, in that it would involve that the plaintiffs acquire rights against the first defendant by virtue of the agreement to which they are not parties, while the first defendant, for want of privity of contract, has no corresponding right to sue the plaintiffs for specific performance or damages. I do not think that this submission is valid. Want of mutuality is merely a factor which a court of equity may have to consider in deciding whether or not to grant a decree of specific performance. It is not an absolute bar to specific performance: see *Price v Strange*[193] [194]

Accordingly, the circumstance of want of mutuality is not a bar to specific performance (or an award of equitable damages in substitution for specific performance).

———◄o►———

9.10 Speculative contracts for the sale of land

Where property is not inherently special to a purchaser who is a party to a speculative contract for the sale of land, an award of common law damages to compensate for lost profits may be an adequate remedy. Where a purchaser has an equity to specific performance, the purchaser may be awarded equitable damages under *Lord Cairns' Act*.[195] In this context there is some controversy as to whether a court will grant specific performance of a speculative contract for the sale of land. There is modern Canadian authority that a purchaser of land will not be granted specific performance of a contract for the sale of land as a matter of course if the land was purchased for a speculative investment.[196] This approach is contrary to the weight of authority that 'the court will almost invariably grant specific performance of a contract regarding land'.[197] There are also sound reasons why a purchaser who is a speculator should ordinarily be granted specific performance. One reason for granting specific performance is the avoidance of a multiplicity of proceedings, such as possible litigation between a purchaser and a sub-purchaser.[198] It has been cogently argued

193   [1978] Ch 337.
194   [1982] 1 WLR 1044 at 1053.
195   *Savill v Chase Holdings (Wellington) Ltd* (1989) 1 NZLR 257 at 317 per McMullin J. See also *Sharma v Hnatiuk* (1987) 58 OR (2d) 345 at 351; P J Brenner, 'Specific Performance Contracts for the Sale of Land Purchased for Resale or Investment', *McGill Law Journal*, vol 24, 1978, 513 at p 561.
196   *Heron Bay Investments Ltd v Peel-Elder Developments Ltd* (1976) 2 CPC 338; *Chaulk v Fairview Construction Ltd* (1978) 3 RPR 116; *McNabb v Smith* (1981) 124 DLR (3d) 547; 132 DLR (3d) 547; *Zalaudek v De Boer* (1981) 33 BCLR 57; *Tanu v Ray* (1982) 20 RPR 22; *McClenaghan v Haley* [1983] 5 WWR 586. The authorities are comprehensively reviewed by Adams J in *Domowicz v Orsa Investments Ltd* (Ontario Court of Justice, No 339/87, 29 September 1993, unreported).
197   P V Baker and P StJ Langan, *Snell's Equity*, 29th ed, Sweet & Maxwell, London, 1990, p 586.
198   P J Brenner, 'Specific Performance of Contracts for the Sale of Land Purchased for Resale or Investment', *McGill Law Journal*, vol 24, 1978, p 513.

by Jones and Goodhart that whether specific performance should be granted should not depend upon whether a purchaser has or has not contracted to sell the land to a third party at the date of the action or whether a purchaser would be liable for breach of contract to a third party if specific performance were denied.[199] A contrary view has been expressed by Sharpe who submits, while recognising the interests of third parties, that a speculator in real estate should be subject to the principle of mitigation.[200] In Canada it has been held that an award of equitable damages will not be made where a purchaser who, because of failure to mitigate, would not be granted specific performance.[201]

---◦---

9.11 Contracts for the loan of money

There is authority from the nineteenth century that a court does not possess jurisdiction to award equitable damages under *Lord Cairns' Act* in a suit for the specific performance of a contract for the loan of money.[202] This was derived from the principle that a court would not decree specific performance of such contracts.[203] Ordinarily a borrower would seek damages for the breach of a contract for the loan of money.[204]

It is now accepted that a court may make an order for the specific performance of a contract for the loan of money where a remedy in damages is clearly inadequate.[205] An example would be where a borrower requires finance to enable the completion of the purchase of land.[206] In such a case the remedy will only be granted where there is evidence that the necessary funds cannot be obtained from another financier and an appropriate adjustment made by the award of damages.[207] A contract with

---

199 G Jones and W Goodhart, *Specific Performance*, Butterworths, London, 1986, pp 93–4. See also P J Brenner, 'Specific Performance of Contracts for the Sale of Land Purchased for Resale or Investment', *McGill Law Journal*, vol 24, 1978, p 513; J Berryman, 'Specific Performance, Uniqueness and Investment Contracts', *Conveyancer and Property Lawyer*, 1984, p 130.

200 R J Sharpe, *Injunctions and Specific Performance*, Canada Law Book, Toronto, 1983, pp 317–19.

201 *Domowicz v Orsa Investments Ltd* (Ontario Court of Justice, Adams J, No 339/87, 29 September 1993, unreported).

202 *Rogers v Challis* (1859) 27 Beav 175 at 180; 54 ER 68; *Crampton v Varna Railway Co* (1872) LR 2 Ch App 562 at 567; *Larios v Bonany Y Gurety* (1873) LR 5 PC 346 at 353 (PC).

203 *Rogers v Challis* (1859) 27 Beav 175; 54 ER 68; *Sichel v Mosenthal* (1862) 30 Beav 371 at 377; 54 ER 932 at 935; *Larios v Bonany Y Gurety* (1873) LR 5 PC 346 (PC); *Western Wagon and Property Co v West* [1892] 1 Ch 271 at 275; *The South African Territories Ltd v MC Logging Ltd* (1967) 65 DLR 300 at 308; *Loan Investment Corp of Australasia v Bonner* [1970] NZLR 724 at 735 (PC).

204 *Aziz v GIFC Ltd* [1988] ANZ ConvR 480.

205 *Starkey v Barton* [1909] 1 Ch 284; *Loan Investment Corp of Australasia v Bonner* [1970] NZLR 724 at 744 per Sir Garfield Barwick *dissentiente* (PC); *Wright v Haberdan Pty Ltd* [1984] 2 NSWLR 280 at 289.

206 *Wright v Haberdan Pty Ltd* [1984] 2 NSWLR 280.

207 *Corpers (No 664) Pty Ltd v NZI Securities Australia Ltd* [1989] ASC 55–714 at 58,419.

a company to take up and pay for debentures of the company may be enforced by an order for specific performance.[208]

There is authority that equitable damages may be awarded where specific performance is sought of a loan agreement. In *Corpers (No 664) Pty Ltd v NZI Securities Australia Ltd*[209] an award of equitable damages was made under the New South Wales equivalent of *Lord Cairns' Act*. The court did not doubt that specific performance could be decreed of a loan agreement. Young J remarked that 'the previous law that equity has no jurisdiction to grant specific performance has now gone'.[210] In that particular case common law damages could not be awarded to the plaintiff because at the time when proceedings were instituted the plaintiff had not accepted the repudiation of the defendant, nor had the plaintiff put an end to the contract.

————◁○▷————

9.12 Contracts for the sale of goods

The traditional attitude of the courts of equity is that damages are an adequate remedy where a commodity is readily available upon the market.[211] However, in an appropriate case a court will make an order for the specific performance of a contract for the sale of goods. This discretionary remedy will be granted where an award of damages would not be a sufficient remedy.[212] As Jacobs J observed in *Aristoc Industries Pty Ltd v RA Wenham (Builders) Pty Ltd*:[213]

> If damages at law are an inadequate remedy then there is no principle which will prevent the interference of a Court of Equity simply because the subject matter is a chattel.[214]

The rarity of a chattel is one aspect of the general question of the inadequacy of damages.[215] A person who has contracted to buy a ship is prima facie entitled to specific performance of the contract.[216] Another instance where specific performance may be decreed is where damages would clearly be inadequate because a defendant is unable to satisfy a judgment.[217] However, such an approach would effectively make a plaintiff

---

208 *Australia:* Corporations Act 1989 (1989 No 109) (now Corporations Law) s 1049; *England:* Companies Act 1985 (1985 c 6) s 195; *India:* Specific Relief Act 1963 (47 of 1963) s 14(3)(a)(ii).
209 [1989] ASC 55–714.
210 [1989] ASC 55–714 at 58,419.
211 *Cohen v Roche* [1927] 1 KB 169; *Price v Strange* [1978] Ch 337 at 359, 369.
212 *Dominion Coal Co Ltd v Dominion Iron and Steel Co Ltd* [1909] AC 293; *Cohen v Roche* [1927] 1 KB 169; *Behnke v Bede Shipping Co Ltd* [1927] 1 KB 649; (1927) 17 Asp MLC 222 (ship). See also G H Treitel, 'Specific Performance in the Sale of Goods', *Journal of Business Law*, 1966, p 211.
213 [1965] NSWR 581.
214 [1965] NSWR 581 at 588.
215 *Aristoc Industries Pty Ltd v RA Wenham (Builders) Pty Ltd* [1965] NSWR 581 at 588.
216 *Behnke v Bede Shipping Co Ltd* [1927] 1 KB 649; (1927) 17 Asp MLC 222 at 225.
217 *Société des Industries Metallurgiques SA v The Bronx Engineering Co Ltd* [1975] 1 Lloyd's Rep 465 at 468.

a preferred creditor. A court may make an order for the specific performance of a contract for the sale of goods under the Sale of Goods Act.[218]

--- ◦ ---

9.13 Contracts for personal services

The courts have traditionally declined to decree specific performance of contracts for personal services because of the difficulties of the continued supervision of any decree by a court.[219] In some instances this relief may be precluded by statute.[220] In *De Francesco v Barnum*[221] Fry LJ remarked that 'the courts are bound to be jealous, lest they should turn contracts of service into contracts of slavery'.[222] In *Scandinavian Trading Tanker Co AB v Flota Petrolera Ecuatoriana*[223] Lord Diplock remarked that 'English Courts have always disclaimed any jurisdiction'.[224] In one Canadian case a rationale for the court declining to decree specific performance was 'that it would be improper to make one man serve another against his will'.[225] There is also authority that an injunction to restrain a breach of a contract for personal services ought not to be granted where its effect would be to decree performance of the contract.[226] In a New Brunswick case which involved an agreement for personal services and for the conveyance of land it was held that there was no jurisdiction under *Lord Cairns' Act* to award damages. The court relied upon authority that specific performance will not be ordered of contracts for personal services.[227]

From an historical perspective the remedy of specific performance has always been available.[228] In an appropriate case a court of equity will grant relief to ensure that an injustice is redressed.[229] There are comparatively recent cases in which a court has made an order for the specific

---

218   Sale of Goods Act 1979 (1979 c 54) s 52.

219   *Ryan v Mutual Tontine Westminster Chambers Assn* [1893] 1 Ch 116; *JC Williamson Ltd v Lukey and Mulholland* (1931) 45 CLR 282 at 298; *Heidke v Sydney City Council* (1952) 52 SR (NSW) 143 at 149; *Price v Strange* [1978] Ch 337 at 369; *McCallum v Mackenzie* (1979) 37 NSR (2d) 328 at 347.

220   *England:* Industrial Relations Act 1971 (1971 c 72) s 128; Trade Union and Labour Relations Act 1974 (1974 c 52) s 16; *Manitoba:* The Court of Queen's Bench Act SM 1988 c 4 CCSM c C280 s 56(1).

221   (1890) 45 Ch D 430.

222   (1890) 45 Ch D 430 at 438.

223   [1983] AC 694.

224   [1983] AC 694 at 701. See also *Warren v Mendy* [1989] 1 WLR 853.

225   *Emerald Resources Ltd v Sterling Oil Properties Management Ltd* (1969) 3 DLR (3d) 630 at 647.

226   *Dataforce Pty Ltd v Brambles Holdings Ltd* [1988] VR 771 at 784; *Warren v Mendy* [1989] 1 WLR 853 at 857.

227   *Rushton v McPherson* (1939) 14 MPR 235.

228   J Berryman, 'The Specific Performance Damages Continuum: An Historical Perspective', Ottawa Law Review, vol 17, 1985, p 295.

229   *Wilson v Furness Railway Co* (1869) LR 9 Eq 28 at 33.

performance of a contract for personal services.[230] A court can make an order for specific performance where such an order is not in vain and is workable as where the necessary relationship of confidence has not broken between the employer and employee.[231] It is accordingly submitted that an award of equitable damages may be made in an appropriate case. An award of equitable damages would not be open to the traditional grounds of objection as no order compelling service would have to be made.

9.14 Contracts for the sale of shares

As a court may make an order for the specific performance of a contract for the sale of shares in a company which are not freely available on the market place[232] or in a partnership,[233] there is jurisdiction to make an award of equitable damages in substitution for an order for the specific performance of such a contract. In one case an award of equitable damages was made in an action for the specific performance of a contract for the purchase of shares where damages were not claimed.[234]

9.15 Expired leases

There is a general reluctance to make an order for the specific performance of an expired lease. In *Singh v Crafter*[235] Murray J remarked:

> ... if ... a lease has expired by the time the decision is to be taken to award specific performance, clearly that would be a case where it was impossible to award the decree and it might be said that on jurisdictional grounds that it was not open to do so.[236]

The reason why a court will generally not make such an order is reflected in the axiom that 'equity does nothing in vain'. However, it is submitted that it may be appropriate in some cases for a court to make a ruling that a plaintiff has an equity to an order for specific performance,

---

230 *C H Giles & Co Ltd v Morris* [1972] 1 WLR 307 at 318; *Tito v Waddell (No 2)* [1977] Ch 106 at 321–2; *Price v Strange* [1978] Ch 337 at 359; *Posner v Scott-Lewis* [1987] Ch 25; *Powell v Brent London Borough Council* [1988] ICR 176.

231 E Macdonald, 'Specific Enforcement of Contracts of Employment', *Northern Ireland Legal Quarterly*, vol 42, 1991, p 374.

232 *Re Schwabacher; Stern v Schwabacher, Koritschoner's Claim* (1907) 98 LT 127; *Llewellin v Grossman* (1950) 83 Ll L Rep 462.

233 *Dodson v Downey* [1901] 2 Ch 620. See also Specific Relief Act 1963 (India) s 14(3)(b)(ii).

234 *Singh v Crafter* (Supreme Court of Western Australia, Full Court, No 8 of 1991, 28 May 1992, unreported).

235 Supreme Court of Western Australia, Full Court, Appeal No 8 of 1991, 28 May 1992, unreported.

236 *Singh v Crafter*, n 235 above, p 71.

not for the purpose of making an order for specific performance for that would be to act in vain, but to provide a jurisdictional basis for an award of equitable damages.

An obstacle to an award of equitable damages in the case of an expired lease is the decision in *McMahon v Ambrose*.[237] In that case the Full Court of Victoria held, by a majority, that there was no jurisdiction to award equitable damages where specific performance was sought of an oral agreement to assign a lease which had expired prior to the commencement of proceedings. The absence of writing in this case precluded an action for common law damages. It is submitted there is much force in the dissenting judgment of McGarvie J who considered that 'the weight of opinion of authors of modern textbooks favours the view that there are interests other than in the future enjoyment of a term or its proceeds which may justify an order for specific performance'.[238] McGarvie J referred, with obvious approval, to the comments of Spry, and Meagher, Gummow and Lehane. Spry says:

> A somewhat different position arises where a plaintiff seeks specific performance of a contract for the execution of a lease for a term that has already expired. Here it has on a number of occasions been held that damages at law are adequate, so that specific enforcement has been refused. But in these cases also it may be argued that ordinarily at least the plaintiff should not be refused, on the ground of alleged futility, the performance that has been agreed upon. In any event, there is no reason why, in some cases of this nature, the plaintiff may not obtain some distinct advantage if the defendant is required to execute a deed or is enjoined from denying that a deed has been executed.[239]

Meagher, Gummow and Lehane state:

> Similarly, specific performance has been refused of agreements for leases for terms which had already expired, and of leases for short terms ... But it cannot be said that specific performance will always be refused in such cases on the ground of futility; the order may not be futile. It may tangibly assist the plaintiff, even in the case of an expired term, to have a legal lease and the rights flowing from it. Indeed, it is hard to conceive of a case where relief is refused on the ground of futility when it could be said that specific performance would afford more complete and perfect justice than damages.[240]

For the purpose of this discussion it would seem to be appropriate to include some other comments of Meagher, Gummow and Lehane:

> ... it is perhaps unnecessarily confusing to maintain that there is a separate defence of futility; in all such cases damages are an adequate remedy.[241]

---

237 [1987] VR 817.

238 [1987] VR 817 at 832. See also J Tooher, 'Case Note: *McMahon v Ambrose*', *Monash University Law Review*, vol 16, 1990, p 122.

239 I C F Spry, *Equitable Remedies*, 4th ed, Law Book Co, Sydney, 1990, pp 133–4.

240 R P Meagher, W M C Gummow and J R F Lehane, *Equity — Doctrines and Remedies*, 2nd ed, Butterworths, Sydney, 1984, p 489 [2039]; 3rd ed, Butterworths, Sydney, 1992, p 512 [2029].

241 See n 240 above.

In a case such as *McMahon v Ambrose*[242] where common law damages were not available at all, the award of equitable damages would give the innocent party a remedy.

———◄○►———

9.16 Contracts which can be terminated on short notice

As equity does nothing in vain, a court will not make an order for the specific performance of a contract which can be terminated on short notice. In *Rosser v Maritime Services Board of New South Wales (No 2)*[243] Young J explained:

> Equity does not, as a general rule, grant specific performance of contracts which can be terminated on relatively short notice. Thus equity will not grant specific performance of a partnership at will, see *Hercy v Birch*[244] and for a more modern example see *Argyle Art Centre Pty Ltd v Argyle Bond & Freestores Co Pty Ltd*,[245] where no equitable relief was granted in respect of a tenancy at will.[246]

Despite the principle that the court will not grant specific performance of contracts at will, it is clear that a court can make an award of equitable damages in respect of such contracts. In *Rosser v Maritime Services Board of New South Wales (No 2)*[247] it was held that the fact that a dredging contract might be terminated by three months' notice on either side tended against the grant of specific performance, and accordingly no order for specific performance was made. However, the court ordered an inquiry into damages before the master. Young J remarked:

> It seems to me that Mr Rosser is entitled to some damages both in lieu of specific performance and in addition to specific performance. These damages are really given under *Lord Cairns' Act* or s 68 of the Supreme Court Act.

In this case the plaintiff had not accepted a repudiation so there was no completed cause of action at common law so that the damages claim was a claim in equity under *Lord Cairns' Act*.[248]

———◄○►———

---

242 [1987] VR 817.
243 Supreme Court of New South Wales, Young J, Eq Div, No 1624 of 1993, 30 August 1993, unreported.
244 (1804) 32 ER 640.
245 [1976] 1 NSWLR 377.
246 *Rosser v Maritime Services Board of New South Wales (No 2)* (Supreme Court of New South Wales, Young J, Eq Div, No 1624 of 1993, 30 August 1993, unreported).
247 See n 246 above.
248 *Rosser v Maritime Services Board of New South Wales (No 2)*, n 246 above, at 46–7.

9.17 Voluntary covenants

The issue of whether equity will enforce a voluntary covenant has generated considerable debate.[249] As a general rule a volunteer cannot obtain the equitable remedy of specific performance.[250] Where a court does not have jurisdiction in a particular case to make an order for specific performance, it follows that equitable damages cannot be awarded either in addition to or in substitution for specific performance.

A court of equity can make an order for the specific performance of certain transactions, which Spry states 'are of an anomalous nature',[251] such as where there is marriage consideration, or where a plaintiff has an equity to have an imperfect disposition perfected[252] or where there is the enforcement of a trust. In these classes of case there is jurisdiction to grant specific performance, and consequently equitable damages.

The fact that an obligation is contained in a deed makes no difference in equity which has no special regard to the form of a seal.[253] This is an illustration of the maxim that 'Equity looks to the intent rather than to the form'.[254] There is one case in which the defendant was sued upon a deed and in which it was submitted that the plaintiff was really seeking equitable damages under s 68 of the Supreme Court Act 1970 of New South Wales and could not be awarded such relief because of the absence of consideration.[255] However, in that case the plaintiff was awarded common law damages for breach of contract; the question of equitable damages did not really arise as there was no suggestion that the plaintiff had an equity to specific relief.

In New Zealand the Law Commission has proposed that a court be empowered to make an order for the specific performance of a voluntary promise made by deed, and that a court could not decline to make an order for specific performance on the ground that there was no valuable consideration for the promise.[256] If such a reform were implemented a court would possess jurisdiction to award equitable damages in the case of a voluntary covenant provided that a plaintiff possessed the requisite equity to specific performance.

---

249 See eg D W Elliott, 'Enforcing Covenants in Favour of Volunteers', *Law Quarterly Review*, vol 76, 1960, p 100; W A Lee, 'The Public Policy of *Re Cook's Settlement Trusts*', *Law Quarterly Review*, vol 85, 1969, p 213; R P Meagher and J R F Lehane, 'Trusts of Voluntary Covenants', *Law Quarterly Review*, vol 92, 1969, p 427.

250 P H Pettit, *Equity and the Law of Trusts*, 7th ed, Butterworths, London, 1993, p 99.

251 I C F Spry, *Equitable Remedies*, 4th ed, Law Book Co, Sydney, 1990, p 56.

252 R P Meagher, W M C Gummow and J R F Lehane, *Equity — Doctrines and Remedies*, 2nd ed, Butterworths, Sydney, 1984, pp 160–73 [614]–[646]; 3rd ed, Butterworths, Sydney, 1992, pp 168–82 [614]–[646].

253 P H Pettit, *Equity and the Law of Trusts*, 7th ed, Butterworths, London, 1993, p 98.

254 P V Baker and P StJ Langan, *Snell's Equity*, 27th ed, Sweet & Maxwell, London, 1990, p 121.

255 *McEwan v Dick* (1985) 9 ACLR 1011 at 1017.

256 Law Commission, *A New Property Law Act*, Wellington, NZLR R29, 1994, pp 12, 17.

10

Procedural Matters

————◁▷————

10.1 Alternative claims for damages and specific performance

A statement of claim containing alternative claims for damages and equitable relief does not cause any procedural difficulties under the Judicature system (as introduced by the *Judicature Acts*[1]).[2] A purchaser can of course claim damages in the alternative to specific performance.[3] The relevant principles were discussed by O'Bryan J in *McKenna v Richey*:[4]

---

1 Supreme Court of Judicature Act 1873 (36 and 37 Vict c 66); Supreme Court of Judicature Act 1875 (38 & 39 Vict c 77).
2 *Minter v Geraghty* (1981) 38 ALR 68 at 85.
3 *McKenna v Richey* [1950] VLR 360 at 371; *Dobson v Winton and Robbins Ltd* [1959] SCR 775 at 779–80; (1959) 20 DLR (2d) 164 at 166–7; *Bosaid v Andry* [1963] VR 465 at 486; *Capital and Suburban Properties Ltd v Swycher* [1976] Ch 319 at 327; *Ogle v Comboyuro Investments Pty Ltd* (1976) 136 CLR 444 at 445, 452; *Johnson v Agnew* [1980] AC 367; *Newmont Pty Ltd v Laverton Nickel NL* [1981] 1 NSWLR 215.
4 [1950] VLR 360.

The apparent inconsistency of a plaintiff suing for specific performance and for common law damages in the alternative arises from the fact that, in order to avoid circuity of action, there is vested in the one Court jurisdiction to grant either form of relief. The plaintiff, in effect, is saying: 'I don't accept your repudiation of the contract but am willing to perform my part of the contract and insist upon your performing your part — but if I cannot successfully insist upon your performing your part, I will accept the repudiation and ask for damages'. Until the defendant's repudiation is accepted the contract remains on foot, with all the possible consequences of that fact. But if, from first to last, the defendant continues unwilling to perform her part of the contract, then, if for any reason the contract cannot be specifically enforced, the plaintiff may, in my opinion, turn around and say: 'Very well, I cannot have specific performance; I will now ask for my alternative remedy of damages at common law'. This, in my opinion, is equally applicable both before and after decree whether the reason for the refusal or the failure of the decree of specific performance is due to inability of the defendant to give any title to the property sold, or to the conduct of the plaintiff which makes it inequitable for the contract to be specifically enforced.[5]

In *Johnson v Agnew*[6] Lord Wilberforce remarked that this passage was 'illuminating'.[7] The analysis of O'Bryan J illustrates two principles. First, there is no inconsistency in a plaintiff concurrently claiming both specific performance and common law damages in the one suit. This principle had not been accepted in some cases.[8] Secondly, an order for specific performance does not preclude a plaintiff from recovering damages where the order cannot be enforced.

Where a plaintiff seeks to pursue a claim for specific performance while concurrently maintaining a claim for damages, difficulties occur in ascertaining whether those damages are common law damages or equitable damages. It should also be noted that a contract of sale may provide for a vendor to elect between determining the contract (and forfeiting the deposit), or suing for damages.[9] An action for specific performance does not put an end to a contract, because the whole purpose of such an action is to obtain the assistance of the court in performing the contract.[10] Where a contract is on foot a plaintiff may be awarded equitable damages, although not common law damages. Common law damages are unavailable where at the time that proceedings are commenced the contract is not terminated because a plaintiff has not accepted a repudiation or rescinded the contract. As Needham J put it in *Newmont Pty Ltd v Laverton Nickel NL*:[11]

> If the claim is for specific performance together with equitable damages, then damages can be given only if the court were able, at the date of commencement of the proceedings, to grant the primary relief. If the claim

---

5 [1950] VLR 360 at 372.
6 [1980] AC 367.
7 [1980] AC 367 at 397.
8 See eg *Conroy v Lowndes* [1958] Qd R 375.
9 *GUS Canada Inc v Oliver* (1980) 24 BCLR 96; *Goulet & Sons Ltd v Lalonde* (1983) 23 Man R (2d) 166; 149 DLR (3d) 577.
10 *Saunders v Multi Builders Ltd* (1981) 30 BCLR 236 at 244.
11 [1981] 1 NSWLR 215.

is for specific performance and, in the alternative, common law damages, then, if the latter claim is open only if the contract has been determined, plainly the two claims are inconsistent and cannot be pursued together even if they can be so pleaded.[12]

Lord Cairns' Act enables an award of equitable damages to be made in substitution for specific performance where a contract has not been determined.[13]

Prior to the introduction of the Judicature system the Court of Chancery would dismiss an application for specific performance (where such relief was inappropriate) without prejudice to the right of a plaintiff to bring proceedings at law.[14] Under the Judicature system if a court declines to order specific performance it would not generally be appropriate to dismiss the proceedings without prejudice to an action for common law damages, even if such an order of dismissal is made so that the plaintiff may appeal on the claim for specific performance.[15] In *Newmont Pty Ltd v Laverton Nickel NL (No 2)*[16] Needham J observed that in this situation there are three possible claims for damages:

(1) One is for equitable damages, and the refusal of the order for specific performance puts equitable damages out of the question.[17]

(2) The second is common law damages ... it may well be that a breach of contract by the defendants would permit the plaintiffs to proceed against them for common law damages for that breach without the plaintiffs being put to the election of rescinding the contract for that breach. It seems to me that, as the plaintiffs have elected not to proceed with any claims for damages in these proceedings, any such claims would be barred by the entry of judgment or even by the dismissal of proceedings.[18]

(3) There is ... a third type of damages, and that is common law damages based upon a rescission of the contract by the plaintiffs for the breach or repudiation by some of the defendants. This claim is not open in these proceedings because the plaintiffs, seeking specific performance, have been careful to maintain the contract in existence. As the right to claim those damages would be based upon a rescission after an acceptance of repudiation by some of the defendants, the claim, if any, for damages in respect of that class was not completely constituted at the time the statement of claim was issued. Accordingly it could not be the subject matter of any order or judgment in these proceedings.[19]

⎯⎯⎯⎯◄○►⎯⎯⎯⎯

12 [1981] 1 NSWLR 215 at 219.
13 *Corpers (No 664) Pty Ltd v NZI Securities Australia Ltd* [1989] ASC 55–714 at 58,419 (Supreme Court of New South Wales, Young J).
14 E R Daniell, *Practice of the High Court of Chancery*, vol 1, 5th ed, Stevens, London, 1871, p 946.
15 *Newmont Pty Ltd v Laverton Nickel NL* [1981] 1 NSWLR 215.
16 [1981] 1 NSWLR 221.
17 [1981] 1 NSWLR 221 at 223. *Semble*, where a plaintiff does not possess the requisite equity to specific relief when proceedings are commenced, or at some later stage in the proceedings.
18 [1981] 1 NSWLR 221 at 223.
19 [1981] 1 NSWLR 221 at 223.

10.2 Election between remedies

As a plaintiff can make alternative claims for relief in the pleading, the question arises of at what time must the plaintiff make an election between alternative claims for damages and specific performance. Obviously a concurrent claim cannot itself constitute an election. In *Dobson v Winton and Robbins Ltd*[20] Judson J explained:

> ... if the claim for specific performance alone is made, that constitutes an affirmation of the contract and, to that extent, an election to enforce the contract. But where the alternative common law claim is made, the writ is equivocal and there is no election.[21]

In a claim for a breach of contract a plaintiff does not have to elect which remedy is sought before the writ is issued or a counterclaim is served. In a claim for common law damages a plaintiff is entitled to elect to treat the contract as repudiated, provided that the facts relied upon for the repudiation occurred before the issue of the writ.[22] It is desirable that any election should be made before or at the trial,[23] and not late in a proceeding.[24] At the latest, an election should be made before a judgment is entered on the record. The doctrine of election only arises where there is no formal entry of judgment, and does not preclude the substitution of a judgment for damages where an order for specific performance is unsuitable.[25] As Lord Atkin emphasised in *United Australia Ltd v Barclays Bank Ltd*,[26] 'on a question of alternative remedies no question of election arises until one or more claims has been brought to judgment'.[27]

10.3 Dissolution of order for specific performance

The question sometime arises whether an award of damages may be made where an order for specific performance has not been complied with or proves to be unsuitable. In *McKenna v Richey*[28] O'Bryan J held that equitable damages or common law damages were available where it was inequitable, by reason of laches, to enforce a decree of specific performance. Subsequently, the Court of Appeal in *Capital and Suburban*

---

20 [1959] SCR 775; (1959) 20 DLR (2d) 164.
21 [1959] SCR 775 at 781; (1959) 20 DLR (2d) 164 at 168. See also *Public Trustee v Pearlberg* [1940] 2 KB 1 at 19.
22 *Tilcon Ltd v Land and Real Estate Investments Ltd* [1987] 1 WLR 46.
23 *Simpson v Kondra* (1982) 42 BCLR 13 at 21.
24 *Kemp v Lee* (1983) 44 BCLR 172 at 182.
25 *Widrig v Strazer* [1964] SCR 376 at 386; (1964) 47 WWR 268 at 277; 44 DLR (2d) 1 at 9.
26 [1941] AC 1.
27 [1941] AC 1 at 30.
28 [1950] VLR 360 at 376.

Properties Ltd v Swycher[29] held that a vendor could not recover common law damages where a purchaser had failed to comply with an order for specific performance. That is why Foster J in *Biggin v Minton*[30] and the Court of Appeal in *Johnson v Agnew*[31] invoked *Lord Cairns' Act* in awarding equitable damages where an order for specific performance had proved useless.[32] In *Biggin v Minton* Foster J remarked: 'I do not see why the plaintiffs should be precluded from seeking damages in lieu of specific performance'.[33]

The House of Lords in *Johnson v Agnew*[34] overruled the decision of the Court of Appeal in *Capital and Suburban Properties Ltd v Swycher*.[35] The error of the decision had been clearly demonstrated.[36] Lord Wilberforce observed: 'if an order for specific performance is sought and is made, the contract remains in effect and is not merged in the judgment for specific performance'.[37] The House of Lords also decided that where a purchaser does not comply with an order for specific performance the vendor may either apply to the court for its enforcement, or for dissolution of the order and rescission of the contract.[38] Such an application is granted under the inherent jurisdiction of the court to grant relief consequential upon an order for specific performance.[39] An award of damages may be made after dissolution of an order for specific performance.[40] Therefore, where it proves impossible to satisfy an order for specific performance, the innocent party may apply to the court to put an end to the contract. In such a case, damages may be assessed as at the date that the court considers just having regard to all the circumstances, including the conduct of the parties. This may be when the contract is finally abandoned,[41] or when the defendant did not comply with an order for specific performance.[42]

Once an order for specific performance has been made a plaintiff has, to use the words of Sir Robert Megarry VC in *Singh (Sudagar) v Nazeer*,[43] 'put it into the hands of the court how the contract is to be carried out'.[44]

---

29 [1976] Ch 319.
30 [1977] 1 WLR 701.
31 [1978] Ch 176.
32 [1980] AC 367.
33 [1977] 1 WLR 701 at 703.
34 [1978] Ch 177.
35 [1976] Ch 319.
36 F Dawson, 'Damages after Specific Performance', *Law Quarterly Review*, vol 93, 1977, p 232.
37 [1980] AC 367 at 393. See also *Vandeleur & Moore v Dargan* [1981] ILRM 75.
38 E R Daniell, *Practice of the High Court of Chancery*, vol 2, Stevens, London, 1914, p 1207; *Vandeleur & Moore v Dargan* [1981] ILRM 75. See also M Hetherington, 'Keeping the Plaintiff Out of His Contractual Remedies: The Heresies That Survive *Johnson & Agnew*', *Law Quarterly Review*, vol 96, 1980, 403 at pp 408–11.
39 *Kenning Investments Pty Ltd v Rusty Rees Pty Ltd* [1992] Q ConvR 54–430.
40 *Hughes v Pellicciari* (1982) 2 BPR 9509; *Gaspari v Creighton Holdings Ltd* (1984) 52 BCLR 30 at 58; 13 DLR (4th) 570 at 576; *Acfold Investments Pty Ltd v Turner* (Supreme Court of Queensland, Weld M, No 727 of 1983, 11 October 1984, unreported).
41 *Sullivan v Darkin* [1986] 1 NZLR 214 at 220.
42 *Gaspari v Creighton Holdings Ltd* (1984) 52 BCLR 30; 13 DLR (4th) 570.
43 [1979] Ch 474.
44 [1979] Ch 474 at 481.

It has long been the case that an order for specific performance may be dissolved or vacated only with the leave of the court.[45]

The dissolution of an order for specific performance is not a mere formality which is granted as a matter of course. In *Johnson v Agnew*[46] Lord Wilberforce remarked:

> Once the matter has been placed in the hands of a court of equity, or one exercising equitable jurisdiction, the subsequent control of the matter will be exercised according to equitable principles. The court would not make an order dissolving the decree of specific performance and terminating the contract (with recovery of damages) if to do so would be unjust in the circumstances then existing, to the other party.[47]

Accordingly, a court would not accede to such an application by a plaintiff if it would result in an injustice to the defendant.[48] It should be appreciated that a discretionary defence, such as laches, may also be relevant where an award of equitable damages is sought in lieu of an order for specific performance which has already been made.[49]

————<o>————

10.4 Rescission while specific performance is pending

The old Chancery rule that a party was not permitted to rescind a contract if an action for specific performance was still pending is of long standing.[50] In *Gray v Fowler*[51] Sir Fitzroy Kelly CB pointed out that:

> ... the whole meaning and essence of that rule (which is a very reasonable rule) is this: "You cannot be acting on the contract and assuming it to exist, and at the same time exercising a right to put an end to it by rescinding it".[52]

The reason for the rule was explained by Goddard LJ in *Public Trustee v Pearlberg*:[53]

---

45 *Halkett v Dudley, Earl of* [1907] 1 Ch 590 at 601; *Facey v Rawsthorne* (1925) 35 CLR 566 at 588; *Cleadon Trust Ltd v Davis* [1940] Ch 940; *Stevter Holdings Ltd v Katra Constructions Pty Ltd* [1975] 1 NSWLR 459; *Sunbird Plaza Pty Ltd v Maloney* (1988) 166 CLR 245 at 260; *Vegret Pty Ltd v Tarko Nominees Pty Ltd* (Supreme Court of Queensland, Full Court, App No 91 of 1990, unreported); *Kenning Investments Pty Ltd v Rusty Rees Pty Ltd* [1992] Q ConvR 54–430.
46 [1978] Ch 176.
47 [1980] AC 367 at 399.
48 *JAG Investment Pty Ltd v Strati* [1981] 2 NSWLR 600 at 606; *Acfold Investments Pty Ltd v Turner* [1985] Q ConvR 54–161; *GKN Distributors Ltd v Tyne Tees Fabrication Ltd* (1985) 275 EG 53 at 54.
49 *Neylon v Dickens* [1987] 1 NZLR 402.
50 *Warde v Dixon* (1858) 28 LJ Ch 315; *Gray v Fowler* (1871) LR 8 Ex 249.
51 (1871) LR 8 Ex 249.
52 (1871) LR 8 Ex 249 at 272.
53 [1940] 2 KB 1.

If one contracting party, either expressly or by conduct, repudiates a contract, the other can either accept the repudiation and treat the contract as rescinded, or can refuse to do so, and regard the contract as still alive, so that his rights will fall to be determined when the time for performance arrives. He cannot, however, insist on performance and at the same time adopt the remedies open to him on rescission. Applying that rule to a case where equity would entertain a claim for specific performance, it follows that if a vendor, by applying for that remedy, asserts that he regards the contract as subsisting, he loses his right to forfeit a deposit, on the footing that the contract has been rescinded by the purchaser's default.[54]

This rule has survived the introduction of the Judicature system.[55] In *Ogle v Comboyuro Investments Pty Ltd*[56] the High Court of Australia reaffirmed its continuing relevance. Gibbs, Mason and Jacobs JJ remarked: 'It is a very understandable rule of equity and is unaffected in principle by the introduction of the Judicature system'.[57] Their Honours added: 'In specific performance there must be mutuality and it is in equity inconsistent with him continuing to seek specific performance that he should rescind the contract'.[58] A differing approach was taken by Barwick CJ who explained the rule on the basis that no case at law antithetic to a suit in Chancery could be permitted. The Chief Justice considered that the procedural rules of Chancery have no place in the Judicature system which permits a concurrent claim for specific performance and, in the alternative, for common law damages.[59] The question sometimes arises whether a court may award damages while an application for specific performance is still on the record. In *Public Trustee v Pearlberg*[60] Goddard LJ considered that an abandonment of a claim for specific performance must be formally entered on the record before a repudiation is accepted:

> But he may resile from the position he has thus taken up, and if he abandons his action by discontinuing it in the manner provided by the Rules of Court he can, if the purchaser is still at fault, accept the repudiation and forfeit the deposit.[61]

In *Ogle v Comboyuro Investments Pty Ltd*[62] Gibbs, Mason and Jacobs JJ disapproved this statement 'if it was intended as a comprehensive statement of the law'.[63] The justices added:

---

54 [1940] 2 KB 1 at 22–3.
55 *Public Trustee v Pearlberg* [1940] 2 KB 1; *Conroy v Lowndes* [1958] Qd R 375 (noted E I Sykes, 'Specific Performance — Claim for Damages at Common Law', *Australian Law Journal*, vol 33, 1959, p 249); *Ogle v Comboyuro Investments Pty Ltd* (1976) 136 CLR 444.
56 (1976) 136 CLR 444.
57 (1976) 136 CLR 444 at 461.
58 (1976) 136 CLR 444 at 461. As to mutuality: see *Price v Strange* [1978] Ch 337.
59 (1976) 136 CLR 444 at 452.
60 [1940] 2 KB 1.
61 [1940] 2 KB 1 at 23.
62 (1976) 136 CLR 444.
63 (1976) 136 CLR 444 at 460.

In our opinion this last statement, if it is thereby meant that the action for specific performance must be abandoned before the repudiation is accepted, is too wide. It may be correct in those cases where the fault of the purchaser is the original continuing breach but not in those cases where the purchaser commits a further breach of contract or evinces an intention never to complete and thus impliedly repudiates the whole contract.[64]

Accordingly the old Chancery rule is not inflexible. Where a party has shown and continues to show an intention never to complete a contract, it must be open to a vendor to rescind, even if there is a pending action, and recover damages for breach of contract.

———◦———

10.5 Pleading a claim for common law or equitable damages

It is important that a plaintiff clarify whether the claim is made for equitable damages or common law damages. A statement of claim must clearly state the relief or remedy which a plaintiff claims.[65] A plaintiff who is seeking common law damages should claim such relief in the statement of claim to allow the defendant adequate notice to obtain appropriate evidence of market value.[66] In some cases a plaintiff who clearly possessed an entitlement to common law damages has been regarded as restricting the claim to one of equitable damages.[67] The danger of unduly restricting such a claim was discussed in *Dobson v Winton and Robbins Ltd*[68] by Judson J who remarked:

> If a plaintiff sues in the alternative for specific performance or damages, he must make sure that his claim for damages is identifiable as one at common law for breach of contract. Otherwise he is in danger of having his claim for damages treated as if it were made in substitution for or as an appendage to the equitable remedy of specific performance and then his claim may be defeated by anything which may bar the equitable remedy, unless an amendment is permitted.[69]

A claim for specific performance 'or in the alternative, damages' would be sufficient where a plaintiff seeks an award of common law damages.[70] In one case a plaintiff amended a simple claim for damages to claim 'damages at common law or alternatively in equity'.[71] A prayer for equitable damages is usually formulated as a claim for 'damages in addition to or in lieu of specific performance' or 'damages in addition to or in lieu of an injunction'. It is submitted that a prayer for equitable damages might also be formulated as a claim for 'damages in addition to or in substitution for specific

---

64   (1976) 136 CLR 444 at 460.
65   RSC 1965 O 18 r 15.
66   *Conroy v Lowndes* [1958] Qd R 375 at 380.
67   *Hipgrave v Case* (1885) 28 Ch D 356; *Conroy v Lowndes* [1958] Qd R 375. See also E I Sykes, 'Specific Performance — Claim for Damages at Common Law', *Australian Law Journal*, vol 33, 1959, p 249.
68   [1959] SCR 775; (1959) 20 DLR (2d) 164.
69   [1959] SCR 775 at 780; (1959) 20 DLR (2d) 164 at 167.
70   *306793 Ontario Ltd in Trust v Rimes* (1979) 25 OR (2d) 79 at 85.
71   *Surrey County Council v Brodero Homes Ltd* [1992] 3 All ER 302 at 315.

performance' to reflect the words of *Lord Cairns' Act*.

A precedent that had been used for some time in New South Wales contained the following prayer for equitable damages:

> That in addition to or in lieu of specific performance of the said agreement the defendant may be ordered to pay to the plaintiff the damages which the plaintiff has sustained by reason of the said refusal and neglect of the defendant to perform his said agreement and that it may be referred to the Master in Equity to enquire what is the amount of such damages.[72]

A later New South Wales precedent contains the following claim for equitable damages:

> In addition to or in lieu of specific performance of the said agreement an order that the defendant pay to the plaintiff the damages which the plaintiff has sustained by reason of the said refusal and neglect of the defendant to perform his said agreement and that an inquiry be held as to the amount of such damages.[73]

A plaintiff may make alternative claims for common law and equitable damages. For instance, in one case a plaintiff claimed:

(a) specific performance of a contract,

(b) equitable damages in addition to or in lieu of specific performance, and

(c) in the alternative, should specific performance not be ordered, common law damages for breach of contract.[74]

It may be advantageous for a plaintiff to make a claim for equitable damages, in addition to common law damages, in a case where there may be an issue as to whether a contract has been effectively repudiated.[75] Also, an assessment of equitable damages may exceed an assessment of common law damages.

In a contractual matter a plaintiff should not confine a claim to one of equitable damages. It would be prudent to make an alternative claim for common law damages. This is because the plaintiff may not possess the requisite equity to specific performance.

———◄◦►———

10.6 Amendment of pleadings

It may be appropriate for a plaintiff who has not included a claim for damages to amend the statement of claim. Whether the leave of the court is required before a pleading may be amended depends upon the rules of court in the particular jurisdiction. A plaintiff may generally amend the

---

72 H H Mason and C A Weston, *Precedents in Equity*, Law Book Co, Sydney, 1915, p 5; E S Miller and J F Horsell, *Equity Forms and Precedents (New South Wales)*, Law Book Co, Sydney, 1934, p 257.

73 A G Nevill and A W Ashe, *Equity Proceedings With Precedents (New South Wales)*, Butterworths, Sydney, 1981, p 260 (Precedent 6(18), Claim For Equitable Damages).

74 *Kelly v Desnoe* [1985] 2 Qd R 477 at 490–1.

75 *Corpers (No 664) Pty Ltd v NZI Securities Australia Ltd* [1989] ASC 55–714 at 58,419 (Supreme Court of New South Wales, Young J).

pleadings without leave before the pleadings are deemed to be closed.[76] If specific performance is no longer sought, the statement of claim should be amended prior to the hearing.[77] Where leave is required, the court will grant leave upon such terms as are reasonable, including an appropriate order for costs.[78] A court may grant leave to amend at the hearing.[79] A defendant given adequate notice of such an application should not be prejudiced by any amendment. Generally an amendment takes effect from the date of the original pleading, so a pleading may not be amended to add a new cause of action which accrued since the date of the original pleading.[80]

10.7 Absence of a prayer for equitable damages

Considerable authority exists that *Lord Cairns' Act* enables a court to award damages in proceedings for an injunction or specific performance even in the absence of a claim for damages in the pleadings.[81] In *Wedmore v Mayor of Bristol*[82] the court declined to restrain a municipality from raising a footpath. The court directed an inquiry into damages, though the bill did not contain a prayer for damages. Sir John Stuart VC said: 'The Court can award damages'.[83] Similarly in *Betts v Neilson*[84] Lord Chelmsford LC observed:

> ... damages may be awarded, though not specifically prayed for by the bill, the statute having vested a discretion in the Judge, which he may exercise when he thinks the case fitting without the prayer of the party.[85]

---

76 *Queensland:* RSC O 32 r 3; *England:* RSC 1965 O 20 r 3.
77 *Ellis v Rogers* (1885) 29 Ch D 661 at 663; *Michie v Drummond* (1913) 32 NZLR 632.
78 *Hipgrave v Case* (1885) 28 Ch D 356 at 360; *McKenna v Richey* [1950] VLR 360.
79 *Nicholson v Brown* [1897] WN 52; *Goldenberg v Lieberman* [1950] OWN 613; *Dell v Beasley* [1959] NZLR 89 at 93.
80 *Eshelby v Federated European Bank Ltd* [1932] 1 KB 254; *Wigan v Edwards* (1973) 47 ALJR 586 at 596 per Mason J.
81 *Wedmore v Mayor of Bristol* (1862) 11 WR 136 at 137; 132 RR 807 at 808; *Catton v Wyld* (1863) 32 Beav 266 at 268; 55 ER 105 at 106; *Betts v Neilson* (1868) LR 3 Ch App 429 at 441; *Stanley of Alderley, Lady v Shrewsbury, Earl of* (1875) LR 19 Eq 616 at 621; *Griffin v Mercantile Bank* (1890) 11 LR (NSW) Eq 231 at 242; *McKenna v Richey* [1950] VLR 360 at 371; *Dell v Beasley* [1959] NZLR 89 at 93; *Willison v Van Ryswyk* [1961] WAR 87 at 90; *Dundee Farm Ltd v Bambury Holdings Ltd* [1976] 2 NZLR 747 at 756; *Minter v Geraghty* (1981) 38 ALR 68 at 84; *McClenaghan v Haley* [1983] 5 WWR 586 at 595; *Barbagallo v J & F Catelan Pty Ltd* [1986] 1 Qd R 245 at 251 per McPherson J; *Singh v Crafter* (Supreme Court of Western Australia, Full Court, No 8 of 1991, 28 May 1992, unreported); *Vanmeld Pty Ltd v Cussen* (1994) 121 ALR 619 at 621 per Einfeld J. See also A Burgess, 'Avoiding Inflation Loss in Contract Damages Awards: The Equitable Damages Solution', *International and Comparative Law Quarterly*, vol 34, 1985, 317 at p 331.
82 (1862) 11 WR 136.
83 (1862) 11 WR 136 at 137.
84 (1868) LR 3 Ch App 429.
85 (1868) LR 3 Ch App 429 at 441.

In *Barbagallo v J & F Catelan Pty Ltd*[86] McPherson J remarked 'the power so conferred may be exercised although damages are not specifically claimed in lieu of an injunction that is expressly sought'.[87]

These decisions are undoubtedly correct as *Lord Cairns' Act* did not provide that the jurisdiction may only be exercised where damages are claimed. As Virtue J explained in *Willison v Van Ryswyk*:[88]

> The express words of the section, conferring as they do a jurisdiction to award damages in all cases where an application for specific performance is entertained, certainly do not suggest any limitation of the discretion to where damages have been actually claimed.[89]

In some early cases a basis for the award of equitable damages was found in the general prayer for relief.[90] This is in accordance with the established Chancery practice as enunciated by Lord Erskine LC in *Hiern v Mill*:[91]

> ... the rule is, that, if the bill contains charges, putting facts in issue, that are material, the Plaintiff is entitled to the relief, which those facts will sustain, under the general prayer.[92]

It is now unnecessary to include a prayer for general or other relief in a statement of a claim.[93] This is because under the Judicature system a court will ensure that all matters in dispute between the parties are completely and finally determined.[94] In *Willison v Van Ryswyk*[95] Virtue J observed:

> The view that it is unnecessary to ask expressly for damages in the pleading also appears to be supported by s 24(7) of the [Supreme Court] Act which in the widest sense empowers the Court to grant such remedies as the parties to an action may be entitled in any claim brought before it.[96]

The fact that equitable damages may be awarded in the absence of a claim does not mean that an award of equitable damages will be made

---

86 [1986] 1 Qd R 245.
87 [1986] 1 Qd R 245 at 251.
88 [1961] WAR 87.
89 [1961] WAR 87 at 90, followed by Murray J in *Singh v Crafter* (Supreme Court of Western Australia, Full Court, Appeal No 8 of 1991, 28 May 1992, unreported).
90 *Catton v Wyld* (1863) 32 Beav 266 at 268; 55 ER 105 at 106; *Stanley of Alderley, Lady v Shrewsbury, Earl of* (1875) LR 19 Eq 616 at 621; *Serrao v Noel* (1885) 15 QBD 549 at 553; *Griffin v Mercantile Bank* (1890) 11 LR (NSW) Eq 231 at 258.
91 (1806) 13 Ves 114; 33 ER 237.
92 (1806) 13 Ves 114 at 119; 33 ER 237 at 239. See also *Wicks v Bennett* (1921) 30 CLR 80 at 100.
93 *Australia: New South Wales:* SCR 1970 Pt 40 r 1; *Queensland:* RSC O 24 r 3; *South Australia:* SCR 1987 O 20 r 4; *Tasmania:* RSC O 22 r 3; *Victoria:* RSC O 20 r 3; *Willison v Van Ryswyk* [1961] WAR 87 at 90; *New Zealand: Dillon v Macdonald* (1902) 21 NZLR 375 at 378. General relief must be consistent with the relief that a plaintiff claims: see *Cargill v Bower* (1878) 10 Ch D 502 at 508; B C Cairns, *Australian Civil Procedure*, 3rd ed, Law Book Co, Sydney, 1992, p 199.
94 See n 119 below.
95 [1961] WAR 87.
96 [1961] WAR 87 at 89, followed by Murray J in *Singh v Crafter* (Supreme Court of Western Australia, Full Court, Appeal No 8 of 1991, 28 May 1992, unreported).

without adequate notice to the parties. A defendant should receive adequate notice of such a claim. In *Minter v Geraghty*[97] Macrossan J observed:

> In the injunction jurisdiction applicable in breach of contract or tort cases and in the specific performance jurisdiction in contract cases, the court is given a discretion to award damages either in addition to or in substitution for an injunction or an order for specific performance. This does not mean that the assessment will be embarked upon without adequate notice to a defendant. Indeed, if a matter is brought within the equity jurisdiction, the control of it is exercised according to equitable principles so that injustice, including injustice to a defendant, would certainly be avoided: cf, per Lord Wilberforce in *Johnson v Agnew*[98].[99]

It would be inappropriate to permit the raising of a claim for equitable damages for the first time by counsel in a final address where a defendant has had no opportunity of calling relevant evidence. This was why in one case such a claim was not permitted where the pleadings did not contain such a claim.[100]

In a number of cases a plaintiff was given leave to amend the statement of claim to include a claim for equitable damages.[101] This may be appropriate in some cases so that the issues between the parties are precisely delineated. However, in all strictness it is not necessary for a plaintiff to seek leave to amend the statement of claim to include a prayer for equitable damages. In *Vanmeld Pty Ltd v Cussen*[102] Einfeld J remarked:

> ... I do not think that it is necessary for the applicants to seek leave to amend the amended application to seek an award of equitable damages, as the authorities indicate that such a specific prayer is not necessary: *Griffin v Mercantile Bank*[103].[104]

———◦———

10.8 Absence of a prayer for equitable relief

There have been suggestions that there must be a claim for equitable relief before jurisdiction under *Lord Cairns' Act* will exist. In *Williamson v Friend*[105] A H Simpson CJ in Eq remarked '... but in all the cases, so far as I am aware, the damages granted have been either in substitution for or supplementary to an injunction which was asked'.[106] Such statements take an unduly narrow view of the jurisdiction. It is accepted that the

---

97   (1981) 38 ALR 68.
98   [1980] AC 367 at 399.
99   (1981) 38 ALR 68 at 84. See also *Dillon v Macdonald* (1902) 21 NZLR 375 at 378.
100 *Odutola v Adeyemo* (Nigeria Court of Appeal, Western State, Ibadan, No I/11/66, 19 April 1974, unreported).
101 *Arbutus Park Estates Ltd v Fuller* [1977] 1 WWR 729 at 739; (1977) 74 DLR (3d) 257 at 266; *Surrey County Council v Bredero Homes Ltd* [1992] 3 All ER 302 at 315.
102 (1994) 121 ALR 619.
103 (1890) 11 LR (NSW) Eq 231 at 248, 258.
104 (1994) 121 ALR 619 at 621.
105 (1901) 1 SR (NSW) Eq 23.
106 (1901) 1 SR (NSW) Eq 23 at 30.

jurisdiction to award damages under *Lord Cairns' Act* may be exercised where the statement of claim does not include a prayer for an injunction or specific performance, provided that the statement discloses a basis for the grant of such relief. It should be appreciated however that equitable damages will only be awarded where it is just in the circumstances. In *Horsler v Zorro*[107] Megarry J observed: 'There are obvious difficulties in awarding damages as a substitute for what is not even claimed'.[108] These cases which uphold the existence of the jurisdiction where there is no claim for an injunction or specific performance were decided in Australia and Canada.

In a New South Wales equity suit, *Dixson v Tange*,[109] the plaintiff claimed only costs and damages. The court could only award damages under the equivalent of *Lord Cairns' Act*[110] as the Judicature system was not in force in the colony. The defendant demurred that the statement of claim raised no equity, and that the plaintiff's remedy was at law. It was held that the statement of claim disclosed a basis for an injunction either restraining the defendants from committing wrongful acts, or a mandatory injunction ordering them to allow the plaintiff to complete the contract. Owen J remarked:

> It appears to me that the plaintiff has, in his statement of claim, set out a wrongful act, in respect of which he might have claimed an injunction, and had he done so the Court would have had jurisdiction to grant the injunction and also damages.[111]

Owen J added that *Lord Cairns' Act* 'provides not that the Court shall grant an injunction, but merely that it shall have jurisdiction to entertain an application for an injunction'.[112]

There are more modern authorities that support the view that equitable damages may be awarded where the statement of claim discloses a case for equitable relief either in the form of an injunction or specific performance. In *Masai Minerals Ltd v Heritage Resources Ltd*,[113] the plaintiff company sought a declaration that it was the beneficial owner of a mining lease. The court considered that an award of equitable damages would adequately compensate the plaintiff. MacPherson J said:

> Although the relief claimed by the present plaintiff is a declaration, I think I may well treat it as a claim for specific performance because the result is the same and in reality that is what it is ... In this respect the Queen's Bench Act, RSS 1965, c 73, s 45(9)[114] authorised the court to award damages or other relief in lieu of or in addition to specific performance. A claim for a declaration should not on the present facts deny this jurisdiction.[115]

---

107 [1975] Ch 302.
108 [1975] Ch 302 at 307.
109 (1891) 12 LR (NSW) Eq 204.
110 Equity Act 1880 (44 Vic No 18) (New South Wales) s 32.
111 (1891) 12 LR (NSW) Eq 204 at 206–7.
112 (1891) 12 LR (NSW) Eq 204 at 207.
113 [1979] 2 WWR 352; (1979) 95 DLR (3d) 488; affirmed *Masai Minerals Ltd v Heritage Resources Ltd* [1981] 2 WWR 140; (1981) 119 DLR (3d) 393.
114 See now Queen's Bench Act RSS 1978 c Q–1 (Saskatchewan) s 45(9): see Appendix at p 289.
115 [1979] 2 WWR 352 at 359; (1979) 95 DLR (3d) 488 at 494.

In *Barbagallo v J & F Catelan Pty Ltd*[116] McPherson J remarked:

> Even the fact that no injunction is sought may not be fatal to an award of damages under the section[117] if the matters relied on show circumstances in respect of which an injunction might be claimed.[118]

———◄○►———

10.9 Multiplicity of proceedings

One object of the *Judicature Acts* was the avoidance of a multiplicity of proceedings. Under the Judicature system the court has jurisdiction to grant all legal and equitable remedies to which a party is entitled so that all matters in controversy may be completely and finally determined in one suit.[119] In *Dunne v Elibank-Murray*[120] Mahoney JA said:

> ... the Court should take such steps, procedural and otherwise, as are necessary, not merely to ensure that all relevant matters are determined, but also to make clear that they are so determined.[121]

While the court must take such procedural steps as are necessary to ensure that a controversy is determined, a plaintiff must in the one action claim all relief that the plaintiff may be entitled to.[122] This principle has been applied to defeat a claim for equitable damages when such relief may have been claimed in a prior suit upon the cause determined.[123] In *Serrao v Noel*[124] the plaintiff had obtained an injunction for the delivery up of shares. In subsequent proceedings the plaintiff was awarded damages under *Lord Cairns' Act*. The Court of Appeal held that the plaintiff was estopped from subsequently obtaining damages which should have been claimed in the earlier action.

---

116 [1986] 1 Qd R 245.
117 Equity Act 1867 (31 Vic No 18) (Queensland) s 62 (*Lord Cairns' Act*).
118 [1986] 1 Qd R 245 at 251.
119 *England*: Supreme Court of Judicature Act 1873 (36 & 37 Vict c 66) s 24(7); Supreme Court of Judicature (Consolidation) Act 1925 (15 & 16 Geo V c 49) s 43; Supreme Court Act 1981 (1981 c 54) s 49(2). Similar provisions are in force in other Commonwealth countries. *Australia: New South Wales:* Supreme Court Act 1970 (1970 No 52) s 68; *Queensland:* Judicature Act 1876 (40 Vic No 6) s 4(8); *South Australia:* Supreme Court Act 1935 (1935 No 2253) s 27; *Tasmania:* Supreme Court Civil Procedure Act 1932 (23 Geo V No 58) s 10(7); *Victoria:* Supreme Court Act 1986 (1986 No 110) s 29; *Western Australia:* Supreme Court Act 1935 (1935 No 36) s 24(7). *Canada: British Columbia:* Law and Equity Act RSBC 1979 c 224 s 10; *Manitoba:* The Court of Queen's Bench Act SM 1988 c 4 CCSM c C280 s 33(3); *Ontario:* Courts of Justice Act SO 1984 c 11 s 148. See also *United States of America v Motor Trucks Ltd* [1924] AC 196 at 201; *Dobson v Winton and Robbins Ltd* [1959] SCR 775 at 778–9; (1959) 20 DLR (2d) 164 at 166; *Wentworth v Woollahra Municipal Council* (1982) 149 CLR 672 at 677; *Beard v Baulkham Hills Shire Council* (1986) 7 NSWLR 273 at 281.
120 New South Wales Court of Appeal, No 12 of 1982 (CA), 2 March 1982, unreported.
121 *Dunne v Elibank-Murray*, n 120 above, at 6.
122 *Serrao v Noel* (1885) 15 QBD 549 at 558–9; *Dillon v Macdonald* (1902) 21 NZLR 375 at 382, 393; *Minter v Geraghty* (1981) 38 ALR 68.
123 *Serrao v Noel* (1885) 15 QBD 549 at 558–9; *Minter v Geraghty* (1981) 38 ALR 68 at 76.
124 (1885) 15 QBD 549.

In *Minter v Geraghty*[125] the plaintiffs obtained an injunction, which was stayed pending an appeal, to restrain a breach of covenant in restraint of trade. The High Court of Australia on appeal upheld the validity of the covenant.[126] The plaintiffs then commenced another action claiming damages, having made no such claim in their original action. It was held that the right to claim damages had merged in the judgment, and that the plea of *res judicata* was an answer to the second action. At trial W B Campbell J remarked:

> Had it been a condition of the stay that the defendants would not object to an amendment of the claim in the first action to include damages the position may have been different. However, this was not a condition of the stay, and it appears that the plaintiffs may have been under the mistaken impression that they could issue further proceedings or commence a fresh action claiming damages. It seems to me that this was a misapprehension of their legal right on the part of the plaintiffs.[127]

This decision was confirmed by a majority of the Full Court of Queensland. The Full Court held that the plaintiffs were precluded from recovering equitable damages, as well as common law damages. Dunn J observed:

> ... what merged with the judgment in the first action was the right to claim an injunction. It logically follows that there also merged with that judgment the right to claim damages in substitution for an injunction, the right conferred by s 2 of *Lord Cairns' Act*.[128]

It was also held that the covenant imposed a continuing duty and that the plaintiffs might claim damages for breaches of the covenant occurring after the injunction was granted and stayed pending an appeal.

———<o>———

10.10 *Limitation of actions*

It is submitted that a claim for equitable damages will not be barred by a limitation statute in the United Kingdom and Australia. Such legislation generally does not apply to a claim for specific performance, an injunction, or other equitable relief, except in so far as the enactment may be applied by analogy.[129] As an award of equitable damages is equitable relief, such a claim is not barred by limitation legislation. In *Joyce v Joyce*[130] it was submitted that for the purposes of limitation legislation equitable damages are to be regarded as equitable relief. Sir Robert Megarry VC commented:

---

125 (1981) 38 ALR 68.
126 *Geraghty v Minter* (1979) 142 CLR 177.
127 *Minter v Geraghty* (Supreme Court of Queensland, W B Campbell J, No 793 of 1978, 26 November 1980, unreported) at 6.
128 (1981) 38 ALR 68 at 76.
129 *Australia: New South Wales:* Limitation Act 1969 (1969 No 31) s 23; *Queensland:* Limitation of Actions Act 1974 (1974 No 75) s 10(6)(b); *Victoria:* Limitation of Actions Act 1958 (1958 No 6295) s 5(8); *England:* Limitation Act 1939 (2 & 3 Geo VI c 21) s 2(7); Limitation Act 1980 (1980 c 58) s 36(1).
130 [1978] 1 WLR 1170.

But, of course, the action is not merely an action for damages, but is primarily an action for the equitable relief of specific performance, with a claim for damages which Mr Purle says is a claim not at common law but under *Lord Cairns' Act.*[131]

In most Canadian jurisdictions (Ontario is the exception) a claim for equitable damages will be barred by a limitation statute, as any common law or equitable claim is covered by these statutes.[132] However, the Ontario Limitation Act does not apply to equitable actions. Accordingly in *M(K) v M(H)*[133] it was held that an action in Ontario for compensation for breach of fiduciary duty was not barred by the Act. Similarly, an action in Ontario for equitable damages should not be barred by the Act.

But even where a claim for equitable damages is not directly barred by limitation legislation a plaintiff may still face difficulties. It may be argued that the limitation provision would apply by analogy to preclude the award of damages under *Lord Cairns' Act.* In England, the Limitation Act 1980 covers most claims, and the scope for applying the statute by analogy is very limited.[134] In *M(K) v M(H)*[135] it was held that a claim for compensation for breach of fiduciary duty was not barred by analogy in equity. La Forest J remarked that 'equity has rarely limited a claim by analogy when a case falls within its exclusive jurisdiction, as in this case for breach of a fiduciary duty'.[136] Where equitable damages are sought for loss which cannot be compensated at law,[137] it is submitted that it would be inappropriate to apply the statute by analogy. In *M(K) v M(H)*[138] La Forest J added, in respect of concurrent actions in equity, that 'equity ... is not bound to follow the law'.[139]

A more fundamental objection to the award of equitable damages would be the reluctance of a court of equity to provide relief to a party guilty of delay. As Goff LJ observed in *Sutton v Spink and Beeching (Sales) Ltd*[140] 'Whether one is considering an injunction or damages in lieu under *Lord Cairns' Act* the problem is one of laches'.[141] From an historical perspective, a court of equity would have regard to a limitation provision in considering the availability of laches as an equitable defence. In

---

131 [1978] 1 WLR 1170 at 1173.
132 *Alberta:* Limitation of Actions Act RSA 1980 c L-15 s 4(1)(g); *British Columbia:* Limitation Act RSBC 1979 c 236 s 3(4); *Manitoba:* Limitation of Actions Act RSM 1987 c L150 s 2(1)(n); *New Brunswick:* Limitation of Actions Act RSNB 1973 c L-8 s 6; *Prince Edward Island:* Statute of Limitations RSPEI 1988 c S-7 s 2(1)(g); *Saskatchewan:* Limitation of Actions Act RSS 1978 c L-15 s 3(1)(j). See *M(K) v M(H)* [1992] 3 SCR 6; (1992) 96 DLR (4th) 289 at 329 per La Forest J.
133 [1992] 3 SCR 6; (1992) 96 DLR (4th) 289.
134 J Weeks, *Preston and Newsom on Limitation of Actions,* 4th ed, Longman, London, 1989, p 52.
135 [1992] 3 SCR 6; (1992) 96 DLR (4th) 289.
136 [1992] 3 SCR 6 at 71; (1992) 96 DLR (4th) 289 at 330.
137 Eg, part performance, prospective loss, etc.
138 [1992] 3 SCR 6; (1992) 96 DLR (4th) 289.
139 [1992] 3 SCR 6 at 74; (1992) 96 DLR (4th) 289 at 332.
140 [1977] 1 All ER 287.
141 [1977] 1 All ER 287 at 293.

Archbold v Scully[142] Lord Wensleydale remarked: 'So far as laches is a defence, I take it that where there is a Statute of Limitations, the objection of simple laches does not apply until the expiration of the time allowed by the statute'.[143] This principle has now been displaced by statute, for limitation legislation expressly does not affect the equitable jurisdiction of a court to refuse relief on the ground of acquiescence or otherwise.[144]

---

142 (1861) 9 HLC 360; 11 ER 769.

143 (1861) 9 HLC 360 at 383; 11 ER 769 at 778. See also *Preston and Newsom on Limitation of Actions*, 4th ed, Longman, London, 1989, p 52.

144 *England:* Limitation Act 1939 (2 & 3 Geo VI c 21) s 29; Limitation Act 1980 (1980 c 58) s 36(2); *Australia: New South Wales:* Limitation Act 1969 (1969 No 31) s 9; *Queensland:* Limitation of Actions Act 1974 (1974 No 75) s 43; *Victoria:* Limitation of Actions Act 1958 (1958 No 6295) s 31; *Canada: British Columbia:* Limitation Act RS 1979 c 236 s 2; *Ontario:* Limitations Act RSO 1980 (c 240) s 2.

11

Monetary Remedies

————◁○▷————

11.1 *Compensation*

The jurisdiction of a court of equity to make an order for the payment of compensation is inherent and does not depend upon the jurisdiction that was conferred by *Lord Cairns' Act.*[1] An award of damages is quite distinct from an award of compensation. In *Jenkins v Parkinson*[2] Lord Brougham LC remarked that the term 'compensation' had a 'less legal and more equitable aspect' than the term 'damages'. Fry commented that 'damages may be said to be a species of compensation ... but they are so distinct a form of relief'.[3]

In equity an order for the payment of compensation could be made in various situations. In suits between a vendor and purchaser the Court of Chancery could grant compensation by way of an abatement of the purchase price. The term 'compensation' is also used to refer to an equitable order for the payment of money, apart from an account of profits, for the breach of an equitable, including a fiduciary, obligation.[4] In

---

1 Compare *McKenna v Richey* [1950] VLR 360 at 373.
2 (1833) 2 My & K 5; 39 ER 846.
3 E Fry, *Specific Performance of Contracts,* 5th ed, Stevens & Sons, London, 1911, p 634.
4 *Nocton v Ashburton, Lord* [1914] AC 932; *McKenzie v McDonald* [1927] VLR 134; *Coleman v Myers* [1977] 2 NZLR 225. See also I E Davidson, 'The Equitable Remedy of Compensation', *Melbourne University Law Review,* vol 13, 1982, p 349; I C F Spry, *Equitable Damages,* 4th ed, Law Book Co, Sydney, 1990, p 608.

equity, orders for monetary payments ordinarily concerned accounts of profits and compensation. These orders were designed to 'even the scales'[5] where it would be unfair to permit a defendant to retain money.

————◄○►————

11.2 Compensation (vendor and purchaser)

In a specific performance suit the Court of Chancery possessed jurisdiction to make an order for the payment of compensation by way of an abatement of the purchase price. An order for compensation was made as ancillary to, and to effectuate, a decree of specific performance.[6] This jurisdiction could be exercised where strict performance of a contract for the sale of land was not possible. A vendor would be non-suited in an action in a court of law where strict performance of a contract was not possible for 'to sustain an action at law performance must be averred according to the very terms of the contract'.[7] Accordingly a vendor would be non-suited at law where a contract was for the sale of a term of 99 years in land of which the vendor had only a term of 98 or 97 years.[8] In *Travinto Nominees Pty Ltd v Vlattas*[9] Menzies J observed:

> At common law, any difference, however trivial, between the land described in the contract and the land produced constituted a defect which entitled the purchaser to rescind.[10]

While a court of law would insist upon the strict performance of a contract, a court of equity was not so constrained. The Court of Chancery would decree specific performance with compensation for a small or immaterial deficiency in the area of land subject to a contract of sale. In *Leighton Properties Pty Ltd v Hurley*[11] Connolly J remarked:

> This was a rule which was evolved as part of the general doctrine of the courts of equity and did not depend upon there being a compensation clause in the contract of sale.[12]

The foundation of this jurisdiction is that a court of equity looks at the substance and not merely the letter of a contract,[13] and will not permit an unconscientious advantage to be taken of a circumstance that does not admit a strict performance of a contract.[14]

The jurisdiction to grant compensation is generally exercised where there is some diminution of the area of the property contracted to be sold,

---

5   *O'Neill v Dept of Health and Social Services (No 2)* [1986] NI 290 at 296 per Carswell J.
6   *Newham v May* (1824) 13 Price 749 at 752; 147 ER 1142 at 1144.
7   *Davis v Hone* (1805) 2 Sch & Lef 341 at 351.
8   *Halsey v Grant* (1806) 13 Ves 73 at 77; 33 ER 222 at 223 per Lord Erskine LC. See also *Anderson v Greenall* (1952) 7 WWR 534 at 538.
9   (1973) 129 CLR 1.
10 (1973) 129 CLR 1 at 27.
11 [1984] 2 Qd R 534.
12 [1984] 2 Qd R 534 at 542.
13 *Rutherford v Acton-Adams* [1915] AC 866 at 869.
14 *Halsey v Grant* (1806) 13 Ves 73 at 77; 33 ER 222 at 223.

or where there is some deterioration of the property. It would not ordinarily be appropriate to decree specific performance with compensation in favour of a vendor where the deficiency required structural additions or alterations to a building.[15] Any deficiency must not be in respect of a matter which is essential to the beneficial use of land. Specific performance with compensation was not granted in *Peers v Lambert*[16] where a wharf and jetty were sold together, but the jetty was liable to be removed by the Corporation of London.

The jurisdiction to grant compensation in a vendor and purchaser suit did not extend to compensation for a misrepresentation that was not part of the contract of sale. In *Rutherford v Acton-Adams*[17] the Privy Council held that the jurisdiction to decree specific performance with compensation is confined to cases where there is a deficiency in the subject matter described in the contract of sale, and does not extend to an oral misrepresentation. Support for a contrary conclusion may appear to be derived from the earlier decision in *Powell v Elliot*.[18] However, the record of earlier proceedings of that case disclosed that the inaccurate description in question was incorporated into the contract of sale.[19] A misdescription, even if included in the contract of sale, will only support the exercise of the jurisdiction if it relates to some diminution or deterioration of the value of the property contracted to be sold.[20] The jurisdiction did not to extend to a case where the contract for the sale of a hotel contained an erroneous statement of the annual sales of beer from the hotel.[21] Where a misrepresentation is fraudulent a representee may recover damages for deceit.[22]

The *locus classicus* of Lord Eldon LC in *Mortlock v Buller*[23] is often quoted in any discussion of the jurisdiction in equity to grant a purchaser compensation. Lord Eldon remarked:

> For the purpose of this jurisdiction, the person contracting under those circumstances, is bound by the assertion in his contract; and, if the vendee chooses to take as much as he can have, he has a right to that, and to an abatement; and the Court will not hear the objection by the vendor, that the purchaser cannot have the whole.[24]

This statement of Lord Eldon illustrates various aspects of the jurisdiction. Lord Eldon said that a party 'is bound by the assertion in his contract'.[25] It is clear that the jurisdiction relates to a misdescription contained in a contract of sale, and not a case of an oral misrepresentation.

---

15 *Southland Investments Ltd v Public Trustee* [1943] NZLR 580 at 610; *Leighton Properties Pty Ltd v Hurley* [1984] 2 Qd R 534 at 544.
16 (1844) 7 Beav 546; 49 ER 1178.
17 [1915] AC 866 at 870.
18 (1875) LR 10 Ch App 424.
19 *Gilchester Properties Ltd v Gomm* [1948] WN 71.
20 *King v Poggioli* (1923) 32 CLR 222 at 246.
21 *Waxman v Yeandale* [1953] 2 DLR 475.
22 *Derry v Peek* (1889) 14 App Cas 337 at 374; *Doyle v Olby (Ironmongers) Ltd* [1969] 2 QB 158.
23 (1804) 10 Ves 292; 32 ER 857.
24 (1804) 10 Ves 292 at 316; 32 ER 857 at 866.
25 (1804) 10 Ves 292 at 316; 32 ER 857 at 866.

Lord Eldon also referred to the remedy of 'an abatement'. In exercising the jurisdiction to grant an abatement of the purchase price the courts grant a purchaser an abatement in proportion to the deficiency of the property.[26]

An example of the grant of a proportionate abatement is *Hooper v Smart*[27] where vendors contracted to sell the entirety of a freehold property of which they were only entitled to a moiety. Sir Charles Hall VC decreed 'that the vendors do submit to an abatement from the purchase-money of one-half the amount'.[28] A modern example is *Topfell Ltd v Gallery Properties Ltd*[29] where a house was sold with an existing tenancy on the first floor, and with vacant possession of the ground floor. Prior to the sale the local authority had served upon the agents of the vendor a statutory notice directing that the house be only occupied by one household. Templeman J held that the purchaser was entitled to specific performance with an abatement of the purchase price assessed with reference to presumed market values.

A vendor may also invoke the jurisdiction in an appropriate case. An early example is *Calcraft v Roebuck*[30] where there was a contract for the sale of 186 acres of freehold, where in fact two acres of the land were held from year to year. Lord Thurlow LC directed a reference to the master to ascertain 'what under the circumstances ought to be allowed as a deduction from the price'.[31] The court will only grant relief to a vendor if a purchaser can obtain substantially what was bought[32] or where a purchaser is willing to accept compensation.[33]

A court of equity will not decree specific performance in favour of a vendor where there is a material deficiency or defect of the property of which a purchaser was unaware.[34] Where a vendor obtains specific performance it would not ordinarily be equitable for a court to order the payment of compensation in favour of a vendor,[35] although the jurisdiction has been exercised in a case where a purchaser was bound to make compensation for an extra quantity of land.[36] A court will ordinarily be reluctant to relieve a vendor if the contract understates the area of the property sold. There may be exceptional circumstances which would justify the exercise of the jurisdiction in favour of a vendor, such as where the purchaser is aware of a vendor's mistake.[37]

---

26   *Milligan v Cooke* (1808) 16 Ves 1; 33 ER 884; *Hill v Buckley* (1811) 17 Ves 394; 34 ER 153.
27   (1874) LR 18 Eq 683.
28   (1874) LR 18 Eq 683 at 686.
29   [1979] 1 WLR 446.
30   (1790) 1 Ves 221; 30 ER 311.
31   (1790) 1 Ves 221 at 226; 30 ER 311 at 314. See also *M'Queen v Farquhar* (1805) 11 Ves 467; 32 ER 1168.
32   *Rutherford v Acton-Adams* [1915] AC 866 at 869; *Watson v Burton* [1957] 1 WLR 19 at 31; *LeMesurier v Andrus* (1986) 25 DLR (4th) 424.
33   *Dyer v Hardgrave* (1805) 10 Ves 505; 32 ER 941.
34   *Flight v Booth* (1834) 1 Bing (NC) 370; 131 ER 1160. For specific performance to be withheld the defect must be material: see *Shepherd v Croft* [1911] 1 Ch 521; *Watson v Burton* [1957] 1 WLR 19 at 27.
35   *Heath v Allen* (1875) 1 VLR (Eq) 176.
36   *Leslie v Tompson* (1851) 9 Hare 268; 68 ER 503.
37   G Jones and W Goodhart, *Specific Performance*, Butterworths, London, 1986, p 237.

The remedy of specific performance is a discretionary remedy which will be denied to a vendor who is guilty of inequitable conduct. A court of equity also will not compel a purchaser to take property under a contract of sale which has been induced by a misrepresentation if the property is different in a material respect from that which the purchaser has been led to expect.[38] This principle is applicable where there has not been full disclosure of the restrictive use that property may be put to, or where there has been a misrepresentation of such a use, and whether the restriction arises because of some restrictive covenant[39] or due to a town planning restriction.[40]

It would seem that a vendor is not entitled in equity to rely upon a condition in a contract of sale which provides that no misstatement shall annul the sale if a material misrepresentation has induced a party to enter into a contract. Such a condition is also subject to the Misrepresentation Act 1967 and the Unfair Contracts Terms Act 1977[41].[42]

On general equitable principles the jurisdiction to grant compensation would not be exercised where to do so would prejudice the interests of a third party,[43] such as a beneficiary under a settlement.[44] However hardship to a third party which is entirely unconnected with the property is irrelevant.[45]

————◄○►————

11.3 Compensation clauses

In some cases the contract of sale provides for the allowance of compensation. The right to compensation under this clause arises from contract. In *Travinto Nominees Pty Ltd v Vlattas*[46] Menzies J remarked:

> The right to compensation under a clause in the contract was independent of the right to compensation in a claim for specific performance.[47]

---

38 *Flight v Booth* (1834) 1 Bing (NC) 370; 131 ER 1160; *Re Arnold* (1880) 14 Ch D 270 at 280–1; *Re Davis & Cavey* (1889) 40 Ch D 601 at 606; *449576 Ontario Ltd v Bogojevski*; *Agincourt Real Estate Ltd* (1984) 9 DLR (4th) 109 at 115. See also *Clermont v Tasburgh* (1819) 1 Jac & W 112 at 120–1; 37 ER 318 at 321.

39 *Flight v Booth* (1834) 1 Bing (NC) 370; 131 ER 1160; *Nottingham Patent Brick and Tile Co v Butler* (1885) 15 QBD 261 at 271; *Faruqi v English Real Estates Ltd* [1979] 1 WLR 963.

40 *Laurence v Lexcourt Holding Ltd* [1978] 1 WLR 1128.

41 1977 (c 50) (Eng).

42 *Walker v Boyle* [1982] 1 WLR 495 at 506–7.

43 *Naylor v Goodall* (1877) 26 WR 162; *Kaunas v Smyth* (1976) 75 DLR (3d) 368; *Cedar Holdings Ltd v Green* [1981] Ch 129 at 147; *Thames Guaranty Ltd v Campbell* [1985] QB 210 at 235.

44 *Thomas v Dering* (1837) 1 Keen 729 at 747; 48 ER 488 at 495.

45 *Gall v Mitchell* (1924) 35 CLR 222 at 230.

46 (1973) 129 CLR 1.

47 (1973) 129 CLR 1 at 28.

In *Stephens v Selsey Renovations Pty Ltd*[48] Mahoney J also recognised that the right to compensation may exist by contract, or independently under 'the general law'.[49]

A compensation clause which provides for the allowance of a proportionate part of the purchase price is generally applicable if there is a deficiency in the area of the property.[50] There must be some error or misdescription of the area or description of the land which is subject to the contract. In *Travinto Nominees Pty Ltd v Vlattas*[51] the omission from an agreement of a statement that a lease over the land contained an option to renew was held not to amount to an 'error or misdescription of the property' which would give rise to a claim for compensation.

At the suit of a purchaser a court will order specific performance with an abatement where a contract contains a compensation clause, notwithstanding that the assessment of compensation would give rise to real and practical difficulties.[52] Compensation will not be ordered against a purchaser, particularly where the misstatement is not as to area but as to the use that property may be put to.[53]

Some contracts of sale contain conditions which provide that in the event of a misdescription a purchaser has no entitlement to compensation from the vendor and that such misdescription shall not annul the sale.[54] Such provisions are usually strictly construed and do not preclude rescission where a vendor has a defective title.[55] A court would be less inclined to order specific performance against a purchaser where there is a misstatement as to area, and a purchaser is unable to claim compensation, than in cases where a condition is adopted which allows a purchaser to claim compensation.[56]

Clauses which preclude any entitlement of the purchaser to compensation in the event of misdescription may also preclude a purchaser from obtaining specific performance with compensation.[57] However such a clause would not exclude the jurisdiction to grant compensation with specific performance where the vendor is in breach of contractual obligations by reason of the misdescription. In *Topfell Ltd v Gallery Properties Ltd*[58] the contract contained such a clause. Specific performance with an abatement of the purchase price was decreed where the vendors

---

48   [1974] 1 NSWLR 273.
49   [1974] 1 NSWLR 273 at 277. See also *Leighton Properties Pty Ltd v Hurley* [1984] 2 Qd R 534.
50   *Flight v Booth* (1834) 1 Bing (NC) 370; 131 ER 1160.
51   (1973) 129 CLR 1.
52   *Goldsmith v Smith* (1951) 52 SR (NSW) 172.
53   *Flight v Booth* (1834) 1 Bing (NC) 370 at 378; 131 ER 1160 at 1163.
54   *England: National Conditions of Sale*, 20th ed, cond 17(1); *Law Society's General Conditions of Sale*, 1984 ed, cond 7(1).
55   *Re Arnold* (1880) 14 Ch D 270; *Jacobs v Revell* [1900] 2 Ch 858; *Watson v Burton* [1957] 1 WLR 19. Similarly 'rescission clauses' which enable rescission where there is a failure to answer requisitions are generally limited to matters of title rather than conveyancing: see *Farantos Development Ltd v Canada Permanent Trust Co* (1975) 56 DLR (3d) 481.
56   *Watson v Burton* [1957] 1 WLR 19 at 25.
57   *Re Terry & White's Contract* (1886) 32 Ch D 14.
58   [1979] 1 WLR 446.

could not give vacant possession in accordance with their contract. Templeman J remarked:

> ... these special and general conditions cannot be allowed to contradict the contractual obligation into which the vendors entered by virtue of the particulars and the contract, the contractual obligation to give vacant possession.[59]

In 1990 new standard conditions of sale were issued in England which provide that there is an entitlement to compensation if there is a material difference between the description or value of the property as represented and as it actually is.[60]

11.4 Compensation in excess of the purchase price

It is not clear whether a court of equity may grant compensation for an amount in excess of the purchase price. This issue would arise when there is an open contract for the sale of property which is subject to encumbrances which secure an amount greater than the purchase price. Such a case was *Grant v Dawkins*[61] where a purchaser was granted the remedy of specific performance together with compensation by way of an abatement of the entire purchase price, and equitable damages under *Lord Cairns' Act* to the extent that the sum required to discharge the encumbrances exceeded the purchase price.

Goff J appeared to assume that compensation could not exceed the purchase price. After referring to comments made by Lord Eldon in *Todd v Gee*,[62] Goff J remarked:

> Lord Eldon seems to me to have been saying that the jurisdiction of a court of equity to grant relief in such circumstances would end when the purchase price was exceeded because, as he said, relief in the shape of damages was "very different from giving compensation out of the purchase-money".[63]

This conclusion may also be fortified by Lord Eldon's earlier judgment in *Mortlock v Buller*[64] which referred to a vendee's right to an 'abatement' of the purchase price.[65] This aspect of the judgment has been criticised and it has been argued that the plaintiff should have been able to recover the full sum claimed, either as equitable damages under *Lord Cairns' Act*, or as compensation.[66] Goff J also apparently considered that the

59 [1979] 1 WLR 446 at 450.
60 *England: Standard Conditions of Sale*, 1st ed, 1990, cond 712.
61 [1973] 1 WLR 1406.
62 (1810) 17 Ves 273; 34 ER 106.
63 [1973] 1 WLR 1406 at 1409.
64 (1804) 10 Ves 292; 32 ER 857.
65 (1804) 10 Ves 292 at 315; 32 ER 857 at 866.
66 C Harpum, 'Specific Performance with Compensation as a Purchaser's Remedy', *Cambridge Law Journal*, vol 40, 1981, 47 at p 70.

jurisdiction in equity to award damages was more extensive than the jurisdiction in equity to grant compensation, and referred to cases which appear to enable the award of damages without any such limitation, namely *Cleaton v Gower*[67] and *Phelps v Prothero*.[68] The cases which Goff J referred to were decided prior to the passing of *Lord Cairns' Act*, and so his Lordship must have been adverting to the inherent jurisdiction in equity to award damages.

The presence of the encumbrances in *Grant v Dawkins*[69] was a matter of conveyancing rather than a matter of title.[70] The rule in *Bain v Fothergill*,[71] which is now abrogated in some jurisdictions,[72] did not apply where the breach of contract was due to a matter of conveyancing where a vendor failed to redeem a prior mortgage,[73] irrespective of whether a purchaser was aware of the existence of a mortgage when entering into a contract of sale.[74] There was therefore no objection to the award of damages in *Grant v Dawkins*[75] to enable discharge of the mortgages.

A concession was made in *Grant v Dawkins*[76] that the measure of damages was limited to the extent that the value of the property exceeded the purchase price. The concession was probably made because the property was subject to the general increase in property values at that time, but it has been pointed out that any increase in the value of the property over the purchase price is really a collateral matter.[77] It has also been suggested that the concession cannot stand in the light of *Johnson v Agnew*[78] where Lord Wilberforce stated that in such circumstances damages under *Lord Cairns' Act* should be assessed on the same basis as damages at common law.[79]

In *Grant v Dawkins*[80] equitable damages were awarded under *Lord Cairns' Act* in reliance on the then recent decision of Megarry J in *Wroth v Tyler*.[81] Megarry J held that equitable damages could be assessed as at the date of judgment to take account of appreciation in the value of the property which was the subject of a contract of sale. Since then the decision of the House of Lords in *Johnson v Agnew*[82] has made it clear that

---

67 (1674) Rep Temp Finch 164; 23 ER 90.
68 (1855) 7 De GM & G 722; 44 ER 280.
69 [1973] 1 WLR 1406.
70 A purchaser cannot resist specific performance where an encumbrance on the land exceeds unpaid purchase moneys: see *Goodchild v Bethel* (1914) 19 DLR 161; *Baxter v Derkasz* [1925] 4 DLR 801.
71 (1874) LR 7 HL 158.
72 See p 123.
73 *Re Daniel, Daniel v Vassall* [1917] 2 Ch 405; *Sharneyford Supplies Ltd v Edge* [1987] Ch 305 at 326.
74 *Thomas v Kensington* [1942] 2 KB 181 at 184.
75 [1973] 1 WLR 1406.
76 [1973] 1 WLR 1406.
77 P H Pettit, *Law Quarterly Review*, vol 90, 1974, 297 at p 301.
78 [1980] AC 367.
79 A J Oakley, 'Pecuniary Compensation for Failure to Complete a Contract for the Sale of Land', *Cambridge Law Journal*, vol 39, 1980, p 62, n 18.
80 [1973] 1 WLR 1406.
81 [1974] Ch 30.
82 [1980] AC 367.

common law damages may also be assessed on that basis. The jurisdiction to award equitable damages is still relevant where a claim of a plaintiff is dependent upon some equitable doctrine such as part performance or equitable estoppel, or for procedural reasons. The jurisdiction may also be available in those cases where there is doubt as to whether a cause of action at law is available.

11.5 Relationship between compensation and damages

The relationship between the remedies of compensation and damages is not easy to deduce from the cases,[83] although it has been suggested that the two remedies are in substance the same as both remedies are compensatory.[84] There is no doubt that both remedies have a compensatory function. Lord Wilberforce in *Johnson v Agnew*[85] remarked that 'the general principle for the assessment of damages is compensatory'.[86] In *Barker v Cox*,[87] where a purchaser was decreed specific performance with compensation, Sir James Bacon VC also adverted to the fact that an innocent purchaser was entitled 'by compensation to be placed in the same position in which he would be entitled to stand'.[88]

Despite the compensatory nature of both remedies, it is clear that the remedies have quite distinct functions. Damages are essentially awarded for the loss or non-performance of a bargain. The measure of damages for the breach of a contract is usually the difference between the purchase price and the value of the property which is assessed as at the date of completion or such date as is appropriate in the circumstances.[89] In *King v Poggioli*[90] Starke J observed:

> Substantially, compensation is given for some diminution or deterioration in the value of the property contracted to be sold.[91]

Thus, in that case, a claim for loss for delay in obtaining possession of property was not properly the subject of a claim for compensation, even if herbage had been destroyed by the delay.

In discussing the remedies of compensation and damages, equitable considerations are relevant. Compensation is an equitable remedy, and the

---

83   C Harpum, 'Specific Performance with Compensation as a Purchaser's Remedy — A Study in Contract and Equity', *Cambridge Law Journal*, vol 40, 1981, 47 at p 67.
84   Harpum, n 83 above, p 82.
85   [1980] AC 367.
86   [1980] AC 367 at 400.
87   (1876) 4 Ch D 464.
88   (1876) 4 Ch D 464 at 469.
89   H McGregor, *McGregor on Damages*, 14th ed, Sweet & Maxwell, London, 1980, p 523, para 745; *Johnson v Agnew* [1980] AC 367.
90   (1923) 32 CLR 222.
91   (1923) 32 CLR 222 at 246. See also *Rutherford v Acton-Adams* [1915] AC 866; *Anderson v Greenall* (1952) 7 WWR 534.

grant of compensation is subject to equitable defences, for example hardship, mistake or prejudice to third parties.[92] Similarly the award of equitable damages under *Lord Cairns' Act* is also subject to equitable defences.[93]

Whether or not the cost of execution of work will be included in an award of compensation or damages is dependent upon the circumstances of each individual case. There is no invariable rule of practice. The remedy of compensation may be granted to restore premises to the state that they were in at the date of the contract if there has been deterioration of the premises since that date.[94] Compensation may be granted for the cost of work on premises to ensure that a purchaser obtains what he had a legitimate expectation of receiving. Therefore, in *Shepherd v Croft*,[95] compensation was decreed for the cost of diverting an underground watercourse that was not disclosed, together with the loss of market value occasioned by such works.[96]

Sometimes it may be inappropriate to award compensation for the cost of work. In *Re Chifferiel*[97] the particulars of sale described a road over land as having been 'made up', which was a misdescription as to the extent to which the road was constructed. It was held that the cost of making the road had nothing to do with the assessment of compensation. North J remarked:

> The damage he has sustained is the difference between the actual value of the estate as it stood at the time of purchase and what the actual value at the same date would have been if Cuddington Avenue had been continued across the lot.[98]

This is a situation where compensation was clearly awarded for the purchaser's loss of bargain.[99] There were particular circumstances in *Re Chifferiel*[100] which inclined North J not to award compensation for the cost of making the road. The road was adequate for pastoral purposes, and if the land was used for building purposes any road would be 'much cut up'.[101]

Damages may be awarded for the cost of the execution of works where the court is satisfied that any damages awarded will be applied towards the execution of those works.[102] However, damages will not necessarily be awarded

---

92 C Harpum, 'Specific Performance with Compensation as a Purchaser's Remedy', *Cambridge Law Journal*, vol 40, 1981, 47 at p 82.

93 I C F Spry, *Equitable Remedies*, 4th ed, Law Book Co, Sydney, 1990, pp 632–3.

94 The precedent in *Seton's Forms of Decrees, Judgments and Orders in Equity*, vol 3, 7th ed, Stevens & Sons, London, 1912, p 2174 provides for an inquiry as to 'what deterioration, if any has taken place in the premises' since the date of the contract, and 'what sum will be required to restore the property to the state in which the same was on the' contract date.

95 [1911] 1 Ch 521.

96 See also *Watson v Burton* [1957] 1 WLR 19 at 27.

97 (1889) 40 Ch D 45.

98 (1889) 40 Ch D 45 at 48.

99 C Harpum, 'Specific Performance with Compensation as a Purchaser's Remedy', *Cambridge Law Journal*, vol 40, 1981, 47 at p 68.

100 (1889) 40 Ch D 45.

101 (1889) 40 Ch D 45 at 48.

102 *Radford v De Froberville* [1977] 1 WLR 1262 at 1284.

for the cost of execution of works, even where a defendant is bound by contract to execute those works. Thus, in *Tito v Waddell (No 2)*[103] Sir Robert Megarry VC observed that where damages are awarded in respect of a contract to do work on a property, the damages would not necessarily equal the cost of execution of those works. The Vice-Chancellor remarked that in assessing damages, 'one always comes back to the fundamental question, that of the loss or injury that the plaintiff has suffered'.[104] In determining that loss it may be relevant to have regard to the difference in market value of the property if the work was executed, the cost of the work and whether the plaintiff had a legitimate interest in the execution of the work. In the circumstances of the particular case the cost of replanting Ocean Island with trees and shrubs was regarded as wasted expenditure.

It has been argued that proceedings in equity would bar any subsequent proceedings for damages at common law.[105] In the Alabama decision of *McCreary v Stallworth*[106] Bouldin J observed: 'It is not questioned that, if full performance is had in equity, it is a bar to an action at law for damages for breach of the contract'.[107] The policy of the Judicature system is to avoid a multiplicity of proceedings, and there is no doubt that a subsequent suit would be precluded by virtue of the doctrine of *res judicata*.[108]

On principle it would seem that there is no objection to the recovery of damages and compensation where both remedies are available, provided that double recovery for the same loss does not occur. The remedies of compensation and damages are not co-extensive as both remedies may be concurrently claimed in the one suit.[109] This was recognised in *Stephens v Selsey Renovations Pty Ltd*[110] where Mahoney J concluded that a purchaser had not merely a right to compensation under the contract for a misdescription of the frontage of land, but also a right to damages for breach of warranty. The view has, however, been expressed that the two remedies are co-extensive. A leading Australian commentator stated: 'It seems that a purchaser who elects to take what the vendor can convey, with an abatement of purchase money for a deficiency in title, quantity, or quality of the estate, is not entitled to damages as well'.[111] The decision of Myers CJ in *Smith v Young*[112] was cited as authority; however, in that case

---

103   [1977] Ch 106.
104   [1977] Ch 106 at 335.
105   C Harpum, 'Specific Performance with Compensation as a Purchaser's Remedy', *Cambridge Law Journal*, vol 40, 1981, 47 at p 69.
106   (1924) 102 So 52.
107   (1924) 102 So 52 at 53. Bouldin J appeared not to distinguish between the remedies of compensation and damages, and there is a reference in the judgment to 'the same measure of damages or compensation recoverable on breach of warranty of title'. Bouldin J also remarked that 'a partial failure of title is a complete bar to specific performance at the suit of the vendor'. This does not reflect the practice in England: see *Calcraft v Roebuck* (1790) 1 Ves 221; 30 ER 311.
108   See p 213.
109   *Gall v Mitchell* (1924) 35 CLR 222; *Anderson v Greenall* (1952) 7 WWR 534; *Stephens v Selsey Renovations Pty Ltd* [1974] 1 NSWLR 273.
110   [1974] 1 NSWLR 273.
111   RM Stonham, *The Law of Vendor and Purchaser*, Law Book Co, Sydney, 1964, p 237.
112   [1941] NZLR 147.

the question of damages was reserved. Nevertheless, Myers CJ considered that the decision in *Ontario Asphalt Block Co v Montreuil*[113] precluded a purchaser recovering both compensation and damages.

The plaintiff in the *Ontario Asphalt* case exercised an option to purchase the fee simple of certain lands of the defendant. The defendant held the fee simple of part of the lands under a grant from the Crown, and only a life interest in the remainder of the lands. At first instance it was decreed that the plaintiff was entitled to a conveyance of the freehold land, a conveyance of the life interest with an abatement of the purchase money and damages for breach of contract. Lennox J remarked:

> If a plaintiff has contracted for the purchase of more land than the defendant is able to make a good title to, the purchaser is entitled to that which the vendor has, with an abatement of the price in respect of that which cannot be conveyed; and with the addition of nominal or substantial actual damages, dependent upon the particular circumstances of the case.[114]

On appeal it was held that a purchaser could not have both remedies.[115] Meredith CJO commented that a purchaser who accepts partial performance of a contract together with an abatement makes an election to accept such relief 'in lieu of the rights he might otherwise have arising out of the contract or the breach of it'.[116] It was conceded that this proposition was not supported by any of the cases, although it was stated that in none of the cases had damages been awarded in addition to an abatement of purchase money.[117] In the *Ontario Asphalt* case Meredith CJO also considered that to award damages would be 'directly contrary to what was decided in *Bain v Fothergill*'[118].[119] However, that rule has now been abrogated in a number of jurisdictions.[120]

———◁o▷———

11.6 Indemnity

The jurisdiction of the Court of Chancery to grant an indemnity to a purchaser was quite distinct from the jurisdiction to award damages or compensation, although Spry has observed that sometimes awards of compensation or an abatement are loosely spoken of as 'indemnities'.[121] The jurisdiction to grant an indemnity may be exercised where there is a defect of title which may enable claims by adverse parties to possibly, but with no certainty, arise in the future, for example an ancient restrictive covenant.[122] In general the court will be reluctant to grant specific

---

113 (1913) 15 DLR 703.
114 (1913) 12 DLR 223 at 225.
115 (1913) 15 DLR 703.
116 (1913) 15 DLR 703 at 710.
117 (1913) 15 DLR 703 at 710.
118 (1874) LR 7 HL 158.
119 (1913) 15 DLR 703 at 712.
120 See p 123.
121 I C F Spry, *Equitable Remedies*, 4th ed, Law Book Co, Sydney, 1990, p 309, n 1.
122 G Jones and W Goodhart, *Specific Performance*, Butterworths, London, 1986, p 237.

performance with an indemnity, irrespective of whether such an order is sought by a purchaser or vendor.[123]

At one time it was thought that an indemnity would not be decreed in the absence of consent from both a vendor and a purchaser. This arose from the decision in *Balmanno v Lumley*[124] where Lord Eldon 'did not apprehend, the Court could compel the Purchaser to take an Indemnity, or the Vendor to give it'.[125] Consequently there is authority that the Court of Chancery could not decree that a purchaser take an indemnity[126] or that a vendor give an indemnity.[127] An early nineteenth century text contains the statement that it is 'unreasonable that a man should have a demand continually hanging over him'.[128] It would be unsatisfactory for a purchaser to be compelled to rely on a personal indemnity which may prove worthless in the event of the insolvency of the vendor.

There may be instances where it would be equitable for a court to grant specific performance with an indemnity irrespective of the absence of consent of both parties. The jurisdiction may be exercised where a purchaser is adequately protected by an indemnity which is secured.[129] An indemnity may be secured by a charge on land,[130] by the payment of part of the purchase price into court[131] or by an indemnity policy.[132]

------◀◉▶------

11.7 *Misrepresentation Act*

In the absence of a special relationship between the parties[133] a representee may not recover damages for an innocent misrepresentation at common law.[134] However the Misrepresentation Act 1967,[135] which has been adopted in some jurisdictions,[136] enables a person who suffers loss by being induced to enter into a contract by a misrepresentation made by another

---

123   I C F Spry, *Equitable Remedies*, 4th ed, Law Book Co, Sydney, 1990, pp 309–10.
124   (1813) 1 Ves & B 224 at 225; 35 ER 88.
125   (1813) 1 Ves & B 224 at 225; 35 ER 88.
126   *Fildes v Hooker* (1818) 3 Madd 193; 56 ER 481; *Ridgway v Gray* (1849) 1 Mac & G 109 at 111; 41 ER 1204 at 1205; *Re Weston and Thomas's Contract* [1907] 1 Ch 244 at 248. However, in some cases a purchaser seeking specific performance may not be entitled to a conveyance unless on the terms of providing a sufficient indemnity: see *Moxhay v Inderwick* (1847) 1 De G & Sm 708; 63 ER 1261.
127   *Balmanno v Lumley* (1813) 1 Ves & B 224; 35 ER 88; *Aylett v Ashton* (1835) 1 My & Cr 105 at 114; 40 ER 316 at 320; *Bainbridge v Kinnaird* (1863) 32 Beav 346 at 347; 55 ER 135 at 136.
128   J Fonblanque, *A Treatise of Equity*, vol I, 5th ed, London, 1820, pp 43–4.
129   I C F Spry, *Equitable Remedies* 4th ed, Law Book Co, Sydney, 1990, p 310.
130   *Horniblow v Shirley* (1806) 13 Ves 81 at 84; 33 ER 225 at 226; *Milligan v Cooke* (1808) 16 Ves 1 at 14; 33 ER 884 at 889 (master directed to settle form of security).
131   *Wilson v Williams* (1857) 3 Jur NS 810; *Mason v Freedman* [1958] SCR 483. (In both cases the wife of the vendor refused to bar her dower.)
132   *Manning v Turner* [1957] 1 WLR 91 at 94.
133   *Hedley Byrne & Co Ltd v Heller & Partners Ltd* [1964] AC 465.
134   *Heilbut, Symons & Co v Buckleton* [1913] AC 30.
135   1967 (c 7).
136   *South Australia:* Misrepresentation Act 1971; *Victoria:* Goods (Sales and Leases) Act 1981; *New Zealand:* Contractual Remedies Act 1979; *Young v Hunt* [1984] 2 NZLR 80 at 89.

person, to recover damages if the person making the representation would be liable in damages in respect thereto had the representation been made fraudulently, unless the other party proves a reasonable belief that the facts represented were true: s 2(1). A purchaser may be granted the remedy of rescission where a contract was induced by an innocent misrepresentation.[137]

While *Lord Cairns' Act* enabled equitable damages to be awarded in lieu of an injunction or specific performance, the statute did not enable the award of damages in lieu of the equitable remedy of rescission.[138] However s 2(2) of the Misrepresentation Act 1967 enables a court to declare a contract subsisting and 'award damages in lieu of rescission, if of opinion that it would be equitable to do so, having regard to the nature of the misrepresentation and the loss that would be caused by it if the contract were upheld, as well as to the loss that rescission would cause to the other party'. The Misrepresentation Act accordingly provides a remedy of damages in lieu of the equitable remedy of rescission.[139] This remedy is only available where the misrepresentation is not fraudulent.[140] The Misrepresentation Act was passed pursuant to recommendations of the Law Reform Committee which drew an analogy with *Lord Cairns' Act*.[141]

————◄○►————

11.8 Account of profits

An account of profits is an equitable remedy. In *Watson v Holliday*[142] Kay J described an account of profits as 'an equitable claim for money had and received'.[143] In *Colbeam Palmer Ltd v Stock Affiliates Pty Ltd*[144] Windeyer J remarked: 'The account of profits was a form of relief peculiar to courts of equity, whereas damages were originally a common law remedy'.[145] Windeyer J had earlier explained the distinction between the two remedies:

> The distinction between an account of profits and damages is that by the former the infringer is required to give up his ill-gotten gains to the party whose rights he has infringed: by the latter he is required to compensate the party wronged for the loss he has suffered. The two computations can obviously yield different results, for a plaintiff's loss is not to be measured by the defendant's gain, nor a defendant's gain by the plaintiff's loss.[146]

---

137 *Leighton Properties Pty Ltd v Hurley* [1984] 2 Qd R 534; *Koszman v Van Dusen* [1989] 4 WWR 73.
138 *Dusik v Newton* (1985) 62 BCLR 1 at 46.
139 As to the assessment of damages: see *William Sindall Plc v Cambridgeshire County Council* [1994] 1 WLR 1016.
140 A J Oakley, 'Pecuniary Compensation for Failure to Complete a Contract for the Sale of Land', *Cambridge Law Journal*, vol 39, 1980, 58 at p 83.
141 Law Reform Committee, *Tenth Report of the Law Reform Committee*, 1962, [Cmnd 1782], para 12. See also *William Sindall Plc v Cambridgeshire County Council* [1994] 1 WLR 1016 at 1037 per Hoffman LJ.
142 (1882) 20 Ch D 780.
143 (1882) 20 Ch D 780 at 784.
144 (1968) 122 CLR 25.
145 (1968) 122 CLR 25 at 33.
146 (1968) 122 CLR 25 at 32.

The Court of Chancery could direct an account of profits as an incident to the award of an injunction.[147] An account could not be directed in the absence of a prayer for an injunction.[148] While in proceedings for an injunction the Court of Chancery could direct an account of profits, such relief was regarded as distinct from an award of damages. Sir William Page Wood VC in *Powell v Aiken*[149] adverted to the distinction between 'damages as such and wrongs attended with profit to the wrongdoer'.[150] However, once *Lord Cairns' Act* had been passed there was no procedural difficulty which prevented a court of equity from granting both remedies. A case in point is *Hunt v Peake*[151] in which an injunction was granted to restrain unlawful mining, an account of profits ordered and damages awarded.

In cases of trade torts an account of profits is regarded as an alternative remedy to an award of damages. This has been so since the Court of Chancery was vested with jurisdiction under *Lord Cairns' Act*. In *De Vitre v Betts*[152] Lord Cairns considered that the jurisdiction under *Lord Cairns' Act* 'was not intended to ... co-exist with, the old relief administered by the Court of Chancery of granting an inquiry as to profits'.[153]

This consequence did not arise from the terms of *Lord Cairns' Act* which did not expressly prohibit the court from awarding damages and directing an account.[154] Instead, the difficulty in awarding damages as well as an account is because an account of profits is directed on the assumption that a plaintiff condones the conduct in question. In *Neilson v Betts*[155] Lord Westbury remarked, 'if you take an account of profits you condone the infringement'.[156]

A Court of Equity decrees an account for an infringement of copyright on the ground that the owner of such property would treat the infringer as having acted as his agent.[157] A plaintiff would be taking up inconsistent positions in challenging an infringement by seeking damages, and also condoning the defendant's infringement by requiring him to account for

---

147 *Baily v Taylor* (1829) 1 Russ & M 73 at 75; 39 ER 28 at 29.
148 See eg *Parrott v Palmer* (1834) 3 My & K 632 at 643; 40 ER 241 at 245 per Lord Brougham LC ('the learned counsel in *Richards v Noble* (1807) 3 Mer 673, whose admission was relied upon in the argument here, concede only that, without the prayer for an injunction, the Plaintiff could have no account').
149 (1858) 4 K & J 343; 70 ER 144.
150 (1858) 4 K & J 343 at 352; 70 ER 144 at 148.
151 (1860) Johns 705 at 713; 70 ER 603 at 606.
152 (1873) LR 6 HL 319.
153 (1873) LR 6 HL 319 at 325.
154 *Betts v Neilson* (1868) LR 3 Ch App 429 at 440.
155 (1871) LR 5 HL 1.
156 (1871) LR 5 HL 1 at 22. See also *De Vitre v Betts* (1873) LR 6 HL 319 at 321, 325; *United Horse-shoe & Nail Co Ltd v Stewart & Co* (1888) 13 App Cas 401 at 412; *Caxton Publishing Co Ltd v Sutherland Publishing Co Ltd* [1939] AC 178 at 198–9; *Reeves Bros v Toronto Quiltings Embroidery Ltd* (1978) 43 CPR (2d) 145 at 167; *Ryde Holdings Ltd v Sorenson* [1988] 2 NZLR 157 at 175.
157 P V Baker and P StJ Langan, *Snell's Equity*, 29th ed, Sweet & Maxwell, London, 1990, p 638; *Saccharin Corp v Chemicals and Drug Co* [1900] 2 Ch 556 at 558. Compare *Larson Jr v Wrigley Jnr* (1928) 277 US 97 at 99 per Holmes J.

his profits.[158] A plaintiff must therefore make an election between these remedies.

It has been argued that there is no compelling reason of policy why a plaintiff in an action for the infringement of intellectual property may not have both remedies, provided that double recovery does not occur.[159] The Canadian Copyright Act[160] allows both remedies to be awarded concurrently. There is however an equitable principle that a plaintiff must not approbate and reprobate. It would be unjust to allow a plaintiff to claim an account in respect of profitable operations, and damages in respect of unprofitable operations.[161]

Legislation which protects intellectual property reflects the equity practice by providing for the alternative remedies of an account or damages.[162] The award of damages or an account where a trade mark or patent is infringed is generally at the option of the plaintiff.[163] In copyright matters a plaintiff who seeks an account will ordinarily be granted such relief.[164] An account can only be obtained for an innocent infringement of copyright.[165]

In some cases the taking of an account may involve procedural difficulties, and an award of equitable damages may be a satisfactory alternative remedy where quantifiable damage has occurred. This may be the case where there is a breach of confidence. In *Attorney-General v Guardian Newspapers Ltd (No 2)* (the *Spycatcher* case)[166] Lord Goff of Chieveley remarked:

---

158 H Street, *Principles of the Law of Damages*, Sweet & Maxwell, London, 1962, p 264. See also *Birn Brothers Ltd v Keene & Co Ltd* [1918] 2 Ch 281; *Caxton Publishing Co Ltd v Sutherland Publishing Co Ltd* [1939] AC 178 at 198; *Van Camp Chocolates Ltd v Aulsebrooks Ltd* [1984] 1 NZLR 354 at 361; (1984) 2 IPR 337 at 345.

159 Institute of Law Research and Reform, *Protection of Trade Secrets (Report No 1)*, Alberta, 1984, p 90 (Trade Secrets Protection Bill cl 4(2)).

160 RSC 1970 cC–30 (Canada) s 20(4).

161 *Heathcote v Hulme* (1819) 1 Jac & W 122 at 132; 37 ER 322 at 325; H A J Ford and W A Lee, *Principles of the Law of Trusts*, 2nd ed, Law Book Co, Sydney, 1990, p 736.

162 *Australia*: Circuit Layouts Act 1989 (Cth) (1989 No 28) s 27; Copyright Act 1968 (Cth) (1968 No 63) s 115(2); Patents Act 1990 (Cth) (1990 No 83) s 122(1); Plant Variety Rights Act 1987 (Cth) (1987 No 2) s 27; Trade Marks Act 1955 (Cth) (1955 No 20) s 65; *England*: Copyright Act 1956 (4 & 5 Eliz II) s 17; Patents and Designs Act 1949 (12, 13 & 14 Geo VI c 87) s 60; Patents Act 1977 s 61; recent English legislation does not expressly provide for the remedies to be alternative remedies, but probably does not disturb the existing practice: Copyright, Designs & Patents Act 1988 (1988 c 48) ss 96(1), 229(1).

163 *Australia*: Patents Act 1990 (Cth) (1990 No 83) s 122(1); Trade Marks Act 1952 (Cth) (1952 No 20) s 65; *England*: Patents and Designs Act 1949 (12, 13 & 14 Geo VI c 87) s 60. The provisions reflect the general law: see *Colbeam Palmer Ltd v Stock Affiliates Pty Ltd* (1968) 122 CLR 25 at 32; *Weingarten Brothers v Charles Bayer & Co* (1905) 92 LT 511 at 513–14. The remarks of Joyce J in *Van Zeller v Mason, Cattley & Co* (1907) 25 RPC 37 at 41 that the *Weingarten Brothers* case decided that the award of an account or damages was in the discretion of the court is contrary to the express remarks in that case of Lord Macnaghten, with whom Lord Lindley agreed.

164 *Ancher, Mortlock, Murray & Woodley Pty Ltd v Hooker Homes Pty Ltd* [1971] 2 NSWLR 278 at 291.

165 *Australia*: Copyright Act 1968 (Cth) (1968 No 63) s 115(3); *England*: Copyright Act 1956 (4 & 5 Eliz II) s 17(2).

166 [1990] 1 AC 109.

This remedy of an account is alternative to the remedy of damages, which in cases of breach of confidence is now available, despite the equitable nature of the wrong, through a beneficent interpretation of the Chancery Amendment Act 1858 (*Lord Cairns' Act*), and which by reason of the difficulties attending the taking of an account is often regarded as a more satisfactory remedy, at least in cases where the confidential information is of a commercial nature, and quantifiable damage may therefore have been suffered.[167]

In some cases it may be necessary to take an account of profits as part of an inquiry into equitable damages.[168]

---

167 [1990] 1 AC 109 at 286.
168 *Noel Leeming Television Ltd v Noel's Appliance Centre Ltd* (1985) 5 IPR 249.

12

England and Ireland

———◁○▷———

12.1 England (and Wales)

High Court

Until 1982 the High Court possessed jurisdiction to award equitable damages under s 2 of the Chancery Amendment Act 1858 (*Lord Cairns' Act*).[1] This jurisdiction survived the repeal of *Lord Cairns' Act*.[2] The High Court now has jurisdiction to award equitable damages under s 50 of the Supreme Court Act 1981.[3] This provision appears to have been derived from s 92 of the Judicature (Northern Ireland) Act 1978.[4]

County Courts

The County Courts have a limited equitable jurisdiction to grant an injunction relating to land,[5] and to make an order for the specific performance of an agreement for the sale of property.[6] This equitable jurisdiction is dependent upon the value of the land or property not exceeding the monetary jurisdictional limit of the County Courts.[7] The County Courts may also, in an appropriate case, award equitable damages under s 50 of the Supreme Court Act. This is because the County Courts under their general ancillary jurisdiction may grant the same relief as the High Court.[8] Equitable damages may be awarded where a plaintiff has an equity to an injunction or specific performance in a matter within the jurisdiction of the County Courts.

———◁○▷———

1　21 & 22 Vict c 27. For the text of s 2 of *Lord Cairns' Act*: see Appendix at p 281.
2　See Chapter 3, above.
3　For the text of s 50 of the Supreme Court Act 1981: see Appendix at p 281.
4　1978 c 23, discussed below.
5　County Courts Act 1984 (1984 c 28) s 23.
6　County Courts Act 1984 s 22.
7　County Courts Act 1984 s 21.
8　County Courts Act 1984 s 38. See also P H Pettit, '*Lord Cairns' Act* in the County Court: A Supplementary Note', *Cambridge Law Journal*, vol 36, 1977, p 369.

12.2 Ireland

The Court of Chancery of Ireland was also vested with jurisdiction under
Lord Cairns' Act.[9] That court was not affected by the *Judicature Acts*, nor
did the Statute Law Revision and Civil Procedure Act 1883, which
repealed *Lord Cairns' Act* in England, extend to repeal a statute having
force in Ireland.[10] The jurisdiction of the Court of Chancery of Ireland
under *Lord Cairns' Act* was transferred to the High Court of Ireland by
virtue of s 21 of the Supreme Court of Judicature (Ireland) Act 1877.[11]
The procedural provisions of *Lord Cairns' Act* and *Sir John Rolt's Act*
regarding the assessment of damages and the trial of questions of fact were
also confirmed under s 42 of the Supreme Court of Judicature (Ireland)
Act.[12] The jurisdiction of the High Court in Ireland that was derived from
Lord Cairns' Act was subsequently transferred to the Supreme Courts of
Southern Ireland and Northern Ireland by ss 39 and 40 respectively of the
Government of Ireland Act 1920.[13] In all strictness the jurisdiction of
those courts to award equitable damages was no longer dependent upon
Lord Cairns' Act which had only vested jurisdiction in the Irish Court of
Chancery. Nevertheless, *Lord Cairns' Act* continued to be on the statute
book in Ireland.

The Statute Law Revision Act 1892[14] omitted any reference in the title
of *Lord Cairns' Act* to the High Court of Chancery and the Court of
Chancery of the County Palatine of Lancaster. After 1892 the title of *Lord
Cairns' Act* read: 'An Act to amend the Course of Procedure in ... the
Court of Chancery in Ireland ...', and the Act was so reprinted in the
Revised Statutes. In the *Leeds* case Viscount Finlay commented that 'the
Act appears there as if it were an Irish statute'.[15] Enactments that related
exclusively to the Irish Free State could be omitted from the *Revised
Statutes* after the enactment of the Statute Law Revision Act 1926.[16]
However *Lord Cairns' Act* appeared in the 1950 edition of the *Revised
Statutes* as the Act was also on the statute book of Northern Ireland.[17] In
1975 Heuston remarked: 'perhaps it is right to emphasise that Ireland is
the only jurisdiction in which it can still be called *Lord Cairns' Act* for it
was repealed in and for England by the Statute Law Revision Act 1883'.[18]
When this comment was written it was undoubtedly correct.

---

9   Chancery Amendment Act 1858 s 8.
10 Statute Law Revision and Civil Procedure Act 1883 s 2. See also *Leeds Industrial Co-
    operative Society Ltd v Slack* [1924] AC 851 at 863.
11 40 & 41 Vict c 57.
12 *De Freyne v Fitzgibbon (No 2)* [1904] 1 Ir R 429 at 430, 432.
13 10 & 11 Geo V c 67. See also H Calvert, *Constitutional Law in Northern Ireland*, Sweet &
    Maxwell, London, 1968, pp 51–2.
14 55 & 56 Vict c 19 s 1 (Schedule).
15 [1924] AC 851 at 863.
16 17 & 18 Geo V c 42 s 3. See also 'Legislation', *Law Times*, vol 164, 1927, p 106.
17 *The Statutes*, 3rd rev ed, 1950, vol 6, pp 751–3. See also Statute Law Revision Act 1950
    (14 Geo VI c 6) s 1.
18 R F V Heuston, 'Hugh McCalmont Cairns', *Northern Ireland Legal Quarterly*, vol 26,
    1975, 269 at p 273.

Lord Cairns' Act was later repealed in Northern Ireland by the Judicature (Northern Ireland) Act 1978.[19] In 1970 the Macdermott Committee had recommended the entire repeal of *Lord Cairns' Act* in Northern Ireland. The Committee had recognised that in *Sayers v Collyer*[20] Baggallay LJ had considered that it was unnecessary to retain s 2 of *Lord Cairns' Act*. However, it is evident that the Committee appreciated that *Lord Cairns' Act* was still relevant, because they had recommended the adoption of the following provision:

> Where an injunction or specific performance is sought, the Court may award damages in addition to or instead of such injunction or specific performance.

Such a provision is manifestly superior in clarity to s 2 of *Lord Cairns' Act*, and also avoids the use of expressions, such as 'party injured', 'wrongful act' or 'the same court', which may arguably impose jurisdictional limitations upon a court. The Committee did not discuss these jurisdictional issues, although their recommendations were related to the embodiment 'in modern dress' of provisions in the *Judicature Acts.*[21]

Section 92 of the Judicature (Northern Ireland) Act 1978 now enables equitable damages to be awarded in Northern Ireland.[22] In *O'Neill v Dept of Health and Social Services (No 2)*[23] Carswell J observed that s 2 of *Lord Cairns' Act* was the 'predecessor provision'[24] to s 92 of the Judicature (Northern Ireland) Act. The latter provision differs from the draft provision recommended by the Committee by enabling equitable damages to be awarded by 'a court' which 'has jurisdiction to entertain an application for an injunction or specific performance'. This provision enables the High Court and the County Courts[25] to award equitable damages.

Lord Cairns' Act continues to be law in the Republic of Ireland.[26] There would be merit if legislation were passed in the Republic which was derived from s 50 of the Supreme Court Act 1981. This would make evident the existence in the Republic of a jurisdiction to award equitable damages.

---

19   1978 c 23 s 122(2), Sch 7.
20   (1884) 28 Ch D 103 at 107.
21   *Report of the Committee on the Supreme Court of Judicature of Northern Ireland,* 1970, Command [4292] (Chairman, Rt Hon Lord Macdermott MC), pp 40–1, para 102.
22   For the text of s 92 of the Judicature (Northern Ireland) Act 1978: see Appendix at p 281.
23   [1986] NI 290.
24   [1986] NI 290 at 296.
25   County Courts Act 1959 (1959 c 25) (Northern Ireland) ss 15, 16; County Courts (Northern Ireland) Order 1980 (1980 No 397) (Northern Ireland) Arts 13, 14.
26   *Solomon v Red Bank Restaurant Ltd* [1938] Ir R 793 at 801; *McGrath v Munster and Leinster Bank Ltd* [1959] Ir R 313; *Cullen v Cullen* [1962] Ir R 268 at 286; *Halpin v Tara Mines Ltd* (High Court, Gannon J, 1973 No 1516 P, 16 February 1976, unreported); *Duggan v Allied Irish Building Society* (High Court, Finlay J, 1974 No 2302 P, 4 March 1976, unreported); *Malone v Clogrennane Lime & Trading Co Ltd* (High Court, McWilliam J, 1977 No 1551 P, 14 April 1978, unreported); *Roberts v O'Neill* [1983] Ir R 47 at 54. See also B M E McMahon and W Binchy, *Irish Law of Torts,* Professional Books, London, 1981, p 592.

13

Australia and New Zealand

----◦----

13.1 New South Wales

Supreme Court

The Supreme Court of New South Wales was constituted in 1824 by
the Charter of Justice that was issued under the New South Wales
Act 1823.[1] This temporary measure was superseded by the Australian
Courts Act 1828[2] which constituted the Supreme Court on a permanent
basis. Section 11 of the Australian Courts Act vested the court with the
same equitable[3] and common law[4] jurisdiction possessed by the Lord

---

1   4 Geo IV c 96. For the text of the Charter of Justice: see *Historical Records of Australia*,
   ser 1, vol IV, Library Committee of the Commonwealth Parliament, Sydney, 1922,
   pp 509–20.

2   9 Geo IV c 83 (Imperial). For a discussion of the Australian Courts Act 1828: see A C V
   Melbourne, *Early Constitutional Development in Australia*, 2nd ed, University of
   Queensland Press, Brisbane, 1963, pp 152–162.

3   See *McManus v Clouter* (1980) 29 ALR 101 at 116 per McLelland J for a discussion of
   the equitable jurisdiction of the early Supreme Court of New South Wales.

4   The established common law jurisdiction of the Lord Chancellor at that time included
   the jurisdiction to repeal a Crown grant under a *scire facias*: see *R v McIntosh* (1851)

Chancellor. This grant of 'equitable' jurisdiction under s 11 of the Act did not include any jurisdiction which had been conferred upon the Court of Chancery under an Imperial statute which had not been adopted in the colony.[5] As a result, this provision did not confer jurisdiction under the Chancery Amendment Act 1858 (*Lord Cairns' Act*).[6] The Supreme Court upon its creation could concurrently grant legal and equitable remedies.[7] However, changes were made to the court to reflect English practice. A separate equity jurisdiction of the court was created by s 20 of the Administration of Justice Act 1840.[8] The equity jurisdiction of the court was vested in a judge who was referred to in later statutes as the 'Primary Judge in Equity'.[9] The Supreme Court in Equity acquired jurisdiction to award equitable damages under s 32 of the Equity Act 1880,[10] which was later superseded by s 9 of the Equity Act 1901.[11] These two provisions were similar except that the words 'if it thinks fit', which merely emphasised the discretionary nature of the jurisdiction,[12] were omitted from the later provision. This omission was not of any consequence, and it has been held that these provisions conferred jurisdiction under *Lord Cairns' Act*.[13] An inquiry as to damages would only be ordered on

---

Legge (NSW) 680. See also J Harrison, *Practice of the Court of Chancery*, vol 1, 8th ed, 1796, p 6. The jurisdiction to annul Crown grants under a *scire facias* was regarded by the Privy Council in *R v Hughes* (1866) LR 1 PC 81 as inapplicable to the colonies where there was no formal enrolment or record of a Crown grant in a court. See also *Osborne v Morgan* (1886) 2 QLJ 113 at 123 per Harding J; *Queensland Investment and Land Mortgage Co Ltd v Grimley* (1893) 4 QLJ Supp 8. A *scire facias* will lie where a Crown grant is deemed by statute to be a record of the Supreme Court: See *R v Redhead Coal Mining Co* (1886) 7 LR (NSW) 279. In Victoria the registration of a Crown grant is deemed to be an enrolment of record of the grant: see Transfer of Land Act 1958 (No 6399) (Victoria) s 29(2). The common law jurisdiction of the Lord Chancellor also related to such matters as traverses of office and petitions of right. See B H McPherson, *The Supreme Court of Queensland 1859–1960*, Butterworths, Sydney, 1989, p 127.

5   Compare *Re Johns* (1873) 7 SALR 101 at 102.
6   21 & 22 Vict c 27.
7   K S Jacobs, 'Law and Equity in New South Wales After the Supreme Court Procedure Act 1957, Section 5', *Sydney Law Review*, vol 3, 1959, p 83; J M Bennett, *A History of the Supreme Court of New South Wales*, Law Book Co, Sydney, 1974, p 94. Compare *Larios v Bonany Y Gurety* (1873) LR 5 PC 346 at 356.
8   4 Vict No 22 (1840) (New South Wales).
9   11 Vict No 22, 11 Vict No 27 (1847) (New South Wales). For a discussion of the office of the Primary Judge in Equity : see J M Bennett, *A History of the Supreme Court of New South Wales*, Law Book Co, Sydney, 1974, pp 96–9.
10 44 Vic No 18 (New South Wales). For the text of s 32 of the Equity Act 1880: see Appendix at p 282. During the passage of the Equity Act 1880 the reform effected in England under *Lord Cairns' Act* (mistakenly referred to as the *Judicature Act*) was mentioned: see *New South Wales Parliamentary Debates (Session 1879–80) (First Series)*, vol 1, 4 December 1879, p 473.
11 1901 No 24 (New South Wales). For the text of s 9 of the Equity Act 1901: see Appendix at p 282.
12 *Aynsley v Glover* (1874) LR 18 Eq 544 at 554.
13 *Horsley v Ramsay* (1889) 10 LR (NSW) Eq 41 at 47; *Weily v Williams* (1895) 16 LR(NSW) Eq 190 at 195; *Boyns v Lackey* (1958) 58 SR (NSW) 395 at 405; *Craney v Bugg* [1971] 1 NSWLR 13 at 16. See also *Goldsborough, Mort & Co Ltd v Quinn* (1910) 10 CLR 674.

the equity side of the Supreme Court where a plaintiff satisfied the jurisdictional requirements of *Lord Cairns' Act*.[14]

The Judicature system was introduced into New South Wales by the Supreme Court Act 1970,[15] the enactment of which was recommended by the Law Reform Commission of New South Wales.[16] The Supreme Court possesses jurisdiction to award equitable damages under s 68 of the Supreme Court Act.[17] The terminology of this provision differs from *Lord Cairns' Act* by conferring jurisdiction upon the court to award equitable damages in a case where the court has 'power' to make an order (in *Lord Cairns' Act* the court has 'jurisdiction to entertain an application') for an injunction or specific performance. This difference in language was not discussed in the report of the Law Reform Commission,[18] and has not been regarded as material.[19] It has been held that s 68 confers jurisdiction under *Lord Cairns' Act*.[20] It has been recognised that a modern provision,

---

14 *Fell v NSW Oil & Shale Co* (1889) 10 LR (NSW) Eq 255; *Want v Moss* (1891) 12 LR (NSW) Eq 101; *Dixson v Tange* (1891) 12 LR (NSW) Eq 204; *Weily v Williams* (1895) 16 LR (NSW) Eq 190 at 195; *Williamson v Friend* (1901) 1 SR (NSW) Eq 23 at 30; *Jones v Pease* (1909) 10 SR (NSW) 64 at 65; *King v Poggioli* (1923) 32 CLR 222; *Wright v Carter* (1923) 23 SR (NSW) 555; *Gall v Mitchell* (1924) 35 CLR 222 at 231; *Western Electric Co (Aust) Ltd v Betts* (1935) 52 WN (NSW) 173; *Boyns v Lackey* (1958) 58 SR (NSW) 395; *Harrigan v Brown* [1967] 1 NSWR 342; *Craney v Bugg* [1971] 1 NSWLR 13. See also J M Bennett, *Equity Law in Colonial New South Wales*, Law School, University of Sydney, 1962, pp 78–84, 325–30.

15 1970 No 52 (New South Wales). See also 'Fusion in New South Wales', *Australian Law Journal*, vol 46, 1972, p 254.

16 New South Wales Law Reform Commission, *Supreme Court Procedure*, NSWLRC 7, 1969.

17 For the text of s 68 of the Supreme Court Act 1970: see Appendix at p 282.

18 New South Wales Law Reform Commission, *Supreme Court Procedures*, NSWLRC 7, 1969, p 103.

19 *ASA Constructions Pty Ltd v Iwanov* [1975] 1 NSWLR 512 at 518.

20 *O'Rourke v Hoeven* [1974] 1 NSWLR 622 at 626; *ASA Constructions Pty Ltd v Ivanov* [1975] 1 NSWLR 512 at 518; *Crockford v Pessego* (Supreme Court of New South Wales, Helsham CJ (in Eq), Eq Div, No 4399 of 1979, 6 May 1980, unreported); *United States Surgical Corp v Hospital Products International Pty Ltd* [1982] 2 NSWLR 766 at 816; *Wentworth v Woollahra Municipal Council (No 2)* (1982) 149 CLR 672 at 676; *Wentworth v Attorney-General (NSW)* (1984) 154 CLR 518 at 523; *Cominos v Rekes* (Supreme Court of New South Wales, Cohen J, Eq Div, No 2065 of 1977, 27 March 1984, unreported), noted [1984] ACLD 555; *Thorne v Doug Wade Consultants Pty Ltd* [1985] VR 433 at 492; *Beard v Baulkham Hills Shire Council* (1986) 7 NSWLR 273 at 280 per Young J; *Dominion Insurance Co of Australia Ltd v Finn* (Supreme Court of New South Wales, Hodgson J, Eq Div, No 1308 of 1984, 18 December 1987, unreported); *Corpers (No 664) Pty Ltd v NZI Securities Australia Ltd* [1989] ASC 55-714 at 58,419; *Filo v Chappuis* (Supreme Court of New South Wales, Young J, Eq Div, No 3997 of 1987, 9 June 1989, unreported); *Spicer v Far South Coast Regional Aboriginal Land Council* (Supreme Court of New South Wales, Needham J, Eq Div, No 1264 of 1986, 18 October 1989, unreported); *Rosser v Maritime Services Board of New South Wales (No 2)* (Supreme Court of New South Wales, Young J, Eq Div, No 1624 of 1993, 30 August 1993, unreported); *Vanmeld Pty Ltd v Cussen* (1994) 121 ALR 619 at 621 per Einfeld J. See also *Madden v Kevereski* [1983] 1 NSWLR 305; *Newmont Pty Ltd v Laverton Nickel NL* [1981] 1 NSWLR 215 at 218; *Newmont Pty Ltd v Laverton Nickel NL (No 2)* [1981] 1 NSWLR 221 at 223; *York Bros (Trading) Pty Ltd v Commissioner of Main Roads* [1983] 1 NSWLR 391 at 399; *McEwan v Dick* (1985) 9 ACLR 1011 at 1017; *Medway v The Heating Centre Pty Ltd* (Supreme Court of New South Wales, Bryson J, Eq Div, No 4972 of 1986, 29 August 1986, unreported).

which avoids possible jurisdictional difficulties, should be substituted for s 68 of the Supreme Court Act.[21]

District Court

The District Court of New South Wales may in some instances exercise the same powers and authority of the Supreme Court, and therefore award equitable damages. The District Court possesses this jurisdiction in proceedings for the specific performance of an agreement for the purchase and lease of property within the jurisdictional limit of the court.[22]

———⟨o⟩———

13.2 Queensland

Supreme Court

The Supreme Court of Queensland was constituted under the Supreme Court Constitution Amendment Act 1861.[23] Section 22 of this Act vested the court with the equitable jurisdiction possessed by the Lord Chancellor or the other equity judges in England, and the common law jurisdiction[24] and lunacy jurisdiction of the Lord Chancellor. The grant of 'equitable' jurisdiction conferred upon the court by s 22 of the Act did not include any jurisdiction under an Imperial statute, such as *Lord Cairns' Act*, which had not then been adopted in Queensland.[25] There was legislative recognition that the New South Wales tradition of a separate equity jurisdiction was to continue after Separation. This was evident from s 68 of the Supreme Court Constitution Amendment Act which enabled general rules to be made in respect of the 'common law, equitable, ecclesiastical or insolvency jurisdiction' of the court. The Supreme Court in equity originally acquired jurisdiction to award equitable damages under s 10 of the Supreme Court Act of 1863,[26] which was later superseded by s 62 of the Equity Act of 1867.[27] Both of these identical provisions were derived from *Lord Cairns' Act*.

The Judicature system was introduced to Queensland by the *Judicature Act* of 1876[28] which was passed on the recommendation of the Civil

---

21 J G Starke, 'A Further Limitation on the Scope of *Lord Cairns' Act*', *Australian Law Journal*, vol 57, 1983, 1 at p 2; J G Starke, 'Date for Assessment of Damages under *Lord Cairns' Act*', *Australian Law Journal*, vol 57, 1983, 537 at p 538.

22 District Court Act 1973 (1973 No 9) (New South Wales) s 134(1)(b).

23 25 Vict No 13 (Queensland). See also B H McPherson, *The Supreme Court of Queensland 1859–1960*, Butterworths, Sydney, 1989, p 27.

24 See n 4 above.

25 Compare *Re Johns* (1873) 7 SALR 101 at 102.

26 27 Vict No 14 (Queensland) (*Pring's Statutes*, vol 3, 1864, p 314). For the text of s 10 of the Supreme Court Act of 1863 (Queensland): see Appendix at p 283.

27 31 Vict No 18 (Queensland). For the text of s 62 of the Equity Act of 1867: see Appendix at p 283.

28 40 Vict No 6 (Queensland).

Procedure Reform Commission.[29] Prior to the passage of the *Judicature Act* a limited reform had been achieved by the Equity Procedure Act of 1873.[30] Section 1 of the Equity Procedure Act empowered the Supreme Court in the common law jurisdiction, and a District Court, to determine an equitable claim or demand for a sum of money or damages. This provision conferred jurisdiction to award equitable damages.[31] After the commencement of the Queensland Judicature Act the source of jurisdiction of the Supreme Court to award equitable damages continued to be s 62 of the Equity Act.

As in England, there was a repeal of the statutory source of jurisdiction to award equitable damages. Section 62 of the Equity Act was initially abrogated under rules in 1900[32] and later repealed by statute in 1908.[33] It has been held that the established jurisdiction of the court to award equitable damages under s 62 of the Equity Act was preserved by savings clauses contained in the rules (rr 2, 3 (Second Schedule)) and in s 2 of the Act.[34] In England s 16 of the *Judicature Act* had transferred the jurisdiction that was vested in the Court of Chancery by *Lord Cairns' Act* to the High Court of Justice.[35] No such provision is to be found in the Queensland Judicature Act which did not create a new court, so there was no need to place reliance on that Act as authority for the survival of the jurisdiction in Queensland.[36] An unsatisfactory consequence of the repeal of s 62 of the Equity Act was that the provision did not appear in any reprints of the Equity Act.[37]

Some recommendations have been made for the re-enactment of *Lord Cairns' Act* in Queensland. In *Conroy v Lowndes*[38] Philp J considered that *Lord Cairns' Act* should be re-enacted 'with appropriate safeguards to a defendant'.[39] Equitable damages may be awarded in the absence of a specific plea for such relief.[40] This may have been the reason why there was a call for 'appropriate safeguards'. However, it would not be necessary to provide any express procedural safeguards in legislation as a court would ensure that a defendant would have adequate notice of a claim for

---

29 'Report of the Civil Procedure Reform Commission (1876)', in *Votes and Proceedings (Legislative Assembly)*, vol 1, 1876, p 775. See also The Civil Procedure Reform Act of 1872 (36 Vict No 23) (Queensland).

30 37 Vict No 3 (Queensland). For a discussion of the Equity Procedure Act of 1873 (Queensland): see B H McPherson, *The Supreme Court of Queensland 1859–1960*, Butterworths, Sydney, 1989, pp 135–6.

31 *Noagues v Hope* (1874) 4 QSCR 57; *Barbagallo v J & F Catelan Pty Ltd* [1986] 1 Qd R 245 at 255–6 per McPherson J and at 265 per Thomas J.

32 *The Repealing Rules of 1900*, vol 74, *Queensland Government Gazette*, 17 October 1900, pp 1145–6.

33 The Statute Law Revision Act of 1908 (8 Edw VII No 18) (Queensland).

34 *Conroy v Lowndes* [1958] Qd R 375 at 383 per Philp J; *Edward Street Properties Pty Ltd v Collins* [1977] Qd R 399 at 400–1 per Douglas J; *Minter v Geraghty* (1981) 38 ALR 68 at 76 per Dunn J and at 84 per Macrossan J; *Barbagallo v J & F Catelan Pty Ltd* [1986] 1 Qd R 245 at 251 per McPherson J.

35 *Chapman, Morsons & Co v Guardians of Auckland Union* (1889) 23 QBD 294.

36 Compare *Smith v Wirth (No 2)* [1945] St R Qd 59 at 65; (1945) 39 QJPR 28 at 32.

37 *Barbagallo v J & F Catelan Pty Ltd* [1986] 1 Qd R 245 at 251 per McPherson J.

38 [1958] Qd R 375.

39 [1958] Qd R 375 at 384.

40 *Minter v Geraghty* (1981) 38 ALR 68 at 84 per Macrossan J; *Barbagallo v J & F Catelan Pty Ltd* [1986] 1 Qd R 245 at 251 per McPherson J.

equitable damages.[41] In 1982 the Law Reform Commission recommended the re-enactment of *Lord Cairns' Act*,[42] and adverted to the jurisdictional issue of whether the term 'wrongful act' in *Lord Cairns' Act* included a breach of an equitable obligation.[43]

In 1990 the Law Reform Commission recommended the adoption of the following provision:

Equitable damages

Where a court has jurisdiction to entertain an application for an injunction or specific performance it may award damages in addition to or in substituiton for an injunction or specific performance.

This provision was derived from s 50 of the Supreme Court Act 1981 of England. The provision was also influenced by s 92 of the Judicature (Northern Ireland) Act 1978, and was expressed to apply to a court that has jurisdiction to entertain an application for an injunction or specific performance.[44] If enacted the provision would have conferred an express jurisdiction to award equitable damages upon not only the Supreme Court, but also the District Court. The adoption of such a provision would avoid the jurisdictional difficulties mentioned in the earlier report of the Commission. It was unfortunate that such a provision was not inserted in the Supreme Court of Queensland Act 1991[45] which markedly deviated from the recommendations of the Commission. The Supreme Court of Queensland Act preserved the jurisdiction of the court: s 9. Accordingly the court continues to possess jurisdiction to award equitable damages under s 62 of the Equity Act of 1867.

District Courts of Queensland

The District Courts, within the monetary limits of the courts, may award equitable damages. This jurisdiction is derived from a number of sources. The District Courts possess jurisdiction to determine an equitable claim or demand for the recovery of a sum of money or damages, whether liquidated or unliquidated, thus enabling the award of equitable damages in an appropriate case.[46] In *Barbagallo v J & F Catelan Pty Ltd*[47] it was held that the jurisdiction to determine an 'equitable claim or demand' included jurisdiction to award equitable damages in lieu of a *quia timet* injunction. The District Courts also possess an express jurisdiction to award equitable damages in addition to or in lieu of specific performance or an injunction.[48]

---

41 *Minter v Geraghty* (1981) 38 ALR 68 at 84 per Macrossan J.
42 Queensland Law Reform Commission, *Report of the Law Reform Commission on a Bill to Consolidate, Amend and Report the Supreme Court Acts, etc*, QLRC 32, 1982, p 20.
43 See n 42 above. See also Chapter 4.
44 Queensland Law Reform Commission, *Supreme Court Acts*, supplementary report, 1990, p 17.
45 1991 No 68 (Queensland).
46 District Courts Act 1967–1989 (Queensland) s 66(1)(a)(i). See also P M McDermott, 'Equitable Claims or Demands — Queensland District and Magistrates Courts, and the Western Australian Local Court', *University of Queensland Law Journal*, vol 16, 1991, p 212.
47 [1986] 1 Qd R 245.
48 District Courts Act 1967–1989 (Queensland) s 66(1)(b)(iii), (xii).

Magistrates Courts

The Magistrates Courts, within the monetary limits of the courts, possess jurisdiction to award equitable damages. This jurisdiction is derived from the jurisdiction that the courts have to determine an equitable claim or demand for the recovery of a sum of money or damages,[49] thus enabling the award of equitable damages where a plaintiff possesses an equity to an injunction or specific performance.[50] This jurisdiction to award equitable damages may be exercised despite the fact that the Magistrates Courts lack an ancillary jurisdiction enabling the grant of remedies that may be granted by the Supreme Court.[51]

------◄◦►------

13.3 South Australia

Supreme Court

The Supreme Court of South Australia was constituted under the Supreme Court Act 1837[52] in a manner similar to the creation of the Supreme Court of New South Wales. Section 8 of the Act vested the court with the equitable jurisdiction that was exercised by the Lord Chancellor. The grant of this 'equitable' jurisdiction did not confer any jurisdiction conferred upon the Lord Chancellor under an Imperial statute that had not been adopted in South Australia.[53] The Equity Act 1866[54] provided for the equity jurisdiction of the court to be vested in the Primary Judge in Equity.[55] The Supreme Court in Equity acquired jurisdiction to award equitable damages under s 141 of the Equity Act.[56] This provision differed from *Lord Cairns' Act* in various respects. The provision conferred jurisdiction 'in any suit arising out of the breach of any trust'. The jurisdiction could also be exercised 'in any suit' for an injunction or specific performance. Despite these minor differences, the provision was regarded as conferring jurisdiction under *Lord Cairns' Act*.[57] In *Van*

---

49 Magistrates Courts Act 1921–1989 (Queensland) s 4(1)(c); McDermott, n 46 above. See also 'Actions on agreements for leases in Magistrates' Courts', *Queensland Justice of the Peace and Local Authorities Journal*, vol 31, 1937, p 113.

50 *Barbagallo v J & F Catelan Pty Ltd* [1986] 1 Qd R 245; *Rapoff v Doropoulos* [1990] 3 WAR 451.

51 In *Noagues v Hope* (1874) 4 QSCR 57 it was held that the Supreme Court on the common law side could award equitable damages in a suit for an equitable claim or demand. This was so even though s 62 of the Equity Act of 1867 (*Lord Cairns' Act*) had only vested jurisdiction in the 'Supreme Court in equity', and not on the common law side of the court. However, the position could be clarified by legislation.

52 7 Will IV No 5 (South Australia).

53 *Re Johns* (1873) 7 SALR 101 at 102.

54 1866–1867 No 20 (South Australia).

55 *Re District Council of Glanville; Ex parte Hindmarsh* (1874) 8 SASR 255 at 270–1.

56 For the text of s 141 of the Equity Act 1866: see Appendix at p 283.

57 *Van Damme v Bloxam* (1875) 9 SALR 27; *White v Taylor* (1874) 8 SALR 1 at 36.

Damme v Bloxam[58] an argument that s 141 of the Equity Act could be invoked despite the lack of any equity in a bill was rejected. Gwynne P J remarked:

> It is now settled by numerous decisions of the English Courts that the question of damages will not be entertained by Courts of Equity except in cases where the court has jurisdiction irrespectively of any right to them.[59]

The jurisdiction to award equitable damages under s 141 of the Equity Act survived the enactment of the Supreme Court Act 1878.[60] This statute introduced the Judicature system into South Australia.[61] The Equity Act was later repealed by the Supreme Court Act 1935.[62]

Jurisdiction to award equitable damages in South Australia is now conferred by s 30 of the Supreme Court Act 1935.[63] This provision differs from *Lord Cairns' Act* by providing that equitable damages may be awarded where there is 'any action' for an injunction or specific performance. It has been argued that damages may be awarded under s 30 irrespective of whether or not a plaintiff possesses an equity to an injunction or specific performance.[64] However, such an argument places no emphasis on the concluding words of s 30 which, like *Lord Cairns' Act*, provide that damages may be awarded 'either in addition to or in substitution' for an injunction or specific performance. Damages can only be awarded 'either in addition to or in substitution' for these remedies where a plaintiff possesses the requisite equity to relief. Section 30 can therefore be seen to confer no greater jurisdiction than *Lord Cairns' Act*. The decision in *Van Damme v Bloxam*[65] is authority for the proposition that such a provision confers jurisdiction under *Lord Cairns' Act*, and it has been held that s 30 confers that jurisdiction.[66] Any revision of the Supreme Court Act should include a provision derived from s 50 of the English Supreme Court Act 1981. The adoption of such a provision would avoid jurisdictional arguments such as arose in one case in which it was held that the words 'party injured' in *Lord Cairns' Act* precluded the court from awarding damages to a plaintiff suing in respect of a public general duty.[67]

---

58 (1875) 9 SALR 27.
59 (1875) 9 SALR 27 at 29.
60 1878 No 116 (South Australia).
61 *Port Adelaide, Corp of the City of v South Australian Railways Commissioner* [1927] SASR 197 at 211.
62 1935 No 2253 (South Australia).
63 For the text of s 30 of the Supreme Court Act 1935: see Appendix at p 284.
64 D C Jackson, *Principles of Property Law*, Law Book Co, Sydney, 1967, p 64.
65 (1875) 9 SALR 27.
66 *Neville Nitschke Caravans (Main North Road) Pty Ltd v McEntree* (1976) 15 SASR 330 at 351; *Dalgety Wine Estates Pty Ltd v Rizzon* (1978) 19 SASR 543 at 556; *Noble v Susta (No 2)* (1980) 26 SASR 586 at 594; *Altmann v Corp of the City of Adelaide* (1986) 43 SASR 353 at 372; *Settlement Wine Co Pty Ltd v National and General Insurance Co Ltd* (Supreme Court of South Australia, Full Court, No 956 of 1988, 31 August 1990, unreported). See also *E Bown Pty Ltd v Florence* (1967) SASR 214 at 225; *Commissioner of Highways v George Eblen Pty Ltd* (1975) 10 SASR 384; *Jackson v Crosby (No 2)* (1979) 21 SASR 280; *Re Claridge House Ltd; Mount v Tomlinson* (1981) 28 SASR 481.
67 *Neville Nitschke Caravan (Main North Road) Pty Ltd v McEntree* (1976) 15 SASR 330 at 351.

Local Court

The Local Courts of South Australia were abolished in 1992. A Local Court, when constituted by a judge, could exercise the jurisdiction and powers and authority of the Supreme Court in an action for specific performance or an injunction.[68] In such cases a Local Court could therefore award equitable damages (*semble* without any monetary limitation) in a case within the jurisdiction of the court. It has been held that equitable damages could be awarded in a case of part performance.[69] A later case cast doubt on the authority of this decision,[70] although the decision may be explained as a case where specific performance could not be decreed on jurisdictional grounds because of the value of the property.[71]

District Court

The District Court of South Australia was constituted under s 4 of the District Court Act 1991.[72] The court has, with certain exceptions, the same civil jurisdiction as the Supreme Court: s 8. Legal and equitable claims and defences may be included in the same action: s 35. The court possesses an express jurisdiction to award equitable damages. Where a party seeks relief by way of injunction or specific performance, the court may award damages in addition to or in substitution for that relief: s 36(2)(a).[73] This modern provision avoids terms such as 'injured party' and 'wrongful act' which are in s 30 of the Supreme Court Act 1935, and which may impose jurisdictional limitations. The interesting consequence follows that the District Court may possess a wider jurisdiction to award equitable damages than is possessed by the Supreme Court.

Magistrates Court

The Magistrates Court of South Australia was constituted under s 4 of the Magistrates Court Act 1991.[74] The court has, with certain exceptions, the civil jurisdiction to hear and determine an action (at law or in equity) for a sum of money which does not exceed $30,000, and property claims which do not exceed $60,000: s 8(1). Legal and equitable claims and defences may be included in the same action: s 30. An express jurisdiction to award equitable damages is conferred upon the court (s 31(2)(a)) in the same terms as s 36(2)(a) of the District Court Act which was discussed earlier.[75]

---

68 Local and District Criminal Courts Act 1926 (1926 No 1782) (South Australia) s 259.
69 *Douglas v Hill* [1909] SALR 28.
70 *Moore v Dimond* [1929] SASR 274. See also H Mayo, 'Statute of Frauds — Part Performance in Relation to Damages', *Australian Law Journal*, vol 6, 1932, p 283.
71 *Moore v Dimond* (1929) 43 CLR 105 at 110.
72 1991 No 70 (South Australia). The District Court Act commenced operation on 7 July 1992.
73 For the text of s 36(2)(a) of the District Court Act 1991: see Appendix at p 284.
74 No 73 of 1991 (South Australia). The Magistrates Court Act commenced operation on 7 July 1992.
75 For the text of s 31(2)(a) of the Magistrates Court Act 1991 (South Australia): see Appendix at p 284.

13.4 *Tasmania*

The Supreme Court of Van Diemen's Land was constituted under the same statutes of 1823 and 1828 which constituted the Supreme Court of New South Wales. The court could, therefore, initially concurrently grant both legal and equitable remedies.[76] In 1856 provision was made for the equitable jurisdiction of the Supreme Court of Tasmania to be separately exercised, as in New South Wales.[77] In 1863 the Supreme Court in Equity was vested with jurisdiction to award equitable damages under s 3 of The Equity Procedure Act No 2.[78] In *Argyle Developments Pty Ltd v Australia and New Zealand Banking Group Ltd*[79] Zeeman J recognised that s 3 was derived from *Lord Cairns' Act*. This provision was in force until the English Judicature system was introduced into Tasmania by the Supreme Court Civil Procedure Act 1932.[80] The Supreme Court is vested with jurisdiction to award equitable damages under s 11(13) of the Supreme Court Civil Procedure Act.[81] This subsection is comprised of two paragraphs which were originally designated as paragraphs I and II. The paragraphs were later designated as paragraphs (a) and (b) respectively in the 1959 reprint of the Tasmanian statutes.[82]

Paragraph (a) of s 11(13) of the Supreme Court Civil Procedure Act is based upon s 3 of the Equity Procedure Act No 2 of 1863. Paragraph (b) of the subsection, which has no counterpart in any other jurisdiction, provides that the jurisdiction conferred by paragraph (a) does not 'empower the Court or a judge to award damages in substitution for an injunction in any case in which no breach of covenant, contract or agreement or no wrongful act (as the case may be), has been committed'. The Bill for the Supreme Court Civil Procedure Act was drafted by A L Clark (later Clark J) when he was in private practice as a barrister.[83] The initial draft of the Bill contained a clause which was identical to s 11(13) of the Act.[84] Paragraph (b) was presumably inserted into the provision to ensure that the then recent decision of the House of Lords in *Leeds Industrial Co-operative Society Ltd v Slack*,[85] where equitable damages were awarded in lieu of a *quia timet* injunction, would not be followed in Tasmania.[86] It is obvious that he considered that *Lord Cairns' Act* should not be able to be invoked so as to interfere with the proprietary rights of a

---

76 See n 7 above.
77 Administration of Justice Act 1856 (19 Vict No 23) (Tasmania) s 1.
78 27 Vict No 21 (Tasmania). For the text of s 3 of The Equity Procedure Act No 2: see Appendix at p 284.
79 Supreme Court of Tasmania, Zeeman J, No 1279/1991, 4 March 1993, unreported.
80 23 Geo V No 35 (Tasmania).
81 For the text of s 11(13) of the Supreme Court Civil Procedure Act 1932 (Tasmania): see Appendix at p 285.
82 Reprint of Statutes Act 1954 (1954 No 33) (Tasmania) s 4(3)(a)(i).
83 *The Mercury*, Hobart, 14 December 1932.
84 Supreme Court Civil Procedure Bill, first draft, 1925, p 19 (A L Clark Papers, University of Tasmania Library, ref c4/L526).
85 [1924] AC 851.
86 *Public General Acts of Tasmania (Reprint) 1826–1936*, vol II, p 87.

plaintiff. This attitude is apparent from *Moore v Corrigan*[87] where Clark J remarked that 'if the Court in this case granted damages in lieu of an injunction it would compel the plaintiff to sell part of his riparian rights at a price fixed by the Court'.[88] The decision in *Leeds Industrial Co-operative Society Ltd v Slack*[89] does not appear to have been applied in a case where there had been a clear abuse of the jurisdiction. Any revision of the Supreme Court Civil Procedure Act should contain a provision which is derived from s 50 of the English Supreme Court Act 1981. The adoption of this provision would remove some words which arguably impose jurisdictional constraints upon a court.[90]

———◆◇◆———

13.5 Victoria

Supreme Court

The Supreme Court of Victoria was constituted under the Supreme Court Act 1852.[91] Section 14 of the Act conferred upon the court the equitable jurisdiction and common law jurisdiction[92] that was possessed by the Lord Chancellor on 6 January 1852. This provision, which was obviously derived from s 11 of the Australian Courts Act 1828, would not have included jurisdiction under *Lord Cairns' Act* which was enacted after 1852. In any event, this grant of equitable jurisdiction under s 11 would not have included any jurisdiction vested in the Court of Chancery under an Imperial statute which had not been adopted in the colony.[93]

The Supreme Court was initially vested with jurisdiction to award equitable damages under s 62(4) of the Supreme Court Act 1928.[94] This provision was later superseded by s 62(3) of the Supreme Court Act 1958.[95] Both provisions differed from *Lord Cairns' Act* by the use of the expression 'in all cases in which the Court entertains', but Sir Owen Dixon did not regard this deviation to be in any respect material.[96] The provision also contained a proviso, which would have been inserted *ex abundanti cautela*, to preserve the existing powers of the court. It has been held that the provisions in the 1928 and 1958 statutes conferred jurisdiction under

---

87 [1949] Tas SR 34.
88 [1949] Tas SR 34 at 73.
89 [1924] AC 851.
90 See p 70.
91 15 Vict No 10 (Victoria).
92 See n 4 above.
93 Compare *Re Johns* (1873) 7 SALR 101 at 102.
94 19 GeoV No 3783 (Victoria).
95 1958 No 6387 (Victoria). For the text of s 62(3) of the Supreme Court Act 1958: see Appendix at p 285.
96 *JC Williamson Ltd v Lukey and Mulholland* (1931) 45 CLR 282 at 295.

Lord Cairns' Act.[97] It would have been at the initiative of Sir Leo Cussen, who was responsible for the 1928 consolidation of the Victorian statutes,[98] that *Lord Cairns' Act* was adopted in Victoria. While the explanatory papers that relate to the 1928 consolidation do not mention *Lord Cairns' Act*,[99] Cussen J had previously observed that *Lord Cairns' Act* had not been adopted in Victoria.[100] However, prior to the enactment of the Supreme Court Act 1928 there had been instances of the award of equitable damages having been made without any apparent jurisdictional basis in cases of part performance.[101]

Jurisdiction to award equitable damages in Victoria is now conferred by s 38 of the Supreme Court Act 1986[102] which is derived from s 50 of the English Supreme Court Act 1981. The adoption of this provision would avoid the jurisdictional issues which had previously arisen with the use of the words 'wrongful act' in s 62(3) of the Supreme Court Act 1958.

County Courts

Formerly, the County Courts possessed a limited equitable jurisdiction.[103] However, the courts now have jurisdiction, within the monetary limit of the courts, to hear and determine any cause of action.[104] The courts can therefore grant equitable relief such as an injunction or specific performance. The courts also have, by virtue of the general ancillary jurisdiction conferred by s 31 of the Supreme Court Act 1986, the same jurisdiction as the Supreme Court to award equitable damages.

Magistrates' Court

The Magistrates' Court has, within certain monetary limits, been vested with general equitable jurisdiction.[105] By virtue of the general ancillary jurisdiction conferred by s 31 of the Supreme Court Act 1986, the court also has the same jurisdiction as the Supreme Court to award equitable damages.

---

97 *Dillon v Nash* [1950] VLR 293; *McKenna v Richey* [1950] VLR 360 at 373; *Grand Central Car Park Pty Ltd v Tivoli Freeholders Ltd* [1969] VR 62 at 77; *Howes v Victorian Railways Commissioners* [1972] VR 103 at 121; *Gas & Fuel Corp of Victoria v Barba* [1976] VR 755 at 766; *Thorne v Doug Wade Consultants Pty Ltd* [1985] VR 433 at 492; *McMahon v Ambrose* [1987] VR 817 at 848. See also *Bosaid v Andry* [1963] VR 465; *Cowan v Cavanagh* [1978] VR 665; *Rojahn Pty Ltd v Ambrose* [1986] VR 499.

98 A A Browne, 'Legislative Summary', *Melbourne University Law Review*, vol 2, 1959, 222 at p 225; F G Brennan, 'Pillars of Professional Practice: Functions and Standards', *Australian Law Journal*, 1987, 112 at p 113.

99 *The General Public Acts of Victoria*, vol 1, 1929, p cvi.

100 *Walker v Walbran* [1917] VLR 231 at 235; *Beswicke v Alner* [1926] VLR 72 at 78.

101 *M'Bean v Brown* (1887) 13 VLR 726; *Kaufman v Michael* (1892) 18 VLR 375.

102 1986 No 110 (Victoria). For the text of s 38 of the Supreme Court Act 1986: see Appendix at p 285.

103 Civil Justice Committee, *The Administration of Civil Justice in Victoria*, vol 1, 1984, pp 132–7.

104 County Court Act 1958 (1958 No 6230) (Victoria) s 37 (as amended by the Courts Amendment Act 1986 (1986 No 16) (Victoria) s 11).

105 Magistrates' Court Act 1989 (Victoria) s 100. See also P M McDermott, 'Equitable Jurisdiction of Magistrates' Courts', *Australian Law Journal*, vol 62, 1988, p 533.

13.6 Western Australia

Supreme Court

The Supreme Court of Western Australia was constituted by the *Supreme Court Ordinance* 1861.[106] Under s 5 of this ordinance the court was constituted as a court of equity with the same equitable jurisdiction possessed by the Lord Chancellor. This grant of 'equitable' jurisdiction would not have included jurisdiction under an Imperial statute which had not been adopted in Western Australia.[107] The court was not thereby vested with jurisdiction under *Lord Cairns' Act*. Although the court was vested with jurisdiction to concurrently grant legal and equitable remedies, the court followed English practice which made it necessary for proceedings to be brought either at law or in equity.[108] The fusion of the administration of law and equity in Western Australia was achieved by the Supreme Court Act 1880[109] which constituted one Supreme Court of Judicature. The court was invested with jurisdiction to award equitable damages under s 25(10) of the Supreme Court Act 1935,[110] which has been held to confer jurisdiction under *Lord Cairns' Act*.[111] The marginal note to the provision indicates that it was derived from s 62(4) of the Supreme Court Act 1928 of Victoria.

District Court

The District Court is constituted by the District Court of Western Australia Act 1969.[112] The court has jurisdiction under s 50(1)(a) of the Act to determine all personal actions where the amount sought to be recovered does not exceed the monetary limit of the court. The court may also, under s 55 of the Act, grant such relief that the Supreme Court may order.[113] This provision enables the court to grant the same relief that the Supreme Court may order where such relief is properly ancillary to a claim for damages which is within the jurisdiction of the court. This ancillary jurisdiction is dependent upon the existence of what Scrutton LJ described in *R v Cheshire County Court Judge*[114] as a 'valid or justifiable money

---

106 24 Vict No 15 (Western Australia).
107 Compare *Re Johns* (1873) 7 SALR 101 at 102.
108 E Russell, *A History of the Law in Western Australia* (ed F M Robinson and P W Nichols), University of Western Australia, Nedlands WA, 1980, p 198.
109 44 Vict No 10 (Western Australia).
110 1935 No 36 (Western Australia): see Appendix at p 286.
111 *Willison v Van Ryswyk* [1961] WAR 87 at 89 per Virtue J; *Elliott v Palmiero* (1978) 1 SR (WA) 173 at 178 per O'Connor DCJ; *Singh v Crafter* (Supreme Court of Western Australia, Full Court, 28 May 1992, unreported). See also *Raffaele v Raffaele* [1962] WAR 29.
112 1969 No 84 (Western Australia).
113 D R Williams, 'Equitable Remedies in the Inferior Courts', *1977 Law Summer School*, University of Western Australia, 1977; S Owen-Conway, 'The Equitable Jurisdiction of the Inferior Courts in Western Australia', *University of Western Australia Law Review*, vol 14, 1979, p 150.
114 [1921] 2 KB 694. See also *Kenny v Preen* [1963] 2 QB 499.

claim'.[115] In *Morgan v Macnamara*[116] Jackson DCJ remarked that:

> ... the District Court has power to grant equitable damages by way of ancillary relief in an action in which there is a money claim within the jurisdiction of the court and that the court cannot grant equitable remedies by way of primary relief.[117]

Consequently the court could grant an injunction to restrain future breaches of contract where that relief was ancillary to a claim for damages for breach of contract.[118] However, the court does not possess a general equitable jurisdiction to entertain a suit for specific performance or any other equitable relief, such as equitable damages, by way of primary relief.[119]

Local Courts

A Local Court constituted under the Local Courts Act 1904[120] possesses jurisdiction under s 32 of the Act to determine an equitable claim or demand where the only relief sought is the recovery of a sum of money or damages, whether liquidated or unliquidated.[121] In *Morgan v Macnamara*[122] Jackson DCJ observed that s 32 of the Act 'gives to Local Courts a limited equitable jurisdiction but only in respect of money claims'.[123] Brinsden J in *Dunlop Olympic Ltd v Ellis*[124] considered that the jurisdiction conferred by s 32 of the Act enabled the determination by a Local Court of a claim for rent under a void lease of which equity would grant specific performance, although a majority of the Full Court declined to express a concluded opinion on this question. Later in *Rapoff v Doropoulos*[125] the Full Court held that the inability of the Local Court to decree specific performance of an oral lease did not prevent a Local Court from awarding equitable damages in respect of that lease under s 32 of the Act. In *Barbagallo v J & F Catelan Pty Ltd*[126] it was held that similar Queensland legislation enabled equitable damages to be awarded in lieu of a *quia timet* injunction. The Law Reform Commission of Western Australia has recommended that the jurisdiction of the Local Courts to

---

115 [1921] 2 KB 694 at 708. See also *Smith v Smith* [1925] 1 KB 144; *De Vries v Smallridge* [1928] 1 KB 482; *Bourne v McDonald* [1950] 2 KB 422; *Thompson v White* [1970] 1 WLR 1434; *Hatt & Co (Bath) Ltd v Pearce* [1978] 2 All ER 474.
116 District Court of Western Australia, Perth, Jackson DCJ, App No 21 of 1986, unreported. (I am indebted to Dr P R Handford, Law School, University of Western Australia for this reference.)
117 *Morgan v McNamara*, n 116 above, at 9.
118 *Hondros v Tholet* [1981] WAR 146.
119 *Elliott v Palmiero* (1978) 1 SR (WA) 173.
120 1904 No 51 (Western Australia).
121 J Martin, *Local Court Procedure*, Law Society of Western Australia, 1990; P M McDermott, 'Equitable Claims or Demands — Queensland District and Magistrates Courts, and the Western Australian Local Court', *University of Queensland Law Journal*, vol 16, 1991, p 212; P M McDermott, 'Equitable Claims and Demands — Western Australian Local Courts', *Brief* (Law Society of WA), vol 18 no 9, 1991, p 11.
122 See n 116 above.
123 *Morgan v Macnamara*, n 116 above, at 10.
124 [1986] WAR 8 at 15.
125 [1990] 3 WAR 451.
126 [1986] 1 Qd R 245.

award equitable damages under *Lord Cairns' Act* should be clarified. The Commission recommended that the Local Courts Act should provide that, for the purpose of determining equitable money claims, Local Courts are deemed to have the equitable jurisdiction of the Supreme Court.[127] The general ancillary jurisdiction of the Local Courts is conferred by s 33 of the Local Courts Act. In *Morgan v Macnamara*[128] it was held that a Local Court does not have jurisdiction to grant an injunction in the absence of a primary claim to which the injunction was ancillary or in aid.

13.7 Australian territories

Australian Capital Territory

The Supreme Court of the Australian Capital Territory is constituted under the Australian Capital Territory Supreme Court Act 1933.[129] Section 11(a) of the Act provides that the Supreme Court has the same original jurisdiction, both civil and criminal, as the Supreme Court of the State of New South Wales had in relation to that state immediately before 1 January 1911. This provision conferred upon the Supreme Court of the Australian Capital Territory jurisdiction to award equitable damages under s 9 of the Equity Act 1901 of New South Wales.[130] It has been suggested that this jurisdiction survives in the Australian Capital Territory by virtue of s 27 of the Australian Capital Territory Supreme Court Act, which applies the practice and procedure of the Supreme Court of New South Wales.[131] It is submitted that a sufficient basis for the survival of this jurisdiction is to be found in s 11(a) of the Act, consequently rendering it unnecessary to inquire whether the award of equitable damages could be properly characterised as a matter of practice and procedure.[132]

Northern Territory

The Supreme Court of the Northern Territory of Australia is constituted under the Supreme Court Act 1979.[133] Section 14(1)(b) of the Act provides that the court has the same original jurisdiction, both civil and criminal, as the Supreme Court of South Australia exercised prior to 1 January 1911. This provision enables the Supreme Court of the Northern Territory to

---

127 Law Reform Commission of Western Australian, *Report on Local Courts*, 1988, pp 37–8, 44.
128 *Morgan v Macnamara*, n 116 above, at 9.
129 Seat of Government Supreme Court Act 1933 (1933 No 34) (Commonwealth) as amended.
130 1901 No 24 (New South Wales). For the text of s 9 of the Equity Act 1901: see Appendix at p 282.
131 D W Grieg and J L R Davis, *The Law of Contract*, Law Book Co, Sydney, 1987, p 1499.
132 Compare *Commonwealth v Crothall Hospital Services Pty Ltd* (1981) 54 FLR 439.
133 1979 No 109 (Northern Territory).

exercise the jurisdiction that was exercised on that date by the Supreme Court of South Australia.[134] Consequently the court has jurisdiction to award equitable damages under s 141 of the South Australian Equity Act 1866–1867[135] which conferred jurisdiction under *Lord Cairns' Act*.[136] The absence from the Supreme Court Act of a provision which is equivalent to *Lord Cairns' Act* has been the subject of comment.[137]

Norfolk Island, Christmas Island, and Cocos (Keeling) Islands

The Supreme Court of Norfolk Island, the Supreme Court of Christmas Island and the Supreme Court of the Territory of Cocos (Keeling) Islands all possess jurisdiction to award equitable damages. Ordinances in force in each jurisdiction confer upon those courts the same jurisdiction as the Supreme Court of the Australian Capital Territory.[138] Accordingly, each court may award equitable damages under s 9 of the Equity Act 1901 (New South Wales).

------◄○►------

13.8 Australian companies, securities and futures legislation

The uniform companies and securities legislation came into operation in Australia in 1982. This legislation conferred jurisdiction upon the Supreme Court of a participating state or territory to issue either a negative or mandatory injunction to prevent the commission of an offence under the legislation.[139] A similar jurisdiction was later vested under uniform legislation relating to futures.[140] The courts were also vested with jurisdiction to award damages in addition to or in substitution for an injunction.[141] The jurisdiction originated from a submission of the

---

134 Compare *Moses v Stephenson* (1981) 10 NTR 32 at 33.

135 30 Vict No 20 (South Australia). For the text of s 141 of the Equity Act 1866: see Appendix at p 283.

136 *Van Damme v Bloxam* (1875) 9 SALR 27.

137 D W Greig and J L R Davis, *The Law of Contract,* Law Book Co, Sydney, 1987, pp 1499–1500.

138 *Christmas Island:* Supreme Court Ordinance 1958 (1958 No 4) s 9(a); *Cocos (Keeling) Islands:* Supreme Court Ordinance 1955 (1955 No 4) s 9(a); *Norfolk Island:* Supreme Court Ordinance 1960 (1960 No 5) s 5(1).

139 Companies Act 1981 (1981 No 89) (Commonwealth) s 574(1); Companies (New South Wales) Code s 574(1); Securities Industry Act 1980 (1980 No 66) (Commonwealth) s 149(1); Securities Industry (New South Wales) Code s 149(1).

140 Futures Industry Act 1986 (1986 No 72) (Commonwealth) s 157(1); Futures Industry (New South Wales) Code s 157(1).

141 Companies Act 1981 (Act No 89 of 1981) (Commonwealth) s 574(8); Companies (New South Wales) Code s 574(8); Securities Industry Act 1981 (1980 No 66) (Commonwealth) as amended s 149(8); Securities Industry (New South Wales) Code s 149(8); Futures Industry Act 1981 (1986 No 72) (Commonwealth) s 157(8); Futures Industry (New South Wales) Code s 157(8). See also R Baxt, 'Company Law and

Institute of Directors in Australia that the companies legislation should confer an express jurisdiction to award equitable damages. The Institute recommended:

> Although damages in lieu of an injunction may be available on the basis of section 68 of the Supreme Court Act [1970 (New South Wales)], this right should be expressed in clause 574(1) to put the matter beyond doubt.[142]

This submission was adopted in s 574(8) of the Companies Act 1981,[143] in the Companies Codes in the various Australian jurisdictions and in s 28 of the Securities Industry Amendment Act (No 2) 1981.[144] There is little reported authority on the application of s 574(8) of the Companies Code. In *Dempster v Biala Pty Ltd*.[145] the Full Court of Western Australia considered that the issue as to whether damages could be awarded under s 574(8) of the Code when no injunction was sought was a question of law which would be just and convenient to deal with in the ordinary course of the proceeding. Kennedy, Franklyn and Nicholson JJ remarked that the issue 'raises questions, it may be suggested, generally similar to those raised under *Lord Cairns' Act*'.[146] In this context there is settled authority that equitable damages may be awarded where a statement of claim does not include a prayer for an injunction, but does allege facts which disclose that a plaintiff has an equity to an injunction.[147] In another case a claim for equitable damages against the directors of a company was not pursued.[148]

In 1991 the Corporations Law[149] conferred jurisdiction upon the Federal Court of Australia and the Supreme Courts of the states or territories to issue either a negative or mandatory injunction to restrain the commission of an offence under the Act: s 1324(1). Those courts possess jurisdiction to award equitable damages in addition to or in lieu of an injunction under s 1324(10) of the Corporations Law.[150] This provision is derived from s 574(8) of the Companies Act 1981. The express conferment of a power to award equitable damages precludes any argument that the jurisdiction is not available in respect of a statutory breach.

———◀▶———

Securities', *Australian Business Law Review*, vol 10, 1982, p 429; R Baxt, 'Will Section 574 of the Companies Code please stand up! (and will Section 1323 of the Corporations Act follow suit)', *Company and Securities Law Journal*, vol 7, 1989, p 388.

142   *The Australian Director*, vol 11 no 1, February 1981, Supplement.
143   1981 No 89 (Commonwealth). For the text of s 574(8) of the Companies Act 1981: see Appendix at p 286.
144   1981 No 96 (Commonwealth) s 28.
145   (1989) 15 ACLR 191.
146   (1989) 15 ACLR 191 at 194.
147   See p 211.
148   *Re Southern Resources Ltd; Ex parte Residues Treatment & Trading Co Ltd v Southern Resources Ltd* (1989) 15 ACLR 770 at 802.
149   Corporations Act 1989 (1989 No 107) (Commonwealth), as amended.
150   For the text of s 1324(10) of the Corporations Law: see Appendix at p 286.

13.9 Australian federal courts

Uniform legislation provides for the cross-vesting of civil jurisdiction between two federal courts (the Federal Court and Family Court) and each state and territory Supreme Court, and between each of the state and territory courts.[151] Under this legislation the Federal Court may exercise original and appellate jurisdiction with respect to state matters.[152] This legislation would, in an appropriate case, allow the Federal Court to award equitable damages under a statutory provision that confers such jurisdiction upon the Supreme Court of a state.[153]

———<o>———

13.10 New Zealand

Supreme Court

The Supreme Court of New Zealand was constituted under the Supreme Court Act 1860.[154] Section 5 of this Act provided for the Supreme Court within the colony to have the same equitable and common law jurisdiction as the Court of Chancery in England. It has been held that the Supreme Court was thereby conferred with jurisdiction under *Lord Cairns' Act*.[155] In *Lange v Lange*[156] Hardie Boys J remarked that 'the undoubted rights of the Court to award damages in lieu of an injunction does not in New Zealand depend on *Lord Cairns' Act*'.[157] These remarks may have been made because in all strictness *Lord Cairns' Act* was not an Imperial statute that was directly received into New Zealand.[158] However, there is authority that the Supreme Court Act effectively incorporated the jurisdiction conferred upon the Court of Chancery by *Lord Cairns' Act* into the jurisdiction of the Supreme Court of New Zealand.[159]

---

151 In 1987 the Commonwealth, State and Northern Territory Parliaments passed uniform legislation entitled the Jurisdiction of Courts (Cross-vesting) Act 1987.

152 See eg Jurisdiction of Courts (Cross-vesting) Act 1987 (New South Wales) s 4.

153 See eg *Vanmeld Pty Ltd v Cussen* (1994) 121 ALR 619 at 621.

154 24 Vic No XVII (New Zealand).

155 *Ryder v Hall* (1905) 27 NZLR 385 at 393; *Laugesen v Spensley* (1910) 12 GLR 719 at 722; *Carpet Importing Co Ltd v Beath & Co Ltd* [1927] NZLR 37 at 65; *Attorney-General v Birkenhead Borough* [1968] NZLR 383 at 392; *Souster v Epsom Plumbing Contractors Ltd* [1974] 2 NZLR 515 at 518. See also *Dillon v Macdonald* (1902) 21 NZLR 375; *Ellis v Rasmussen* (1910) 30 NZLR 316; *Algie v Leaning* [1927] GLR 284; *Moore v Dunn* [1927] GLR 361; *Dell v Beasley* [1959] NZLR 89; *Sullivan v Darkin* [1986] 1 NZLR 214 at 220; G W Hinde, D W McMorland and P B A Sim, *Land Law*, vol 2, Butterworths, Wellington, 1979, p 1094.

156 [1966] NZLR 1057.

157 [1966] NZLR 1057 at 1060.

158 Imperial statutes as existing on 14 January 1840 were generally received into New Zealand: see English Laws Act 1908 (1908 No 55) (New Zealand).

159 *Ryder v Hall* (1905) 27 NZLR 385 at 393. See also *Attorney-General v Birkenhead Borough* [1968] NZLR 383 at 392.

The Supreme Court Act 1860 was later repealed by the Supreme Court Act 1882.[160] However, a savings clause in s 16 of the Supreme Court Act 1882 operated to preserve the jurisdiction of the Supreme Court under *Lord Cairns' Act*.[161] The Supreme Court Act 1882 was consolidated into the *Judicature Act* 1908.[162]

The jurisdiction of the Supreme Court to award equitable damages is now conferred by s 16A of the *Judicature Act* 1908 as inserted by the Judicature Amendment Act 1988.[163] This provision is derived from s 50 of the English Supreme Court Act 1981. The enactment of such a provision, together with the repeal of *Lord Cairns' Act*, was originally proposed in cl 26 of the Imperial Law Application Bill 1986.[164] The Law Commission of New Zealand in its report on Imperial legislation had later recommended that *Lord Cairns' Act* be preserved and not 'be the subject of unnecessary amendment'.[165] However, the adoption of s 50 of the English Supreme Court Act 1981 has the advantage of avoiding possible jurisdictional arguments which may arise from the presence in *Lord Cairns' Act* of words such as 'party injured', 'the same Court' and 'wrongful act'.[166]

District Courts

The District Courts, within their monetary limits, possess a limited equitable jurisdiction to determine proceedings for the specific performance of contracts in respect of property.[167] In such proceedings the courts, by virtue of the general ancillary jurisdiction,[168] also possess the same jurisdiction that the High Court possesses to award equitable damages.

New Zealand statute law

Within the context of statute law in force in New Zealand, some commentators have highlighted a number of relevant issues.[169] First, it has been mentioned that s 43 of the Fair Trading Act 1986[170] enables a court to make an order for the payment of compensation for past or future losses. Accordingly where a plaintiff seeks to recover damages for prospective loss it may be useful to make a claim under the Fair Trading Act where that Act applies. That is because the ability to recover damages

---

160 (1883 No 29) s 41, First Sch (New Zealand).
161 *Ryder v Hall* (1905) 27 NZLR 385 at 394.
162 1908 No 89 (New Zealand).
163 1988 No 117 (New Zealand). For the text of s 16A of the Judicature Act: see Appendix at p 287.
164 Law Commission, *Imperial Legislation in Force in New Zealand*, Report No 1, 1987, pp 156–7.
165 Law Commission, *Imperial Legislation in Force in New Zealand*, Report No 1, 1987, p 29.
166 *Attorney-General v Birkenhead Borough* [1968] NZLR 383 at 393; *Stininato v Auckland Boxing Association Inc* [1978] 1 NZLR 1 at 23.
167 District Courts Act 1947 (1947 No 16) (New Zealand) s 34.
168 District Courts Act 1947 (1947 No 16) (New Zealand) s 41.
169 S M D Todd, J F Burrows, R S Chambers, M A Mulgan and M A McGregor Vennell, *The Law of Torts in New Zealand*, Law Book Co, Sydney, 1991, pp 898–9.
170 1986 No 121.

for prospective loss is not dependent upon a plaintiff having the necessary equity to an injunction or specific performance. Another issue is whether or not an award of equitable damages is barred by s 27 of the Accident Compensation Act 1982.[171] That section provides that no proceedings for damages arising directly or indirectly out of the injury or death of a person 'shall be brought in any Court in New Zealand independently of this Act, whether by that person ... or any other person, and whether under any rule of law or any enactment'. It is submitted that in this context a claim for equitable damages under s 16A of the *Judicature Act* is not a claim under 'any enactment' within the meaning of s 27 of the Accident Compensation Act. The object of a suit would be to obtain an injunction or specific performance. An award of equitable damages may be made irrespective of any claim for such relief.

Niue

The New Zealand Parliament has conferred jurisdiction upon the High Court of Niue to award 'damages in lieu of injunction'.[172] This provision confers jurisdiction upon the court to award equitable damages in substitution for an injunction, although not in substitution for specific performance.

---

171 1982 No 181.
172 Niue Act 1966 (1966 No 38) (New Zealand) s 67(1). For the text of s 67(1) of the Niue
     Act 1966: see Appendix at p 287.

14

Canada[*]

———◁◦▷———

14.1 Alberta

After the creation of Alberta in 1905, the Supreme Court of the Northwest Territories continued to exercise jurisdiction in the province.[1] In 1907 the Supreme Court of Alberta was created and vested with the jurisdiction formerly exercised in Alberta by the Supreme Court of the Northwest Territories.[2] This grant of jurisdiction included jurisdiction to award equitable damages under s 10(9) of The Judicature Ordinance 1898.[3] Successive revisions of The Judicature Act in Alberta have contained provisions[4] which confer jurisdiction under *Lord Cairns' Act.*[5] The

---

* See generally E Veitch, 'An Equitable Export – *Lord Cairns' Act* in Canada', *Ottawa Law Review*, vol 12, 1980, p 227.

1   The Alberta Act 1905 (4–5 Edw VII c 3) s 16.

2   Supreme Court Act 1907 SA 1907 c 3 (Alberta) s 10(9).

3   CO N-WT 1898 c 21 (Northwest Territories).

4   Judicature Ordinance COA 1915 c 21 (Alberta) s 10(9); The Judicature Act 1919 c 3 (Alberta) s 37(9); The Judicature Act RSA 1922 c 72 (Alberta) s 37(i); The Judicature Act RSA 1942 c 129 (Alberta) s 36(i); The Judicature Act RSA 1955 c 164 (Alberta) s 34(11); The Judicature Act RSA 1970 c 193 (Alberta) s 34(11); The Judicature Act RSA 1980 c J-1 (Alberta) s 20.

5   *E J H Holdings Ltd v Bougie* (1977) 3 Alta LR (2d) 244 at 246; 7 AR 213 at 216. See also

Supreme Court of Alberta may award equitable damages under s 20 of The Judicature Act.[6] This provision also enables the court to 'grant such other relief as may be deemed just'. This jurisdiction to grant ancillary relief originated in Ontario before the adoption of the Judicature system,[7] and is now unnecessary as the court may grant the parties such relief to which they are entitled so as to avoid a multiplicity of proceedings.[8]

——◦——

14.2 British Columbia

On 19 November 1858 Sir James Douglas, the first Governor of British Columbia, made a proclamation under the British Columbia Government Act 1858[9] declaring that English law was in force in British Columbia. The Douglas Proclamation provided:

> ... that the Civil and Criminal Laws of England, as the same existed at the date of the said Proclamation of the said Act, and so far as they are not, from local circumstances, inapplicable to the Colony of British Columbia, are and will remain in force within the said Colony, till such times as they shall be altered.[10]

This provision of the Douglas Proclamation was repeated in successive enactments of the English Law Act,[11] and provides the basis for the reception of English law in British Columbia.[12] English law is now in force in British Columbia by virtue of s 2 of the Law and Equity Act[13] which provides that:

Canadian Pacific Railway Co v Canadian Northern Railway Co (1912) 5 Alta LR 407 at 412–3; 3 WWR 4; 7 DLR 120; *Brownscombe v Public Trustee of Alberta* (1968) 69 DLR (2d) 107; 64 WWR 559; *Martens v Burden* [1974] 3 WWR 522 at 544; 45 DLR (3d) 123 at 142; *Hyder v Edgar* (1979) 10 Alta LR (2d) 17 at 23; *Olympia & York Developments Ltd v Fourth Avenue Properties Ltd* (1982) 20 Alta LR (2d) 187 at 191; [1982] 5 WWR 88 at 92; *Trawick v Mastromonaco* (1983) 24 Alta LR (2d) 389 at 392; 45 AR 276 at 278; *Carma Developers Ltd v Groveridge Imperial Properties (Calgary) Ltd* (1985) 36 Alta LR (2d) 355.

6   R S A 1980 c J-1 (Alberta). For the text of s 20 of the Judicature Act 1980 (Alberta): see Appendix at p 287.

7   For the text of s 2 of the Court of Chancery Act Amendment Act 1865 (28 Vict c 17) (Ontario): see Appendix at p 289.

8   The Judicature Act RSA 1970 c 193 (Alberta) s 32 (k).

9   21 & 22 Vict c 99.

10   D R Verchere, *A Progression of Judges — A History of the Supreme Court of British Columbia*, University of British Columbia Press, Vancouver, 1988, p 175.

11   *English Law Ordinance* 1867 (No 7 1867) (British Columbia) s 2; English Law Act CA 1888 c 69 (British Columbia) s 2; English Law Act RSBC 1897 c 115 (British Columbia) s 2; English Law Act RSBC 1911 c 75 (British Columbia) s 2; English Law Act RSBC 1924 c 80 (British Columbia) s 2; English Law Act RSBC 1936 c 88 (British Columbia) s 2; English Law Act RSBC 1948 c 111 (British Columbia) s 2; English Law Act RSBC 1960 c 129 (British Columbia) s 2.

12   The reception of English law in British Columbia is comprehensively discussed in J S Marshall, *The Reception of English Law as a Modern Legal Problem* (LLM thesis, Faculty of Law, University of British Columbia, 1977).

13   RSBC 1979 c 224 (British Columbia).

... the Civil and Criminal Laws of England, as they existed on November 19, 1858, so far as they are not from local circumstances inapplicable, are in force in the Province.

The English Law Act vested the Supreme Court of British Columbia with the statutory jurisdiction possessed by the English Court of Chancery on 19 November 1858.[14] *Lord Cairns' Act* was assented to on 1 November 1858, and was thus received in British Columbia on 19 November 1858.[15] In a number of cases the existence of jurisdiction under *Lord Cairns' Act* appears to have been assumed.[16] Some writers have commented upon the absence of an express statutory jurisdiction to award equitable damages in British Columbia.[17]

---◄○►---

14.3 Manitoba

The Court of Queen's Bench initially possessed jurisdiction under *Lord Cairns' Act* through its acquisition of the powers and authority of the 'Court of Chancery at Lincoln's Inn'.[18] The court was vested with an express jurisdiction to award equitable damages by s 6(14) of the Queen's Bench Act 1880[19] which was based on an Ontario provision. In *Boultbee v Shore*[20] Wood CJ confirmed that *Lord Cairns' Act* 'is in force in this Province'.[21] The Chief Justice also assumed that a plaintiff in a suit for specific performance could be awarded damages where the action was brought after the land had been sold to a third party. This decision was based upon the assumption that law and equity were fused in Manitoba. However, it was later held that the court had to adopt English practice as at 1870.[22] It was not until 1895 that the Judicature system was

---

14 *Oasis Hotel Ltd v Zurich Insurance Co* [1981] 5 WWR 24 at 28; (1981) 124 DLR (3d) 455 at 457–8.

15 *Rombough v Crestbrook Timber Ltd* (1966) 55 WWR 577 at 587, 598; 57 DLR (2d) 49 at 57, 67; *Kemp v Lee* (1983) 44 BCLR 172 at 182; 28 RPR 141 at 159; *Gaspari v Creighton Holdings Ltd* (1984) 52 BCLR 30 at 59; *Ansdell v Crowther* (1984) 55 BCLR 216 at 217–8; 11 DLR (4th) 614 at 615; 34 RPR 73 at 75; *Dusik v Newton* (1985) 62 BCLR 1 at 46. In *Zalaudek v De Boer* (1981) 33 BCLR 57 at 67 the court did not have the benefit of argument on this issue. See also Law Reform Commission, *The Statute of Frauds*, LRC 33, 1977, p 22.

16 *Gross v Wright* [1923] SCR 214; [1923] 1 WWR 882; [1923] 2 DLR 171; *Clark v McKenzie* [1930] 1 WWR 67; [1930] 1 DLR 226; *Mines Ltd v Woodworth* (1941) 56 BCR 219; [1941] 3 WWR 40; [1941] 4 DLR 101; *Robinson v MacAdam* [1948] 2 WWR 425; *Re 140 Developments Ltd v Steveston Meat & Frozen Food Lockers (1973) Ltd* (1975) 59 DLR (3d) 470.

17 S M Waddams, *The Laws of Contracts*, Canada Law Book Co, Toronto, 1976, p 436, n 6; G H L Fridman, *The Law of Contract in Canada*, 2nd ed, Carswell, Toronto, 1986, p 652, n 79.

18 Queen's Bench Act SM 1874 (38 Vic c 12) (Manitoba) ss 1, 2.

19 CCSM 1880 c 31 (Manitoba).

20 (1882) Man Rt Wood 376.

21 (1882) Man Rt Wood 376 at 379.

22 *Real Estate Loan Co v Molesworth* (1886) 3 Man R 116.

introduced in Manitoba.[23] Prior to then a limited reform had been achieved by s 1 of the Queen's Bench Act 1886[24] which permitted an action at law for a monetary demand where the plaintiff's right to recover was equitable.[25] Successive revisions of the Queen's (or King's) Bench Act have contained provisions based upon s 6(14) of the 1880 Act[26] which conferred jurisdiction under *Lord Cairns' Act.*[27] The court possesses jurisdiction to award equitable damages under s 36 of The Court of Queen's Bench Act[28] which is derived from s 50 of the English Supreme Court Act.

---◀○▶---

14.4 New Brunswick

The Supreme Court of New Brunswick acquired the jurisdiction of the colonial Court of Chancery in 1854.[29] It acquired jurisdiction to award equitable damages by s 25 of the Supreme Court in Equity Act 1890,[30] which was replaced by s 33 of the Supreme Court in Equity Act 1903.[31] Both of these provisions were derived from *Lord Cairns' Act.* The Judicature system was introduced to New Brunswick by the Judicature Act 1906[32] which created a Supreme Court of Judicature which was vested with the equitable jurisdiction of the former Supreme Court. Subsequent enactments of the Judicature Act have continued to preserve the jurisdiction of the court,[33] so that the jurisdiction to award equitable

---

23 See Queen's Bench Act RSM 1895 c 6 (Manitoba).

24 SM 1886 c 14 (Manitoba).

25 This provision originated in Ontario: see Administration of Justice Act RSO 1877 c 49 (Ontario) s 4. See also n 66 below.

26 Queen's Bench Act 1885 (48 Vict c 15) (Manitoba) s 9(14); Queen's Bench Act RSM 1891 c 36 (Manitoba) s 11(n); Queen's Bench Act 1895 (58–59 Vict c 6) (Manitoba) s 26(l); King's Bench Act RSM 1902 c 40 (Manitoba) s 39(p); King's Bench Act RSM 1913 c 46 (Manitoba) s 26(p); King's Bench Act RSM 1931 c 6 (Manitoba) s 59; King's Bench Act RSM 1940 c 44 (Manitoba) s 59; Queen's Bench Act RSM 1954 c 52 (Manitoba) s 59; Queen's Bench Act RSM 1970 c C 280 (Manitoba) s 60; Queen's Bench Act RSM 1987–1988 c C 280 (Manitoba) s 57. For the text of s 57 of the Queen's Bench Act RSM 1987–1988 c C 280: see Appendix at p 288.

27 *Wright v City of Winnipeg* (1887) 4 Man R 46 at 49–50. See also *Miguez v Harrison* (1914) 7 WWR 650 at 651; *Tenning v Manitoba* (1983) 23 Man R (2d) 227 at 228; *Obirek v Manitoba* (1984) 32 Man R (2d) 110.

28 CCSM c C 280 SM 1988–89 c 4 (Manitoba). For the text of s 36 of The Court of Queen's Bench Act 1988 (Manitoba): see Appendix at p 288.

29 Supreme Court in Equity Act 1854 SNB 1854 (17 Vict) c 18 (New Brunswick).

30 SNB 1890 (53 Vict) c 4 (New Brunswick).

31 CSNB 1903 c 112 (New Brunswick).

32 CSNB 1906 c 37 (New Brunswick).

33 Judicature Act SNB 1906 c 37 (New Brunswick) s 6; Judicature Act SNB 1909 c 5 (New Brunswick) ss 3, 55(2); Judicature Act RSNB 1927 c 113 (New Brunswick) s 3(1); Judicature Act RSNB 1952 c 120 (New Brunswick) s 2(1); Judicature Act RSNB 1973 c J-2 (New Brunswick) s 2(1). See also *Societe Des Acadiens Du Nouveau Brunswick Inc v Minority Language School Board, No 50* (1984) 54 NBR (2d) 198 at 205, para 11.

damages has been preserved.[34] The Supreme Court of Canada in *St Anne Nackawic Pulp & Paper Co Ltd v Canadian Paper Workers' Union, Local 219*[35] observed that 'the New Brunswick Judicature Act ... carries forward the equitable jurisdiction established in England by *Lord Cairns' Act*'.[36] In *Bridges Brothers Ltd v Forest Protection Ltd*[37] it was held that the source of this jurisdiction continues to be s 33 of the Supreme Court in Equity Act 1903.[38] Some Canadian commentators have recognised the absence of an express statutory jurisdiction to award equitable damages in New Brunswick.[39]

———◦———

14.5 Newfoundland

A 'supreme court of civil jurisdiction' was initially constituted under an Imperial statute in 1791.[40] The Commonwealth (Newfoundland) Act 1824[41] later provided for the constitution of the Supreme Court of Newfoundland which was to 'have all Civil and Criminal Jurisdiction ... as His Majesty's Courts of King's Bench, Common Pleas, Exchequer, and High Court of Chancery ... have, or any of them hath'. This statute did not vest the Supreme Court with jurisdiction under *Lord Cairns' Act*. Successive enactments of the Judicature Act confirm that the Supreme Court possesses the jurisdiction conferred by the Imperial statute of 1824.[42] The Supreme Court of Newfoundland was thus never vested with jurisdiction under *Lord Cairns' Act*. In some trespass cases it has been assumed that the court has jurisdiction to award equitable damages for

---

34 *Lounsbury v Sutherland Motor Bus Co* (1928) 54 NBR 7 at 12; *Bridges Brothers Ltd v Forest Protection Ltd* (1976) 14 NBR (2d) 91 at 140, para 129; 72 DLR (3d) 335 at 366–7.

35 [1986] 1 SCR 704; (1986) 28 DLR (4th) 1; 73 NBR (2d) 236.

36 [1986] 1 SCR 704 at 727; (1986) 28 DLR (4th) 1 at 19; 73 NBR (2d) 236 at 262.

37 (1976) 14 NBR (2d) 91 at 140, para 129.

38 For the text of s 33 of the The Supreme Court in Equity Act 1903 (New Brunswick): see Appendix at p 288.

39 S M Waddams, *The Law of Damages*, Canada Law Book Co, Toronto, 1983, p 52, para 93, n 192; G H L Fridman, *The Law of Contract in Canada*, 2nd ed, Carswell, Toronto, 1986, p 652, n 79.

40 An Act Establishing a Court of Civil Jurisdiction in the Island of Newfoundland, for a Limited Time (31 Geo III c 29) (1791). See also C English and C P Curran, *A Cautious Beginning, The Court of Civil Jurisdiction 1791*, Newfoundland Law Reform Commission, St John's, 1991.

41 Commonwealth (Newfoundland) Act 1824 (5 Geo IV c 67) s 1. Although the Imperial Act was passed in 1824, the Supreme Court was not duly constituted until 2 January 1826: see D W Prowse, *A History of Newfoundland*, 2nd rev ed, Eyre and Spottiswoode, London, 1896, p 422.

42 Administration of Justice Act CSN 1872 c 9 (Newfoundland) s 1; Judicature Act CSN 1892 c 50 (Newfoundland) s 2; Judicature Act CSN 1916 c 83 (Newfoundland) s 4; Judicature Act RSN 1952 c 114 (Newfoundland) s 4; Judicature Act RSN 1970 c 187 (Newfoundland) s 4; Judicature Act RSN 1986 c 42 (Newfoundland) s 3.

future loss.[43] It has also been held that damages may be awarded in a case of part performance.[44] However, these cases were based upon a substratum of English cases decided upon *Lord Cairns' Act*.

The absence of *Lord Cairns' Act* in Newfoundland has been recognised by Fridman who has raised the issue of whether the jurisdiction may arise 'on general principles'.[45] It may be held that the jurisdiction is statutory in origin, and could not be exercised in a jurisdiction which had never adopted *Lord Cairns' Act*. However, there may be an argument that the jurisdiction is part of an inherent equity jurisdiction. *Lord Cairns' Act* was not part of the inherited body of Imperial statutes that was received into Newfoundland on 26 July 1832 as it was passed after that date.[46] No warrant for the award of equitable damages could be found in a procedural provision such as s 258 of the Judicature Act SN 1970 c 187 which provided for the adoption of the practice and procedure of the High Court in England.

14.6 Nova Scotia

In the colony of Nova Scotia the Governor was the Chancellor of the colony. This was common practice in British colonies.[47] In 1833 the Master of the Rolls was empowered to exercise primary jurisdiction in Chancery. All decrees that had to be enrolled still had to be signed by the Governor as Chancellor.[48] The Court of Chancery was abolished in 1859. At that time the Supreme Court was created and vested with common law and equitable jurisdiction.[49] An 1864 statute vested the Supreme Court with Chancery jurisdiction.[50] Section 1 of this statute provided:

> The Supreme Court shall have within this province the same powers as are exercised by the courts of queen's bench, common pleas, chancery and exchequer in England.

---

43 *Mayo v Hefferton* (1972) 3 Nfld & PEIR 236; *Luedee v Nova Construction Co Ltd* (1973) 4 Nfld & PEIR 361; *Murphy v Knight* (1983) 42 Nfld & PEIR 304; *Tucker v Gosse* (1984) 48 Nfld & PEIR 163.

44 *Arns v Halliday* (1982) 36 Nfld & PEIR 337.

45 G H L Fridman, *The Law of Contract in Canada*, 2nd ed, Carswell, Toronto, 1986, p 652, n 79.

46 J T Robertson, *Discussion Paper on the Statute of Frauds*, 1677, NLRC — WP 4, 1991, p 23, n 96.

47 A Stokes, *Constitution of the British Colonies*, London, 1788, p 185; J Chitty, *Prerogatives of the Crown*, Butterworth, London, 1820, p 36. See also J T Horton, *James Kent: A Study in Conservatism, 1763–1847*, Appleton-Century Co, New York, 1939, p 199.

48 Chancery Act 1833 (An Act for amending the Practice of the Court of Chancery and diminishing the Expenses thereof) (3 Will IV c 52) (Nova Scotia) s 6. The revised statutes of 1851 continued the requirement for the Chancellor to sign all decrees to be enrolled: see RSNS 1851 c 127 (Nova Scotia) s 5.

49 RSNS 1859 c 127 (Nova Scotia). See also *McAgy v Gray* (1859) 4 NSR 52.

50 An Act in Respect of Courts and Judicial Officers, and Proceedings in Special Cases, RSNS 1864 c 123 (Nova Scotia).

It is not clear whether this provision referred to the statutory jurisdiction vested in the Court of Chancery. An 1873 statute[51] provided for the equity jurisdiction of the court to be confined to the 'Court of the Equity Judge': s 1. That this equity jurisdiction was to be separately exercised was evident from s 22 of this consolidating statute which provided:

> No cause of action heretofore denominated legal shall be contained in a writ or declaration which seeks equitable relief.

An exception was provided in s 53 where a plaintiff sought 'a writ of injunction against the repetition or continuance of such breach of contract or other injury, or the committal of any breach of contract or injury of a like kind arising out of the same contract or relating to the same property or right'. Section 53 enabled a plaintiff 'in the same action' to 'include a claim for damages or other redress'. This section appears to have originated in the 1859 revision of the Nova Scotia statutes.[52] It did not confer jurisdiction to award equitable damages as it did not, unlike *Lord Cairns' Act*, enable damages to be awarded 'in substitution' for an injunction. It appears that no statutory provision corresponding to *Lord Cairns' Act* was ever enacted in Nova Scotia.

The Supreme Court of Nova Scotia was later constituted by The Nova Scotia Judicature Act 1884.[53] Section 8(1) of that Act provided:

> The Supreme Court shall have within this Province the same powers as were formerly exercised by the Courts of Queen's Bench, Common Pleas, Chancery and Exchequer, in England; and also such and the same powers as were on the nineteenth day of April, A.D. 1884, exercised in England by the Supreme Court of Judicature, save in respect of Probate and Surrogate Courts.

This provision would undoubtedly be the source of jurisdiction in the court to award equitable damages under *Lord Cairns' Act*. By including a reference to 'the nineteenth day of April, A.D. 1884' it would presumably be construed as including any statutory jurisdiction possessed by the English High Court on that date. Successive revisions of the Judicature Act have provided for the continuation of the court as constituted in 1884.[54] Consequently, the jurisdiction of the court under *Lord Cairns' Act* has been preserved.[55] The courts have recognised the existence of

---

51 CSNS 1873 c 95 (Nova Scotia) (Procedure in Equity).
52 RSNS 1859 c 127 (Nova Scotia) s 25.
53 RSNS (5th ser) 1884 c 104 (Nova Scotia).
54 Judicature Act RSNS 1900 c 155 (Nova Scotia) s 3; Judicature Act SNS 1919 c 32 (Nova Scotia) s 3; Judicature Act SNS 1950 (Nova Scotia) s 3; Judicature Act SNS 1972 c 2 (Nova Scotia) s 2. See also *Deruelle v Children's Aid Society of Cape Breton* (1978) 26 NSR (2d) 125 at 128.
55 Compare *St Anne-Nackawic Pulp & Paper Co Ltd v Canadian Paper Workers' Union, Local 219* [1986] 1 SCR 704 at 727; (1986) 28 DLR (4th) 1 at 19; 73 NBR (2d) 236 at 262 where the Supreme Court of Canada considered similar legislation which constitutes the Supreme Court of New Brunswick.

jurisdiction under *Lord Cairns' Act* in Nova Scotia.[56] Canadian commentators have noted the absence of an express statutory jurisdiction to award equitable damages in Nova Scotia.[57]

———◦———

14.7 Ontario

Court of Chancery

In 1837 the Court of Chancery of Upper Canada was constituted.[58] The Court of Chancery Act 1859[59] continued the existence of this court. The court later acquired jurisdiction to award equitable damages under s 3 of the Court of Chancery Amendment Act 1865.[60] This provision differed from *Lord Cairns' Act* in providing that 'the Court may grant such other relief as it may deem just', thereby enabling the grant of ancillary relief. In 1871 the court became 'The Court of Chancery for Ontario'.[61] The court followed English authority by declining to award equitable damages where a plaintiff lacked the requisite equity to specific relief.[62] A later reform based upon *Sir John Rolt's Act*[63] provided that where the court had cognisance of the rights of the parties to an agreement, it was required to ascertain the damages to which a party was entitled.[64] The court later became the Court of Chancery of Ontario[65] and acquired jurisdiction to award equitable damages under s 40 of the Chancery Act 1877. Prior to the adoption of the Judicature system a limited reform, which was later adopted in Manitoba, was achieved by the *Administration of Justice Acts* which enabled a plaintiff to proceed at law for a money demand where the right of the plaintiff to recover was equitable.[66]

---

56 *Dominion Supply & Construction Co v Foley Brothers* (1919) 53 NSR 333 at 348; *Carter v Irving Oil Co Ltd* [1952] 4 DLR 128; *Lockwood v Brentwood Park Investments Ltd* (1970) 1 NSR (2d) 669 at 705; *Gallant v MacDonald* (1970) 3 NSR (2d) 137 at 145; *Dempsey v JES Constructions Ltd* (1976) 15 NSR (2d) 448 at 453; *Andrews v RA Douglas Ltd* (1975) 17 NSR (2d) 209 at 216; *McCallum v MacKenzie* (1979) 37 NSR (2d) 328 at 346–7; *MacDonald v Lawrence* (1980) 38 NSR (2d) 319 at 326–7; 40 NSR (2d) 626; *Brean v Thorne* (1982) 52 NSR (2d) 241 at 244. See also P M McDermott, 'Equitable Damages in Nova Scotia', *Dalhousie Law Journal*, vol 12, 1989, p 131.
57 S M Waddams, *The Law of Damages*, Canada Law Book Co, Toronto, 1983, p 52, para 93, n 192; G H L Fridman, *The Law of Contract in Canada*, 2nd ed, Carswell, Toronto, 1986, p 653, n 79.
58 Chancery Act 1837 (An Act to establish a Court of Chancery in this Province) (7 Will 4 c IV c 2) (Upper Canada) s 16.
59 22 Vict c 12 (Upper Canada) s 1.
60 28 Vict c 17 (An Act to amend the Consolidated Statute respecting the Court of Chancery) (Ontario). For the text of s 3 of the Court of Chancery Amendment Act 1865 (Ontario): see Appendix at p 289.
61 SO 1870–1871 c 8 (An Act to alter the names of the Superior Courts in Ontario) (Ontario) s 3.
62 *Brockington v Palmer* (1871) 18 Gr 488; *O'Donnell v Black* (1873) 19 Gr 620.
63 Chancery Regulation Act 1862 (25 & 26 Vict c 42).
64 Administration of Justice Act of 1873 (36 Vict c 8) (Ontario) s 32. See also *Casey v Hanlon* (1875) 22 Gr 445.
65 Chancery Act 1877 RSO 1877 c 40 (Ontario).
66 Administration of Justice Act of 1873 (36 Vict c 8) (Ontario) s 2; Administration of

Supreme Court

The Court of Chancery was consolidated into the Supreme Court of Judicature for Ontario by the Ontario Judicature Act 1881[67] upon the adoption of the Judicature system. A plaintiff could thereafter be awarded common law damages in a case where specific performance was not available.[68] The jurisdiction of the Court of Chancery was transferred to the Supreme Court under s 9 of the Act and the Supreme Court as a result acquired jurisdiction to award equitable damages. An express jurisdiction to award equitable damages was conferred upon the Supreme Court by s 53(9) of the Judicature Act 1887.[69] This subsection was in the same terms as s 40 of the Chancery Act which empowered the court to grant 'other relief'. This conferral of jurisdiction to grant ancillary relief was unnecessary as the court could grant the parties such relief to which they were entitled to avoid a multiplicity of proceedings.[70] Successive enactments of the Judicature Act have contained provisions which were derived from s 53(9) of the Judicature Act 1887.[71] The words 'if it thinks fit', which merely emphasised the discretionary aspect of the jurisdiction,[72] were omitted from statutes enacted after 1913. This omission was of no consequence as the courts have always regarded the provisions as conferring jurisdiction under Lord Cairns' Act.[73]

Justice Act RSO 1877 c 49 (Ontario) s 4, repealed by the Ontario Judicature Act 1881 (44 Vict c 5) (Ontario). See also Soules v Soules (1874) 35 UCQB 334; Bank of Hamilton v Western Assurance Co (1876) 38 UCQB 609; Cole v Bank of Montreal (1876) 39 UCQB 54; Kavanagh v Corp of the City of Kingston (1876) 39 UCQB 415; Kelly v Isolated Risk and Farmers' Fire Insurance Co (1876) 26 UCCP 299; Parkinson v Clendinning (1878) 29 UCCP 13. Similar legislation was at this time enacted in Queensland, and later in Western Australia: see Barbagallo v J & F Catelan Pty Ltd [1986] 1 Qd R 245 at 254–5; P M McDermott, 'Equitable Claims and Demands — Queensland District and Magistrats Courts and the Western Australian Local Courts', University of Queensland Journal, vol 16, 1991, p 212.

67 SO 1881 44 Vict c 5 (Ontario).
68 Corp of the City of St Thomas v Credit Valley Railway Co (1885) 12 OAR 273 at 279; Stuart v McVicar (1898) 18 PR 250 at 254.
69 RSO 1887 c 44 (Ontario).
70 Judicature Act RSO 1877 c 44 (Ontario) s 53. See now Courts of Justice Act RSO 1984 c 11 (Ontario) s 148.
71 Judicature Act SO 1895 (58 Vict c 12) (Ontario) s 53(9); Judicature Act RSO 1897 c 51 (Ontario) s 58(10); Judicature Act SO 1913 (3–4 Geo V c 19) (Ontario) s 18; Judicature Act RSO 1914 c 56 (Ontario) s 18; Judicature Act RSO 1927 c 88 (Ontario) s 17; Judicature Act RSO 1937 c 100 (Ontario) s 17; Judicature Act RSO 1950 c 190 (Ontario) s 18; Judicature Act RSO 1960 c 197 (Ontario) s 18; Judicature Act RSO 1970 c 228 (Ontario) s 21; Judicature Act RSO 1980 c 223 (Ontario) s 21.
72 Aynsley v Glover (1874) LR 18 Eq 544 at 554.
73 Snider v McKelvey (1900) 27 OAR 339 at 344; McIntyre v Stockdale (1912) 27 OLR 460; Feinberg v Weisfeld (1924) 27 OWN 363; Duchman v Oakland Dairy Co Ltd (1928) 63 OLR 111 at 120, 127, 134; KVP Co Ltd v McKie [1949] SCR 698 at 702; [1949] 4 DLR 497 at 500; Tozer v Berry [1955] OWN 68; Dobson v Winton and Robbins Ltd [1959] SCR 775 at 778; JG Collins Insurance Agencies Ltd v Elsley [1978] 2 SCR 916 at 934; (1978) 83 DLR (3d) 1 at 13. See also Tolton v Canadian Pacific Railway Co (1892) 22 OR 204; Arthur v Grand Trunk Railway Co (1894) 25 OR 37; Appleby v Erie Tobacco Co (1910) 22 OLR 533 at 538; Haggerty v Latreille (1913) 29 OLR 300 at 312; Chadwick v City of Toronto (1914) 32 OLR 111 at 113; Campbell v Township of Morris (1923) 54 OLR 358 at 394;

The Supreme Court of Ontario may award equitable damages under s 99 of the Courts of Justice Act[74] (which is identical to s 112 of the Courts of Justice Act 1984[75]). This provision is derived from s 50 of the Supreme Court Act 1981 (Eng).

District Court

The District Court may determine an action where the sum claimed or the value of the property does not exceed a specified monetary limit. The court may grant the same remedies as the Supreme Court, excepting prerogative remedies.[76] The court may therefore grant an injunction or specific performance. As s 99 of the Courts of Justice Act confers jurisdiction to award equitable damages upon 'a court that has jurisdiction to grant an injunction or order specific performance', the court can award equitable damages.

---<o>---

14.8 Prince Edward Island

The Governor of Prince Edward Island originally presided as the Chancellor of the colony.[77] This was in accordance with the practice in other British colonies. In 1848 a Master of the Rolls was appointed to exercise all jurisdiction in equity. In 1859 a Vice-Chancellor and an Assistant Judge of the Supreme Court were appointed to have Chancery jurisdiction with the Master of the Rolls.[78] Jurisdiction to award equitable damages was initially vested in the Court of Chancery under s 9 of the Chancery Act 1900.[79] This provision was derived from *Lord Cairns' Act*. Successive revisions of the Chancery Act have contained provisions which were derived from s 9 of the Chancery Act 1900.[80]

Point v Dibblee Construction Co Ltd [1934] OR 142 at 149; *Bottom v Ontario Leaf Tobacco Co Ltd* [1935] OR 205 at 209; *WC Pitfield & Co Ltd v Jomac Gold Syndicate Ltd* [1938] OR 427 at 446; *Godfrey v Good Rich Refining Co Ltd* [1940] OR 190; *Walker v McKinnon Industries Ltd* [1949] OR 549; *City of Toronto v Hutton* [1953] OWN 205 at 207; *Maker v Davanne Holdings Ltd* [1954] OR 935; *Denison v Carrousel Farms Ltd* (1981) 129 DLR (3d) 334 at 341–2; *Bowes & Cocks Ltd v Aspirant Investments Ltd* (1984) 31 RPR 63 at 72.

74 RSO 1990 c C 43. The Revised Statutes of Ontario 1990 have renumbered what used to be s 112 of the Courts of Justice Act as s 99.

75 SO 1984 c 11 (Ontario). For the text of s 99 of the Courts of Justice Act RSO 1990 c C 43 (Ontario): see Appendix at p 289. See also *Children's Aid Society of Hamilton-Wentworth v Burrell* (1986) 56 OR (2d) 40 at 56; 9 CPC (2d) 298 at 320; *Sharma v Hnatiuk* (1987) 58 OR (2d) 345 at 351.

76 Court of Justice Act 1984 (Ontario) ss 32, 35.

77 F MacKinnon, *The Government of Prince Edward Island*, University of Toronto Press, Toronto, 1951, pp 27, 36.

78 MacKinnon, n 77 above, p 261. The office of Master of the Rolls ceased in 1924: see Sir R Evershed, 'Government under Law in Post-War England', *Law Quarterly Review*, vol 72, 1956, p 42.

79 63 Vict c 2 (An Act to diminish unnecessary delay and expense in the Court of Chancery) (Prince Edward Is).

80 Chancery Act 1910 c 8 (Prince Edward Is) s 56; Chancery Act RSPEI 1940 c 11 (Prince Edward Is) s 45; Chancery Act RSPEI 1951 c 21 (Prince Edward Is) s 45.

The Judicature system was introduced into Prince Edward Island in 1974. Before 1974 the Supreme Court had an ancillary jurisdiction to determine equitable claims or defences in a suit which was properly before the court.[81] Upon the introduction of the Judicature system, the jurisdiction of the Court of Chancery was transferred to the Supreme Court by s 9(1) of the Judicature Act.[82] This general transfer of jurisdiction included jurisdiction that was conferred upon the Court of Chancery under the Chancery Act (with certain exceptions which were specified in s 9(2) of the Judicature Act, namely ss 71–8, 81, 107–13). Accordingly the jurisdiction to award equitable damages under s 45 of the Chancery Act 1951 was transferred to the Supreme Court.[83] In 1987 the Judicature Act was repealed by the Supreme Court Act.[84] Section 32 of the Supreme Court Act provides that the Supreme Court has jurisdiction to award damages in addition to or in substitution for an injunction or specific performance.[85] Prior to the enactment of the Supreme Court Act, some Canadian commentators had recognised the absence of an express statutory jurisdiction to award equitable damages in Prince Edward Island.[86]

14.9 Saskatchewan

Upon the creation of Saskatchewan, the Supreme Court of the Northwest Territories continued to exercise jurisdiction in the province (as in Alberta).[87] That court could award equitable damages under s 10(9) of the Judicature Ordinance 1898. The Supreme Court of Saskatchewan was constituted by the Judicature Act 1907.[88] The court was empowered to award equitable damages under s 31 of the Judicature Act which was identical to s 10(9) of the Judicature Ordinance. Identical provisions, which have been held to confer jurisdiction under *Lord Cairns' Act*,[89] are to be found in the Judicature Act 1909[90] and successive revisions of the

---

81 Judicature Act RSPEI 1974 c J-3, s 14(1). See *Solomon v Currie* (1965) 51 MPR 252.

82 RSPEI 1974 c J-3 (Prince Edward Is) (as inserted by s 2 of the Chancery Jurisdiction Transfer Act 1974 (23 Eliz II c 65)) s 2.

83 For the text of s 45 of the Chancery Act 1951 (Prince Edward Is): see Appendix at p 289.

84 1987 c 66.

85 For the text of s 32 of the Supreme Court Act (Prince Edward Is): see Appendix at p 289.

86 S M Waddams, *The Law of Damages*, Canada Law Book Co, Toronto, 1983, p 52, para 93, n 192; G H L Fridman, *The Law of Contract in Canada*, 2nd ed, Carswell, Toronto, 1986, p 652, n 79.

87 Saskatchewan Act 1905 4-5 EdwVII c 42 (Canada) s 16.

88 1907 c 8 (Saskatchewan).

89 *McKenzie v Hiscock* [1967] SCR 781; (1967) 65 DLR (2d) 123 at 130; *Kopec v Pyret* [1987] 3 WWR 449 at 461; (1987) 36 DLR (4th) 1 at 11; 55 Sask R 172. See also *Masai Minerals Ltd v Heritage Resources Ltd* [1979] 2 WWR 352; *Ulmer v Ulmer* (1979) 5 Sask R 3; *Shindelka v Rosten* [1982] 5 WWR 395; *McClenaghan v Haley* [1983] 5 WWR 586; (1983) 148 DLR (3d) 577; 23 Sask R 212; *Kopec v Pyret* [1983] 4 WWR 246; (1983) 146 DLR (3d) 242; 25 Sask R 280.

90 Judicature Act RSS 1909 c 52 (Saskatchewan) s 31(9).

Queen's (or King's) Bench Act.[91] The court may award equitable damages under s 45(9) of the Queen's Bench Act.[92] This provision differs from *Lord Cairns' Act* by enabling the court to 'grant such other relief as may be deemed just'. This jurisdiction to grant ancillary relief was exercised in *Shindelka v Rosten*[93] where the court granted an easement to the defendant during the 'life' of an encroaching building where the plaintiff had received a damages award in a prior judgment. The jurisdiction to grant ancillary relief originated in Ontario before the adoption of the Judicature system,[94] and is now unnecessary as the court may grant the parties such relief to which they are entitled so as to avoid a multiplicity of proceedings.[95]

———◁▷———

14.10 *Canadian Territories*

The Supreme Court of the Northwest Territories and the Supreme Court of the Yukon Territory possess jurisdiction to award equitable damages. Successive revisions of the Judicature Ordinance in the Northwest Territories[96] and the Yukon Territory[97] conferred this jurisdiction on those courts. The provisions differ from *Lord Cairns' Act* by providing that the court 'may grant such other relief as it may deem just'. This express conferral of jurisdiction to grant ancillary relief is unnecessary as under the Judicature system the courts may grant the parties to a suit such relief to which they are entitled so as to avoid a multiplicity of proceedings.[98] The provision originated in Ontario before the English Judicature system was adopted in the province.[99]

---

91 *Saskatchewan:* King's Bench Act RSS 1915 c 10 s 25(9); King's Bench Act RSS 1930 c 49 s 27(9); King's Bench Act RSS 1940 c 61 s 28(9); Queen's Bench Act RSS 1953 c 67 s 44(9); Queen's Bench Act RSS 1965 c 73 s 45(9); Queen's Bench Act RSS 1978 c Q-1 s 45(9).

92 *Saskatchewan:* RSS 1978 c Q-1. For the text of s 45(9) of the Queen's Bench Act 1953: see Appendix at p 289.

93 [1982] 5 WWR 395 at 405–6.

94 Court of Chancery Act Amendment Act 1865 (28 Vict c 17) (Ontario) s 3: see Appendix at p 289.

95 Queen's Bench Act RSS 1978 c Q-1 (Saskatchewan) s 44 r 7. See *Childs v Montreal Trust Co of Canada* [1988] 1 WWR 746; (1988) 59 Sask R 310; 45 DLR (4th) 282.

96 *Northwest Territories:* Judicature Ordinance RONWT 1888 c 58 s 9(9); Judicature Ordinance ONWT 1893 c 6 s 10(9); Judicature Ordinance CONWT 1898 c 21 s 10(9); Judicature Ordinance ONWT 1905 c 21 s 10(9); Judicature Ordinance RONWT 1970 c 5 s 20(i); Judicature Act RSNWT 1974 c J-1 s 19(i); Judicature Act RSNWT 1988 s 42. For the text of s 42 of the Judicature Act RSNWT 1988 c J-1: see Appendix at p 290.

97 *Yukon:* Judicature Ordinance COYT 1902 c 17 s 10(9); Judicature Ordinance COYT 1914 c 48 s 8(9); Judicature Ordinance ROYT 1958 c 60 s 10(i); Judicature Ordinance ROYT 1971 c J-1 s 10(1)(i); Judicature Ordinance ROYT 1978 c J-1 s 10(1)(i); Judicature Act RSY 1986 c 96 s 27. See also *Treadgold v Rost* (1912) 7 DLR 741 at 753. For the text of s 27 of the Judicature Act RSY 1986 c 96: see Appendix at p 290.

98 Judicature Act SNWT 1974 c J-1 (Northwest Territories) s 18(e); Judicature Ordinance ROYT 1978 c J-1 (Yukon) s 8(e).

99 See Judicature Ordinance ONWT 1888 c 58 (Ontario) s 10(9) (footnote).

15

Commonwealth Jurisdictions

15.1 *General*

In most Commonwealth countries the superior courts have jurisdiction to award equitable damages under the Chancery Amendment Act 1858 (*Lord Cairns' Act*),[1] or a statutory successor. This is the case in the United Kingdom, Ireland, Australia, New Zealand and Canada.

In a number of Commonwealth countries the superior court of record (usually designated as the Supreme Court or High Court) possesses the jurisdiction of the High Court of Justice in England. This is the case in Fiji,[2] The Gambia,[3] Gibraltar,[4] various West Indian jurisdictions[5] and

---

1   21 & 22 Vict c 27.

2   Supreme Court Ordinance Revised Laws 1978 s 18 (Fiji).

3   Courts Act Rev Laws 1966 c 36 (L/N 9/1965) s 3(1) (Gambia).

4   Supreme Court Ordinance 1960 No 2 s 12 (Gibraltar).

5   Antigua and Barbuda: Supreme Court Act (20/1939) Revised Laws 1962 c 81 s 22; West Indies Associated States Supreme Court Act 1969 (No 26 of 1969) s 7(1); The Bahamas: Supreme Court Act Revised Laws 1957 c 54 s 29; *Grenada*: Supreme Court Ordinance (L1 2/1928) Revised Laws 1961 c 28 s 25(1) (Grenada); see also Supreme Court Act 1913 (4/13) Rev Laws 1927 c 22 (Leeward Islands) s 33(2); *St Christopher (St Kitts) and Nevis*: Supreme Court Ordinance (28 of 1896) Revised Laws 1934 c 220 ss 3, 6; *St Vincent and the Grenadines*: Supreme Court Ordinance (28 of 1896) Revised Laws 1966 c 7 s 4; *Trinidad and Tobago*: Supreme Court of Judicature Act (No 12 of

---

269

Zambia.[6] In these countries the courts may award equitable damages under *Lord Cairns' Act* as the High Court would have possessed this jurisdiction when the relevant provisions became law. An exception is Gibraltar where the Supreme Court may exercise the jurisdiction which is vested in the English High Court 'from time to time'.[7] Consequently in Gibraltar equitable damages may be awarded under s 50 of the English Supreme Court Act 1981.

In some countries a basis for the award of equitable damages under *Lord Cairns' Act* can be found in provisions which apply English statutes of general application. For example, this is the case in Kenya[8] and Tonga.[9]

The remainder of this chapter examines the position in Barbados, Bermuda, Hong Kong, India and Pakistan, Jamaica, Malaysia, Nigeria and Singapore.

———◦———

15.2 Barbados

In 1859 the Chief Justice of Barbados was constituted as the Vice-Chancellor with jurisdiction to determine proceedings in the Court of Chancery, thereby assuming the jurisdiction which was vested in the Governor as Chancellor.[10] The Court of Chancery was vested with jurisdiction under *Lord Cairns' Act* by s 18 of the Chancery Act 1889.[11] This provision was adopted in successive revisions of the Chancery Act.[12] In 1956 the Judicature system was adopted in Barbados upon the constitution of the Supreme Court of Barbados. The jurisdiction of the Court of Chancery was transferred to the Supreme Court under s 11(2) of the Supreme Court of Judicature Act 1956.[13] The jurisdiction to award equitable damages would have been included in this general transfer of Chancery jurisdiction. The Supreme Court may therefore award equitable damages under s 73 of the Chancery Act 1906.[14] In *Saunders v Haymans Sugar Factory Ltd*[15] Chenery VC declined to award equitable damages in substitution for an injunction to restrain a nuisance caused by pollution from a sugar factory.

———◦———

1962) LRO 1980 c 401 s 9; *Turks and Caicos Islands*: Supreme Court Ordinance (No 5 of 1903) Revised Statutes c 3 s 3.

6 High Court Act (41 of 1960) Revised Laws c 50 (Zambia) s 9. See also High Court Ordinance (1 of 1913) Rev Laws 1930 c 3 (Northern Rhodesia).

7 Supreme Court Ordinance 1984 Edition (Gibraltar) s 12.

8 Judicature Act Revised Statutes c 8 (Kenya) s 3.

9 Civil Law Act (No 12 of 1966) Revised Statutes 1977 c 14 (Tonga) s 3.

10 No 341, 12 October 1859 (Barbados).

11 Session of 1888–1889, cap XLIII, 20 July 1889 (Barbados).

12 See eg Chancery Act 1891 No 51 (Barbados) s 71; Chancery Act 1906 No5 (Barbados) s 73.

13 1956–1956. See LRO 1985 cap 117 (Barbados).

14 For the text of s 73 of the Chancery Act 1906 (Barbados): see Appendix at p 291.

15 (1955) 1 Barb LR 51.

15.3 Bermuda

The Court of the General Assize was constituted as the Court of Chancery under s 4 of the Court of Chancery Act 1876,[16] thereby acquiring the Chancery jurisdiction formerly exercised by the Governor as Chancellor. The court was also vested with the jurisdiction of the Chancery Division of the High Court of Justice in England. The Court of Chancery therefore acquired jurisdiction to award equitable damages under *Lord Cairns' Act*. In 1905 the jurisdiction of the superior courts in Bermuda, including the Court of Chancery, was transferred to the Supreme Court of Bermuda by virtue of s 10(1) of the Supreme Court Act 1905.[17] The jurisdiction under *Lord Cairns' Act* was included in this general transfer of jurisdiction.

15.4 Hong Kong

The Court of Appeal and the High Court possess jurisdiction to award equitable damages under s 17 of the Supreme Court Ordinance.[18] This provision is derived from s 50 of the English Supreme Court Act 1981. Section 17 was inserted into the Ordinance in 1987 following a review of the Ordinance to ascertain whether reforms in the United Kingdom should be adopted in Hong Kong.

15.5 India and Pakistan

The Specific Relief Act 1877[19] conferred jurisdiction upon the courts of British India to grant specific and compensatory relief in cases of breach of contract. Section 19 of the Act, in part, provides:

> Any person suing for the specific performance of a contract, may also ask for compensation for its breach, either in addition to, or in substitution for, such performance ... Compensation awarded under this section may be assessed in such manner as the Court may direct.[20]

The provision contained the following explanation:

> EXPLANATION — The circumstance that the contract has become incapable of specific performance, does not preclude the Court from exercising the jurisdiction conferred by this section.

---

16 1876 No 25 (Bermuda).
17 1905 No 4 (Bermuda).
18 Cap 4 revised ed 1987 (Hong Kong) as amended by Supreme Court (Amendment) Ordinance (52/87) (Hong Kong). For the text of s 17 of the Supreme Court Ordinance 1987 (Hong Kong): see Appendix at p 291.
19 Act No 1 of 1877 (British India).
20 For the text of s 19 of the Specific Relief Act 1877 (British India): see Appendix at p 291.

The following illustrations of the explanation were included in the Act:

A, a purchaser, sues B, his vendor, for specific performance of a contract for the sale of a patent. Before the hearing of the suit the patent expires. The Court may award A compensation for the non-performance of the contract, and may, if necessary, amend the plaint for that purpose.

A sues for the specific performance of a resolution passed by the Directors of a public company, under which he was entitled to have a certain number of shares allocated to him, and for compensation for the non-performance of the resolution. All the shares had been allotted before the institution of the suit. The Court may, under this section, award A compensation for the non-performance.

The explanation was applied to award compensation in one case where the relevant property had since the trial, and before the appeal, been vested in the state by compulsory acquisition.[21] However, an award of compensation would not be made where a plaintiff had elected to sue for specific performance knowing that land acquisition proceedings were pending.[22]

The first illustration to the explanation of s 19 of the Specific Relief Act 1877 is obviously based upon the case of *Davenport v Rylands*.[23] In that case it was held that damages may be awarded under *Lord Cairns' Act* where a plaintiff sought an injunction to restrain the infringement of a patent, although the patent had expired before the hearing. In this respect the Specific Relief Act conferred jurisdiction under *Lord Cairns' Act*.

The second illustration to the explanation was obviously based upon the case of *Ferguson v Wilson*[24] in which it was held that damages under *Lord Cairns' Act* could not be awarded where a bill for the specific performance of a contract for the allotment of shares had been filed after the shares had been allotted. In this respect the Specific Relief Act conferred a wider jurisdiction than *Lord Cairns' Act*.

It is obvious that the draftsman of the Specific Relief Act was familiar with the early English authorities on *Lord Cairns' Act*. The Specific Relief Act was introduced by Lord Hobhouse who was the Law Member of the Governor-General's Council (1872–1877). Lord Hobhouse had informed the Council that the Specific Relief Act 'consisted mainly of the law administered by the Court of Chancery'.[25] His biographers have remarked that the Specific Relief Act was 'pre-eminently the work of Mr Hobhouse himself, who, owing to his having practised so long in courts of equity in England, was singularly qualified for such a task'.[26] Lord Hobhouse was one of a number of distinguished lawyers who held the office of Law Member of the Council. Others included Sir James Stephen, Sir Henry Maine and Lord Macauley. The office of Law Member was established

---

21   *Salim Beg v Krishna Ballabh* AIR 1954 MB 76.
22   *Mohamed Abdul Jabbar v Lalmia* AIR 1947 Nag 254.
23   (1865) LR 1 Eq 302.
24   (1866) LR 2 Ch App 77.
25   *Proceedings of the Council of the Governor General of India 1877*, vol XVI, 1878, p 23.
26   L T Hobhouse and J L Hamond, *Lord Hobhouse — A Memoir*, Edward Arnold, London, 1905, p 87. See also *Dictionary of National Biography*, vol II, Smith, Elder & Co, London, 2nd supp, 1912, p 272.

through the influence of James Mill of the East India Company who was a disciple of Bentham.[27]

The various Indian Codes had to be administered by civil servants who had no access to a law library, and who had only elementary legal training. The task of administering the Codes was assisted by the use of illustrations to show how various provisions had application in particular situations. This was particularly evident in the Evidence Act which was drafted by Sir James Stephen.

Although in British India the courts could concurrently administer legal and equitable remedies, the Specific Relief Act emphasised the elective nature of these remedies. Specific performance of a contract could not be enforced in favour of a person 'who has already chosen his remedy and obtained satisfaction for the alleged breach of contract': s 24(c). Similarly the Act provided that the dismissal of a suit for the specific performance of a contract 'shall bar the plaintiff's right to sue for compensation for the breach of such contract': s 29. It was however clear that the mere fact that a plaintiff in the pleadings sought alternative relief of an award of compensation did not prejudice the right of that plaintiff to obtain a decree of specific performance.[28] An alternative prayer for compensation is ordinarily made by way of precaution, as granting of a decree of specific performance is discretionary with the court even if the plaintiff has proved a breach of contract.[29]

Although the Specific Relief Act did not expressly provide that an averment of readiness and willingness to perform a contract is necessary in a specific performance action, the Privy Council in *Mama v Sassoon*[30] considered that, on principle, there was no difference between English and Indian practice in this respect.[31] The Privy Council also held that, apart from the divergence from *Ferguson v Wilson*,[32] s 19 of the Specific Relief Act 'embodies the same principle as *Lord Cairns' Act*'.[33] The Privy Council came to this conclusion because of the close correspondence of the terms of s 19 with those of s 2 of *Lord Cairns' Act*, coupled with the presence in the Specific Relief Act of ss 24(c) and 29 indicating the old distinction between the equitable and legal forms of remedy. The Board accordingly held that compensation could not be awarded under s 19 of the Specific Relief Act where the plaintiff had debarred himself from asking at the hearing for specific performance.

The Indian courts also adopted other English principles. For example, there is authority that compensation may be awarded even though not specifically claimed in the plaint.[34] However, the correctness of this approach may be doubted because s 19 required a plaintiff to 'ask for compensation'.[35]

---

27 Sir L Stephen, *Life of Sir James Fitzjames Stephen*, Smith Elder & Co, London, 1895, pp 246-8.
28 *Devendra v Sonubai* AIR 1971 Mys 217; *Zaibun Sa Binti Syed Ahmad v Loh Koon Moy* [1982] 2 MLJ 92 at 94 (PC).
29 *Kumaraswamy v Rudraradhya* AIR 1966 Mys 215.
30 (1928) LR 55 IA 360; 52 Bom 597.
31 See also *Karsandas v Chhotalal* (1923) 25 Bom 1037 at 1050.
32 (1866) LR 2 Ch App 77.
33 (1928) LR 55 IA 360 at 376; 52 Bom 597 at 623.
34 *Gokul Chandra v Haji Mohammed* AIR 1938 Calcutta 136.
35 *Somasundaram v Chidambaram* AIR 1951 Madras 282 at 283.

Section 21(5) of the 1963 Act now provides that a claim for compensation should be made in a plaint before an award can be made.[36] It is not enough for a plaintiff in a suit for specific performance to merely establish that a contract has been broken. It is also necessary for a plaintiff to prove some loss or damage before a court may award compensation.[37] In reliance on *Mama v Sassoon*[38] it would still be necessary for a plaintiff to prove willingness and readiness to perform a contract. It is submitted that authorities on the Malaysian Specific Relief Act may also be relevant.

The Specific Relief Act 1877 is still in force in Pakistan.[39] In India the Specific Relief Act 1877 was repealed by s 44 of the Specific Relief Act 1963.[40] In India, compensation in addition to or in substitution for specific performance may now be awarded under s 21 of the Specific Relief Act 1963.[41] This provision was derived from s 19 of the Specific Relief Act 1877. One reform which was introduced by the Specific Relief Act 1963 was the conferral of jurisdiction to award compensation in a suit for an injunction. This jurisdiction is of particular relevance where a *quia timet* injunction is sought. The Indian courts have assumed that they have the same jurisdiction in this regard as the English High Court.[42] However, the Specific Relief Act 1877 did not correspond to *Lord Cairns' Act* by enabling compensation to be awarded where an injunction was sought. This was recognised by the Law Commission of India which stated that 's 19 was not extended by the framers of the Act to an action for an injunction'.[43] The Law Commission accordingly proposed the conferral of an express statutory jurisdiction to award compensation where an injunction is sought. The Law Commission concluded:

> In the circumstances it is advisable to make a specific provision in the Act for that purpose. We recommend that a new provision on the lines of s 19 of the Act be added to cover cases arising under sections 54 and 55 of the Specific Relief Act.[44]

Sections 54 and 55 of the 1877 Act related to the jurisdiction of the courts to grant perpetual and mandatory injunctions respectively. This recommendation of the Law Commission was reflected in s 40 of the Specific Relief Act 1963.[45] Subsections (1) and (2) of s 40 of the Specific Relief Act 1963 were essentially derived from the recommendations of the

---

36 Compare *AP Pradeshak Sabba v Lahori* (1924) 5 Lah 509; *Salim Beg v Krishna Ballabh* AIR 1954 MB 76 at 78.

37 *Ramchandra v Chinubhai* AIR 1944 Bom 76 at 86.

38 (1928) LR 55 IA 360; 52 Bom 597.

39 S M I K Mokai, *The Specific Relief Act, 1877*, Lahore, 1978; M Mahmood, *The Specific Relief Act, 1877*, Lahore, 1979.

40 47 of 1963 (India).

41 For the text of s 21 of the Specific Relief Act 1963 (India): see Appendix at p 292. See also *AP* [1977] Labour and Industrial Cases 1583.

42 *Callianji Hirjivan v Narsi Tricum* (1895) ILR 19 Bom 764; *Kalliandas v Tulsidas* (1899) ILR 23 Bom 786; *Krishnan Pillai v Kilasathommal* AIR 1928 Madras 810; *Kalyandas Gokaldas v Hiralal Karnsdas* AIR 1954 Sau 139.

43 Law Commission of India, *Specific Relief Act, 1877*, Ninth Report, 1958, p 53.

44 Law Commission of India, *Specific Relief Act, 1877*, Ninth Report, 1958, p 53.

45 For the text of s 40 of the Specific Relief Act 1963 (India): see see Appendix at p 292.

Law Commission.[46] The proviso to s 40(2) and (3) were amendments made to the draft Bill by the Government of India.

Another reform recommended by the Law Commission related to the method of assessment of compensation. There were a number of decisions that the word 'compensation' in s 19 of the Specific Relief Act 1877 referred to damages under s 73 of the Indian Contract Act 1872.[47] However, in *Sassoon v Ardeshir*[48] Macleod CJ considered that the word 'compensation' was used to emphasise the fact that the courts were not bound to follow the ordinary rules relating to damages for breach of contract. To clarify the position the Law Commission concluded:

> In these circumstances, we think it desirable to provide that compensation under the present section should be assessed on the same principles as are followed under s 73 of the Contract Act.[49]

The Law Commission proposed the adoption of the following provision:

> Compensation awarded under this section may be assessed according to the principles laid down in s 73 of the Indian Contract Act, 1872, and under such procedure as the court may direct.[50]

This recommendation was reflected in s 21(4) of the Specific Relief Act 1963 which provides for the court to be guided by the principles specified in s 73 of the Indian Contract Act 1872. An award of compensation may include loss sustained by delay in performing a contract.[51]

———◦———

15.6 *Jamaica*

The Governor of Jamaica originally exercised jurisdiction as Chancellor of the colony.[52] It was a common practice for the Governor of a British colony to be constituted Chancellor of a colony.[53] Section 9 of the Judicial Amendment Act 1855[54] provided for the jurisdiction of the Court of Chancery to be vested in the Chief Justice who was thereby appointed as the Vice-Chancellor of Jamaica.[55] The jurisdictions of the superior courts

46 Law Commission of India, *Specific Relief Act, 1877*, Ninth Report, 1958, pp 76–7.
47 *Pratapchand v Raghunath* AIR 1937 Nag 243; *Dwarkaprasad Florence v Kathelen* AIR 1955 Nag 28.
48 AIR 1926 Bom 189.
49 Law Commission of India, *Specific Relief Act, 1877*, Ninth Report, 1958, p 18.
50 Law Commission of India, *Specific Relief Act, 1877*, Ninth Report, 1958, p 65.
51 *Kamaraswamy v Rudraradhya* AIR 1966 Mys 215 at 217.
52 *The Laws of Jamaica*, 1683, Preface, p c3. ('His Majesty has also constituted in this Island a Court of Chancery wherein the Governour himself always sits as Chancellour, assisted by several discreet Gentlemen of Eminency as Masters.')
53 A Stokes, *Constitution of the British Colonies*, 1788, p 185; J Chitty, *Prerogatives of the Crown*, Butterworths, London, 1820, p 36.
54 19 Vict c 10 (Jamaica).
55 H V T Chambers, *Essays on the Jamaican Legal System*, Metro Press, Kingston, 1974, p 42.

of the colony, including the High Court of Chancery, were later consolidated into the Supreme Court of Judicature of Jamaica under the Judicature Law 1879.[56] The Supreme Court upon its creation did not acquire any statutory jurisdiction to award equitable damages. This is because no provision corresponding to s 2 of *Lord Cairns' Act* was ever enacted in Jamaica. This was recognised by the Federal Supreme Court in *Gloucester House Ltd v Peskin.*[57]

————◁○▷————

15.7 Malaysia

In Malaysia, compensation in the nature of equitable damages may be awarded under the Specific Relief Act 1950[58] (formerly the Specific Relief (Malay States) Ordinance 1950) which was derived from the Indian Specific Relief Act. Section 18 of the Specific Relief Act allows a court to award compensation either in addition to or in substitution for the specific performance of a contract.[59] This provision is derived from *Lord Cairns' Act.*[60]

The Malaysian courts cite precedents upon the Indian Specific Relief Act, such as the decision in *Mama v Sassoon.*[61] Accordingly it has been held that an award of compensation can only be made where a plaintiff has claimed specific performance.[62] An award of compensation can also be made under s 18(3) of the Act where an order of specific performance is not sufficient to satisfy the justice of the case.[63] Specific performance or an award of compensation cannot be ordered where a plaintiff fails to prove readiness and willingness to perform a contract,[64] where any order for specific performance would require an impractical degree of supervision by the court[65] or where a plaintiff has accepted the rescission of a contract.[66] It is also suggested that the courts will follow those Indian authorities which have held that compensation may be awarded where a writ does not contain a claim for damages in the alternative.[67] However, in

---

56 24 of 1879 (Jamaica). See now Judicature (Supreme Court) Act Cap 180 (Jamaica) s 4, Revised Laws of Jamaica, 1974 Edition.
57 (1961) 3 WIR 375.
58 Act 137 (Revised 1974) (Malaysia).
59 For the text of s 18 of the Specific Relief Act 1950 (Malaysia): see Appendix at p 293.
60 V Sinnadurai, *The Law of Contract in Malaysia and Singapore: Cases and Commentary*, 2nd ed, Butterworths, Singapore, 1987, p 783.
61 (1928) LR 55 IA 360.
62 *Lee Hoy v Chen Chi* [1971] 1 MLJ 76 at 77.
63 *City Investment Sdn Bhd v Koperasi Serbaguna Cuepacs Tanggungan Bhd* [1985] 1 MLJ 285 at 293 per Mohamed Azmi FJ; *Rasiah Munusamy v Lim Tan & Sons Sdn Bhd* [1985] 2 MLJ 287 at 297 per Mohamed Azmi SCC.
64 *Ganam D/O Rajamany v Somoo S/O Sinnah* [1984] 2 MLJ 290. See also *Tan Meng San v Lim Kim Swee* (1962) 28 MLJ 174.
65 *Lee Sau Kong v Leow Cheng Chiang* (1961) 27 MLJ 17 at 20.
66 *Chin Kim v Loh Boon Siew* [1970] 1 MLJ 197.
67 *Salim Beg v Krishna Ballabh* AIR 1954 MB 76 at 78.

one case the Privy Council did not have to determine this issue, which Lord Cross of Chelsea regarded as a 'difficult question', as the appellant by accepting the repudiation of a contract had disentitled himself to a decree for specific performance.[68]

The Privy Council has also emphasised that the commonplace fact of an alternative claim for damages in an action by a purchaser for specific performance of a contract cannot be relevant as to whether specific performance ought to be ordered.[69]

Section 18(5) of the Specific Relief Act provides that the circumstance that a contract has become incapable of specific performance shall not preclude the court from exercising the jurisdiction conferred by the section.[70] This subsection was originally constituted in the explanation which followed s 18 of the Specific Relief Ordinance 1950.

In assessing compensation under s 18 of the Specific Relief Act the courts in Malaysia would rely upon s 74 of the Contracts Act 1950,[71] which was derived from the Indian Contract Act.[72]

———◦———

15.8 Nigeria

Chapter VII of the Constitution of Nigeria[73] (decreed by the Federal Military Government in 1978) relates to the Judicature of Nigeria. Section 234 of the Constitution provides that there shall be a High Court for each state of the Federation. The High Court is the superior court in each state.[74] Section 236 of the Constitution provides that the High Court of a state shall have unlimited jurisdiction to hear and determine any civil proceedings. The House of Assembly of each state may make laws conferring jurisdiction upon the High Court of each state. The High Court of a state generally possesses the same jurisdiction as the High Court of Justice in England. The relevant legislation usually provides that the High Court shall 'possess and exercise all the jurisdiction, powers and authorities which are vested in or capable of being exercised by the High Court of Justice in England'.[75] This conferral of jurisdiction would enable the Nigerian High Courts to exercise jurisdiction under *Lord Cairns' Act*. A number of commentators have recognised that damages

---

68 *Loh Boon Siew v Chin Kim* [1972] 1 MLJ 139 at 143; [1972] 2 PCC 763 at 774 (PC).

69 *Zaibun Sa Binti Syed Ahmad v Loh Koon Moy* [1982] 2 MLJ 92 at 94; [1982] 4 PCC 49 at 54 (PC).

70 *Lee Hoy v Chen Chi* [1971] 1 MLJ 76 at 79.

71 Act 136 (Malaysia).

72 V Sinnadurai, *Law of Contract in Malaysia and Singapore: Cases and Commentary*, 2nd ed, Butterworths, Singapore, 1987, p 785.

73 *Constitution of the Federal Republic of Nigeria (Enactment) Decree*, 1978–1978, No 25.

74 The High Courts are discussed by Dr D I O Ewehukwa in his essay 'Administration of Justice' in *Introduction to Nigerian Law*, ed C O Okonkwo, Sweet & Maxwell, London, 1980, pp 118–28.

75 See eg High Court Law s 9 Revised Laws 1976 cap 65 (Bendel); High Court Law s 10 Revised Laws 1973 cap 52 (Lagos); High Court Law s 9 Rev Laws 1978 cap 45 (Ondo).

under *Lord Cairns' Act* may be awarded in Nigeria.[76] In a trespass case it was recognised that a court has a discretion to award damages in lieu of an injunction.[77]

————◄○►————

15.9 Singapore

Lord Cairns' Act was an Imperial statute which was received as part of the law of Singapore as it was passed after the Second Charter of Justice of 1826. However, at one time the Supreme Court of the Straits Settlements possessed jurisdiction under *Lord Cairns' Act*. In *Tan Seng Qui v Palmer*[78] it was assumed that this jurisdiction had been conferred by s 10 of the Courts Ordinance 1878[79] which conferred upon the Supreme Court the jurisdiction and authority of judges in England in civil and criminal matters. Later the High Court of Singapore was vested with the jurisdictions of the High Court of Chancery, the Court of Queen's Bench, Common Pleas and Exchequer.[80] Various revisions of the Courts Ordinance vested the court with the same jurisdiction as the High Court of Chancery.[81] For instance, s 17 of the Courts Ordinance 1955 vested the Supreme Court with the jurisdictions of the Chancery and Queen's Bench Divisions of the High Court of Justice in England.[82] Under that provision, which was repealed in 1964, the Supreme Court would have continued to possess jurisdiction to award equitable damages under *Lord Cairns' Act*.

Upon the passage of the Supreme Court of Judicature Act[83] the jurisdiction under *Lord Cairns' Act* was abrogated. The jurisdiction of the High Court is now conferred by the Supreme Court of Judicature Act which confers upon the court such jurisdiction and powers as are vested in it by any written law for the time being in force in Singapore: ss 16 and 18. No written law is in existence which confers jurisdiction under *Lord Cairns' Act*. In *Shiffon Creations (Singapore) Pte Ltd v Tong Lee Co Pte Ltd*[84] Thean J held that the Supreme Court did not have 'the equitable jurisdiction conferred by *Lord Cairns' Act*'.[85] In a Privy Council appeal it

---

76 M I Jegede, *Principles of Equity*, Ethiope Publishing Corp, Benin City, 1981, pp 78–80; J O Fabunmi, *Equity and Trusts in Nigeria*, University of Ife Press, Ife Ife, 1986, p 230. See also *Williams v Smith* (1948) 19 NLR 21.
77 *Odutola v Adeyemo* (Court of Appeal, Western State, Ibadan, 19 April 1974, unreported).
78 (1887) 4 Ky 251.
79 No 3 of 1878 (Straits Settlements).
80 R StJ Braddell, *The Law of the Straits Settlements*, Oxford University Press, New York, 1982, p 67.
81 Ordinance No 101 (Courts) No 30 of 1907 (Singapore) s 8; Courts Ordinance (1934 No 17) (Singapore) s 11. This revision may have been intended to overcome the decision in *Tunku Mahmoud v Tunku Ali* (1897) 5 SSLR 96 which held that the court did not possess jurisdiction under the Chancery Procedure Act 1852.
82 Laws of Singapore 1955 (Singapore) cap 3.
83 Act 24 of 1969 (Revised St c 322 (1985 ed)) (Singapore).
84 [1988] 1 MLJ 363.
85 [1988] 1 MLJ 363 at 371.

is mentioned that a purchaser was awarded damages 'in lieu of specific performance',[86] however it is submitted that this is merely an instance of the award of common law damages for breach of contract. No basis for the exercise of the jurisdiction is to be found in s 5 of the Civil Law Act,[87] which applies English law in mercantile matters.[88] It has been recognised that Singapore should adopt a provision which is derived from s 50 of the Supreme Court Act 1981 (England).[89]

---

86 *Meng Leong Development Pte Ltd v Jip Hong Trading Co Pte Ltd* [1985] AC 511.

87 Ord 8 of 1909 as amended (Revised St c 43 (1985 ed)) (Singapore).

88 See also V Sinnadurai, *The Law of Contract in Malaysia and Singapore: Cases and Commentary*, 2nd ed, Butterworths, Singapore, 1987, p 22.

89 S K Bun, 'Jurisdiction to Award Equitable Damages in Singapore', *Malaya Law Review*, vol 30, 1988, p 79.

Appendix

Statutory Provisions

1 England and Ireland

2 Australia and New Zealand

New South Wales
Queensland
South Australia
Tasmania
Victoria
Western Australia
Commonwealth statutes
New Zealand

3 Canada

Alberta
Manitoba
New Brunswick
Ontario
Prince Edward Island
Saskatchewan
Northwest Territories
Yukon Territory

4 Commonwealth Jurisdictions

Barbados
Hong Kong
India and Pakistan
Malaysia

———◦———

1 England and Ireland

Chancery Amendment Act 1858 (Lord Cairns' Act)
(21 & 22 Vict c 27)
Section 2

In all cases in which the Court of Chancery has Jurisdiction to entertain an Application for an Injunction against a Breach of any Covenant, Contract, or Agreement, or against the Commission or Continuance of any wrongful act, or for the Specific Performance of any Covenant, Contract or Agreement, it shall be lawful for the same Court, if it shall think fit, to award damages to the Party injured either in addition to or in substitution for such Injunction or Specific Performance, and such damages may be assessed in such manner as the Court shall direct.

Judicature (Northern Ireland) Act 1978
(1978 c 23)
Section 92

Where a court has jurisdiction to entertain an application for an injunction or specific performance it may award damages in addition to or in substitution for such injunction or specific performance.

Supreme Court Act 1981
(1981 c 54)
Section 50

Where the Court of Appeal or the High Court has jurisdiction to entertain an application for an injunction or specific performance, it may award damages in addition to, or in substitution for, an injunction or specific performance.

———◄○►———

2 Australia and New Zealand

New South Wales

Equity Act 1880
(44 Vict No 18)
Section 32

In all cases in which the Court in Equity has jurisdiction to entertain an application for an injunction against a breach of any covenant contract or agreement or against the commission or continuance of any wrongful act or for the specific performance of any contract covenant or agreement it shall be lawful for the Court if it shall think fit to award damages to the party injured either in addition to or in substitution for such injunction or specific performance and such damages may be assessed in such manner as the Court shall direct.

Equity Act 1901
(1901 No 24)
Section 9

In all cases in which the Court has jurisdiction to entertain an application for an injunction against a breach of any covenant, contract, or agreement, or against the commission or continuance of any wrongful act or for the specific performance of any contract, covenant, or agreement the Court may award damages to the party injured either in addition to or in substitution for such injunction or specific performance.

Supreme Court Act 1970
(1970 No 52)
Section 68

Where the Court has power —

(a)   to grant an injunction against the breach of any covenant, contract or agreement, or against the commission or continuance of any wrongful act; or

(b)   to order the specific performance of any covenant, contract or agreement,

the Court may award damages to the party injured either in addition to or in substitution for the injunction or specific performance.

———◦———

Queensland

Supreme Court Act of 1863
(27 Vict No 14)
Section 10

In all cases in which the Supreme Court in equity has jurisdiction to entertain an application for an injunction against a breach of any covenant contract or agreement or against the commission or continuance of any wrongful act or for the specific performance of any covenant contract or agreement it shall be lawful for the same court if it shall think fit to award damages to the party injured either in addition to or in substitution for such injunction or specific performance and such damages may be assessed as the court shall direct.

Equity Act of 1867
(31 Vict No 18)
Section 62

In all cases in which the Supreme Court in equity has jurisdiction to entertain an application for an injunction against a breach of any covenant contract or agreement or against the commission or continuance of any wrongful act or for the specific performance of any covenant contract or agreement it shall be lawful for the same court if it shall think fit to award damages to the party injured either in addition to or in substitution for such injunction or specific performance and such damages may be assessed as the court shall direct.

———<o>———

South Australia

Equity Act 1866
(1866–1867 No 20)
Section 141

In any suit in the said Court arising out of the breach of any trust, covenant, contract, or agreement, or instituted to prevent the commission or continuance of any wrongful act, or for the specific performance of any covenant, contract, or agreement, the Court or Primary Judge may award damages to the party injured, either in addition to, or substitution for, the relief prayed, and such damages shall be assessed in such manner as the Court or Primary Judge shall direct.

Supreme Court Act 1935
(1935 No 2253)
Section 30

In any action arising out of the breach of any covenant, contract, or agreement, or instituted to prevent the commission or continuance of any wrongful act or for the specific performance of any covenant, contract, or agreement, the court shall have power to award damages to the party injured either in addition to or substitution for the injunction or specific performance, and those damages may be assessed by the court or in such manner as it directs.

District Courts Act 1991
(1991 No 70)
Section 36(2)(a)

(a)   Where a party seeks relief by way of injunction or specific performance, the Court may award damages in addition to or in substitution for such relief;

Magistrates Court Act 1991
(1991 No 73)
Section 31(2)(a)

(a)   where a party seeks relief by way of injunction or specific performance, the Court may award damages in addition to or in substitution for such relief.

————◄○►————

Tasmania

The Equity Procedure Act No 2 (1863)
(27 Vict No 21)
Section 3

In all cases in which the Court has Jurisdiction to entertain an application for an injunction against a breach of any covenant, contract, or agreement, or against the commission or continuance of any wrongful act, or for the specific performance of any covenant, contract, or agreement, it shall be lawful for the Court, if it thinks fit, to award damages to the party injured, either in addition to or in substitution for such injunction or specific performance, and such damages may be assessed in such manner as the Court directs.

Supreme Court Civil Procedure Act 1932
(23 Geo V No 58)
Section 11(13)

(a) In all cases in which the Court or any judge thereof now has jurisdiction to entertain an application for an injunction against a breach of any covenant, contract, or agreement, or against the commission or continuance of any wrongful act, or for the specific performance of any covenant, contract, or agreement, it shall be lawful for the Court or any judge thereof, if it or he thinks fit, to award damages to the party injured, either in addition to or in substitution for such injunction or specific performance, and such damages may be assessed in such manner as the Court or judge directs;

(b) But paragraph (a) of this subsection shall not be so construed as to empower the Court or a judge to award damages in substitution for an injunction in any case in which no breach of covenant, contract, or agreement, or no wrongful act (as the case may be), has been committed.

————◦————

Victoria

Supreme Court Act 1958
(1958 No 6387)
Section 62(3)

In all cases in which the Court entertains an application for an injunction against a breach of any covenant contract or agreement or against the commission or continuance of any wrongful act or for the specific performance of any covenant contract or agreement the Court may if it thinks fit award damages to the party injured either in addition to or in substitution for such injunction or specific performance and such damages may be assessed in such manner as the Court directs.

Nothing in this paragraph shall limit or affect the jurisdiction or powers which the Court has apart from this paragraph.

Supreme Court Act 1986
(1986 No 110)
Section 38

If the Court has jurisdiction to entertain an application for an injunction or specific performance, it may award damages in addition to, or in substitution for, an injunction or specific performance.

————◦————

Western Australia

Supreme Court Act 1935
(1935 No 36)
Section 25(10)

In all cases in which the Court entertains an application for an injunction against a breach of any covenant contract or agreement, or against the commission or continuance of any wrongful act, or for the specific performance of any covenant contract or agreement, the Court may, if it thinks fit, award damages to the party injured, either in addition to or in substitution for such injunction or specific performance, and such damages may be assessed in such manner as the Court directs:

Provided that nothing in this subsection shall limit or affect the jurisdiction or powers which the Court has apart from this subsection.

————◁◦▷————

Commonwealth Statutes

Companies Act 1981
(1981 No 89)
Section 574(8)

Where the Court has power under this section to grant an injunction restraining a person from engaging in particular conduct, or requiring a person to do a particular act or thing, the Court may, either in addition to or in substitution for the grant of the injunction, order that person to pay damages to any other person.

Corporations Law
(1989 No 107)
Section 1324(10)

Where the Court has power under this section to grant an injunction restraining a person from engaging in particular conduct, or requiring a person to do a particular act or thing, the Court may, either in addition to or in substitution for the grant of the injunction, order that person to pay damages to any other person.

————◁◦▷————

New Zealand

Judicature Act 1908
(1908 No 87)
Section 16A

Power to award damages as well as, or in substitution for, injunction or specific performance —
Where the Court has jurisdiction to entertain an application for an injunction or specific performance, it may award damages in addition to, or in substitution for, an injunction or specific performance.

Niue Act 1966
(1966 No 38)
Section 67(1)

The High Court may exercise by way of order in the ordinary course of its civil procedure the same jurisdiction as that possessed and exercised for the time being by the Supreme Court of New Zealand by way or in lieu of injunction, certiorari, mandamus, and prohibition, including the power of awarding damages in lieu of injunction.

———◄○►———

3 Canada

Alberta

Judicature Act RSA 1980 c J–1

Section 20

In all cases in which the Court has jurisdiction to entertain an application

- (a) for an injunction against
  - (i)   a breach of a covenant, contract or agreement, or
  - (ii) the commission or continuance of a wrongful act, or
- (b) for the specific performance of a covenant, contract or agreement, the Court if it thinks fit may award damages to the injured party either in addition to or in substitution for the injunction or specific performance, and the damages may be ascertained in any manner the Court may direct, or the Court may grant any other relief that it considers just.

Manitoba

The Queen's Bench Act RSM 1987–1988 c C280

Section 57

Where the court has jurisdiction to entertain an application for an injunction against a breach of covenant, contract, or agreement, or against the commission or continuance of a wrongful act, or for the specific performance of a covenant, contract, or agreement, the court may award damages to the party injured either in addition to, or in substitution for, the injunction or specific performance; and the damages may be ascertained in such manner as the court directs, or the court may grant such other relief as may be deemed just.

The Court of Queen's Bench Act CCSM c C280
(SM 1988–89 c 4)

Section 36

The Court may award damages in addition to, or in substitution for, an injunction or specific performance.

————◄○►————

New Brunswick

The Supreme Court in Equity Act CSNB 1903 c 112

Section 33

In all cases in which the Court has jurisdiction to entertain an application for an injunction against a breach of any covenant, contract or agreement, or against the commission or continuance of any wrongful act or for the specific performance of any covenant, contract or agreement, it shall be lawful for the Court to award damages to the party injured either in addition to or in substitution for such injunction or specific performance, and such damages shall be assessed by the Court. Provided, however, that it shall be lawful for the Court on the application of either party to the suit to cause the amount of such damages, in any case, to be assessed by a jury, and such jury shall be summoned and paid, and the enquiry before them conducted in the manner hereinafter provided as to the trial of an issue, and subject to the same right of applying for a new trial as upon the trial of an issue.

————◄○►————

Ontario

Court of Chancery Amendment Act 1865
(28 Vict c 17)
Section 3

In all cases in which the Court has jurisdiction to entertain an application for an injunction against a breach of any covenant, contract or agreement or against the commission or continuance of any wrongful act, or for the specific performance of any covenant, contract or agreement, the Court, if it thinks fit, may award damages to the party injured either in addition to or in substitution for such injunction or specific performance, and such damages may be ascertained in such manner as the Court may direct, or the Court may grant such other relief as it may deem just.

Courts of Justice Act RSO 1990 c C 43
Section 99

A Court that has jurisdiction to grant an injunction or order specific performance may award damages in addition to, or in substitution for, the injunction or specific performance.

———◦———

Prince Edward Island

The Chancery Act RSPEI 1951 c 21
Section 45

Upon an application for an injunction against a breach of any covenant, contract or agreement, or against the commission or continuance of any wrongful act, or for the specific performance of any covenant, contract or agreement, the Court may award damages to the party injured, either in addition to or in substitution for such injunction, or specific performance, and such damages may be assessed as the Court shall direct.

Supreme Court Act 1987 c 66
Section 32

The court has jurisdiction to grant injunctions or order specific performance and may award damages in addition to, or in substitution for, the injunction or specific performance.

———◦———

Saskatchewan

The Queen's Bench Act RSS 1978 c Q–1
Section 45(9)

The law to be administered in this province as to the matters next hereinafter mentioned shall be as follows:

... In all cases in which the court has jurisdiction to entertain an application for an injunction against a breach of any covenant, contract or agreement or against the commission or continuance of any wrongful act or for the specific performance of any covenant, contract or agreement, the court may if it thinks fit award damages to the party injured either in addition to or in substitution for such injunction or specific performance, and such damages may be ascertained in such a manner as the court may direct, or the court may grant such other relief as it may deem just.

————◁○▷————

Northwest Territories

Judicature Act RSNWT 1988 CJ–1

Section 42

Where a court has jurisdiction to entertain an application for:

- (a) an injunction against a breach of any covenant, contract or agreement or against the commission or continuance of any wrongful act; or
- (b) the specific performance of any covenant, contract or agreement,

the court may if it thinks fit award damages to the party injured either in addition to or in substitution for the injunction or specific performance, and the damages may be ascertained in such manner as the court may direct, or the court may grant such other relief as it deems just.

————◁○▷————

Yukon Territory

Judicature Act RSY 1986 c 96

Section 27

Where the Court has jurisdiction to entertain an application for an injunction against a breach of any covenant, contract or agreement, or against the commission or continuance of any wrongful act or for the specific performance of any covenant, contract or agreement, the Court may if it thinks fit award damages to the party injured either in addition to or in substitution for the injunction or specific performance, and the damages may be ascertained in such manner as the Court may direct, or the Court may grant such other relief as it may deem just.

————◁○▷————

4 Commonwealth Jurisdictions

Barbados

Chancery Act 1906
(1906–1902)
Section 73

In all cases in which the Court has jurisdiction against a breach of any covenant, contract, or agreement, or against the commission or continuance of any wrongful act, or for the specific performance of any covenant, contract, or agreement, it shall be lawful for the Court, if it shall think fit, to award damages to the party injured, either in addition to or in substitution for such injunction or specific performance, and such damages may be assessed in such manner as the Court shall direct.

————<o>————

Hong Kong

Supreme Court Ordinance
(Cap 4 rev ed 1987)
Section 17

Where the Court of Appeal or High Court has jurisdiction to entertain an application for an injunction or specific performance, it may award damages in addition to, or in substitution for, an injunction or specific performance.

————<o>————

India and Pakistan

Specific Relief Act 1877
(1 of 1877) (British India)
Section 19

Power to award compensation in certain cases
Any person suing for the specific performance of a contract may also ask for compensation for its breach, either in addition to, or in substitution for, such performance.

If in any such suit the Court decides that specific performance ought not to be granted, but that there is a contract between the parties which has been broken by the defendant and that the plaintiff is entitled to compensation for that breach, it shall award him compensation accordingly.

If in any such suit the Court decides that specific performance ought not to be granted, but that it is not sufficient to satisfy the justice of the case, and that some compensation for breach of the contract should also be made to the plaintiff, it shall award him compensation accordingly.

Compensation awarded under this section may be assessed in such manner as the court may direct.

Explanation — The circumstance that the contract has become incapable of specific performance does not preclude the court from exercising the jurisdiction conferred by this section.

Specific Relief Act 1963
(47 of 1963) (India)
Section 21

(1) In a suit for specific performance of a contract, the plaintiff may also claim compensation for its breach, either in addition to, or in substitution of, such performance.
(2) If, in any such suit, the court decides that specific performance ought not to be granted, but that there is a contract between the parties which has been broken by the defendant, and that the plaintiff is entitled to compensation for that breach, it shall award him such compensation accordingly.
(3) If, in any such suit, the court decides that specific performance ought to be granted, but that it is not sufficient to satisfy the justice of the case, and that some compensation for breach of the contract should also be made to the plaintiff, it shall award him such compensation accordingly.
(4) In determining the amount of any compensation awarded under this section, the court shall be guided by the principles specified in s 73 of the Indian Contract Act, 1872.
(5) No compensation shall be awarded under this section unless the plaintiff has claimed such compensation in this plaint:

Provided that where the plaintiff has not claimed any such compensation in the plaint the court shall, at any stage of the proceeding, allow him to amend the plaint on such terms as may be just, for including a claim for such compensation.

Explanation — The circumstance that the contract has become incapable of specific performance does not preclude the court from exercising the jurisdiction conferred by this section.

Section 40

(1) The plaintiff in a suit for perpetual injunction under s 38, or mandatory injunction under s 39, may claim damages either in addition to, or in substitution for, such injunction and the court may, if it thinks fit, award such damages.
(2) No relief for damages shall be granted under this section unless the plaintiff has claimed such relief in his plaint:

Provided that where no such damages have been claimed in the plaint, the court shall, at any stage of the proceedings, allow the plaintiff to amend the plaint on such terms as may be just for including such claim.

(3) The dismissal of a suit to prevent the breach of an obligation existing in favour of the plaintiff shall bar his right to sue for damages for such breach.

———◄◊►———

Malaysia

Specific Relief Act, 1950
(Revised — 1974)
Section 18

(1) Any person suing for the specific performance of a contract may also ask for compensation for its breach, either in addition to, or in substitution for, its performance.

(2) If in any such suit the court decides that specific performance ought not to be granted, but that there is a contract between the parties which has been broken by the defendant and that the plaintiff is entitled to compensation for that breach, it shall award him compensation accordingly.

(3) If in any such suit the court decides that specific performance ought to be granted, but that it is not sufficient to satisfy the justice of the case, and that some compensation for breach of the contract should also be made to the plaintiff, it shall award him such compensation accordingly.

(4) Compensation awarded under this section may be assessed in such a manner as the court may direct.

(5) The circumstance that the contract has become incapable of specific performance does not preclude the court from exercising the jurisdiction conferred by this section.

Select Bibliography

Parliamentary References

Third Report of Her Majesty's Commissioners appointed to inquire into the Process, Practice and System of Pleading in the Court of Chancery & c, 1856, Command [2064].

Hansard's Parliamentary Debates (3rd series), Volumes CXL, IX and CL, 1858.

Law Commission, *Breach of Confidence*, Law Com No 110, Cmnd 8388, 1981.

Report of the Committee on the Supreme Court of Judicature of Northern Ireland, 1970, Command [4292] (Chairman, Rt Hon Lord MacDermott MC).

Books

R Dean, *The Law of Trade Secrets*, Law Book Co, Sydney, 1990.

F Gurry, *Breach of Confidence*, Oxford University Press, Oxford, 1984.

H McGregor, *McGregor on Damages*, 15th ed, Sweet & Maxwell, London, 1988.

R P Meagher, W M C Gummow and J R F Lehane, *Equity — Doctrines and Remedies*, 2nd and 3rd ed, Butterworths, Sydney, 1984 and 1992.

R E Megarry and H W R Wade, *The Law of Real Property*, 5th ed, Sweet & Maxwell, London, 1984.

P H Pettit, *Equity and the Law of Trusts*, 6th ed, Butterworths, London, 1993.

I C F Spry, *Equitable Remedies*, 4th ed, Law Book Co, Sydney, 1990.

Articles and notes

R P Austin, 'Contract for Sale of Land: Two Recent English Cases', *Australian Law Journal*, vol 48, 1974, p 273.

R N Barber, 'The Operation of the Doctrine of Part Performance, in Particular to Actions for Damages', *University of Queensland Law Journal*, vol 8, 1973, p 79.

A Bradbrook, 'Nuisance and the Right of Solar Access', *University of Western Australia Law Review*, vol 15, 1983, p 148.

R A Brewer, 'A Comparison of *Lavery v Pursell*, and *McIntyre v Stockdale*', *University of New Brunswick Law School Journal*, vol 1, 1947, p 25.

M G Bridge, 'The *Statute of Frauds* and Sale of Land Contracts', *Canadian Bar Review*, vol 64, 1986, p 58.

S K Bun, 'Jurisdiction to Award Equitable Damages in Singapore', *Malaya Law Review*, vol 30, 1988, p 79.

A Burgess, 'Avoiding Inflation Loss in Contract Damages Awards: The Equitable Damages Solution', *International and Comparative Law Quarterly*, vol 35, 1985, p 317.

W Cornish, 'Confidence in Ideas', *Intellectual Property Journal*, vol 1, 1990, p 3.

P D Finn, 'A Road Not Taken: The Boyce Plaintiff and *Lord Cairns' Act*', *Australian Law Journal*, vol 57, 1983, 493 at p 571.

T Ingham, 'Damages in Equity — A Step in the Wrong Direction', *Conveyancer and Property Lawyer*, 1994, p 110.

T Ingham and J Wakefield, 'Equitable Damages under *Lord Cairns' Act*', *Conveyancer and Property Lawyer*, 1981, p 286.

J A Jolowicz, 'Damages in Equity — A Study of *Lord Cairns' Act*', *Cambridge Law Journal*, vol 34, 1975, p 224.

P M McDermott, 'Equitable Claims or Demands', *University of Queensland Law Journal*, vol 16, 1991, p 212.

P M McDermott, 'Equitable Claims and Demands — Western Australian Local Courts', *Brief* (Law Society of Western Australia), vol 18, 1991, p 11.

P M McDermott, 'Equitable Damages in Nova Scotia', *Dalhousie Law Review*, vol 12, 1989, p 131.

P M McDermott, 'Jurisdiction of the Court of Chancery to Award Damages', *Law Quarterly Review*, vol 108, 1992, p 652.

P M McDermott, 'Survival of Jurisdiction under the Chancery Amendment Act 1858 *(Lord Cairns' Act)*', *Civil Justice Quarterly*, vol 6, 1987, p 348.

R D Mulholland, 'Part Performance and Common Law Damages', *New Zealand Law Journal*, 1981, p 211.

K G Nicholson, '*Riches v Hogben*: Part Performance and the Doctrines of Equitable and Proprietary Estoppel', *Australian Law Journal*, vol 60, 1986, p 345.

M H Ogilvie, 'Sale of Land — Defect in Title — Limitation and Measure of Damages — Common Law of Equity', *Canadian Bar Review*, vol 58, 1980, p 394.

P H Pettit, '*Lord Cairns' Act* in the County Court: A Supplementary Note', *Cambridge Law Journal*, vol 36, 1977, p 369.

B J Reiter and R J Sharpe, '*Wroth v Tyler*: Must Equity Remedy Contract Damages', *Canadian Business Law Journal*, vol 3, 1979, p 146.

P A Ridge, 'The Equitable Doctrines of Part Performance and Equitable Estoppel', *Melbourne University Law Review*, vol 16, 1988, p 725.

J G Starke, 'Further Limitation on the Scope of *Lord Cairns' Act*', *Australian Law Journal*, vol 57, 1983, p 1.

J G Starke, 'Date for Assessment of Damages under *Lord Cairns' Act*', *Australian Law Journal*, vol 57, 1983, p 537.

E I Sykes, 'Specific Performance — Claim for Damages at Common Law', *Australian Law Journal*, vol 33, 1959, p 249.

J Tooher, 'Case Note: *McMahon v Ambrose*', *Monash University Law Review*, vol 16, 1990, p 122.

E Veitch, 'An Equitable Export — *Lord Cairns' Act* in Canada', *Ottawa Law Review*, vol 12, 1980, p 227.

Index